Agreement

Agreement in language occurs when grammatical information appears on a word which is not the source of that information. In simple examples like *she runs*, the form *runs* is singular, agreeing in number with *she*. This is information about the number of runners (just one), and it matches that expressed in its source *she*. Patterns of agreement vary dramatically cross-linguistically, with great diversity in expression and types of variation found. This clear introduction offers an insight into how agreement works, and how linguists have tried to account for it. Comparing examples from a range of languages, with radically different agreement systems, it demonstrates agreement at work in a variety of constructions. It shows how agreement is influenced by the conflicting effects of sentence structure and meaning, and highlights the oddities of agreement in English. *Agreement* will be essential reading for all those studying the structure and mechanisms of natural languages.

GREVILLE G. CORBETT is Distinguished Professor of Linguistics at the University of Surrey. His previous books include *Gender* (1991), *Number* (2000) and *The Syntax-Morphology Interface* (with Matthew Baerman and Dunstan Brown, 2005), all published by Cambridge University Press.

Agreement

In this series:

Agreement

GREVILLE G. CORBETT

University of Surrey

CAMBRIDGE UNIVERSITY PRESS
Cambridge, New York, Melbourne, Madrid, Cape Town, Singapore, São Paulo, Delhi

Cambridge University Press
The Edinburgh Building, Cambridge CB2 8RU, UK

Published in the United States of America by Cambridge University Press, New York

www.cambridge.org
Information on this title: www.cambridge.org/9780521001700

First published 2006

A catalogue record for this publication is available from the British Library

ISBN 978-0-521-80708-1 hardback
ISBN 978-0-521-00170-0 paperback

Transferred to digital printing 2009

For Judith, David, Ian and Peter

Contents

Figures

Tables

Preface

Agreement is a fascinating phenomenon. In many languages it is evident in almost every sentence and involves several different linguistic components. Yet it is not something we would include in the design of an artificial language. It therefore tells us a good deal about human languages. This book is intended for all who are interested in how languages really work, from final-year undergraduates to seasoned theoreticians and fieldworkers. It has been in the making for some time: reaching a consistent typology has involved many rounds of reanalysing, restructuring and rewriting.

I want to thank several colleagues and friends who have contributed substantially. Bernard Comrie and Edith Moravcsik have worked on agreement for at least as long as I have. Both have generously shared their knowledge and interest as the book has progressed. All of the following have also read a draft of the whole book, and given helpful comments from their different perspectives: Jenny Audring, Matthew Baerman, Marina Chumakina, Greg Stump and Claudia Wegener. Others have shared their expertise on substantial areas of the topic or on some of the chapters, namely Jonathan Bobaljik, Dunstan Brown, Nicholas Evans, Anna Kibort, Aleksandr Kibrik, Gabriella Vigliocco and Stephen Wechsler. I am most grateful to you all. The Surrey Morphology Group Agreement Project (1999–2002) produced a database, bibliography and edited volume (see §1.6.1), which readers may wish to use. Those involved, Carole Tiberius, Julia Barron, Dunstan Brown, Nicholas Evans, Andrew Hippisley, Elena Kalinina and Marianne Mithun, deserve special thanks, as do Lisa Mack and Alison Long, for careful help with preparing the typescript.

I am most grateful to the Cambridge team for their expertise and support, especially to Andrew Winnard, Helen Barton and Jackie Warren, to Steve Barganski for fine copyediting, and to Prachi Joshi for typesetting a complex script.

I have presented material from the book in various lectures and seminars, and am grateful for all the comments and discussion which resulted, especially to the enthusiastic audiences at the Third Winter Typological School, Moscow District (February 2002), the Vilem Mathesius Lecture Series, Prague (March 2002), the Association for Linguistic Typology Summer School at Cagliari (September 2003), the Netherlands Graduate School in Linguistics Winter School in Amsterdam (January 2004), and the Morphology and Typology Seminar, Vilnius (May 2005). And more generally, thank you to everyone who provided an example, a reference or an objection.

The research was supported by the ESRC (grants R000238228 and RES051270122) and by the Max Planck Institute for Evolutionary Anthropology, Leipzig, through visits kindly hosted by Bernard Comrie. The support of both bodies is gratefully acknowledged.

Abbreviations

The abbreviations follow the Leipzig Glossing Rules
(http://www.eva.mpg.de/lingua/files/morpheme.html)
with additions for items not in that list.

A_OBL	associating oblique
ABL	ablative ('from')
ABS	absolutive
ACC	accusative
ACT	active
AD	adessive ('on', 'about')
ADJ	adjective
ADV	adverb(ial)
AFF	affective
AGR	agreement
ALL	allative ('onto', 'to')
ANIM	animate
AOR	aorist
ART	article
ATTRIB	attributive
AUX	auxiliary
CLF	classifier
COM	comitative
COMN	common gender
CONN	connective
CONT	contessive ('contact' localization)
COP	copula
CVB	converb
D_SBJ	different subject
DAT	dative
DECL	declarative
DEF	definite
DIMIN	diminutive
DIST	distal
DU	dual
ERG	ergative

ESM	epistemic status marker
EXCL	exclusive
F	feminine
FOC	focus
FUT	future
GEN	genitive
HAB	habitual
HON	honorific
HUM	human
ILL	illative ('into')
IMP	imperative
IN	'in' localization
INAN	inanimate
INCL	inclusive
IND	indicative
INDF	indefinite
INESS	inessive ('in')
INF	infinitive
INS	instrumental
INTENS	intensifier
INTER	'inter' localization ('in', 'within')
INTR	intransitive
IPFV	imperfective
IRR	irrealis
LOC	locative
M	masculine
M.PERS	masculine personal
MOD_ABL	modal ablative (case)
MOD_PROP	modal proprietive (case)
N	neuter
NEG	negation, negative
NMLZ	nominalizer/nominalization
NOM	nominative
NON_OBJ	non-object
OBL	oblique
OPT	optative
PASS	passive
PERS	personal
PFV	perfective
PL	plural
POSS	possessive
POT	potentialis
PRF	perfect
PROG	progressive

PRS	present
PRV	preverb
PST	past
PTCL	particle
PTCP	participle
Q	question particle/marker
RED_AGR	reduced agreement
REFL	reflexive
REL	relative
RES	resultative
RLS	realis
S_SBJ	same subject
SBJ	subject
SG	singular
SUB	'sub' localization
TR	transitive
V_DAT	verbalizing dative (case)
VOC	vocative
1	first person
2	second person
3	third person
I–IV	genders I, II, III, IV

1 Introduction: canonical agreement

Agreement is a widespread and varied phenomenon. In some of the world's languages it is pervasive, while in others it is absent. Despite extensive research, agreement remains deeply puzzling. There was a time when it was treated mainly as a tool for researching other syntactic phenomena. Yet there has also been a tradition of recognizing it as a challenging problem in its own right. Indeed agreement presents serious problems for all our theories of syntax. It is therefore worth looking first at the reasons for the continuing interest in agreement (§1.1). Part of this comes from the way in which it involves so many components of grammar (§1.2). The terminology has become somewhat confused, so I clarify the terms I shall use (§1.3). The substantial part of this chapter lays out the canonical approach to agreement (§1.4), which will form the basis for my typology. I then outline the way in which the book is structured (§1.5), and present background information which should be of value to the reader (§1.6).

1.1 The special interest of agreement

Consider the following idea:

Hypothesis I: Grammatical information will be found only together with the lexical item to which it is relevant. (False)

This hypothesis suggests a situation which is iconic, functional, sensible and understandable. Compare *dog* and *dogs*, where number is marked in accordance with the hypothesis, or *compute* and *computed*, where tense is similarly marked. This entire book presents evidence to show that Hypothesis I is also wrong.

It is surprising that grammatical meaning can be 'displaced' (Moravcsik 1988: 90), in other words, that one word can carry the grammatical meaning relevant to another. This is what happens in agreement:

(1)   Mary makes pancakes.

Here *makes* is singular because *Mary* is an individual; even if she makes pancakes frequently, the number of 'pancake making events' will not affect the agreement of the verb. The verb form tells us how many Marys there are, not how many makings there are. Thus the number information on the verb is displaced. This displaced information, or 'information in the wrong place', is not a minor issue. Agreement affects different components of grammar, as we shall see in the next section.

1.2   The place of agreement

Take another simple example like:

(2)   The cooks make pancakes.

We need to specify that the form *make* ~ *makes* varies according to the subject (there is no effect if we change the object *pancakes* to *bread*, for example). Clearly, then, agreement is a matter of **syntax**, since the syntactic role of the items involved is of importance. But now compare:

(3)   The committee has agreed.
(4)   The committee have agreed.

Here there is a choice in some varieties of English, notably in British English. That is, there is a choice here, but not with *Mary* in (1) above. Why not? Because *Mary* is an individual, whereas *committee* may be conceptualized as an entity or as several individuals. Clearly, then, agreement is also a matter of **semantics**.

Particularly if we start from English data, we might think that agreement is all a matter of semantics, an idea put most consistently in Dowty & Jacobson (1989). We could argue that the singular verb in (1) results from semantic compatibility with a singular actor, and the plural in (2) similarly from a plural actor. However, there are three types of problem with such a view.

Consider first these examples from Morgan (1984: 235):

(5)   More than one person has failed this exam.
(6)   Fewer than two people have failed this exam.

Here we can see that the agreement of the verb depends on the grammatical number of the subject (shown by *person* versus *people*) and not on the meaning of the sentence (semantic plural in (5) and singular in (6));[1] another type of supporting example is given in §5.6.3.

There is a more general second argument that agreement cannot be entirely semantic which involves agreement in grammatical gender, in languages like Russian:

Russian
(7)   Lamp-a   stoja-l-a   v   ugl-u
         lamp(F)-SG stand-PST-F.SG in corner-SG.LOC
         'The lamp was standing in the corner.'

---

[1] For the form of pronouns with such phrases see Gil (2001).

In this example there is no semantic reason for *lampa* 'lamp' to be of feminine gender.[2] A similar argument can be made with grammatical number in English. The use of plural agreement with English *scissors* does not, for many linguists at least, have a semantic justification.

The third argument is that even when there are semantic reasons for a particular type of agreement, the domain in which this is possible is determined by syntax. *The committee have agreed* is fine in British English (as in (4)), which suggests that *committee* takes agreement according to its meaning. And yet **these committee* is quite unacceptable. It is syntax which determines when agreement according to meaning is possible. We shall see many more examples of such mismatches in agreement in chapter 5. And evidence from acquisition also supports the syntactic basis of agreement in English (§9.3). Thus an adequate theory requires reference both to syntactic and to semantic information (Pullum 1984).

Now consider for contrast:

(8)   The committee agreed.
(9)   Mary made pancakes.
(10)   The cooks made pancakes.

Here we see no evidence of agreement. Past tense verbs in English do not show agreement. Clearly, then, agreement is a matter of **morphology** (word structure) since we require the morphology to provide the opportunity for agreement to be indicated. Indeed agreement is arguably the major interface problem between morphology and syntax, and hence appears particularly difficult when viewed from the heartland of either component.

There is a single exception to the statement about the past tense in English, namely the verb *be* which distinguishes number in the past (*was* ~ *were*). This is something that has to be stated individually for this verb, in its lexical entry. We conclude that agreement is a matter which may have to be specified in the lexicon; it is a matter of **lexicology**.

It is tempting to try to treat all such specific irregularities within the lexicon, but some apply so broadly that this approach cannot be right. Consider this example:

Russian (19th century, from Turgenev's *Nakanune* 'On the Eve', 1860)

(11)   «Mamen´ka **plač-ut**, — šepnu-l-a   ona vsled uxodivš-ej
         Mother   cry-3PL   whisper-PST-F.SG she after   leaving-F.SG.DAT

         Elene,   a   papen´ka **gnevaj-ut-sja** . . .»
         Elena.DAT and father   be.angry-3PL-REFL

         'Your mother is crying', she whispered after Elena, who was leaving,
         'and your father is angry . . .'

The speaker is a maid, talking in turn about her mistress and her master. Here the plural verbs with singular subjects indicate that the speaker is showing respect

---

[2] Dowty & Jacobson (1989: 98–101) discuss the problem of gender and attempt to meet the objection, by suggesting that a real-world property of objects is the word which is used by convention to denote that class of objects. This is hardly convincing, in my view.

for the people referred to. There are all sorts of items which could appear in this construction. They cannot be restricted to particular lexical items, rather a range of noun phrases may be involved. The generalization involves the situation: this agreement occurs when the speaker wishes to show respect (to the referents of the noun phrases agreed with). Hence agreement can be a matter of **pragmatics**.

Agreement is increasingly recognized as of interest not just for core areas of linguistics like syntax and morphology, but also more widely, in work on acquisition and in psycholinguistics, for instance, which are topics I take up in the final chapter. Given this interest from 'outside', it is particularly important that we should be talking about the same thing. Unfortunately, the terminology is muddled, and important choices in analysis are made sometimes as much by tradition as by argument. I therefore will pay attention to key terms and to the analytic choices available.

1.3   Defining terms

I have just argued for the need for clarity in terminology. What then is it that unites the examples of agreement we have considered so far? Anderson (1992: 103) points out that agreement is 'a quite intuitive notion which is nonetheless surprisingly difficult to delimit with precision'. Indeed, while several definitions have been proposed, none is fully satisfactory; see the suggestions by Keenan (1978: 167), Lehmann (1982: 203) and Lapointe (1988). There is detailed discussion of definitional issues in Mel'čuk (1993) and a formal approach can be found in Avgustinova & Uszkoreit (2003). We shall start from a suggestion by Steele:

> The term *agreement* commonly refers to some systematic covariance between a semantic or formal property of one element and a formal property of another.
> Steele (1978: 610)

This covers the instances we have seen. The essential notion is covariance. It is not sufficient that two items happen to share properties; the sharing must be systematic, and we see this by the fact that as one element varies so will the other.

Some terms will be useful at this stage, to allow us to generalize about different types of agreement. We call the element which determines the agreement (say the subject noun phrase) the **controller**. The element whose form is determined by agreement is the **target**. The syntactic environment in which agreement occurs (the clause for instance) is the **domain** of agreement. And when we indicate in what respect there is agreement, we are referring to agreement **features**. Thus number is an agreement feature, it has the values: singular, dual, plural and so on. This is diagrammed in Figure 1.1.

Features are directly reflected in agreement. There can be other factors (like word order) which have an effect on agreement but are not directly reflected like

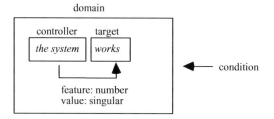

Figure 1.1   *Framework of terms*

features. Such factors are called agreement **conditions**. Thus, within a particular domain, a target agrees with a controller in respect of its feature specifications (that is, the features and their values); this may be dependent on some other condition being met.

These terms are now fairly standard among those working on agreement. For controller, the term 'trigger' or 'source' is sometimes found. 'Category' may be found in place of 'feature', and 'conditioning factor' for condition. For 'probe' and 'goal' see §4.2.5. As our terms suggest, there is a clear intuition that agreement is asymmetric. In *Mary laughs*, most accept that *laughs* is singular because *Mary* is singular. However, it does not follow that we should model it in this way. Older accounts of agreement captured the intuition directly by copying feature specifications from the controller to the target. More recent accounts use techniques like unification, and model the asymmetry less directly. This issue is considered in §1.4.3, and discussed more fully in §4.1.

I shall further clarify what is covered by agreement. First I deal with the term 'concord' (§1.3.1) and then I examine the relation of agreement to government (§1.3.2). The main way forward, however, will be using the notion of canonical agreement (§1.4), which will allow us to work with the full range of agreement, from the core instances of the phenomenon to those at the fringe.

1.3.1   Agreement and concord

These innocent terms have led to considerable confusion. For many linguists they are synonymous; the trend is towards the use of 'agreement',[3] which is the term I shall use. Some others have distinguished the terms, but they have done so in contradictory and potentially confusing ways. Since some of this confusion remains in the literature, I shall outline two positions, so that readers can be alert to the issues. Readers for whom this is not an issue should go straight to §1.3.2.

---

[3] In a survey of the topic, Moravcsik (1978: 333) gives 'agreement (or concord) phenomena'. Similarly Trask (1997: 10) has '**agreement** (also **concord**)'. Somewhat earlier, Lyons (1968: 239) had '*concord* (or 'agreement')'; this suggests that 'agreement' is on the rise, an impression supported by Anderson (1992: 103), who writes 'just what is "agreement" (or as it is often called in the traditional literature, "concord")?'

Some linguists, following Bloomfield (1933: 191–4), treat agreement as the superordinate term. According to Bloomfield (1933: 191), 'In a rough way, without real boundaries, we can distinguish three general types of agreement.' These are 'concord' or 'congruence', which includes agreement within the noun phrase and the agreement of predicate verbs, government and cross-reference.[4] As was predictable, this system of terms has not survived unchanged. One development has been to restrict concord to the noun phrase, which means that the domain of agreement is the key part of such definitions.[5]

In contrast to the position of Bloomfield, and developments from it, Greenberg (1978: 50) treats concord as the wider term:

> It would be useful, then, to distinguish the wider notion of concord from agreement, the latter being a subtype in which the choice of alternative concord elements depends on the class to which the stem of the governing item belongs, whether marked by an affix or not.

Greenberg would include matching in case within the noun phrase as an instance of concord. When, however, matching is determined by 'the class to which the stem of the governing item belongs', then we have agreement. Greenberg cites gender here, and is clearly talking of what we would term a lexical feature.

Note the contrast between this definition and Bloomfield's. Most obviously the subset relations are different: for Bloomfield concord is a subset of agreement, while for Greenberg agreement is a subset of concord. But the criteria on which the relation is based differ too. Bloomfield and several followers draw a distinction according to domain: concord exists in a 'smaller' domain than cross-reference. For Greenberg the distinction is based on the type of feature involved: agreement involves lexical features, while concord can involve matching of other features.[6]

Thus no distinction is drawn consistently between the terms 'agreement' and 'concord', indeed they are used in opposing ways. I shall therefore use just

---

[4] Bloomfield puts certain pronominal constructions and pro-drop together as cross-reference, and includes them with concord and government under 'agreement', but he treats antecedent-anaphor relations separately.

[5] For example:

> The term *concord* traditionally distinguishes this pattern of agreement within DP from the canonical specifier-head type: agreement theory as developed in Chomsky 1993 and related work accounts only for the latter.   (Carstens 2000: 323)

Note the distinction; what for Bloomfield counted as concord is cut down to agreement within the determiner phrase, and part of what he treated as concord is treated as the 'canonical' type of agreement. The difference in the definitions depends on what is considered the domain of agreement.

[6] The domain is not a defining criterion here, indeed Greenberg later talks of 'three types of concordial phenomena' and distinguishes in what he calls a 'somewhat rough and heuristic fashion' between agreement within the noun phrase, predicate agreement and anaphoric use (1978: 75–6). There are other ways in which the terms are used. Thus Lehmann (1982: 206, 249–50) also distinguishes agreement from concord: agreement is the core syntactic phenomenon, which he defines, and the term 'concord' is then used for instances of semantic compatibility, certain classifier-noun relations, for example. But still others use both terms without definition.

'agreement', as the more current term. There is no particular reason to determine my terms primarily according to the domains of agreement or to the features involved: both should be a part of the account (as will be the case in my 'canonical' approach). Any subdivision of agreement, whether or not 'concord' is used as the term, will require a careful definition, since there is no generally accepted terminology here.

1.3.2   Agreement and government

In the clearest instances of agreement (those I shall later treat as 'canonical'), agreement can be distinguished from government rather readily. The differences can be illustrated by this example taken from a corpus of spoken Russian.

Russian conversation (Zemskaja & Kapanadze 1978: 251)

(12)   Zna-eš´   kak-oj   mne   vsegda   dava-l-a
         know-2SG   what-M.SG.ACC   1SG.DAT   Always   give-PST-F.SG

         sovet   moj-a   mam-a ?
         advice (M)[SG.ACC]   my-F.SG.NOM   mother(FEM)-SG

         'Do you know what advice my mother always gave me?'

The subject is *moja mama* 'my mother', and the verb agrees with it. In agreement the feature specification of the target is in the relevant respects the same as that of the controller (here feminine singular).[7] In turn the verb governs the split noun phrase *kakoj sovet* 'what advice'.[8] For government it is simply the presence of the verb *davat´* 'give' which requires the accusative case for this noun phrase; changing the form of the verb to, say, the present, does not affect its government requirement (this is point 1 in (13) below). Another way of expressing this is to say that the agreement controller has the feature specification required of the target (i.e. the subject is indeed feminine and singular in my example), while the governor does not (the verb is not accusative), as in point 2 below. The controller of agreement is usually nominal, while targets are of various sorts; conversely, the governor can be varied, but items which are governed are nominal (point 3). The features involved in agreement, typically gender, number and person have direct semantic relevance, to varying degrees (discussed further in §4.2.4), while government canonically involves case, which is not directly involved in semantic interpretation (point 4). And finally, if there are multiple targets for an agreement controller, they will in the canonical instance share the same values (when they realize the same features); thus *moja* 'my' and *davala* 'gave' are both feminine singular.[9] However, when a single governor governs two governees, they will

---

[7] This is a further important aspect of 'systematic covariance' in the definition above, namely that it is in respect of the same feature. Thus if the case of an argument varies according to the aspect of the verb, this would not qualify as agreement any more than does normal government (thanks to Atle Grönn for pointing out this issue).

[8] We discuss the glossing of phrases like this showing syncretism in §1.6.3 below.

[9] As we shall see in §1.4.4, hybrid controllers are non-canonical in this regard.

normally have different feature values; thus the noun phrase *kakoj sovet* 'what advice' is accusative, while *mne* 'to me' is dative, as in point 5.

(13)   Summary of differences: canonical agreement and canonical government

	AGREEMENT	GOVERNMENT
1. feature specification of target/governee is determined by:	feature specification of controller	presence of governor
2. controller/governor:	has the relevant feature specification	does not have the relevant feature specification[10]
3. element which is normally nominal:	controller	governee
4. features involved are:	gender, number, person, i.e. 'direct' features (§4.2.4)	case, i.e. an 'indirect' feature
5. multiple targets/governees are:	same as each other	different from each other

In the canonical instances agreement and government are rather different, agreement being characterized by matching, and government lacking this.[11] However, they share the characteristic of being syntactic relations of an asymmetric type. Indeed, in recent work in Minimalism, the operation Agree is given a major role, covering both agreement and case government (see Chomsky, 2000: 101). I shall here restrict myself to agreement in the narrower sense, retaining the sharper notion of the covariance of features, not found in government. Adopting the broader definition would blur this important distinction. While I have treated the canonical instances, there are difficult phenomena falling between these idealizations, as we shall see when we consider data from Kayardild (§4.5.2). We return to the issue of agreement in case in §4.4.1, and for 'collaborative agreement', which involves an interaction with case, see §3.3.5.

1.4   Canonical agreement

To clarify some of the conceptual problems and misunderstandings that have characterized the topic of agreement I shall adopt a 'canonical' approach. This means that I shall take definitions to their logical end point and build a

---

[10] Strictly speaking, it does not *necessarily* have the relevant feature specification; it may have it coincidentally. For example, if we have a verb which governs the genitive, a participle formed from it may be in the genitive. The fact that this participle then governs the genitive is still a matter of it being present, and does not depend on its being in the genitive.

[11] For extended discussion of definitions of agreement and government see Schmidt & Lehfeldt (1995).

theoretical space of possibilities. Only then do I ask how this space is populated. It follows that canonical instances, which are the best and clearest examples, those most closely matching the 'canon', may well not be the most frequent. They may indeed be extremely rare. However, they fix a point from which occurring phenomena can be calibrated. Then I discuss weakenings of the criteria, which allow for less canonical instances. As these instances no longer fully match the definitions, they will include some which not all linguists would accept as instances of agreement. At several points I introduce here interesting phenomena which are then taken up in more detail in later chapters.

To start from an instance of canonical agreement, consider agreement in gender in the Italian noun phrase:

Italian (Pierluigi Cuzzolin, personal communication)[12]

(14)   il   nuov-o   quadr-o
         DEF.M.SG   new-M.SG   picture(M)-SG
         'the new picture'

(15)   i   nuov-i   quadr-i
         DEF.M.PL   new-M.PL   picture(M)-PL
         'the new pictures'

(16)   la   nuov-a   tel-a
         DEF.F.SG   new-F.SG   painting(F)-SG
         'the new painting'

(17)   le   nuov-e   tel-e
         DEF.F.PL   new-F.PL   painting(F)-PL
         'the new paintings'

I shall discuss canonical aspects of such examples in turn. As a brief summary, the canonical aspects of these examples are as follows:

controller: is present, has overt expression of features, and is consistent in the agreements it takes, its part of speech is not relevant (this is a vacuous criterion in (14)–(17))

target: has bound expression of agreement, obligatory marking, doubling the marking of the noun, marking is regular, alliterative, productive; the target has a single controller and its part of speech is not relevant

domain: agreement is asymmetric (the gender of the adjective depends on that of the noun), local, and the domain is one of multiple domains

features: lexical (in one instance), matching values, not offering any choice in values

conditions: no conditions

For some readers examples like (14)–(17) will seem familiar; however, it is worth reflecting on how interesting they are. Each is a clear counter-example to

---

[12] Glossing conventions are discussed in §1.6.3. Inherent features (§4.2.3) are given in parentheses. Thus gender is glossed with the noun stem; it is true that -*a* on the noun often implies feminine gender by the assignment rules (§4.3.1) of Italian, but this is not necessarily so, as with *poeta* 'poet' (masculine); similarly -*o* often implies masculine, but this is not always the case, as with *mano* 'hand' (feminine). This glossing may seem over-careful. However, when discussing agreement it is important to distinguish between what is inherent and what is contextual.

Hypothesis I. As we shall see, the different canonical aspects of agreement con-
agreement in gender of the modifier with the noun in the noun phrase
as the canonical instance. Phenomena which extend the instances
e now grouped under the five components (Figure 1.1) of my account

ontrollers

everal of the criteria relate to the controller. An important one is that
ntrollers are present.

*-1: controller present > controller absent
(where '>' means 'more canonical than')

Compare these two similar examples:

Russian
(18)   ty   čita-eš´
           2SG.NOM   read-2SG
           'you are reading'

Serbian/Croatian/Bosnian
(19)   čit-aš
           read-2SG
           'you are reading'

In such sentences in Russian the controller is typically present, while in
Serbian/Croatian/Bosnian[13] typically it is not. I treat as canonical what is sometimes called 'grammatical agreement' rather than 'anaphoric agreement' (Bresnan
& Mchombo 1987, Siewierska 1999, Bresnan 2001a: 151). An effect of adopting criterion 1 is that, for the construction we are discussing, the canonical type
is restricted to relatively few languages, since the omission of subject pronouns
(often referred to as 'pro drop') is common. It is important to stress that canonical
is not necessarily what is 'normal' or 'common'. Several familiar examples of
languages where pronominal subjects are normally included come from northern
Europe (English and German being obvious examples).[14]

While discussions of 'dropping' concentrate on pronouns, I am making a more
general point here: it is more canonical for any controller to be present rather
than absent. For agreement of the adjective with the noun within the domain
of noun phrase, it is more canonical for the noun to be present; similarly in

---

[13] I use this designation for the South Slavonic varieties spoken in Bosnia-Hercegovina, Croatia,
Montenegro and Serbia, since linguistically they show considerable similarity. An account of the
breakup of Serbo-Croat is given in Greenberg (2004).

[14] A particularly interesting less familiar example is Skou (New Guinea), which has elaborate
agreement marking (to be discussed in §3.2.3 and §3.2.4) and which normally includes subject
pronouns: the third person pronouns are regularly included and first and second person pronouns
are present more often than not (Mark Donohue, personal communication). Siewierska (2004b:
268–70) suggests in addition: the Papuan languages Au, Ekari, Koiari and Vanimo, and the
Austronesian languages Anejom, Fehan and Labu.

possessor-possessed agreement it is more canonical for the 'possessed' to be present.

> *C-2: controller has overt expression of agreement features > controller has covert expression of agreement features*

Compare these French examples:

French

(20)　　　elle　　est　　　　　content-e
　　　　　3SG.F　be.PRS.3SG　happy-F.SG
　　　　　'she is happy'

(21)　　　je　　suis　　　　content / content-e
　　　　　1SG　be.PRS.1SG　happy[M.SG] / happy-F.SG
　　　　　'I am happy'

In (20) the controller is overtly feminine: the pronoun *elle* 'she' contrasts with *il* 'he'. In (21) there is no distinction in the controller for gender (it is underspecified for gender). We treat examples like (20) as canonical in this respect, rather than those like (21). Another way of stating this criterion is that a canonical controller marks at least as many distinctions as the target. It does so in two respects: in terms of the number of features and in terms of their values. These examples make clear that I am comparing constructions and even particular examples in terms of canonicity: even within a given language one construction can show more canonical agreement than another.

On the basis of these criteria, and others to be considered below, a more general principle may be suggested (compare Moravcsik 1988: 90):

> *Principle I: Canonical agreement is redundant rather than informative*

This principle fits well with the definition of agreement in §1.3. In the French example *elle est contente* 'she is happy' the feminine feature is available from the controller (criterion 2). In *je suis content(e)* 'I am happy' it is not. Agreement in the canonical example is redundant. Similarly, English examples like *the horse is / the horses are* are more canonical than *the sheep is / are*. The situation where there is no controller present, and hence the only information about the controller is that supplied by the target, is non-canonical (though, as we noted, it is commonly found); this is the point of criterion 1.

Let us continue with other criteria relating to controllers.

> *C-3: consistent controller > hybrid controller*

A consistent controller is one which controls a consistent agreement pattern. This is more canonical than one which controls different feature values. The notion 'consistent agreement pattern' is intuitively straightforward, but not quite so easy to define (for the details see Corbett 1991: 176–81 and §5.4.1 below). As a first characterization, a consistent agreement pattern is the set of agreements controlled by a typical regular controller. A hybrid controller, on the other hand, takes agreements from more than one such pattern. It controls different feature values on different targets. An example can be found in Bulgarian:

Bulgarian (Osenova 2003: 666)
(22)   Negov-o   Veličestv-o   e   došăl
        his-N.SG   Majesty(N)-SG AUX.3SG come.PST[M.SG]
        'his Majesty has come'

Neuter agreement is found in the noun phrase, but masculine in the verbal predicate, and so the same controller takes different agreements according to the target. A consistent controller would take either neuter or masculine (or feminine) agreements, irrespective of the target: that is, it would have a consistent agreement pattern.

> *C-4: controller's part of speech is irrelevant > is relevant (given the domain)*

The idea is that given a domain, for instance, subject-predicate agreement, in the canonical case we do not need further information on the part of speech of the controller. For instance, in Russian we do not need to have different rules for a subject noun phrase headed by a noun as compared to one headed by a pronoun. Sometimes, however, the difference is substantial. A good example is Bayso, where the rules are rather different for pronouns as compared with nouns. This complex situation will be analysed in §5.9.

These two criteria fall under a second general principle:

> *Principle II: Canonical agreement is syntactically simple*

Agreement varies from examples which can be captured by a relatively simple rule, to those which are exceptionally complex. The two criteria, C-3 and C-4, both point to agreement phenomena which can be captured by simple and general rules.

1.4.2   Targets

The largest number of criteria relate to the target. This makes sense, since it is the target which is the locus of agreement. These target criteria are often intertwined, though as we shall see they can be untangled in some systems.

I begin with the nature of the expression of agreement on the target, something I shall discuss in more detail in chapter 3. Stated in the most general terms, a major criterion is:

> *C-5: bound > free*

We are concerned with the *expression* of agreement here. Some define agreement such that its expression must be bound to the target; for example, Källström (1993: 272). Matthews' definition of agreement also has this effect: 'Syntactic relation between words and phrases which are compatible, in a given construction, by virtue of inflections carried by at least one of them.' (1997: 12). Others are more liberal. To discuss alternative possible stances on this, let us expand out the criterion:

C-5´: inflectional marking (affix) > clitic > free word

The canonical expression of agreement is through affixes bound to the target, that is, through concatenative inflectional morphology. Let us accept this 'anchoring' of the hierarchy (we shall return to the means of inflectional marking below) and consider the other possibilities. Some treat certain uses of clitics as agreement. According to Halpern (1998: 105) verbal clitics 'are often assumed to be types of inflectional affixes themselves, perhaps simply agreement markers'. On the other hand: 'there are also several respects in which clitics are not like canonical agreement affixes'.

There seems to be no argument about inflectional marking being more canonical than the use of clitics; some consider clitics (particularly in clitic doubling constructions) to be an expression of agreement, some exclude them.[15] Here is an example from the South Slavonic language Macedonian:

Macedonian (Victor Friedman 1993: 285 and personal communication)
(23)   kuče-to   ja=kasa   mačka-ta
         dog-DEF.N.SG   3SG.F.ACC=bite[3SG] cat-DEF.F.SG
         'the dog bites the cat'

In (23) the clitic *ja* 'doubles' the noun phrase *mačkata* 'the cat'; I mark clitic boundaries with '='. The clitic is singular and feminine, like its controller. In such examples, where the object is definite (which is an example of an agreement condition, the topic of chapter 6), there must be a doubling clitic pronoun (Friedman 1993: 285). Of course, clitics vary as to 'how bound' they are; verbal clitics are 'more bound' than second position clitics, and so are somewhat closer to being canonical agreement. I take up this issue in §3.2.3.

We should now ask whether a free word can be an expression of agreement. It is important to be clear that we are looking at the expression of agreement, not just at a potential stem or host. A predicate verb is a common target, but it acts as a stem (for inflectional marking) or a host (for a clitic), but is not itself the expression of agreement. (The distinction merges particularly easily with pronouns, where an anaphoric pronoun may function as such, and be a target for agreement, or may develop into a form which loses its anaphoric function and be considered, at least by some, to be entirely an expression of agreement: see Lehmann 1982: 234–41 for early discussion, Siewierska 1999, and §9.1 below).

Potentially convincing examples of free words as the expression of agreement are found in Daly languages of north Australia. For instance, Ngan'gityemerri

---

[15] See Harris (2002: 110–13) for discussion. Woolford (2003) uses 'cross-referencing' as a general term covering referencing of arguments by clitics and by inflection, with 'agreement' reserved for the latter; this is a good convention, when one is concerned primarily with the domain of the clause.

(Reid 1997), a Daly language with two dialects, Ngan'gikurunggurr and Ngan'giwumirri, and with 100 speakers, 300 miles south-west of Darwin, Australia, has arguably fifteen genders. Of these, six genders have optional free-form generics/classifiers:

Ngan'gityemerri (Reid 1997: 177)
(24)   (syiri) magulfu   (syiri) marrgu
         STRIKE cylindrical.fighting.stick STRIKE new
         'a new cylindrical fighting stick'

Syiri is the free-form generic for weapon-like objects which have a striking type of contact. In its first use in (24) it is analogous to a classifier. In its second use it is more like an agreement marker. The repetition of this free form in the noun phrase is, according to one's point of view, an example of agreement with a free word as the expression of agreement, or else a phenomenon on the edge of agreement.[16] There is strong evidence that such free-form generics can develop into agreement markers, as shown by Ngan'gityemerri, where the generics are still feeding the gender system (Reid 1997: 211–22); we return to this in §9.1.1.

> *C-6: obligatory > optional*

Canonical agreement is marked obligatorily; optional marking is less canonical. This criterion is linked to the previous one (since inflectional marking is usually obligatory), but the two can vary independently. We find optional inflectional marking of agreement, if rarely, while less canonical types of marking are more likely than inflectional marking to be optional. An example is again Ngan'gityemerri (Reid 1997). Of the fifteen genders, nine are distinguished by the agreements found on agreement targets, such as adjectives:

(25)   a-syensyerrgimi   a=tyentyenmuy
         ANIM-white.rock.wallaby   ANIM=tame
         'a tame white rock wallaby'

Reid argues that the marker on the head noun is a prefix, while that on the agreement target is a proclitic, on the basis of stress and assimilation processes (1997: 212–15). The important point for us is that the use of these agreement markers on targets is optional (1997: 168). (We might think the language has two different systems, based on generics and on proclitics, but this is not the case, since in some genders there is a generic available in addition to a proclitic agreement marker.) As noted earlier, like the proclitic agreement markers, the generics/classifiers are optional.

These instances of optionality of agreement are less canonical than, for example, the Italian examples (14)–(17), where agreement is obligatory. We shall meet

---

[16] If it is agreement, we must ask what the target is. A possible answer would be that it is the additional classifier 'slot' in the noun phrase which is made available by the presence of the qualifying element.

further examples in §6.7.1. Examples are frequent when we look at clitic doubling. The closely related South Slavonic languages Macedonian and Bulgarian both have clitic doubling for objects (as well as inflectional subject agreement). Earlier we looked at Macedonian and noted that clitic doubling is obligatory under certain circumstances. In Bulgarian clitic doubling is 'generally optional' (Scatton 1993: 234). There are circumstances in which it is required, but overall it is found less than in Macedonian. Thus, if clitic doubling is included as a type of agreement, we can say that the type found in Macedonian is closer to canonical agreement than that of Bulgarian.

Let us move on to the morphology of the agreement marking. There are three relevant criteria here, which we consider in turn.

C-7: regular > suppletive

The canonical marking is by regular inflectional morphology (affixation). Perhaps surprisingly, we also find instances of agreement being expressed by suppletion.

Norwegian (Bokmål, Tore Nesset, personal communication)
(26)   en   lit-en   bil
         one/a   small-M.SG   car[SG]
         'one small car'

(27)   to   små   bil-er
         two   small.PL   car-PL
         'two small cars'

Here we see number agreement expressed through suppletion; for other adjectives it is expressed regularly.

This criterion is logically independent of the others, which is worth bearing in mind below when, in the discussion of domains, I ask whether the English pronouns *he/she/it/they* show agreement with their antecedent. One reason why some say this cannot be agreement, almost automatically, is that the pronouns would then show suppletive expression of gender and number. We can examine the domain question in other languages where the suppletion issue can be factored out, for instance in Russian where the third person pronoun *on/ona/ono/oni* 'he/she/it/they' is not suppletive (at least in the nominative); we continue with this point about pronouns in the discussion of (37) below.

C-8: alliterative > opaque

This criterion is related to the last but differs from it. Consider this example from Swahili; here '7' indicates the singular of the Swahili 7/8 gender (Corbett 1991: 43–49):

Swahili (Welmers 1973: 171)
(28)   ki-kapu   ki-kubwa   ki-moja   ki-lianguka
         SG-basket(7/8) 7-large   7-one   7-fell
         'one large basket fell'

Two characteristics of this type of agreement system deserve attention, and both may be found to a greater or lesser degree.

> 1. the agreement marker on the target is identical to a formant of the controller[17]

In (28) the initial *ki-* on the noun *kikapu* 'basket' is indeed identical to the marker found on various agreement targets in the sentence. But this is not invariably the case in Swahili, as we see if we look at a different gender, the 3/4 gender:

(29)   m-shale   u-lianguka
         sG-nail(3/4) 3-fell
         'a nail fell'

Here the agreement marker does not match the noun prefix, and so the system is not fully alliterative. English has a particularly opaque system in this respect, in having -*s* and allomorphs as the marker of the plural on controllers, but as the marker of the singular on verb targets.[18]

The second characteristic of alliterative agreement is:

> 2. the same agreement marker is used for different agreement targets

In a fully canonical system all targets take the same form. If we have, say, an adjective, numeral and verb agreeing in gender with a given noun, the agreement marker will be identical, and there will be no variation in agreement within word classes (for example, all verbs will behave identically). In example (28) we found *ki-* on each target. Contrast this with Swahili gender 1/2 (Welmers 1973: 171):

(30)   m-tu   m-moja   a-likuja
         sG-person(1/2) 1-one   1-came
         'one person came'

The numeral takes an alliterative form, while the verb, with the prefixed form *a-*, does not. Again languages vary: some have identical or extremely similar agreement forms, others show considerable variation (see, for instance, the discussion of Tsakhur in §3.3.3).

Thus alliterative agreement is one pole of a scale along which agreement systems can be measured. It may be that no language has totally consistent alliterative agreement, but many Bantu languages show the phenomenon to a high degree, with systems considerably more consistent than that of Swahili. Particularly

---

[17] This point relates back to the second criterion, according to which overt expression of agreement features on the controller is more canonical than covert expression. That criterion is concerned with the *fact* of overt marking; such marking may or may not be reflected in phonologically similar forms of the target, which is what criterion 8 is about. The second point is independent of criterion 2; the targets may have the same marker, even if this is not found on the controller.

[18] For the different status of this inflection in African American Vernacular English see Poplack & Tagliamonte (1989, 1994) and Green (2002: 99–102); see particularly Godfrey & Tagliamonte (1999) for references, for an account of the origins of the system of African American English, and for the 'Northern Subject Rule' (discussed in §7.7.4). The general oddness of the various English systems is pointed out by Hudson (1999).

consistent alliterative systems are found elsewhere in the Niger-Congo group (see §3.5.1 for references).

> *C-9: productive marking of agreement > sporadic marking*

The canonical situation is for each potential target of a given type to show agreement. Thus in Russian every verb shows agreement in number. Compare this with the Nakh-Daghestanian languages Chechen and Ingush, where only around 30% of the verbs show agreement (Bickel & Nichols forthcoming; Ingush is discussed in §3.3.3). Agreement may be much more sporadic. As an extreme case, in Kuwaa, a Kru language (a group within Niger-Congo), only one adjective retains agreement in number.[19] This criterion is distinct from criterion 6 (obligatory agreement is more canonical than optional agreement), in that here we are comparing items across the lexicon, whereas for criterion 6 we assume that agreement is possible and ask whether it is then obligatory or not.

These last five target criteria we have discussed can be seen as aspects of a single principle:

> *Principle III: The closer the expression of agreement is to canonical (i.e. affixal) inflectional morphology, the more canonical it is as agreement.*

I develop the notion of canonical inflectional morphology in §3.2. We now go on to three criteria which concern the target from a wider perspective, and which fall under the principle of syntactic simplicity. The first relates back to the earlier discussion of doubling:

> *C-10: target always agrees > target agrees only when controller is absent*

A target shows more canonical agreement if the agreement occurs irrespective of the presence or absence of the controller. That is, the target must agree, rather than doing so only when the controller is absent. This criterion relates to and further specifies the controller criterion C-1 *'controller present > controller absent'*. We need two criteria in order to generalize both over types of controller and over types of target.

My example concerns the agreement of possessive forms in Chukchi, which are formed from nouns by suffixation (Skorik 1961: 240–1). When functioning as an attributive, such possessives can agree in number with the head noun, but they do so only rarely (this is therefore another example of optional agreement, which is less canonical than obligatory agreement, according to criterion 6). The main point here is that these forms are more likely to take the plural marker when the noun controller is absent than when it is present (Skorik 1961: 233).

---

[19] The Kuwaa adjective is cited in Marchese (1988: 335), acknowledging a personal communication from R. Thompson. More generally on criterion 9, it might be thought that this criterion is of a different order, that any phenomenon is better illustrated by non-sporadic instances. The criterion has more weight than this, in that we find that those languages which have agreement which is canonical according to a significant number of other criteria tend to be those in which it is also expressed by productive morphology.

> *C-11: target agrees with a single controller > agrees with more than one*
> *controller*

Canonically, a target has a single controller, as in examples (1)–(4). Sometimes the target may mark agreement more than once, in fact it may mark it up to four times as we shall see in §3.2.4. What is less canonical is for a single target (of whatever type) to agree simultaneously with more than one controller. An example of this is found in associative/possessive constructions in some Bantu languages. I shall take examples from Shona:

Shona (Welmers 1973: 178)
(31)   Imbwa   na-v-ana   v-a-dz-o
         dogs(9/10) and-PL-young(1/2) 2-ASSOCIATIVE-10-ASSOCIATIVE
         'the dogs and their pups'

The last item, the associative -*a-o*, has two slots for agreement, and agrees with both nouns. The head noun *imbwa* 'dog(s)' belongs to gender 9/10, it does not change for number, but its plural (class 10) agreement marker is -*dz*-, hence 'dogs' is intended. The associated noun *v-ana* 'children, young' is gender 1/2 and takes the plural (class 2) agreement marker *v*-.

And finally, in this section on targets:

> *C-12: target has no choice of controller > target has choice of controller (is*
> *'trigger-happy')*

This criterion is due to Comrie (2003). The idea is that in canonical agreement a target has just one potential controller. In some less canonical instances, in a given construction there can be different controllers (as alternatives, rather than simultaneously as in the last section). Comrie gives an example from the Nakh-Daghestanian language Tsez. The target in question is the matrix verb with a sentential complement. Example (32) shows the expected construction. The complement is treated as the controller of agreement, and so the agreement is in the default gender, gender IV (the genders are given in Roman numerals). The experiencer argument, as with most verbs of this type, stands in the dative, hence *eni-r* 'mother-DAT'. (Following Polinsky & Comrie, for clarity the embedded complement is given in square brackets.)

Tsez (Polinsky & Comrie 1999: 116–117, Comrie 2003)
(32)   eni-r   [už-ā   magalu   b-āc'-ru-łi]
         Mother(II)-DAT boy(I)-ERG   bread(III)[ABS] III-eat-PST_PTCP-NMLZ[ABS]
         r-iy-xo.
         IV-know-PRS
         'The mother knows that the boy ate the bread.'

Remarkably, however, in Tsez a matrix verb can instead agree with a nominal in the absolutive, which is inside the complement. In (33) the matrix verb has gender III agreement, marking agreement with *magalu* 'bread', an absolutive phrase which is within the sentential complement:

(33) eni-r [už-ā magalu b-āc'-ru-łi]
Mother(II)-DAT boy(I)-ERG bread(III)[ABS] III-eat-PST_PTCP-NMLZ[ABS]

b-iy-xo.
III-know-PRS

'The mother knows that the boy ate the bread.'

We return to this interesting construction in §2.4.7, and for the conditions on its use in §6.7.1. For now the important point is that, rather than having a single possible controller, the matrix verb has two potential controllers (or triggers) and so is 'trigger-happy'. Another example is Skou (Donohue 2003a: 486–7) where some verbs (which in any case agree with the subject) may additionally show further agreement marking for the subject or agree with the object (according to the feature values of the subject and object).

C-13: target's part of speech is irrelevant > is relevant (given the domain)

The intuition here is that it is more canonical to be able to specify targets at a high level, as a general part of a domain, rather than having to make additional stipulations for subtypes. Thus we treat it as canonical to specify, for instance, that attributive modifiers agree with their head noun. Thus when we discussed Swahili (28), we noted that attributive adjective and numeral both agreed. Being able to give a rule for attributive modifiers in general is a more canonical situation than that in a language like English where one would have to specify that certain types of attributive modifier agree while some do not (we shall meet the particularly non-canonical situation in Michif in §9.1.2). Criterion 13 differs from criterion 9 (productive marking of agreement is more canonical than sporadic marking) in that the latter operates within a part of speech (do all adjectives behave alike?), while the current criterion compares across parts of speech (do all targets of a particular type behave alike, irrespective of part of speech?). Criterion 13 for targets mirrors criterion 4 for controllers.

1.4.3 Domains

There are few criteria concerning domains, but they are substantial. We consider these criteria here, then in §2.3 we return to domains in more detail, justifying the need for domains in addition to controllers and targets, and investigating their variety.

C-14: asymmetric > symmetric

The use of the terms 'controller' and 'target', and indeed the arrow in Figure 1.1, imply that agreement is an asymmetric relation. We might treat this as a defining characteristic, or we may see it as a property of canonical agreement. If two items match for the same external reason, this is not canonical agreement. If one stands in a particular form because of the properties of the first, then this is potentially canonical agreement. An analogy may be helpful. If houses numbered 10 and 12 are both white because it has snowed on both, this is not canonical agreement. If Mrs White paints number 10 white and Mrs Green in number 12 paints her house white too, that is, potentially, canonical agreement.

Seeing agreement as an asymmetric relation fits well with the idea that agreement is essentially a matter of 'displaced' information. The logical asymmetry is seen in two interrelated ways. First, the controller may have no choice of feature value, while the target does, as in these examples:

Russian
(34)   nov-yj   avtomobil´
        new-M.SG car(M)[SG]
        'a new car'

(35)   nov-aja   mašin-a
        new-F.SG car(F)-SG
        'a new car'

(36)   nov-oe   taksi
        new-N.SG taxi(N)[20]
        'a new taxi'

Here we have an adjective agreeing with the head noun in gender. The adjective has different morphological forms available to match the gender of the noun, while the noun does not accommodate the adjective in any comparable way. Logically, then, the relation is asymmetric, with the adjective being controlled by the noun. Examples of the verb agreeing in person with the pronoun would make the point equally well.

The second part of the logical asymmetry of agreement concerns the contribution of the agreement features to semantic interpretation. In examples (34)–(36) gender is not based on semantics but depends on assignment based on form (§4.3.1). If, however, in place of *avtomobil´* 'car' and *mašina* 'car' we have *byk* 'bull' and *korova* 'cow', then we have semantically based gender. Yet the gender marking on the adjective does not affect the interpretation of *nov-* 'new'. The contribution to semantic interpretation is related to the controller rather than to the target. Again this points to the asymmetry of the agreement relation (see also Nichols 1985, 1986).

This is a logical asymmetry, which does not determine how the relation should be modelled. There have been different means for doing so. Formerly the asymmetry was handled directly by copying, but there are serious problems with that approach: the controller may be absent (as in pro-drop languages, example (19)); or it may be present but be underspecified, as in (21); or the feature specifications on the controller and the target may simply not match, as we shall see in §1.4.4. More modern approaches are based on unification, which does not capture the asymmetry directly, and so leads to the question of how it is to be captured. We discuss this important issue in §4.1.

---

[20] This noun is indeclinable and so does not mark number (see §5.1.1).

If we accept that agreement is canonically an asymmetric relation, that leads to the problem of agreement in case. For linguists who have a view of syntax which is based on the notion of constituency, the traditional instances of 'agreement in case' are not agreement: matching of case values within the noun phrase results from government of the whole noun phrase by an external governor (see (13)). For those who accept a dependency view of syntax, the opposite conclusion follows, namely that there is agreement in case. I conclude that canonical agreement is asymmetric. Which instances count as asymmetric, and therefore potentially canonical, depends on other assumptions about syntax. We consider the agreement features in chapter 4, and we look specifically at the question of agreement in case in §4.4.1.

C-15: local domain > non-local domain

This criterion implies that the 'smaller' the domain the more canonical it is. That is, the smaller the structural distance between controller and target the more canonical is the instance of agreement. The most canonical is agreement within the phrase, as in examples like *these books*, and in (14)–(17); some would call this 'concord' (§1.3.1). Less canonical would be agreement beyond the phrase but within the clause, as in *Mary sings*, showing agreement of the verb with one of its arguments. Then we have agreement beyond the clause but within the sentence; this would be agreement of the relative pronoun with its antecedent (which we meet in §2.2.2). Finally we have the more controversial domain which goes potentially beyond the sentence, namely agreement of the anaphoric (personal) pronoun with its antecedent, as in *Mary sings because* she *is happy*.

The question as to whether agreement is only a local phenomenon is rarely asked. Opposing views are stated, almost as facts, with little discussion. There is a divide here, though by no means an absolute one, between those who have treated agreement as a prime focus of study as opposed to those who come to it as one of a set of syntactic phenomena to be accounted for. The former, for instance Moravcsik (1978: 334) and Lehmann (1982: 211), typically assume that the feature values of anaphoric pronouns are determined by agreement mechanisms. They cite examples of anaphoric pronouns within the discussion of agreement. On the other side, those who come to agreement as just one syntactic phenomenon of many often assume that it is a local phenomenon, and so exclude examples like (*Mary . . . she*). This is a convenient delineation for syntax, but we shall see evidence to question it. The only extended discussion of the issue of which I am aware is found in Barlow (1991, 1992: 134–52), who concludes that there are no good grounds for distinguishing between agreement and antecedent-anaphor relations. Agreement cannot be restricted only to local domains. This conclusion is confirmed in Siewierska (1999: 225).[21]

There are two main types of evidence supporting this conclusion: the type of features involved, and the distribution of syntactic and semantic agreement. The

---

[21] For the agreeing pronouns of Fula, which show special patterns, see Culy (1996).

simple argument is that canonical agreement and antecedent-anaphor relations are often based on the same features. This can be illustrated from a Russian example, from the transcript of a conversation:

Russian (Zemskaja & Kapanadze 1978: 242)

(37)   Mama   a   **čajnik**   kipjačen-yj?
         Mummy PARTICLE kettle(M)[SG] boiled.PST.PTCP.PASS-M.SG
         'Mummy has the kettle boiled?'

         Da-a. **On**   uže   naverno   čas   sto-it.
         Yes. 3[M.SG.NOM] already probably hour stand-3SG
         'Yes. It's probably been standing for an hour.'

The anaphoric pronoun *on* is masculine singular, because those are the feature values of its antecedent *čajnik* 'kettle'. Here the participle *kipjačenyj* 'boiled', like an adjective, distinguishes number (two values) and gender (three values: masculine, feminine and neuter, but only in the singular). The anaphoric pronoun does the same. It is not always the case, cross-linguistically, but it is extremely common that the anaphoric pronoun has the same feature possibilities as other agreement targets. If agreement and antecedent-anaphor relations are split, then there are two distinct phenomena which for no principled reason utilize identical features.

The second argument must wait until additional concepts have been introduced, so we will only preview it here. The four domains mentioned above constitute the Agreement Hierarchy, which will be discussed extensively in chapter 7. The hierarchy constrains the distribution of syntactic and semantic agreement. This distribution is a gradient phenomenon, across the range of domains. Evidence from the Agreement Hierarchy shows that there is no one point at which agreement phenomena can be neatly divided into two in a principled way. Rather there are several different domains for agreement, related in hierarchical fashion.

Anticipating the discussion in §2.2.2 and §7.6.1, I conclude that agreement covers feature covariance in a range of domains, from within the noun phrase to antecedent-anaphor relations. This is accepted in Head-Driven Phrase Structure Grammar, HPSG (Pollard & Sag 1994: 74), and in Lexical-Functional Grammar, LFG (Bresnan 2001a: 151). And as we shall see in §9.4.6, there is some psycholinguistic evidence to support this conclusion. Others limit agreement, more or less drastically. If we are to draw a boundary, then we need to be clear whether this is based on evidence from agreement itself (which would be hard to justify), or whether the boundary is being drawn as a result of other considerations within the syntactic model adopted. If such a boundary is proposed, then we should ask whether it claims to handle the distribution of syntactic versus semantic agreement (again such a claim seems unlikely to be well founded). However, even if one excludes antecedent-anaphor relations as part of agreement, this is likely to be because they are not local links, thus taking criterion 15 as categorical rather than gradient. Within the domains there are other sources of considerable variety. We discuss these in §2.3; the interesting issue of 'long-distance' agreement (a term suggesting that controller and target are more distant syntactically than we would expect) will be taken up in §2.4.7.

If we accept anaphoric pronouns as agreement targets, treating antecedent-anaphor as a domain, it is worth noting that an anaphoric pronoun is a pronoun which also agrees. Since I am using the criteria to separate out overlapping factors, I have concentrated in this section on the syntactic position of such pronouns. However, their morphology can also vary, and in part independently of their syntax. Thus anaphoric pronouns can be morphologically free or bound, the latter often being termed 'pronominal affixes' or 'incorporated pronouns' (discussed in §3.8). Pronominal affixes are less canonical in terms of their domain than, say, subject-verb agreement, since they are part of a non-local domain; on the other hand, they are more canonical than free pronouns in being morphologically bound. It is generally accepted that diachronically pronouns provide a major source of agreement morphology, progressing from full pronouns, to clitics, to inflections, as we shall see in §9.1.

Finally in this section on domains we shift from looking at individual relations to looking at the system, hence our last criterion is couched in terms of a given domain (and its being one of several).

C-16: domain is one of a set > single domain

In canonical instances, a given domain will be a member of a set of domains (agreement with a given controller may be expressed by different targets), following a general rather than a specific syntactic rule. Thus if we take Russian subject-verb agreement, this is one domain of several (attributive modifier agreeing with head noun, relative with antecedent . . .). This is a more canonical situation than that in a language where, say, subject-verb is the only agreement domain.

This criterion links back to the notion of redundancy: information concerning a given controller can be expressed more than once in different domains. An interesting implication related to this criterion is that multiple domains may well be a sufficient but not necessary condition for showing that particular markers are agreement markers rather than pronominal affixes (incorporated pronouns). Where different targets can show what is claimed to be agreement with a single controller, it is much more likely that these are instances of agreement rather than being pronominal affixes (§3.8.2).

1.4.4   Features

Here we find three criteria, one relating to features as a whole, and two relating to their values. Features are discussed in detail in chapter 4.

C-17: feature is lexical > non-lexical

Agreement in gender (where lexical) is considered the canonical type (see further §4.2.3, where I show that lexical features are the core of the 'inherent' features). The reason is that the target could not be marked with the feature independently, if it is lexical, and so this links to the asymmetry of agreement. Thus in (34)–(36) there is no independent source of the gender feature apart from the controller. Another way of stating this criterion is that features which are based at least in part on formal assignment are more canonical for agreement than features where assignment is more semantically based (§4.3.1). This criterion therefore falls under the principle of redundancy.

An interesting consequence concerns anaphoric pronouns; the fact that in many languages these can covary according to lexical gender strongly suggests they are part of the phenomenon of agreement, as discussed in relation to (37).

C-18: features have matching values > non-matching values

This seems obvious: some would claim that the definition of agreement must refer to the matching of values (§1.3). However, once a construction is identified as involving agreement, because there is a covariance of features, we would not want to rule out the analogous instances where the features do not match.[22] Specifically, since English subject and predicate verb regularly have matching features, we have to address examples like this one where they do not:

(38)   the committee have decided

We cannot simply say that *committee* is plural, since we find *this committee* and not **these committee*. We need to invoke a notion of semantic agreement for such cases, that is, agreement consistent with the meaning of the controller (discussed in detail in §5.4). From this point of view, we can say that examples like (38) are less canonical instances of agreement than those where the feature values match straightforwardly (*the committee has decided*); for further discussion see Corbett (2000: 188–91). Mismatches are analysed in chapters 5 and 7.

If we accept that semantic agreement is non-canonical, then we should include here instances of resolution, which specifies the feature values of targets when the controller consists of conjoined noun phrases. Consider this example from Slovene (Priestly 1993: 433):

Slovene (Priestly 1993: 433)
(39)   Milk-a   in   njen-o   tele   sta   bi-l-a   zunaj
         Milka(F)-SG and   her-N.SG   calf(N)[SG]   AUX.3DU   be-PST-M.DU   outside
         'Milka and her calf were outside.'

Here we have a feminine singular and a neuter singular conjoined; the verb is dual and masculine. Clearly, then, the features do not match. It is resolution which specifies these particular feature values (as we shall see in chapter 8). The fact that such instances are taken to be non-canonical fits with §8.6, where the peripheral nature of resolution rules is discussed.

The general effect of this criterion is to claim that syntactic (formal) agreement is more canonical than semantic agreement. An interesting consequence is

---

[22] Mel'čuk (1993: 329–31) stresses that the definition of agreement must allow for such instances; in Steele's definition this is covered by the reference to a semantic property of the controller.

that unification is an adequate mechanism for formalizing canonical instances of agreement (discussed further in §4.1). This consequence demonstrates well that criterion 18 falls under the principle of syntactic simplicity. The criterion is also consonant with the 'redundancy' principle.

Non-matching values can arise in various circumstances, from those which can be related directly to the lexical item (as in (38)), through those involving a construction (39), to those which depend on the use of the item, the pragmatics (as in (11)). There are systems in which mismatching is widespread, systems which Bickel (2000) calls 'associative', which are less canonical than the more familiar 'integrative' systems (of languages like Russian). We return to mismatches in chapter 5.

C-19: no choice of feature value > choice of value

In sentences such as the following, English allows no choice of form:

(40)   The five applicants arrive tomorrow.

Similarly in Hungarian predicate agreement with numeral phrases does not allow an option. The form, however, differs from that of English:

Hungarian (Edith Moravcsik, personal communication)
(41)   hat   fiú   érkez-ett
            six   boy[SG]   arrive-PST[3SG]
            'six boys have arrived'

The plural of *fiú* 'boy' is *fiúk*, and the plural of *érkezett* 'arrived' is *érkeztek*; neither would be used in (41).[23]

In Russian, the situation is more complex. Let us take just one type: these Russian examples are both fully acceptable:

Russian
(42)   voš-l-o   pjat´   devušek
            come.in-PST-N.SG   five[NOM] girl[PL.GEN]
            'five girls came in'
(43)   voš-l-i   pjat´   devušek
            come.in-PST-PL   five[NOM] girl[PL.GEN]
            'five girls came in'

The essential point here is that, given the same controller, target, domain and feature specification of the controller, there remains a choice of agreement. Taking a set of the quantifiers, I counted all relevant examples in a corpus of texts from the nineteenth and twentieth centuries (details in Corbett 1983: 150–3) and found 235 relevant examples, of which 54% showed singular agreement as in (42) and 46% showed plural agreement as in (43). (We return to conditions on the choice

---

[23] Amharic combines the possibilities of English and Hungarian. In construction with a quantifier, a noun may be singular or plural. If the noun phrase is subject, the verb then agrees, being singular if the noun is singular, and plural if it is plural (Leslau 1995: 179–80).

in §1.4.5.) Therefore the situation found in English and Hungarian (no choice of feature value) is more canonical than that found in Russian (choice of value).

This criterion links to the last, but is distinct from it. While choices typically involve semantic agreement in one option, semantic agreement may or may not involve an agreement choice for a particular target. For instance, in the example

(44)   this man and woman have travelled all day to meet you

The use of *have*, the result of number resolution, is an instance of semantic agreement, but is obligatory (at least for some speakers).

While many accounts ignore them, agreement choices are rampant. In §5.5, I investigate the factors which can give rise to them. As we shall see in chapter 7, however, while choices are frequent, the variation we find is far from random.

1.4.5   Conditions

Here the criterion is straightforward and intuitive:

C-20: no conditions > conditions

That is to say, in the canonical situation, when the controller, target, domain and features have been specified for a particular agreement construction, that constitutes a full specification. If we need in addition to specify a condition, that is less canonical. For example, we noted the agreement choice in examples (42) and (43) above. There is good evidence that controllers denoting animates in such constructions are more likely to take agreement forms with a greater degree of semantic justification (plural here) than are those referring to inanimates. Similarly, controllers which precede their targets are more likely to take agreement forms with a greater degree of semantic justification than are those which follow. Chapter 6 is devoted to conditions on agreement and so I can be brief here. We should note, however, that agreement conditions are particularly prevalent when agreement is non-canonical in some other way. In the Russian examples the condition interacts with an agreement choice, itself a non-canonical characteristic.

1.4.6   Three general principles

Three general principles were introduced earlier, and deserve brief discussion here. It is important to note that they never conflict; on the contrary, like all the criteria which they cover, they converge on the notion 'canonical agreement'. We have no need to rank them nor to specify what happens in situations of conflict, because the criteria are mutually compatible.[24]

Principle I: Canonical agreement is redundant rather than informative

---

[24] Canonical is thus a more abstract notion than prototypical; canonical can be clearly defined, but in principle there need not be a real instance, only approximations, while prototypical implies real instances.

Several separate criteria (numbers 1, 2, 10, 17, 18 and 19, and secondarily number 16) converge on this principle. It may be that it is this principle which leads to canonical agreement being relatively rare among the world's languages.

As a partial restating of this principle, we might add that the greater the reliance on formal properties the more canonical the agreement. This view of it is best seen by imagining its opposite. If we had fully semantic agreement, then it would hardly exist as a distinct phenomenon, since all the forms could be predicted directly from semantics; the matching effect would arise from controller and target corresponding simply by virtue of having a common semantic source. It is in the converse cases, for example in agreement in gender in instances where the gender is not assigned by a semantic rule, that we most evidently require special rules of agreement.

Principle II: Canonical agreement is syntactically simple

This principle is that canonical agreement can be described in straightforward rules, while non-canonical instances typically involve an additional complication. It is a generalization of criteria numbers 3, 4, 10, 11, 12, 13, 14, 15, 16, 18, 19, 20 and partially of number 6. It is reflected in criteria relating to each aspect of agreement (controller, target and so on).

Principle III: The closer the expression of agreement is to canonical (i.e. affixal) inflectional morphology, the more canonical it is as agreement.

Different criteria converge on this principle, namely numbers 5, 6, 7, 8 and 9. Note that they all relate to the target. There are different views as to which target types are legitimately considered to be a part of agreement, but no-one, I think, would exclude the type of targets with canonical inflectional morphology from an account of agreement. The criteria which fall under this principle have application beyond agreement, in that they are part of a typology of inflectional morphology, based on canonicity.

I wished to clarify some of the conceptual problems and misunderstandings that characterize this area. We have seen how different properties cluster, which makes it particularly important that we specify which properties are the basis for our analytical decisions. Seeing the gradient nature of many of the properties (as well as the ways in which they overlap), makes the question of 'drawing the line' between agreement and other phenomena appear secondary. It is more important to understand agreement and its related phenomena than to draw a precise line at which we might claim agreement 'stops' and some other phenomenon begins.

1.5   Scope and structure of the book

Given the importance of the topic and its diversity across languages the book could have run to many volumes. It could have been filled with details of different theories of syntax and how they fail to cover the data presented by agreement. However, that would not be a fruitful approach. In the early days of generative grammar agreement was used as a convenient test for investigating apparently more complex problems (e.g. verb agreement was a test for subjecthood, which allowed us to work on subject raising). Then various papers (including Morgan 1972, Corbett 1979) showed that agreement was itself much too poorly understood for it to be treated as an easy diagnostic. Now the wheel has turned, and it is rather agreement which is a major test of our theories of syntax. So I aim to present the agreement data in a clear and where possible neutral way, so that the established patterns of agreement can serve as a measure for theory-building.

The problems with terms go deeper than many realize. For this reason my 'canonical' approach is valuable. Individual readers may wish to exclude certain phenomena, but the position of what is being presented within the overall conceptual space should be clear, so that readers can include it as relevant or not.

I am tackling an area that for some would be up to three areas. There is agreement within noun phrases, which we have seen is the most canonical. For some, agreement in person is the major type, where the domain is the clause. Some work exclusively on this type of agreement, and ignore the others. And then there is the question of pronouns, which are assumed to be part of the area by some and are excluded by others. I shall discuss these issues carefully; we shall see that these three parts of the problem are linked in interesting ways, and that it makes sense to treat them together, rather than trying to draw unmotivated boundaries between them.

There are various areas involving some notion of identity which have been associated with agreement. Though I have taken a broad approach, I still need to exclude some phenomena which show only superficial resemblances to agreement. I list these here.

Switch reference is distantly related to agreement. It involves indicating (usually by morphological marking on the verb) whether the subject stays constant or switches from one clause to the next. This can be illustrated from Haruai, a Papuan language of the Piawi family, spoken in the south-west of Madang province, Papua New Guinea:

Haruai (Comrie 1989a: 41)

(45)   Ha   döyw   nwg^w-ön, bör dw-a.
        child rat   see-s_sbj   run go.prs.3sg-dec
        'The child saw the rat and he ran away.'

(46)   Ha   döyw   nwg^w-mön, bör dw-a.
        child rat   see-d_sbj   run go. prs.3sg-dec
        'The child saw the rat and it ran away.'

In (45) the same subject (s_sbj) marker -*ön* on the dependent verb tells us that the clauses must have coreferential subjects. The subject of the dependent clause is 'child', so the other clause will have the same subject, therefore it is the child who ran away. In (46) on the other hand, we know that the subject of the clause 'ran away' cannot be 'the child'. The likely interpretation is that 'the rat' ran away, since this is an available referent, but it is possible that there could be some other subject (provided it were third person and singular). This is not agreement because we do not find the 'systematic covariance' of features required by the definition. Agreement and switch reference are connected in that both contribute towards reference tracking (§9.2).

Negative concord is seen in examples of this type:

French
(47)   Personne n'=est   venu
         nobody   NEG=AUX.3SG come.PST.PTCP
         'Nobody came.'

Negative concord shares with agreement the repetition of information, in that the negative markers (*personne* and *n(e)*) express a single negation. However, there is no 'systematic covariance', no range of features available to controller and target. Rather the controller is there or not, and when it is there, it requires the presence of the second negation marker.[25] 'Concord' is a good term for such instances (which is another reason to avoid its use for agreement). A somewhat analogous phenomenon is so-called 'agreement in voice' in Maori, where some manner particles take passive morphology when the verb does (Bauer 1993: 92, 478–9). Again this is a matter of the presence of a controller of the phenomenon, not an instance of systematic covariance.

Preposition doubling can be illustrated from some varieties of Russian, as in this example:

Russian (some varieties; Turgenev, *Stuk . . . stuk . . . stuk!.. *'Knock . . . knock . . . knock!'
XIV, 1870)
(48)   ot   èt-oj   ot   sam-oj   ot   baryšn-i
         from   this-F.SG.GEN from   very-F.SG.GEN from   lady(F)-SG.GEN
         'from this very lady'

Here we see the preposition occurring before each element of the noun phrase. There is no 'systematic covariance' here, but simple repetition of a particular class of items.

Classifiers are of several types. Typically they involve a set, sometimes quite large, of semantically general elements which serve to classify the full range of possible referents. Thus even in English we have expressions like: *forty head of cattle*, where *head* is used for various livestock but not for other items. This is not agreement, since we have to do with selection of a lexical item, not systematic covariance. However, where the classifier is repeated (as in (24) above), this is arguably non-canonical agreement, or at least a possible source of agreement.

Sequence of tenses, as found in English, is sometimes annexed to agreement. However, this is hardly justified. Consider this example:

---

[25] I am grateful to Richard Ingham for discussion of negative concord.

(49)   Mary said that John had come. (Mary said: 'John has come'.)

There is no matching of tenses; rather the tense in the subordinate clause is shifted back to the pluperfect, and this shift is determined by the past tense in the main clause.

If we view syntax abstractly enough, a great deal of it is to do with required identities. Agreement is the central instance of identities, and there are numerous analogies to more distant phenomena. It therefore proves a good entry point to much of what syntax is about.

1.5.1   Outline of the book

Having set out the five components we need in order to describe agreement (Figure 1.1), we can explore each in turn. In chapter 2 we investigate the diversity of controllers, targets and domains. At this point issues about the realization of agreement become pressing, and so chapter 3 is devoted to the morphology of agreement. We then return to agreement features in chapter 4. This naturally brings us to the challenge of the instances where feature values do not match, which we address in chapter 5. We then have all the necessary material in place to tackle the remaining component, namely conditions, in chapter 6. We next look in detail at constructions in which there is a choice of agreements (chapter 7). Chapter 8 is devoted to the specific, but very interesting issue of resolution. And finally in chapter 9 we look at other perspectives on agreement. Each chapter builds on what has gone before. However, to help readers who prefer to begin in the middle, there is a good deal of cross-referencing.

1.5.2   Key languages

I shall draw data from a wide range of interesting languages. However, for continuity, three will play a special role. **Russian** is a member of the Slavonic family, which is a relatively conservative branch of Indo-European. It has substantial inflectional morphology of a fusional nature. Case is marked on noun phrases, where there is agreement in gender (masculine, feminine and neuter) and number (singular and plural), and verbs agree with subject noun phrases; the language is clearly of the nominative-accusative type. Within the noun phrase word order is relatively fixed, with determiners and attributive adjectives normally preceding the noun, and modifying phrases following. Discontinuity of elements is possible (as in (12)), with varying degrees of stylistic effect. On the other hand, order within the clause is relatively free, in that it is sensitive to information structure: given information typically precedes new information. Since subjects frequently represent given information, subject-verb-object emerges as the canonical word order. A fine overview of Russian is provided by Timberlake (1993); this is a good pointer to more detailed accounts. The development of Russian over the twentieth century is traced in Comrie, Stone & Polinsky (1996), and Timberlake

(2004) is a useful reference grammar. Russian earns its place as a language which frequently shows constructions which are close to canonical. Yet it has plenty of surprises too, with many choices of agreement forms and complex conditions on choices.[26]

Tsakhur is a Nakh-Daghestanian language of the Lezgian group. Estimates of the number of speakers vary, with the official figure being around 30,000, in southern Daghestan and in Azerbaijan. There is considerable dialectal variation. The recent substantial grammar (Kibrik 1999) is based on the language as spoken in Mishlesh, the largest Tsakhur settlement, with around 1,000 inhabitants.[27] All the examples cited in this book come from that settlement. Mishlesh is situated on the River Samur, somewhat higher up the valley than the settlement of Tsakhur itself, at about 1,800 metres. Tsakhur is the language normally heard in Mishlesh, though many people know Russian, to varying degrees, and some know other languages too, notably Azerbaijani.

The phonological inventory is impressive, with over 70 consonantal phonemes.[28] The inflectional morphology is extensive, with rich verbal paradigms, both finite and non-finite, based on a perfective-imperfective aspectual distinction, with a third stem indicating epistemic modality. There are eighteen cases, two numbers and four genders. Assignment to genders I and II is relatively straightforward: I is for male humans (but also gods, angels and so on) while II is for female humans (and female mythical beings). The other two genders are more difficult. Most of the remaining animates are assigned to gender III. Just a few, however, are in gender IV, along with some mythical beings. And inanimates are found both in genders III and in gender IV.

Tsakhur has ergative syntax: subjects of transitive clauses are marked with the ergative case; intransitive subjects and direct objects take the absolutive. The basic word order is subject-object-verb, as is usual for a Daghestanian language, but the Tsakhur of Mishlesh shows rather free word order. Tsakhur is remarkable for the sheer amount of agreement it has. As we shall see, agreement seems to appear everywhere we might imagine, and then in additional places too. Even among the luxuriant agreement systems of Daghestanian languages, Kibrik (1999: 354) gives Tsakhur the top place for the variety of the agreements it displays. We shall also meet some of Tsakhur's relatives, notably Archi and Tsez.

Our third key language is **Kayardild**, a member of the Tangkic family, described in Evans' (1995) extensive grammar. Kayardild is highly endangered, with a handful of speakers in Queensland, Australia, in the Wellesley Islands and adjoining mainland. Kayardild's relatives are Lardil and Yukulta (plus the

---

[26] Russian orthography is largely morphophonemic and so examples will be given in the standard linguistic transliteration of the orthography.

[27] I wish to thank again the people of Mishlesh for their hospitality and their help with working on their language.

[28] For transcribing Tsakhur, as in Kibrik (1999: 14–17, 27) the following deserve mention:

> **I** indicates pharyngialization; **macron** indicates length of vowels and intensive pronunciation of consonants; for consonants: ' marks ejectives, subscript **j** shows palatalization; **G** is a voiced uvular stop, **R** a voiced uvular fricative, and **X** an unvoiced uvular fricative.

extinct Yangkaal and Nguburindi). The Tangkic family is only distantly related to other Australian languages. Kayardild has a moderate phoneme inventory, with six vowels and seventeen consonants; it has parallel series of stops and nasals, each distinguishing six points of articulation. Kayardild is a typical Australian language in having a rich case system and very free word order. Cases can be 'stacked' to a remarkable degree. Moreover, the displacement of information on tense/aspect/mood/polarity means that Kayardild poses a serious challenge to traditional and current accounts of agreement.

These three languages are in many respects as different as one can imagine, both in their external circumstances and in their linguistic characteristics. An introduction to these three gives some sense of the scale of diversity of the world's languages. By including them at strategic points I will ensure that my view of agreement systems is broadly based. We should not forget too that English can have a useful role (Morgan & Green 2005). Its agreement system is at the typological extreme, particularly in the role of semantics; it should certainly not determine our approach, but it will prove very useful as a familiar language which exhibits an exotic agreement system.

1.6   Helpful background for the reader

1.6.1   Resources

There are considerable resources available for research into agreement. First there are several collections on the topic. Barlow & Ferguson (1988), and Brentari, Larson & MacLeod (1988) are still regularly cited. More recent collections are Corbett (1999a) and Brown, Corbett & Tiberius (2003). There is an on-line bibliography containing over 550 items (Tiberius, Corbett & Barron 2002). Then there is a typological database, which attempts to cover agreement exhaustively in fifteen genetically diverse languages (Tiberius, Brown & Corbett 2002a). This is freely available for on-line searching. It is described in Tiberius, Brown & Corbett (2002b), and analytical issues concerning the database are discussed in Corbett (2003b).

1.6.2   Assumptions

While I have gone to great lengths to make the material available to readers of different persuasions, readers should be aware of my own position, particularly in three key areas, so that they can adjust as necessary. The first is the nature of morphology, which clouds many discussions, when linguists have assumptions which are often unspoken and unanalysed. I think of morphology in realizational terms, that is, it realizes the feature specifications determined by syntax. There is therefore no need in our typology for agreement markers to be treated separately from targets and the feature specifications which are realized on targets. This view is discussed in §3.1. Second, as raised briefly in §1.4.3, I think of agreement as cumulating information from different sources, not as a matter of copying. We return to this issue in §4.1. For now we should bear in mind that a good deal has been written with the assumption that agreement is copying, and much of this (particularly writings on phenomena which were claimed not to be agreement) is rendered somewhat unconvincing once the alternative perspective of cumulation becomes available. And third, I take a canonical view, believing that there are clearer and less clear instances of agreement, and that in some areas it may not be productive to draw definitional lines; rather we need to see how the phenomena are related. This issue has been aired in the current chapter, and will inform the rest of the book.

1.6.3   Conventions

For presenting examples the Leipzig Glossing Rules are adopted (for details see http://www.eva.mpg.de/lingua/index.html). The essentials have probably been absorbed from the examples already given. Where the material can be segmented morphologically, this is done with '-' in the example and in the gloss (thus 'cat-s' is glossed as 'cat-PL'). There is a standard set of abbreviations (for items such as 'SG'), which promise to save linguists time as they are adopted more generally. Those used in this book, including necessary additions not in the list, are given on pages xvi–xviii. Where there is a many-to-one relationship, as in *were* indicating both past and plural, this is normally indicated with a stop, thus 'be.PST.PL' (but person and number are not separated in this way). For us it will be important that non-overt elements are indicated with '[ ]', thus 'cat' can be glossed 'cat[SG],' and inherent non-overt features are given in '( )', notably for the gender of nouns (§4.2.3). Explanations will be deliberately repeated when the key point of the example might otherwise be lost.

Glossing is always a compromise, since more and more information may be added, but this may obscure the point at issue.[29] For agreement, features are of key importance and all necessary detail will be given for them. Occasionally I shall simplify glosses in otherwise complex examples. Glossing is sometimes uncomfortable, because of the need to segment linguistic material and to assign information to particular segments. This segmentation is only to help the reader; it is not an issue in a realizational approach to morphology (§1.6.2, §3.1). Bold face may be used in examples, particularly complex ones, to draw attention to the relevant part; it has no linguistic significance.

The glosses are morphosyntactic, in the sense that syncretisms (morphological ambiguities) are normally resolved in the gloss in the light of the syntactic context. Thus in the example *they have decided*, the verb *have* will be glossed as third

---

[29] I note from the Leipzig Glossing Rules: 'Glosses are part of the analysis, not part of the data. When citing an example from a published source, the gloss may be changed by the author if they prefer different terminology, a different style or a different analysis.'

person plural, though out of context *have* represents various other feature specifications. There was an instance in (12) above, where the phrase *kakoj . . . sovet* 'what advice' was glossed as being accusative, even though out of context the morphological forms could have realized nominative case. In (12) the agreement of the verb unambiguously identifies subject from object, hence accusative is the only appropriate gloss in context. Where such syncretisms are of relevance, they are discussed in the text following the example.

We also need a convention for presenting evidence here, since I have written previously on related topics. The books on Gender (Corbett 1991) and Number (2000) had particular features as their focus, and demonstrating their nature depended in part on agreement. In this book there will be occasional overlaps, where the main argument line requires it. Whenever supporting evidence from those books can be referred to rather than needing to be directly cited, a reference across will be given. Other papers of mine on agreement are superseded by this book, though there will often be additional supporting material in the original paper.

1.7   Conclusion

I have mapped out the area of agreement in broad outline, and we can now begin to look in more detail. As we do so, we shall examine a wider range of languages than is usual in discussions of agreement. For this reason it will be important to be consistent in our use of terms, and to be clear about any analytical decisions. This will also make it easier to have fruitful collaboration with others interested in agreement, such as psycholinguists, those in acquisition and those in computational linguistics.

2   Controllers, targets and domains

We shall look in turn at controllers, targets and domains, starting with canonical examples and moving on to instances that are increasingly far from canonical (and occasionally quite exotic). Here we are investigating where agreement is possible: there may be further constraints on the instances described, and these will be investigated in subsequent chapters. We might not have expected displacement of information, as discussed in §1.1, to be possible at all. So we could try retreating to this weaker hypothesis:

Hypothesis II: The ways in which grammatical information can be displaced will be
                 tightly constrained. (False)

As we shall see, there is in fact a great range of instances of displacement; in this chapter I map out the possibilities in respect of controllers, targets and domains.

2.1   Controllers

Controllers are typically nominal in nature. We start with canonical types, and then move on to various problematic controllers.

2.1.1   Canonical controllers

Within the noun phrase, we may find a noun controlling agreement:

Russian
(1)   nov-aja   knig-a
           new-F.SG   book(F)-SG
           'a new book'

Recall that the controller here is *kniga* 'book' (feminine singular), the target is *novaja* 'new', which is also feminine singular. The domain in which the agreement operates is the phrase. Here the feminine gender is found on the adjective because *kniga* 'book' is a noun in that gender. Following the Leipzig Glossing Rules (§1.6.3), we mark the inherent gender of the noun as '(F)'. The feminine gender on the target is in a sense secondary.

For agreement beyond the phrase (as in (2)), the controller is usually taken to be the noun phrase (which may be constructed around a noun, pronoun, or other element):

(2)   moj-a   mam-a   ljub-it   roman-y
        my-F.SG.NOM   mother(F)-SG.NOM   love-3SG   novel-PL.ACC
        'my mother loves novels'

Within the domain of the clause in (2), the controller is *moja mama* 'my mother' and the target is *ljubit* 'loves', which agrees in the features person and number.[1]

The issue of which noun phrase in the clause is the controller is a domain question, considered in §2.3. However, controllers, targets and domains are closely connected, and to understand some of the interesting instances we shall need to know about ergative-absolutive agreement systems. I therefore make a brief excursus to include these systems here, before discussing them further in §2.3.2. In the Russian example (2) we have a transitive clause in which the subject is marked with nominative case and the object with accusative. In an intransitive sentence (like *moja mama spit* 'my mother is sleeping') the subject is in the same case, the nominative. This system, in which the intransitive subject is treated just as the transitive subject, is a nominative-accusative case marking system. In the canonical instance agreement works in the same way as the case system. Indeed in Russian the verb agrees with the subject in both sentences, showing that we also have a nominative-accusative agreement system. Our second key language, Tsakhur, behaves very differently:

Tsakhur (Kibrik 1999: 350, 829)
(3)   za-s   ham-ni   anna wasilewn-ē . . . dars   hiwo.
        1SG.OBL-DAT   this-ATTRIB.OBL   Anna Vasil'evna-ERG lesson(IV)[ABS] IV.give.PFV
        'This Anna Vasil'evna . . . gave me lesson(s).' (taught me)

Here the transitive subject is marked by the ergative case (which counts as an oblique case in Tsakhur as the modifier *ham-ni* 'this' indicates). The transitive object *dars* 'lesson' takes the absolutive case, which is the bare stem form. In an intransitive sentence, the subject stands in the absolutive. In other words, the system treats the intransitive subject and the object similarly for case marking. Tsakhur also has ergative-absolutive agreement. In (3) the verb *hiwo* 'give' shows gender IV, agreeing with the absolutive argument *dars* 'lesson'. It cannot be agreeing with the ergatively marked noun phrase, since then the form would be **hīwo* 'II.give.PFV'.

We return to these systems in §2.3.2 below. We should note that Kayardild, our third key language, has an unusual type of nominative-accusative case

---

[1] Some reflect the distinction between (1) and (2) in their terminology, treating agreement within the phrase as 'concord', and reserving the term 'agreement' for agreement beyond the phrase (as discussed in §1.3.1). As we shall see (§7.6.2), it is not possible to draw a clear line, and I shall term both 'agreement'. Lehmann (1982: 227–8) uses 'internal agreement' for agreement within the phrase, and 'external agreement' for agreement outside the phrase. Several have adopted this usage, but the reader should be aware of a less common usage which is to use 'internal' to mean within the clause, and 'external' for outside the clause. Some suggest that, even within the noun phrase, it is the phrase as a whole which is the controller (Lehmann 1982: 221–4), but examples of stacked modifiers showing different agreements (§7.7.2) would cause problems for such a view.

marking, and the verb does not agree with its arguments, so it is not relevant here. We have considered straightforward noun phrases here: there are also various types of complex noun phrase (conjoined noun phrases, comitative constructions, quantified noun phrases) which cause interesting complications for agreement. (The question of choices induced by controllers is taken up in §5.5 and §7.3.) However, these are all noun phrases and so are already included in our current list of possible controllers. We now turn to some less obvious types of controller.

2.1.2   Defective controllers

These are overt controllers which are not canonical noun phrases and which lack agreement features, for example, clauses and infinitive phrases:

(4)   [That he came so early] was very surprising.
(5)   [To err] is human.

Here the controllers (indicated '[ ]') lack agreement features; however, targets which *can* agree often *must* agree, and so here we find third person singular agreement (the default agreement form for English, see §3.6.3 for defaults).[2] We shall see other instances of controllers which can be treated as defective in §5.2.2.

2.1.3   No possible controller

The extreme case of defectiveness is shown by absent controllers that cannot have any surface expression. In languages like Italian there is no possibility of an overt subject for 'weather verbs', for instance:

Italian
(6)   piov-e   (*lui   piov-e   *ciò   piov-e)
           rain-3SG   (it   rain-3SG   that   rain-3SG)
           'it's raining'

Here there is no possible controller, but the target must still show agreement features. We expect to find that default agreement forms in such instances will be as for a defective controller.

2.1.4   Possessive adjectives as controllers

In Upper Sorbian, a Slavonic language of eastern Germany, the possessive adjective can control an attributive modifier, as in this example:

---

[2] To see that these controllers are not just singular, it is sufficient to experiment with conjoining them (*to err and to repent is human*), when agreement is (in the straightforward cases) singular, as opposed to plural for the conjoining of 'real' singulars.

Upper Sorbian (Faßke 1981: 382–3; Corbett 1987)
(7)   moj-eho   muž-ow-a   sotr-a
       my-M.SG.GEN   husband-POSS-F.SG.NOM   sister(F)-SG.NOM
       'my husband's sister'

In (7), the possessive suffix -ow- may be thought of as marking the phrase *mój muž*
'my husband'. To it is added the inflection to mark the feature values nominative
singular feminine, in agreement with the noun *sotra* 'sister'. The particularly
interesting form is *mojeho*; this is masculine since *muž* 'husband', which is the
source of *mužowa*, is masculine. It is singular for the same reason (the formation of
the possessive adjective requires a singular referent). Thus we have the possessive
adjective as a controller of agreement, taking another attributive modifier as its
target. The construction has been discussed in detail in Corbett (1987, 1995a);
see those sources for references, and for the distribution of the construction in
the Sorbian dialects see Faßke (1996: 66–73). This Upper Sorbian construction
is indeed remarkable, since we have an adjective (though of a special type) as
controller. It is a challenge to notions of lexical integrity, since the syntax appears
to require access to the internal structure of the word. The only other modern
Slavonic language which has constructions like (7), though to a more limited
extent, is Slovak. Control of the relative pronoun by the possessive adjective is
much more common than by the attributive, and control of the personal pronoun
is found throughout Slavonic, though with limitations for Polish (as we shall see
in §7.5.2). Here then we have a non-canonical controller which operates normally
in less canonical domains.

2.1.5   Qualitative adjectives as controllers

Basaá is a Bantu language of southern Cameroon. The data are from
Larry Hyman (2003 and personal communications). Basaá has a system of eight
genders, which I indicate according to the singular-plural class agreements (1/2,
3/4, 3a/6, 5/6, 7/8, 9/10, 9/6, 19/13). It has a set of 'adjectival nouns' (Hyman has
identified 77 to date), whose behaviour is unexpected:

Basaá (Hyman 2003: 268–72)
(8)   mí-n-laŋgá mí   dí-nuní   míní   / *tíní
       4-3-black   4.CONN   PL-bird(19/13)   4.this   / 13.this
       'these black birds'

The connective (CONN) must be used between nouns in a genitive construction.
Note that the plural form of -*laŋgá* 'black' in gender 3/4 is based on the singular
form (the 3 form). The adjective is plural, agreeing with the noun *dí-nuní* 'birds'
(for which 13 is the plural for singular class 19; this noun has the same singular-
plural pairing as diminutives). However, the adjective has its own gender (it is
in gender 3/4) and the connective and the demonstrative agree with the adjective
in gender and number (the 4 form is plural), rather than with the noun. A form

agreeing with the noun *(*tíní)* is unacceptable. The same situation is found with the possessive adjective:

(9) mí-n-laŋgá mí   dí-nuní   ŋwêm / *cêm
     4-3-black   4.CONN PL-bird(19/13) 4.my / 13.my
     'my black birds'

The agreement is not affected by word order, as these examples show (compare with (8) and (9)):

(10) míní mi-n-laŋgá mí   dí-nuní
      4.this 4-3-black 4.CONN PL-bird(19/13)
      'these black birds'

(11) ŋwêm mi-n-laŋgá mí   dí-nuní
      4.my 4-3-black 4.CONN PL-bird(19/13)
      'my black birds'

For comparison, we now consider a noun and an adjectival noun which are of different genders to those we have seen so far:

(12) lí-kéŋgé lí   mût   líní
      5-clever 5.CONN SG.person(1/2)   5.this
      'this clever person'

-kêŋgɛ 'clever' is of gender 5/6, while *mût* 'person' is in 1/2. When the noun stands in the plural, so does the adjectival noun, but in the plural of its own gender:

(13) ma-kéŋgé má   ɓôt   máná
      6-clever 6.CONN PL.person(1/2) 6.this
      'these clever people'

In the previous examples the demonstrative or possessive agrees with the adjectival noun and not with the noun. What then if there is more than one adjectival noun? The preferred version is for agreement to be with the adjectival noun closest to the noun:

(14) bi-lóŋgɛ bí   mí-n-laŋgá mí   dí-nuní   míní / ?bíní / *tíní
      8-good   8.CONN 4-3-black 4.CONN PL-bird(19/13) 4.this / ?8.this / 13.this
      'these good black birds'

In (14), *míní* 'these' agrees with *mínlaŋgá* 'black'. As the alternatives indicate, agreement with the further adjectival noun is less preferred, while agreement with the noun (which is what we might have expected) is excluded. It appears that these constructions have arisen from nouns, so the phrase in an example like (12) may originally have meant an 'intelligence of person' (Hyman 2003: 269).[3]

---

[3] A construction showing some similarities is found in the Chapakuran language Warí' (Everett & Kern 1997: 152).

2.2   Targets

Possible targets form a varied and interesting array. I focus on items which themselves show agreement, rather than acting as hosts for clitics (§3.2.3) which agree (since in the latter case the clitic is the target). The distinction is sometimes hard to draw, for two reasons. First because different theoretical positions can lead researchers to describe the same data as clitics or as agreement; and second because over time clitics can develop into canonical agreement markers and so there are genuinely difficult borderline instances (Lehmann 1982: 234–41; Siewierska 1999). This should be borne in mind, particularly when we consider more exotic targets.

2.2.1   Canonical targets

In different domains targets which frequently show the behaviour of canonical targets are adjectives and verbs. We also find articles, demonstratives and various types of pronoun showing agreement. Examples follow, and many more will be found throughout the book.

We begin with the adjective (and there are also verbal forms which behave like adjectives, namely participles):

Russian
(15)   star-yj   žurnal
        old-M.SG   magazine(M)[SG]
        'an old magazine'

Recall that we mark the inherent feature values, here the gender of the noun, inside '( )'.

(16)   star-aja   gazet-a
        old-F.SG   newspaper(F)-SG
        'an old newspaper'

(17)   star-oe   pis′m-o
        old-N.SG   letter(N)-SG
        'an old letter'

To take a less familiar example, here are examples of agreement of the adjective in gender in the Kunwinjku dialect of Bininj Gun-Wok (or Mayali), a non-Pama-Nyungan language of northern Australia. There are four genders:

Bininj Gun-Wok, Kunwinjku dialect (Evans, Brown & Corbett 2002: 117)
(18)   bininj   na-mak
        man(I)   I-good
        'good man'

(19)   daluk   ngal-mak
        woman(II) II-good
        'good woman'

(20)   kamarn   man-mak
        cheeky.yam(III) III-good
        'good cheeky yam'

(21)   kukku   kun-mak
        water(IV) IV-good
        'good water'

Adjectives may occur within noun phrases, as in the Russian and Bininj Gun-Wok examples given. Often they occur in other positions, notably in the predicate. We also frequently find articles (definite and indefinite) and determiners as agreement targets. For instance, French has the definite articles *le* (masculine singular), *la* (feminine singular) and *les* (plural). It also has determiners such as: *ce* (masculine singular), *cette* (feminine singular) and *ces* (plural).

Within the clause the verb is typically the central target for agreement:

Russian
(22)   Svetk-a   risu-et   xorošo
        Svetk-SG.NOM   draw-3SG well
        'Svetka draws well'

Such examples are commonplace. We shall consider the possible controllers for verbal agreement further in §2.3.2. The verb is often a host for clitics and for pronominal affixes (§3.8).

2.2.2   Pronouns

The other frequent type of target is the pronoun, of which there are various types. Consider first the personal pronoun:

Russian (Zemskaja & Kapanadze 1978: 245)
(23)   Alla! Ty   govori-l-a   tam   načat-aja
        Alla 2SG.NOM say-PST-F.SG there begin.PST.PTCP.PASS-F.SG.NOM

        koric-a   est', gde   **on-a**?
        cinnamon(F)-SG.NOM   be   where 3-F.SG.NOM

        'Alla! You said there was some started cinnamon there, where is it?'

The last word, the third person pronoun *ona*, is feminine singular because its antecedent phrase is headed by *korica* 'cinnamon', which is feminine singular. (It cannot be that the pronoun takes its gender directly from the referent because there is no semantic reason for it to be feminine.) Some would not wish to include such instances within agreement, since the pronoun can be arbitrarily far from its antecedent. On the other hand, it takes agreement features like other targets, and when we consider the topic of agreement choices we see that there is no non-arbitrary point at which to draw the line between such pronouns and more canonical agreement. We discuss this issue further in §7.6.1; for now we note that pronouns can be found in various domains. They are less canonical than the other targets discussed so far. For recent discussion of the agreement of pronouns see Wechsler & Zlatić (2003: 197–225).

Finally, though relative pronouns are restricted in their distribution, they are common agreement targets:

Russian (Bunin, *Gospodin iz San-Francisko* 'The Man from San Francisco')

(24)   . . . by-l-a   izjaščn-aja   vljublenn-aja   par-a,   za

be-PST-F.SG elegant-F.SG.NOM loving-F.SG.NOM couple(F)-SG.NOM after

kotor-oj   vs-e   s   ljubopytstv-om   sledi-l-i

which-F.SG.INS all-PL.NOM with curiosity-SG.INS follow-PST-PL

'there was an elegant loving couple, who everyone watched with curiosity . . .'

Here the relative pronoun takes its gender and number from the antecedent (*para* 'couple'), while its case is determined within the clause, by the preposition *za* 'behind, after'.

Apart from these familiar targets, there is a surprising variety of other possible targets. We review the less common types here.

2.2.3   Numerals and other quantifiers

Cardinal numerals sometimes show agreement; typically this is restricted to lower numerals.[4] For numerals, higher numerical value correlates with having more noun-like qualities (Corbett 1978), and so higher numerals are more frequently agreement controllers than agreement targets. In Russian the numeral *odin* 'one' behaves like an adjective in terms of agreement:

Russian

(25)   odin   žurnal
          one[M.SG] magazine(M)[SG]
          'one magazine'

(26)   odn-a   gazet-a
          one-F.SG   newspaper(F)-SG
          'one newspaper'

(27)   odn-o   pisʹm-o
          one-N.SG   letter(N)-SG
          'one letter'

It also agrees in number (*nožnicy* 'scissors' has no singular):

(28)   odn-i   nožnic-y
          one-PL   scissors-PL
          'one pair of scissors'

---

[4] Ordinal numerals, like Russian *pjat-yj* 'fifth', are often a type of derived adjective, and are therefore a frequently found type of agreement target.

Thus with *odin* 'one' we see agreement in number and in all three genders, as we would find with an adjective (only the forms are irregular). The numeral *dva* 'two' agrees in a more limited way:

(29)　　dv-a　　　　žurnal-a
　　　　two-M.NOM　magazine(M)-SG.GEN
　　　　'two magazines'

(30)　　dv-e　　　　gazet-y
　　　　two-F.NOM　newspaper(F)-SG.GEN
　　　　'two newspapers'

(31)　　dv-a　　　　pis´m-a
　　　　two-N.NOM　letters(N)-SG.GEN
　　　　'two letters'

The numeral *dva* 'two' agrees, but does not make as many gender distinctions as a typical adjective, nor indeed as many as *odin* 'one'; the forms marked masculine in (29) and neuter in (31) are identical (they are syncretic, see §3.4.1). For more of the complex story of Russian numerals see Corbett (1993). We return to the use of the genitive of the noun in §3.3.5.

Now consider Chichewa, a Bantu language spoken in Malawi; it is a variety of the language called Chinyanja in neighbouring Zambia, Zimbabwe and Mozambique. Here the numerals one to five show agreement in gender:

Chichewa (Sam Mchombo, personal communication)

(32)　　fupa　　　　　li-modzi
　　　　[SG]bone(5/6)　5-one
　　　　'one bone'

(33)　　ma-fupa　　　a-wiri
　　　　PL-bone(5/6)　6-two
　　　　'two bones'

Fupa 'bone' is a gender 5/6 noun, which means that in the singular, as in (32), it takes class 5 agreements, and when plural, as in (33), it takes the plural, class 6 markers. Compare this with *chingwe* 'rope, string':

(34)　　chi-ngwe　　chi-modzi
　　　　SG-rope(7/8)　7-one
　　　　'one rope'

(35)　　zi-ngwe　　　zi-wiri
　　　　PL-rope(7/8)　8-two
　　　　'two ropes'

As was mentioned, higher numerals are more likely, cross-linguistically, to be agreement controllers and lower ones to be agreement targets; however, there are various 'in between' cases which lead to complex patterns. These appear at different points in §6.5.2, §6.6 and §6.7.2. While I have given examples of numerals, there are various other quantifiers which in different languages may be adjectival in their syntactic behaviour and may show agreement, for example, French *tout* 'all', Russian *každyj* 'every' and many more.

2.2.4   Adverbs

Several languages have items which according to their syntactic behaviour and according to their semantics are adverbs and which show agreement. Such languages are found in various parts of the world. We begin with this example from the Daghestanian language Archi (Kibrik 1994: 349):[5]

Archi (Kibrik 1994: 349):
(36)   buwa-mu   b-ez   **dīta<b>u**   χ̄ʷalli   a<b>u
        mother(II)-ERG   III-1SG.DAT   early<III>   bread(III)[ABS] made<III>
        'Mother made bread for me early.'

This is a fascinating example; for now it is the form *dīa-b-u* 'early' which is of special interest. This is an adverb, with an internal agreement marker *-b-*, showing gender III singular. Note the Leipzig convention of indicating infixed markers with '<>'; we discuss infixes further in §3.2.1. If we change the example, we find different agreement:

(37)   dija-mu   ez   **dīta<t'>u**   nokɬ'   a<ø>w[6]
        father(I)-ERG   [IV]1SG.DAT early<IV>   house(IV)[ABS] made<IV>
        'Father made a house for me early.'

Here we have the gender IV singular *-t'-*. In both examples we have agreement with the absolutive noun phrase (we return to another domain found in these examples in §2.3.2 below).

The following example from Tsakhur is particularly telling:

Tsakhur (Aleksandr Kibrik 1999: 367, 828, Text 5: 209, and personal communication)
(38)   anna   wasilewna-nī   wo-r-na   inₐā   malʔallim,   **gē-r**
        Anna   Vasil'evna-ESM   be-II-ATTRIB.II[7] here   teacher   very-II

        uftan-da   dars   hel-e-na
        beautiful-ADV.IV   class(IV)[ABS] IV.give-IPFV-ATTRIB.II

        'Anna Vasil'evna was a teacher here, (and she) gave classes very beautifully.'

'ESM' indicates an epistemic status marker; the one used here, *-nī*, must refer to the past (Kibrik 1999: 705–12). In (38) we have two forms to consider. *Uftanda*

---

[5] The transcription of Archi is updated (thanks to Aleksandr Kibrik and Marina Chumakina, personal communications). kɬ is a palato-velar voiceless lateral affricate; 'marks ejectives, hence kɬ' is a palato-velar voiceless lateral ejective. The macron indicates a tense (fortis) consonant (as in ī). χ̄ʷ is a voiceless labialized uvular tense fricative. Stresses are given (marked ´) in the textual example in §2.4.10.

[6] Normally I avoid the use of Ø since it can lead to sloppy analyses; when a particular feature value is indicated by a bare stem I indicate this by giving the non-overt information within [ ], as with the pronoun *ez*. When there is an internal slot, as with *a<Ø>w*, I use Ø to aid readability.

[7] *-na* the ATTRIButive marker is the same for genders I, II and III: here it is gender II. This marker is used, for instance, in forming adjectives; in Tsakhur, unlike related languages, the range of these forms is extended to include predicative use also (Aleksandr Kibrik, personal communication).

'beautifully' agrees in gender IV with the constituent in the absolute case (§2.1.1), namely *dars* 'class'. Such forms have various adverbial and predicative functions (Kibrik 1999: 99–104), and so are not fully clear instances of agreeing adverbs. More surprisingly, the degree adverb 'very' has agreement forms, namely *gē-r* (genders I and II), *gē-b* (III) and *gē-d* (IV) (Kibrik 1999: 357, 367). This adverb (*gē-r* 'very-II') is ultimately controlled by the noun phrase *anna wasilewna* in the preceding clause. The example is not fully clear, but the effect of agreement in gender II, according to Kibrik's consultants, is to emphasize that the quality of the lessons was due to the teacher, Anna Vasil´evna, and did not come about by chance.

Examples of agreeing adverbs are found in more familiar languages (though they may be analysed differently). Consider first a construction found in Romance languages, such as Catalan:

Catalan (Wheeler 1995: 210, citing Fabra 1956: 82):

(39) l'   he   trobad-a   **tot-a**   trist-a
      3SG.OBJ have.1SG found-F.SG all-F.SG sad-F.SG
      'I found her all sad.'

Here again a degree adverb marks agreement. Wheeler evidently has the intuition that this is out of the ordinary because he labels it 'false inflectional agreement or "misagreement"' (1995: 210). He gives further examples from other Romance languages. In Catalan, however, there is the word *tot-* 'all', which agrees as an adjective. We might not have expected it to be used in examples like (39), but since it does function in this use too, we have an example of the use being extended in an unexpected way, and agreement being retained.[8] In Italian too adverbs agree to a limited degree (Napoli 1975).

We find a similar extension in Dutch. The attributive adjective distinguishes gender (common versus neuter) just for indefinite singular controllers. Most

---

[8] Something similar is found in Russian, as discussed by Mel´čuk (1993: 343–4). Russian superlatives are most commonly formed as follows:

Russian
(i)   sam-yj   interesn-yj   žurnal
       the.very-M.SG interesting-M.SG magazine(M)[SG]
       'the most interesting magazine'

(ii)   sam-aja   interesn-aja   gazet-a
       the.very-F.SG   interesting-F.SG   newspaper(F)-SG
       'the most interesting newspaper'

(iii) sam-oe   interesn-oe   pis´m-o
       the.very-N.SG   interesting-N.SG   letter(N)-SG
       'the most interesting letter'

Here we have what Mel´čuk calls a pronominal adjective (*sam-yj* 'the very'), which is used to form the superlative, and which remains an agreement target in that role.

For Mel´čuk this gives a new domain, since he argues that in (i) *sam-yj* 'the very' agrees with the adjective *interesn-yj* 'interesting'. This would be a remarkable domain. However, though *sam-yj* 'the very' may function as a modifier of this adjective, it does not follow that it need agree with it; it is simpler to say that it agrees normally with the noun which is head of the noun phrase.

adjectives can also function as adverbs, in which case they remain uninflected, as in this opposition of adjectival and adverbial use:

Dutch (Booij 2002: 48)

(40)   een   echt-e   flink-e   jongen
        INDF.SG   real-COM.SG   tough-COM.SG   boy(COM)[SG]
        'a real tough boy'

(41)   een   echt   flink-e   jongen
        INDF.SG   real.ADV   tough-COM.SG   boy(COM)[SG]
        'a really tough boy'

A small number of such adverbs are used as degree modifiers; for instance *echt* has come also to mean 'very'. Thus (41) can also be 'a very tough boy'. However, instances are also found of the agreeing form, as in (40), being used as the degree adverbial. This is found only with those adverbs which have a semantically corresponding adjectival counterpart, and never with those which do not (like *helemaal* 'absolutely' and *zeer* 'very' (Booij 2002: 48–50)).

Adverbs of various sorts are agreement targets in the following languages: Lak (a Daghestanian language, like Archi, Xajdakov 1980: 206), Kala Lagaw Ya (the language of the western Torres Straits Islands, Bani 1987: 189, 199), Bhitrauti (Hook & Chauhan 1988) and Gujarati (Hook & Joshi 1991).

2.2.5   Adpositions

Tsakhur has around thirty postpositions, of which two are agreement targets, namely *a-* 'in, inside' (which governs the inessive case) and *awu-* 'under' (which takes the contessive, the case for contact localization). In both instances they agree with the absolutive argument of the clause:

Tsakhur (Kibrik 1999: 125)

(42)   ši   wo-b-nī   centr-ē   **a-b**
        1PL   be-I/II.PL-ESM   centre(IV)-INESS   in-I/II.PL[9]
        'we were in the centre'

(43)   Xoče   Gaje-j-k$_j$ **awu-b**   wo-b-na
        snake(III)[ABS]   stone-OBL-CONT[10]   under-III   be-III-ATTRIB.III
        'the snake is under the stone'

In other languages adpositions may also agree with the noun phrase they govern, as in postpositions of the Northwest Caucasian language Abkhaz (Hewitt 1979: 113–14, 125–37). Most of the modern Indic languages have at least one postposition (generally 'of') agreeing with the noun governed (Payne 1995). Celtic languages have agreeing prepositions (see Sadler 2003: 88 for Welsh). The Iwaidjan languages Ilgar, Iwaidja and Maung, of north-western Arnhem Land, Australia, arguably have inflecting prepositions (Evans 2000: 127–32).

---

[9] In Tsakhur in the plural, genders I and II share the same form, and III and IV also share a form; see chapter 3 example (34) for the forms and §5.1.2 for discussion.

[10] This noun can be of gender III or IV, so this example is not as clear as the previous one.

2.2.6   Nouns

In addition to their frequent role within controllers, nouns may also be the target of agreement. This is not unusual in possessive constructions, where the possessum may agree with the possessor, and vice versa. In Bagwalal, a Daghestanian language of the Andi group, we find the possessor agreeing with the possessum:

Bagwalal (Kibrik 2001: 139–40)

(44)   ehun-šu-**w**   waš
       blacksmith(M)-OBL-**M.SG**   brother(M)
       'blacksmith's brother'

(45)   ehun-šu-**j**   jaš
       blacksmith(M)-OBL-**F.SG**   sister(F)
       'blacksmith's sister'

(46)   ehun-šu-**b**   misa
       blacksmith(M)-OBL-**N.SG**   house(N)
       'blacksmith's house'

(47)   ehun-šu-**ba**   waš-ibadi
       blacksmith(M)-OBL-**HUM.PL** brother(M)-PL
       'blacksmith's brothers'

(48)   ehun-šu-**r**   mis-ibi
       blacksmith(M)-OBL-**N.PL**   house(N)-PL
       'blacksmith's houses'

(49)   ehun-dar-alu-**r**   mis-ibi
       blacksmith(M)-PL-OBL.PL-**N.PL** house(N)-PL
       'blacksmiths' houses'

We return to Bagwalal at the end of this section. Tsakhur similarly has an agreeing possessive, but it agrees with the absolutive argument (Kibrik 1999: 357, 792 ex. 1, 803 ex. 14).

The opposite situation, where the possessum agrees with the possessor, can be found in, for instance, Tundra Nenets (a member of the Samoyedic branch of Uralic):

Tundra Nenets (Nikolaeva 2005):

(50)   Wata-h   ti   / te-da
       Wata-GEN   reindeer / reindeer-3SG
       'Wata's reindeer'

With a noun possessor, as here, agreement is optional (§1.4.2, criterion 6), and in fact the lack of agreement is more usual. With a pronoun possessor (even if itself absent) marking on the possessum is obligatory:

(51)   (pidør°)   te-r°
       you.SG.NOM reindeer-2SG
       'your reindeer'

We return to person agreement in Tundra Nenets in §4.6. For agreement with the possessor, but in gender and number, see Paumarí in the Arawá family of Brazil, described by Chapman & Derbyshire (1991: 257–8).

Another situation which might arguably be considered agreement of nouns arises in various languages of Australia, as documented by Nicholas Evans (1994 and personal communications). It involves body parts. In familiar European languages body parts have a gender unaffected by that of the 'possessor'. Thus Russian *nos* 'nose' takes masculine agreements, irrespective of whose nose is intended. This strategy is found in Australia too, for instance in the Gun-djeihmi dialect of Bininj Gun-Wok *kun-mim* 'eye' is in the vegetable gender, irrespective of possessor. However, in Nungali (an Australian language of the upper Daly River area, related to Jaminjung) there is an interesting construction restricted to possessed body parts, in which a noun denoting the body part agrees in gender with the noun denoting the possessor:

Nungali (Bolt, Hoddinott & Kofod 1970, analysed in Evans 1994)
(52)   ni-ya-manga   d-uŋunin
          IV-I-ear   I.ABS-man
          'the man's ear'

Here the gender IV noun for 'ear' has a gender I marker to show agreement with *d-uŋunin* 'man'. Note that the overt marker of the noun's lexical gender (IV) appears outside the agreement gender, a curious pattern found because the marking of the agreement gender appears to have arisen earlier. The following example shows a gender II possessor:

(53)   ni-na-wa   ɲa-ŋaru[11]
          IV-II-foot   II.ABS-woman
          'the woman's foot'

Though we are mainly concerned here with agreement of nouns, we should note that an agreeing adjective, more conventionally, takes the inherent gender of the noun denoting the body part:

(54)   mi-nad   mi-ya-ŋargin
          III-big   III-I-eye
          'big eye (of man)'
(55)   mi-nad   mi-na-ŋargin
          III-big   III-II-eye
          'big eye (of woman)'

The data are remarkable. However, we might treat the pairs as derivationally related, with the noun in (54) simply meaning 'eye of male' and that in (55) as 'eye of female'. For discussion of part-whole relations in Yawuru see §5.5.1.

Recall that the most frequent adposition to show agreement appears to be 'of', and the grammaticalization of such an adposition may give rise to possessive

---

[11] Evans points out that a final -ŋ would be expected here and suggests a misprint or transcription error; this is not relevant to the point at issue.

constructions with agreement. However, noun targets are not limited to possessive constructions. Several of the Daghestanian languages allow a noun marked in a particular case to take an agreement marker. Thus in Lak, the allative marker (ALL), which is added to the lative marker, brings with it an agreement slot:

Lak (Kibrik 1979: 76)
(56)   q̄at-lu-wu-n-**m**-aj
           house-OBL-IN-LATIVE-III-ALL
           'into the house'

In this example, the -*m*- is a gender III singular marker for agreement; the controller will be a noun phrase in the absolute. Kibrik (1979: 76) gives an example of a construction with two arguments in the absolutive (agent and theme), each of which can act as controller, with different emphases. In Dargi (Lak's closest relative, also known as Dargwa), the essive similarly adds an agreement slot, but has no distinct marker itself; thus the presence of agreement signals essive case:

Dargi (Helma van den Berg and Aleksandr Kibrik, personal communications)
(57)   urši   ši-li-zi-w   le-w
           boy(M)[ABS]   village(N)-OBL-INTER-M   be-M
           'the boy is in the village'

(58)   rursi   ši-li-zi-r   le-r
           girl(F)[ABS]   village(N)-OBL-INTER-F   be-F
           'the girl is in the village'

(59)   č'ič'ala   GarGa-li-ʔu-b   le-b
           snake(N)[ABS]   stone(N)-OBL-SUB-N   be-N
           'the snake is under the stone'

In these examples the gender marker (-*w*, -*r* or -*b*) indicates position of rest (giving inter-essive (57) and (58), and sub-essive (59)); without it the local case forms would indicate motion, 'into' or 'under' (lative cases). Agreement is with the absolutive argument.

Let us go back to Bagwalal. Some nouns have an 'ordinary' genitive, while those that we saw earlier in the section have an agreeing genitive. For the latter type, rather like the essive in Dargi, it is agreement which is the indicator of the genitive.[12]

2.2.7   Complementizers

Remarkably enough there is good evidence that complementizers can agree. The best evidence to date comes from West Flemish, a dialect of Dutch spoken in rural West Flanders (Liliane Haegeman 1992 and personal communication). Consider the following forms (they are not fully glossed so as not to prejudge the analysis):

---

[12] For an example of the two different genitives stacked, and a surprising agreement, see Kibrik (2001: 464, ex. 4.261).

West Flemish (Haegeman 1992: 48–51)

(60)   K=peinzen dan=k   (ik) morgen   goan.
         1SG=think   that=1SG (I) Tomorrow go
         'I think that I'll go tomorrow.'

(61)   K=peinzen da=j   (gie) morgen   goat.
         1SG=think   that=2SG (you) tomorrow go
         'I think that you'll go tomorrow.'

(62)   K=peinzen da=se   (zie)   morgen   goat.
         1SG=think   that=3SG.F (she)   tomorrow go
         'I think that she'll go tomorrow.'

(63)   K=peinzen da=me   (wunder) morgen   goan.
         1SG=think   that=1PL (we)   tomorrow go
         'I think that we'll go tomorrow.'

(64)   K=peinzen da=j   (gunder) morgen   goat.
         1SG=think   that=2PL (you)   tomorrow go
         'I think that you'll go tomorrow.'

(65)   K=peinzen dan=ze   (zunder) morgen   goan.
         1SG=think   that=3PL (they)   tomorrow go
         'I think that they'll go tomorrow.'

(66)   K=peinzen da   Valère morgen   goat.
         1SG=think   that Valère tomorrow go
         'I think that Valère will go tomorrow.'

(67)   K=peinzen dan Valère en Pol morgen   goan.
         1SG=think   that Valère and Pol tomorrow go
         'I think that Valère and Pol will go tomorrow.'

Let us look first at the verb 'go'. It has limited inflection: *goat* is found in the second person singular and plural, and in the third singular, while *goan* is found in the remaining paradigm cells (it is also the infinitive). Now let us turn to the complementizer. In most examples it has an attached subject clitic: =*k* '1sg', =*j* '2sg', and so on. Note that this subject clitic occurs whether the subject pronoun is omitted or whether it is stressed and so is included (1992: 60); in both cases inclusion of the clitic is normal, if not fully obligatory (1992: 75). However, it does not co-occur with a full noun phrase (66) and (67). Some would treat this as agreement, some would not (§1.4.2).

It is the form of the complementizer itself which is of greatest interest. In examples (60)–(67) we find the forms *dan* when the verb has -*n*, and *da* when the verb has -*t*, with one exception. This is the first plural, where we would have expected **dan=me*. However, we find exactly the same with the verb when it is followed by a subject clitic, hence *goa=me (wunder)* 'we go'. Thus the complementizer agrees in the same limited way as the verb, distinguishing two forms, spread over person and number. The complementizer is even more similar to the verb than first appears: for both, *-t* occurs before a vowel, but not before a consonant (1992: 218n5). This was not evident in (60)–(67), because of the subject clitics. Compare the following where there is an object clitic, which is vowel-initial (1992: 50):

(68)   K=peinzen dat=et   Valère goa kuopen.
         1sɢ=think that=3sɢ.ɴ Valère goes buy
         'I think that Valère is going to buy it.'

(69)   K=peinzen dan=t   Valère en Pol   goan kuopen.
         1sɢ=think that=3sɢ.ɴ Valère and Pol   go   buy
         'I think that Valère and Pol are going to buy it.'

In (68) the clitic is vowel initial, and so the *-t* is found on the complementizer (but note that the verb 'go' is now followed by a consonant initial word and so there is no *–t* here, which shows that the rule is indeed shared). With the third plural subject in (69) we again find *-n*. These examples also show that the subject need not be adjacent to the complementizer to trigger agreement.

Finally note that this agreement is obligatory; all of Haegeman's informants reject examples without the appropriate agreement:

(70)   K=vinden dan die   boeken te diere   zyn.
         1sɢ=find that those books too expensive be.
         'I find that those books are too expensive.'

(71)   *K=vinden da die   boeken te diere   zyn.
         1sɢ=find that those books too expensive be.
         'I find that those books are too expensive.'

We therefore have a clear case of a complementizer which agrees. There are languages for which similar claims are made, though in some there may not be canonical agreement but clitic doubling. There is other work on Dutch (Hoeksema 1986), on other Dutch dialects (see references in Haegeman 1992: 51, 218n6), and on German dialects (Kathol 2001: 43–5); see Getty (1997) for arguments that the Germanic complementizers take inflectional agreement (as well as being host to clitics). Examples from Dutch and German dialects, and from West Frisian, are given by Zwart (1993) and Weiß (2005). For work on complementizer agreement in Bantu languages see Rizzi (1990: 51–60).

2.2.8   Coordinating conjunctions

We are now into rather unexpected domains. Indeed Lehmann (1982: 206) wrote that possible targets include 'all the major word classes; excluded from the list are only conjunctions, particles, interjections, and the like'. It turns out that Tsakhur arguably has an agreeing conjunction. It is a particle used for coherence-related meanings, including 'and' and 'both … and'. It consists just of agreement in gender and number, with a link vowel if the host ends in a consonant (Kibrik 1999: 608–20):

Tsakhur (Kibrik 1999: 610)

(72)   bes,   halšdille hiӡ̄ō-n   haʔ-as,   dawar-ā-r=**id**
        well, now   what.IV-Q   do.IV-POT   sheep(III)-PL-ABS.PL= **III/IV.PL**

        maša   hel-e   deš   balkan-ā-r=**id**   deš?
        sell   III/IV.PL.give.IPFV   not.be   horse(III)-PL-ABS.PL= **III/IV.PL**   not.be

        'Well, what can you do?, (both) you can't sell sheep, and there aren't any horses.'

The agreement marker attaches, with a link vowel, to the two parallel elements, and would be translatable as the equivalent of 'and . . . and' in some languages, or 'both . . . and' in English. It agrees with the absolutive argument (in (72) it is attached to absolutive arguments but this is not always so). In (72) we have non-human animate plurals, which are in gender III, and the agreements for genders III and IV are syncretic in the plural. This Tsakhur item appears to be a counter-example to Lehmann's claim.

A second type of example comes from Walman, a Torricelli language of New Guinea:

Walman (Lea Brown and Matthew Dryer, personal communications)

(73)   wru   chuto   rounu   alpa   w-aro-l   nyanam
        3SG.FEM woman   old   one.FEM   3SG.FEM-and-DIMIN   child

        nngkal   ngo-l   pa   y-an   nakol
        small   one-DIMIN   that   3PL-be.at   house

        'Only one old woman and a small child were left behind.'

Observe how -aro- 'and' agrees with both conjuncts: it has the third singular prefix w- to agree with the first conjunct and the diminutive suffix -l to agree with the second (just as Walman verbs can mark subject and object). It is morphologically a verb (and can be used as a verb with the sense 'be with'), though syntactically it can behave like a conjunction.

2.2.9   Particles

Further counter-examples to Lehmann's suggestion are various agreeing particles of Tsakhur (Kibrik 1999: 182–3, 376, 410–12, 608–20). Consider this restrictive particle:

Tsakhur (Kibrik 1999: 182)

(74)   malhammad   čoӡ-u-s-qa   ӡa-**b**   balkan
        Mohammed(I)[ABS]   brother(I)-OBL-AD-ALL   restrictive-III   horse(III)[ABS]

        hi<w>l-es   qaljqʼan-o-r
        <III>give-POT   I.fear.IPFV-be-I

        'Mohammed is afraid to give the horse to his BROTHER.'
        'Mohammed is afraid to give the horse just to his brother.'

The restrictive particle ӡa- indicates that he is afraid to give the horse precisely to his brother. Note, however, that it agrees with the absolutive argument *balkan* 'horse', a point we return to in §2.4.8 and §2.5.2 below.

Tsakhur also has an agreeing focus marker, in the sense that it uses the copula (which agrees) to mark focus (Kibrik 1999: 582–608). Unusually, however, there is a language even more luxuriant than Tsakhur, and so we turn to that. A remarkable case of agreeing **focus markers** is found in Lavukaleve, a Papuan language of the Solomon Islands (described in Terrill 2003). Lavukaleve has pervasive focus marking: around 35% of clauses have a focus marker (Terrill 2003: 269), and there can be two focus markers in the same sentence (see (76) and (77) below). There are three focus markers, *meo, heo* and *feo* (cited in the third singular feminine form) with different uses, *feo* being the unmarked one. Each has a substantial inflectional paradigm for agreement, with fifteen different forms, ranging over three persons, three numbers and three genders (with some syncretisms). Different types of constituent can be focussed; Terrill provides ample discussion and textual examples.[13] For our purpose, the important point is to illustrate the agreement of these markers, with the focussed element. Contrast the following examples:

Lavukaleve (Terrill 2003: 290–1)

(75)   Aira   la   **fo'sal   na**   o-u-m   **fin.**
        woman(F)   ART.F.SG fish(M)   ART.M.SG   3SG.SBJ-eat-M.SG   FOC.3SG.M
        'The woman **ate the fish**.' (answers: 'What did the woman do?')

(76)   Aira   la   **fo'sal   fin**   o-u-m   **hin.**
        woman(F)   ART.F.SG fish(M)   FOC.3SG.M   3SG.SBJ-eat-M.SG   ECHO_FOC.3SG.M
        'The woman ate **a fish**.' (answers: 'What did the woman eat?')

'ECHO_FOC' indicates a focus marker from the *heo* paradigm, used in different environments. These include, as in (76), being the second focus marker in focus-echo constructions. In this use it agrees like the first focus marker (Terrill 2003: 291).

(77)   **Aira**   **la**   **feo**   fo'sal   na   a-u-a
        woman(F)   ART.F.SG   FOC.3SG.F   fish(M)   ART.M.SG   3SG.M.OBJ-eat-F.SG

        heo.
        ECHO_FOC.3SG.F

        '**The woman** ate the fish.' (answers: 'Who ate the fish?')

Terrill describes (75) as a basic sentence-final focus construction, showing predicate focus. The others show argument focus, determined by the first focus marker: (76) has a focussed object (the fish) and (77) has a focussed subject (the woman). The important thing for our purposes is that in each case the focus marker shows agreement; and in the focus-echo construction in (76) and (77) the second focus marker also agrees and so matches the first.

---

[13] These focus markers probably arose from copulas in cleft constructions (Malcolm Ross, personal communication).

2.3   Domains

I first need to justify having domains as part of my typology. It might seem that if we can list the possible controllers and the possible targets we merely need to combine the two. While in principle the relations between controllers and targets are many to many, it is certainly not the case that all theoretically possible combinations are found. Indeed, domains may be both more general and more specific than the relevant combinations of controllers and targets.[14] Thus we may find targets such as adjectives, determiners and some quantifiers in a particular language which might be part of a more general domain (attributive modifiers agree within the noun phrase). Conversely, if we say that a noun phrase is a possible controller and a verb is a possible target, we still need to specify the domain: the verb will not agree with any noun phrase. We also find instances where a particular lexical category agrees but only if it is in an appropriate domain; for instance, German adjectives agree in attributive position (78) but not in the predicate (79):

German
(78)   kalt-es   Wasser
         cold-N.SG.NOM   water(N)[SG.NOM]
         'cold water'

(79)   das   Wasser   ist   kalt
         the.N.SG.NOM   water(N)[SG.NOM] be.PRS.3SG   cold
         'the water is cold'

A more complex example is found in Spanish dialects, such as the Lena dialect, where we find 'mass' agreement (for agreement with controllers with mass interpretation). This is available in domains outside the noun phrase, but also inside the noun phrase given an agreement condition involving word order (see Corbett 2000: 124–6 and references there).

We have seen that there are four broad domains, namely: within the noun phrase, beyond the noun phrase but within the clause, beyond the clause but within the sentence, and domains that can extend beyond the sentence. Since these domains are increasingly less local, they are according to that criterion increasingly less canonical (§1.4.3). Within domains other criteria come into play, and so we can have more canonical and less canonical constructions within each.

We shall review previous work on delimiting possible domains (§2.3.1); then we need to look in more detail at the clausal domain, since there is particular scope for variety here (§§2.3.2–2.3.3).

---

[14] I have treated controllers and targets in terms of categories. One could treat, for instance, 'subject noun phrase' as a controller type, but doing so would incorporate the domain into the definition of controller, since appealing to the notion 'subject' requires the domain to have been specified.

2.3.1   Possible domains

There is an interesting tradition of work attempting to define possible domains. These attempts are valuable, but we shall discuss this work relatively briefly since they fail to include some of the more surprising domains. There are several problematic phenomena, and new agreement domains are still being found. I shall list the more challenging domains in §2.4, and these suggest that the notion 'possible domain' must be substantially widened. This will be a move toward a more complete basic typology (which is an essential step if there is eventually to be a more adequate definition of possible domain).

The domains question was raised by Moravcsik (1978). She proposed the 'coreferentiality principle':

> there is one generalization that holds for all constituents that agree with nominals whether in the same language or not and whether in the same sentence or not: that all such constituents are understood as including reference to the nominal. The particular content of this claim is that in no sentence of any language is there a constituent that agrees with a nominal such that that constituent includes reference to a nominal other than the one it agrees with or that does not include reference to any nominal at all.   (1978: 362–3)

Once pointed out, this principle appears to be self-evidently true. It rules out having a referring expression agreeing with a nominal with a different referent. We do not expect to find a language in which an expression like *the large cat chased the small mouse* would include agreement of *small* with *the large cat*. Of course not. And yet we shall see that Moravcsik's principle does not hold, when we examine Archi in §2.4.9.[15]

Taking a different approach to the domains question, Keenan (1978) considered the relation between surface syntax and logical form and concluded that we would expect greater similarities between the two than linguistic theory suggested. As an instance Keenan proposed that function-argument structure in semantics was a predictor for possible agreement in syntax. Thus verb phrases are functions which take determined noun phrases (in Keenan and Faltz's Logical Types) as their arguments, and verb phrases can indeed agree with noun phrases. (Keenan was aware of the possibilities of flipping functions and arguments within logic; he attempted to construct the logic according to the evidence of natural language.) Keenan's is probably the best-known attempt to define possible agreement domains. It fed directly into Generalized Phrase Structure Grammar (GPSG), in that it is the basis for the Control Agreement Principle (Gazdar, Klein, Pullum & Sag 1985: 83–94), which specifies possible domains. The Control Agreement Principle runs into problems with some of the domains we shall see below, notably agreement with possessives as in Maithili (§2.4.1).

---

[15] Moravcsik also provides (1978: 364–5) nine implicational statements about domains within the sentences of a given language.

The problems of specifying possible domains are discussed further in Schmidt (forthcoming). A radical suggestion is that of Koopman (2003), who argues for the 'strong agreement' hypothesis, according to which the specifier-head configuration is the only agreement configuration. The specific instance of long-distance agreement (§2.4.7) undermines this claim, as shown by Polinsky & Potsdam (2001), and more generally the diversity of domains shown in this chapter as a whole does not fit readily under the specifier-head configuration. Rather than spending more time on the problems with particular suggestions, it is more important that I specify as completely as possible what agreement domains are actually found, which I shall continue in §2.4 and §2.5. We should note too that for some researchers there are further domains which for us will count as conditions (chapter 6). I treat notions like 'topic' as a matter of pragmatics, and describe it as a condition on agreement; others represent it directly in the syntax, thus giving a more complex picture of domains than that presented here.

2.3.2   Nominative-accusative and ergative-absolutive systems

Given a language with agreement within the clause, a basic question is which of the possible elements of the clause will be the controller. Languages have different systems for organizing the arguments of the verb, and these are reflected in agreement domains. We discuss grammatical relations further in §2.3.3; in order to introduce the major systems I will for now assume that notions like 'subject' are relevant to agreement. In the more familiar systems the subject is privileged. In the well-known nominative-accusative systems the subjects of transitive and of intransitive verbs are treated alike: they both are marked with the nominative case and both control agreement of the verb (§2.1.1).

The less familiar ergative-absolutive systems deserve fuller attention. In canonical ergative-absolutive systems, case and agreement work in parallel, both in a sense favouring the absolutive. Such systems are found in Daghestanian languages, as in Archi which I use for illustration here, since some crucial examples will be from Archi in the succeeding sections. As we saw in §2.1.1, ergative-absolutive systems treat intransitive and transitive clauses differently. If there is a single argument, it will be in the absolutive, and the verb agrees with it. We see this from gender agreement: Archi has four genders (Corbett 1991: 27–9), like Tsakhur (§1.5.2), and the noun phrases in these examples are all singular:

Archi (Kibrik 1994: 349)
(80)   Buwa   d-arχ arši   d-i
        mother(II)[ABS] II-lie.down II-be
        'Mother is lying down.'

(81)   dija   w-arχ arši   w-i
        Father(I)[ABS] I-lie.down   I-be
        'Father is lying down.'

Both the main verb and the auxiliary in these examples show agreement with the absolutive argument (and note that the absolutive takes zero marking in the singular).[16] When there are two arguments, it is the object which stands in the absolutive case and controls verb agreement. The subject stands in the ergative, which is morphologically marked:

(82) buwa-mu   b-ez   dīta<b>u   x̄ʷalli   a<b>u
      mother(II)-ERG III-1SG.DAT early<III> bread(III)[ABS] made<III>
      'Mother made bread for me early.'

(83) dija-mu   Ø-ez   dīt<t'>u   noL'   a<Ø>w
      Father(I)-ERG IV-1SG.DAT early<IV>   house(IV)[ABS] made<IV>
      'Father made a house for me early.'

Here the verb agrees with the absolutive argument, as do other targets; we noted agreement of the adverb in §2.2.4, and we return to the agreement of the pronoun in §2.4.9.

Like nominative-accusative systems, ergative-absolutive systems are canonical to varying degrees (see Kibrik 1985 for discussion of differences in ergative systems). Some systems allow clauses with two absolutive arguments, as indeed in Archi (Kibrik 2003: 562–3) and in Tsakhur (Kibrik 1999: 368–70).

I have labelled systems 'canonical' where case marking and agreement run in parallel. In an ergative-absolutive system this means that the verb agrees with the absolutive argument. This is another instance where what is canonical is not particularly frequent; there are many less canonical examples. A particularly interesting one is Nias, an Austronesian language spoken on Nias, one of the Barrier Islands along the west of Sumatra. This system was pointed out by Brown (2003); for more detail on Nias generally see Brown (2005). Nias distinguishes two modes, realis and irrealis, and the construction of interest occurs in the realis mode:

Nias (Brown 2003)
(84) I-tolo   zi'ila   ama-gu.
      3SG.RLS-help   ABS.village.advisor   [ERG]father-1SG.POSS
      'My father is helping/helped a/the/some village advisor(s).'

This example shows agreement with the ergative, the agent argument *ama-gu* 'my father'. This is unexpected. We can see this from the information on number. Nouns do not themselves mark number, but the sentence is understood as having a singular subject ('father') and a singular or plural object ('village advisor(s)'), according to context. Furthermore, and also unusually, the ergative is the morphologically unmarked case, while the absolutive is marked by an initial mutation.

---

[16] When analysing these systems, rather than the terms 'absolutive' and 'ergative', some prefer the terms 'nominative' and 'ergative', arguing that 'nominative' should indicate the case for naming and for the single argument of an intransitive verb, as in nominative-accusative systems (Kibrik 2003: 147n21). This is a good point. I use 'absolutive' partly because this usage is widespread and partly because it immediately reminds the reader of the type of system in question. Since my typology requires us to compare examples from many languages, the fact that 'absolutive' provides an instant prompt as to the syntactic system is valuable for exposition.

Thus *zi'ila* 'village advisor' is the absolutive form of *si'ila* (ergative). This ergative form is found in the next example, and the verb agrees with it:

(85)   **La**-tolo   n-ama-gu   **si'ila.**
        3PL.RLS-help ABS-father-1SG.POSS [ERG]village.advisor
        'The village advisors are helping/helped my father.'

Here the vowel-initial *ama* 'father' takes *n-* in its mutation form (absolutive). My final example shows that the verb does not agree with the argument in the absolutive:

(86)   Mofanö n-ama-gu.
        leave   ABS-father-1SG.POSS
        'My father is leaving/left.'

Thus we see that in Nias the ergative is the morphologically unmarked form, and that in the realis mode the verb agrees just with the argument in the ergative.

While for clarity I have emphasized the two main types of system, there are considerable complications: languages may combine nominative-accusative and ergative-absolutive systems in various ways (in 'split-ergative systems', Dixon 1994: 70–110), and case marking and agreement do not always run smoothly in parallel (Woolford 2000).[17] When case marking and agreement diverge, agreement runs on a nominative-accusative basis.

2.3.3   The role of grammatical relations: preliminary considerations

The notion 'grammatical relation' is well established (see Blake 1994: 48–93, Palmer 1994, Givón 2001: 173–232, Kibrik 2003: 109). It has a continuous tradition in European linguistics, while the attempt in transformational grammar to treat sentence structure in terms of dominance and linear order led to a reaction, particularly in America, in which the need for grammatical relations was carefully justified, rather than being assumed. This is most evident in Relational Grammar, where grammatical relations are central (see Perlmutter 1983a, Perlmutter and Rosen 1984, Postal and Joseph 1990, Blake 1990). A parallel reaction is found in the typology of Keenan and Comrie (1977).

Grammatical relations are treated hierarchically, as in the Relational Hierarchy (Johnson 1977: 156):

subject > direct object > indirect object > other object

The Accessibility Hierarchy of Keenan and Comrie (1977: 66) is comparable, but extends to further categories. In subsequent years grammatical relations have been embedded in different theories, with somewhat different interpretations. They

---

[17] Silverstein (1976) is an important early paper on split ergativity; see also Garrett (1990: 290) and for discussion and further references see Van Valin & LaPolla (1997: 352–76). It may be helpful to think of split systems as systems in which (agreement) conditions apply. The systems found in the Chukotko-Kamchatkan languages Itelmen, Chukchi and Koryak are particularly challenging; see Bobaljik (1998) and Spencer (2000) for analysis.

have a major role in Lexical Functional Grammar, as 'grammatical functions' (Bresnan 2001a: 44–60).

It is worth going back to early ideas on grammatical relations and agreement, since the claims made then were attractively simple. The Relational Hierarchy was considered directly relevant to agreement. Thus Moravcsik (1978: 364) claimed that if a language shows agreement, then there will be cases of agreement with the intransitive subject; only if there is such agreement will there be agreement with the direct object, and agreement of this type is a precondition for agreement with the indirect object. This is a typological claim at the level of possible languages. A related claim was made by Johnson (1977: 157):

(87)   THE AGREEMENT LAW: *Only terms can trigger verbal agreement.*
          (Where 'term' covers the first three items on the hierarchy.)

Moreover, there are instances where grammatical relations appear to be the natural way to state agreement rules; thus in the Daghestanian language Udi Harris (1984: 246) states that there is agreement with the subject, though this may be marked ergative or absolutive. Such instances were discussed in detail with regard to Georgian, notably by Harris (1981); for later analyses giving a greater role to morphology see Anderson (1984) and Kathman (1995). An interesting instance reported recently involves Icari Dargi (Daghestanian), where with a few affective verbs person agreement can in the right construction be controlled by the experiencer noun phrase in the superlative case (Sumbatova & Mutalov 2003: 79).

If Johnson's claim could be maintained, we would indeed have a highly restricted theory of agreement, and a fine basis for a typology.[18] However, there are three types of serious counter-examples. In each of them the term-controller fails to control agreement, and another noun phrase 'usurps' its position. These are: 'back' agreement (§2.4.4), 'brother-in-law' agreement (§2.4.5) and instances of the lack of agreement with possessor phrases, which we discuss in terms of the role of case in §6.6. All three problematic constructions share two characteristics. First, the subject is not a prototypical subject, according to Keenan's criteria (1976). Second, the noun phrase which controls the agreement is in the expected case of the subject (nominative or absolutive). We return to grammatical relations and case in §6.6, in the context of possible conditions on agreement.

2.4   A schema for non-canonical domains

We have started to explore the diversity of domains. As we shall see, there are many more domains of agreement, which show that previous typologies and suggestions for defining domains were too restrictive. In order to come to grips with their diversity I shall plot them in terms of their distance from the

---

[18] It should be pointed out that much of the early discussion dealt with verbal affixes, whose status has since been under scrutiny as to whether they are agreement markers or pronominal affixes (see Corbett 2003b for discussion).

canonical type. First I organize them by 'overall' domain (within the phrase
or within the clause). Within those divisions, are we dealing with a canonical
controller (canonical in respect of the domain)? If so, is control of agreement
dependent on the canonical component of the controller? These distinctions are
laid out in (88).

(88)

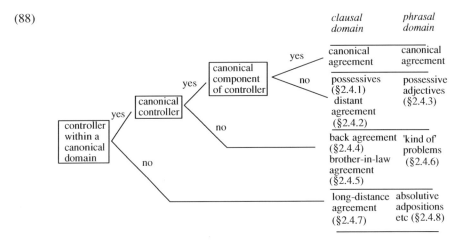

	clausal domain	phrasal domain
canonical component of controller — yes	canonical agreement	canonical agreement
canonical component of controller — no	possessives (§2.4.1) distant agreement (§2.4.2)	possessive adjectives (§2.4.3)
canonical controller — no	back agreement (§2.4.4) brother-in-law agreement (§2.4.5)	'kind of' problems (§2.4.6)
controller within a canonical domain — no	long-distance agreement (§2.4.7)	absolutive adpositions etc (§2.4.8)

The schema in (88) gives a convenient map for investigating unusual domains.
Note that the agreement of pronouns, discussed under §2.2.2, is outside this
scheme, since it involves the largest domains (it goes beyond normal syntactic domains). I have divided the domains into those within the phrase and
those within the clause. There is more scope for non-canonical domains within
the looser bounds of the clause, and so the distinctions are easier to spot.
For exposition, therefore, I shall consider each type of non-canonical domain
first within the overall domain type of the clause, and then within the phrase.
And the non-canonical elements can be 'stacked up', giving more complex
situations.

The schema in (88) also provides a way of classifying agreement errors, a subject taken further in §9.4.2. Of course, non-canonical does not mean we are dealing
with errors; and the examples to be considered in the subsections below are not
errors. However, as an example, the famous error in English known as attraction,
where the verb agrees with the nearer part of a complex noun phrase, would fit as
agreement with a canonical controller but with a non-canonical component. For
example:

Headline in Guardian newspaper, 4 August 2001, page 2
(89)   Rise in email viruses threaten net.

Austin & Bresnan (1996: 244*n*21)
(90)   Copies of all this data is available for study at the Australian Institute of
         Aboriginal and Torres Strait Islander Studies, Canberra.

Example (89) shows agreement with *email viruses*, and (90) with *this data*.

2.4.1   Verb agreement with possessives

Verbs can agree with a range of noun phrases. While noun phrases may have surprising functions in some instances, we expect the head of the noun phrase to determine the relevant features. What is surprising about agreement with possessors is that we find agreement with a part of a complex noun phrase which is not the lexical head. This is found in various languages, in differing circumstances (for instance, it may be optional or obligatory, and all persons or only first and second may be involved). Stump & Yadav (1988) pointed out the construction in Maithili specifically as a domain problem (claiming it as a counter-example to the Control Agreement Principle of GPSG), so it is appropriate to start with Maithili. They give the following examples (1988: 309):

Maithili (Stump & Yadav 1988)
(91)   tohar   bāp   aelthun
          your.MID_HON   father.HON   came.3_HON.2_MID_HON
          'Your (mid-honorific) father (honorific) came.'

Here the verb agrees with both parts of the noun phrase, the head and the possessor. This is not always the case, however, because in (92), if we look at the object, the verb agrees just with the possessor, and not with the head:

(92)   ham torā   betā-ke   dekhaliau
          I   your.NON_HON   son-OBJ   saw.1.2_NON_HON
          'I saw your (non-honorific) son.'

The Maithili situation is discussed at length in Bickel, Bisang & Yādava (1999); see also Yadav (1996) and Subbarao (2003: 3–4).

   This phenomenon (with variants) is found in different parts of the world. According to Dan Everett (personal communication), Banawá (and other Arawá languages) have subject-verb agreement in person and number. Agreement is with the head of the subject noun phrase, and it is marked by a prefix on the verb. The verb also agrees in gender with the topic noun phrase, which is marked by a suffix on the verb. This gives an interesting effect with inalienable possession, as in phrases such as 'my hand'. If this is used in subject position, the verb agrees in person and number with 'hand', but in gender with 'I'. The situation in the closely related Jarawara is described in Dixon (2000); we return to Jarawara in §5.6.4. Then for possessors as controllers in Tabasaran (a Daghestanian language) see Kibrik & Seleznev (1982) and Harris (1994: 121).

2.4.2   Distant first conjunct agreement

   In agreement with conjoined noun phrases, there are typically two possibilities: agreement with all conjuncts (in which case resolution operates) or agreement with just the nearest conjunct (as discussed in §5.7). There is, however, a further rare possibility: *distant first conjunct* agreement (sometimes just called 'distant' agreement). This is agreement with the first conjunct, which, with subject-verb word order, is not the nearest. Occasional examples occur in Slovene:

Slovene (Lenček 1972: 59)
(93)   **knjig-e**   in   peres-a   so   se   **podražil-e**
        book(F)-PL and pen(N)-PL AUX.PL REFL got.dear-F.PL
        'Books and pens have become more expensive.'

This must be an instance of agreement with the first conjunct; agreement with all would require the masculine plural (a result of resolution). Similar examples occur in Serbian/Croatian/Bosnian; the most extensive source is Megaard (1976), see also Corbett (1983: 99–103 and references there) and Leko (1986: 230). It is also attested in Latin (Kühner & Stegmann 1955: 53, 55, 58–9). The general situation of distant agreement may be represented like this:

(94)   Agreement with the first (most distant) conjunct

           NP   NP   NP   **TARGET**

It is worth stressing that distant agreement is rare, and that agreement with the nearest noun phrase or agreement with all (resolution) is much more common.

2.4.3   Possessive adjectives

We have already met the Upper Sorbian possessive adjective since it is a highly unusual controller (§2.1.4). It also fits here in that part of its unusual nature is that it typically controls agreement in respect of a non-canonical component. Consider again a typical example:

Upper Sorbian (Šewc-Schuster 1976: 27)
(95)   w   naš-eho   nan-ow-ej   chez-i
        in our-M.SG.GEN father-POSS-F.SG.LOC house(F)-SG.LOC
        'in our father's house'

Recall that the adjective *nanow*-'father's' agrees normally with the noun. However it can control an adjective itself, and this adjective will be genitive and singular, and it will be masculine because *nan* 'father' is masculine. It is as though *naš* 'our' agrees with a part of the controller, which is certainly unusual behaviour. We expect agreement with 'all of' a controller, and certainly when the controller is a single word.

Interestingly, besides the normal agreement as in (95) above, examples showing 'attraction', like (96), are also found:

(96)   w   **naš-ej**   nan-ow-ej   chez-i
        in our-F.SG.LOC father-POSS-F.SG.LOC house(F)-SG.LOC
        'in our father's house'

Here *naš* 'our' agrees completely with the head noun, in all features. This might be thought of as a relapse to canonical agreement, agreeing in all features with the head noun of the phrase. (As for the conditions under which this attraction occurs, it is known that the possessive adjective must be in the singular, but otherwise it remains somewhat mysterious.)

2.4.4 'Back' agreement

In sentences with the structure [subject noun phrase plus copula plus nominal predicate] we expect agreement with the subject. However, we may find agreement of the copula with the noun phrase in the predicate. This phenomenon is called *back* or *backward agreement*, or *attraction*. There are various brief references to the phenomenon in the literature, but many are unconvincing. For example, in some languages claimed to show back agreement predicate-subject order is common, which means that it is not sufficient merely to find examples of agreement with the postverbal noun phrase. Examples of back agreement can be found in Russian.[19] However, demonstrating that we do indeed have back agreement in Russian is not simple, whereas in the West Slavonic language Czech, a relative of Russian, the case is clear-cut. Consider these sentences, from Vanek (1970: 53) and confirmed subsequently by several speakers (also by Panevová 1991: 326–7):

Czech (Vanek 1970: 53)

(97)   jedna a   dvě **jsou**   tři
        one   and two be.3PL   three
        'one and two are (make) three'

(98)   jedna a   tři   **jsou**   čtyři
        one   and three be.3PL   four
        'one and three are four'

(99)   dvě   a   tři   **je**   pět
        two   and three be.3SG five
        'two and three are five'

(100)   tři   a   tři   **je**   šest
        three and three be.3SG six
        'three and three are six'

The regularity concerns the numeral in the predicate, that is, the one on the right in our examples. If it is 'two', 'three' or 'four', then the copula takes plural agreement, while if it is 'five' or above, then the singular is found.[20] Moreover, there are syntactic tests to show that the numeral in question is part of the predicate (Corbett 1986: 1002–3). More needs to be done to specify the factors which allow

---

[19] The evidence is assessed in Corbett (1986: 1019–20) and references there; see also Crockett (1976: 406–7) and Paducěva & Uspenskij (1997).

[20] There is a split after 'four' in that the lower numerals inflect more like adjectives and those above inflect more like nouns. This is general in Slavonic (see §2.2.3 and §3.3.5).

this type of agreement to occur in different languages. For Slavonic languages, this is made more difficult by the fact that its 'habitat' is being eroded by the rise of the instrumental predicate; when the nominal predicate is in the instrumental case we never find back agreement. But this is significant in that the 'usurper' controller must be in the right case (see §6.6 for discussion).

Tsakhur also shows examples of back agreement (Kibrik 1999: 442–3, and for a further example see p. 825 ex. 189):

Tsakhur (Kibrik 1999: 841)

(101) rōc   ušaR   Galₐ?-a-n[21]
       cradle(III)[SG.ABS] baby(IV)[SG.ABS] IV.SG.put-IPFV-ATTRIB.IV.SG

       kar   wo-d-un
       thing(IV)[SG.ABS] be-IV.SG-ATTRIB.IV.SG

       'A cradle is a thing (into which) you put a baby.'

Here the copula agrees with the predicate noun *kar* 'thing' and not with the subject *rōc* 'cradle'. Thus we clearly find examples of back agreement, that is, the predicate nominal takes the place of the subject as the controller of agreement.[22]

2.4.5   Brother-in-law agreement

This is originally a Relational Grammar term, introduced by Perlmutter (1983b); it was taken up by Aissen in various papers and definitively in (1990). Consider this example:

(102)   There are cows in next door's garden.

Such constructions have a dummy element (English *there*) in what Relational Grammar called the term position; we can see that it is in the term position from the evidence of raising constructions. Yet the agreement controller is *cows*, which Aissen called the 'brother-in-law' of the term (in Minimalism it is called an 'associate'). Perlmutter (1983b) permits 'silent' dummies, which allows for analyses in which apparent terms are analysed as brothers-in-law of zeroes. The construction has been problematic in other frameworks too: see van Gelderen (1997: 87–123), Sobin (1997) and Lasnik (2002) for discussion of Minimalist approaches.

Note that agreement with the brother-in-law is not obligatory (see Schütze 1999); we also find in some registers:

(103)   There's cows in next door's garden.

Here expletive *there* controls agreement. Constructions which are related to this one more or less closely provoked an interesting set of squibs, starting from Dixon's (1977) paper concerned with examples like *Where's my pants?*, which led to squibs entitled: 'What's these facts about?' (Nathan 1981) and 'Here's a

---

[21] This verb agrees with its absolutive argument *ušaR* 'baby' by internal stem change.

[22] For examples from Biblical Hebrew and from Modern Hebrew see Levi (1987: 125–7).

few more facts' (Sparks 1984). A survey of the agreements in American English based on corpora totalling over 12 million words can be found in Crawford (2005).

2.4.6 *kind of* problems

An instance of agreement within the phrase, controlled by the 'wrong' controller, is provided by complex noun phrases where the first noun is functionally like a qualifier. A scan of the web provides many thousands of instances of expressions like:

(104)   these sort of things
(105)   these kind of people

The demonstrative agrees with the semantically significant noun.[23] These examples are frequent, though frowned on by the style guides. Examples with *this kind*, *this sort* are also found, of course. Furthermore, there may be no overt *of*-phrase in context (*those kind are the best*).

2.4.7 Long-distance agreement

This phenomenon was originally called 'transparent agreement' (Russian *prozračnoe soglasovanie*), starting from the notion of a predicate being transparent, used by Kibrik in Bergel'son, Zaliznjak & Kibrik (1982: 49). Other terms include 'non-local agreement' and 'cross-clausal agreement' (see Polinsky 2003 for recent terms and for a helpful typology of these constructions). Long-distance agreement is well attested in Daghestanian languages (Testelec 2001: 401), in Bagwalal (Kibrik 2001: 483), Godoberi (Haspelmath 1999), Hunzib (van den Berg 1995)[24], Tsakhur (Kibrik 1999: 373, 495–6) and Tsez (Polinsky & Comrie 1999; Polinsky & Potsdam 2001). It has also been reported in the Algonquian languages Innu-aimûn (Branigan & MacKenzie 2002) and Passamaquoddy (Bruening 2001).[25]

I take an example from Tsez (Polinsky & Comrie 1999: 116–17). The construction concerns sentential complements, and example (106) shows the expected agreement. The complement is treated as the controller of agreement, and so the agreement is in the default gender, gender IV. The experiencer argument, as with most verbs of this type, stands in the dative, hence *eni-r* 'mother-DAT'. (Following Polinsky & Comrie, for clarity the important agreement target is in bold, and the embedded complement is in square brackets.)

---

[23] These examples are the extreme instance of the semantic head of the noun phrase taking over the syntactic function of head too. We discuss examples where things have not gone so far in §7.4.2.

[24] Examples on pages 190, 211, 240, which were identified by Polinsky & Potsdam (2001: 606n9).

[25] There are interesting related constructions in Hindi-Urdu (Davison 1988, Mahajan 1989) and in Itelmen (Bobaljik & Wurmbrand 2002); in Polinsky's (2003) typology these are instances of restructuring and not of full-blown long-distance agreement. See Bobaljik & Wurmbrand (2005) for further discussion.

Tsez (Polinsky & Comrie 1999: 116–17, Polinsky & Potsdam 2001: 584)

(106)   eni-r   [už-ā   magalu   b-āc'-ru-ɬi]   **r-iy-xo.**
          mother(II)-DAT boy(I)-ERG   bread(III)[ABS]   III-eat-PST_PTCP-NMLZ[ABS] IV-know-PRS
          'The mother knows that the boy ate the bread.'

Surprisingly, however, in Tsez a matrix verb can alternatively agree with a nominal in the absolutive which is inside the complement. In (107), the matrix verb has gender III agreement, marking agreement with *magalu* 'bread', an absolutive phrase which is within the sentential complement:

(107)   eni-r   [už-ā   magalu   b-āc'-ru-ɬi]   **b-iy-xo.**
          mother(II)-DAT boy(I)-ERG   bread(III)[ABS]   III-eat-PST_PTCP-NMLZ[ABS] III-know-PRS
          'The mother knows that the boy ate the bread.'

Thus the target has two potential controllers (it is 'trigger-happy', §1.4.2, criterion 12). The conditions under which this option is employed will be discussed in §6.7.1. For our typology, the important thing is the nature of the domain in (107). One way of viewing it is that the controller and target are more distant syntactically than we would expect, hence the name 'long-distance agreement'.[26] Another view of it is that we have something comparable to possessor agreement (§2.4.1), in that we have an unexpected element within the normal controller supplanting the expected one. That is, the whole complement is the expected controller, but in (107) a part of it (the absolutive nominal) takes over that role.[27]

2.4.8 Adpositions, adverbs and particles agreeing with absolutive arguments

We have already seen instances of these surprising targets. However, in some examples there was also an interesting domain, and we return to this now:

Tsakhur (Kibrik 1999: 182): example repeats (74)

(108)   maɬhammad   čoǯ-u-s-qa   **ǯa-b**   balkan
          Mohammed(I)[ABS] brother(I)-OBL-AD-ALL restrictive-III horse(III)[ABS]

          hi<w>l-es   qaɬjq'an-o-r
          <III>give-POT   I.fear.IPFV-be-I
          'Mohammed is afraid to give the horse to his BROTHER.'
          'Mohammed is afraid to give the horse just to his brother.'

The particle *ǯa-* indicates that Mohammed is afraid to give the horse precisely to his brother. We might have expected agreement, if it occurs at all, to be within this pragmatically relevant constituent. In fact, as with other surprising domains we have seen in Daghestanian languages, agreement is with the absolutive argument, in this instance *balkan* 'horse'. We return to this in §2.5.2.

---

[26] The domain is just larger than the clause, while the anaphoric pronoun can be in principle indefinitely far from its antecedent.

[27] For very interesting data on agreement in the backward control construction in Tsez see Polinsky & Potsdam (2002).

2.4.9 Agreement of arguments one with another

This remarkable domain is found in Archi. We find agreement of certain pronouns with an absolutive noun phrase:

Archi (Kibrik 1972: 124; Kibrik 1994: 349; Corbett 1991: 114–15)

(109) **b**-ez   dogi   kɬ'an-ši b-i
       III-1SG.DAT donkey(III)[ABS] like-CVB III-is
       'I like the donkey'

(110) ez   motol   kɬ'an-ši i
       [IV]1SG.DAT young.goat(IV)[ABS] like-CVB [IV]is
       'I like the kid'

(111) **w**-ez   dija   kɬ'an-ši w-i
       I-1SG.DAT father(I)[ABS] like-CVB I-is
       'I like father'

(112) **d**-ez   buwa   kɬ'an-ši d-i
       II-1SG.DAT mother(II)[ABS] like-CVB II-is
       'I like mother'

Since Archi is an ergative language, the part of the verb which shows agreement (the auxiliary in these examples) agrees with the object of a transitive verb; the different forms in (109) to (112) correspond to the four genders of Archi. With verbs of emotion and perception, the experiencer phrase stands in the dative case (as in the Tsez examples earlier); in (109) to (112) the experiencer is expressed by a personal pronoun with an agreement slot, and this also agrees with the object. Note that the agreement slot is made available by the target irrespective of its syntactic role: it also agrees when functioning as an indirect object (Kibrik 1994: 349):

(113) buwa-mu   **b**-ez   diī̄a<b>u χ̄ʷalli   a<b>u
       mother(II)-ERG III-1SG.DAT early<III> bread(III)[ABS] made<III>
       'Mother made bread for me early.'

(114) dija-mu   ez   diī̄a<t'>u nokɬ'   a<Ø>w
       father(I)-ERG [IV]1SG.DAT early<IV> house(IV)[ABS] made<IV>
       'Father made a house for me early'.

The first plural inclusive pronoun also has an agreement slot in the ergative case, which allows possibilities such as the following:

(115) nena<b>u   χ̄ʷalli   a<b>u
       1PL.INCL.ERG<III> bread(III)[ABS] made<III>
       'We (inclusive) made bread.'

A similar phenomenon is found in Andi according to Testelec (2001: 387–8), and a comparable situation of agreement between arguments was found in Coahuilteco (Troike 1981). The Archi examples and similar data are clearly problematic for Moravcsik's 'coreferentiality principle' (§2.3.1). They show the wide range of possible domains.

2.4.10   Pronominal agreement with itself

Going on from the Archi data above, we find another surprise; the remarkable domain of an element agreeing with itself. At first this seems an impossibility. However, if arguments can agree one with another, then the chances of finding this remarkable domain are increased. However, if an item agrees with itself, we would expect it to have a single form, hence it would be difficult to show that we have an instance of agreement. Archi gives just the data we need.

We have seen that some pronouns have gender/number agreement slots in particular cases. The important one is the first person plural inclusive, which agrees when in the ergative, absolutive, dative and genitive. As we have already seen, these pronouns will agree with the absolutive argument. Let us return to example (115). The agreement forms available for the first plural inclusive pronoun, when in the ergative, are as follows:

(116)   Forms of the first plural inclusive ergative in Archi
            according to the absolutive argument: Kibrik (1977a: 125)

	singular	plural
gender I	nenaw	nenabu
gender II	nenaru	nenabu
gender III	nenabu	nént'u
gender IV	nent'u	nént'u

We can see that in (115) the pronoun agrees with the absolutive noun phrase, which is gender III singular. There is an additional complication when the controller of agreement is a pronoun. First and second person plural pronouns control forms which are identical to the plural for genders III and IV (as will be discussed in §4.2.1).

Let us now move on to the absolutive. In principle if the absolutive first plural inclusive pronoun has an agreement slot it should agree with itself. And it does (Kibrik 1977a: 125). Consider this example from a recorded text (Kibrik, Kodzasov, Olovjannikova & Samedov 1977b: 106, text 30, sentence 14):[28]

(117)   č'éba χará-ši   baqI'á   **nént'u**
          let's back-ALL return.RFV 1PL.INCL.ABS.**1pl**
          'let's go back'

The form of *nént'u* in the absolutive is the one appropriate for agreeing with a first plural. However, since it must agree with itself, how can we show that it is in fact agreeing? The evidence comes from the ergative case: for all the other

---

[28] I am grateful to Marina Chumakina and Aleksandr Kibrik for help with this example. Aleksandr Kibrik informs me (personal communication) that the agreeing suffix in *nén-t'u* goes back to an emphatic particle which includes an agreeing gender marker. There is an analogical particle in Tsakhur, for which see §2.2.8.

first and second person pronouns, except the first singular (Kibrik 1977a: 125), absolutive and ergative are the same, and we assume this will be so also for the first plural inclusive pronoun. We established above that the agreement form for a first or second person plural pronoun will be as for the gender III/IV plural. In this instance it will be *nént'u*. This is what we have in (117), hence we have a target agreeing with itself. This item therefore marks information which is displaced and 'replaced'.

2.5 Further domains

There are two further issues. The first involves multiple domains, and the second is a radical rethink of the more problematic domains we have encountered.

2.5.1 Multiple domains

We have considered a range of separate domains, but we have also seen that domains can be combined. That is, a single word is the target of more than one controller, as first discussed in §1.4.2, criterion 11. From one perspective that is merely the combination of domains which are each to be described in their own right. From another angle, however, these are specially interesting, since they suggest a more demanding task for the speaker, well worthy of psycholinguistic investigation. Examples include Shona associative/possessive constructions (§1.4.2), Bagwalal relatives and gerunds (Kibrik 2001: 481–3), and the issue of stacking, a special type of multiple domain, is raised in §4.4.1.

How many multiple domains we recognize depends of course on how close to canonical we require the agreements to be. Those who accept clitics as indicating agreement and then treat the host as the target will find many multiple domains, while those who take only inflectional marking as agreement will find far fewer. If one takes the strictest view of agreement (occurring obligatorily, and necessarily accompanied by a controller) then, according to Siewierska (1999), we do not find verbs which agree with two arguments, since object agreement appears not to reach the final stage of grammaticalization.

2.5.2 Verbs as agreement controllers

We have seen several problematic domains, particularly in Daghestanian languages. These involved various targets which match the features of the absolutive argument, even though there is no evident syntactic link between controller and target. A striking example was the restrictive particle of Tsakhur (108), but the Archi examples (109)–(115) are also difficult. Another way of thinking about them is to treat the verb as the controller (as suggested by Kibrik 2003: 564). A possible approach would be to treat the verb as agreeing with the absolutive argument, and to treat other targets (particles, adverbs and so on) as agreeing with the verb, as the head of the clause.

This move would need working out, since it would have varying effects in different theories. It dramatically expands the range of possible domains. On the other hand, there are challenging data to be considered from Kayardild, where also we might treat the verb as the controller (Evans 2003: 215). With Kayardild, the agreement features are also unexpected, and so I shall treat it in the chapter on features, in §4.5.2.

2.6   Conclusion

Languages have substantially different inventories of agreeing items. At first the possibilities for controllers seemed relatively restricted, being nominal in nature. This initial impression was challenged by the Basaá adjectival nouns, and then more seriously by the Daghestanian data suggesting we might have to allow for verbs as controllers. Targets are remarkably diverse, and Lehmann's minor restrictions on them proved too restrictive; even discourse particles can agree. With domains, the range of possibilities is again extensive, and the data go beyond what the promising theories of Keenan and Moravcsik allowed for. At this stage we must respect the diversity, and begin to look for implicational claims, relating the apparently exotic domains found in languages like Tsakhur to the more expected ones.

3   The morphology of agreement

We now turn to the role of morphology in agreement, which is to mark the agreement information (whether formal or semantic/pragmatic in nature) on targets. Given the asymmetric nature of agreement, this means that agreement morphology will mark on targets information which relates primarily to controllers.

3.1   Models of morphology

The way we think of morphology pervades our view of language. Often people make decisions about syntax without realizing that they are prompted by unexamined opinions about morphology. To enable readers to situate their particular view, and to make clear the writer's underlying assumptions, I give a typology of approaches to morphology, from Stump (2001: 1–9).

We can approach the different types of morphological theory from a basic question: how do we relate an inflected form, like English *sits*, to the stem *sit*? I first distinguish lexical theories from inferential theories. In **lexical** theories, the affix -*s* has a lexical entry, which specifies it as 'third-person singular subject agreement', 'present tense' and 'indicative mood', rather as *sit* has a lexical entry. Thus *sits* corresponds to two lexical entries. In **inferential** theories, on the other hand, the systematic relations between a stem like *sit* and an inflected form like *sits* are expressed in terms of rules or formulas. The existence of an inflected form like *sits* is inferred from the existence of *sit* by a rule which associates the appearance of -*s* with the feature specification 'third-person singular', and so on.

There is a second distinction, cross-cutting the first, which contrasts incremental and realizational theories. In **incremental** theories words gain morphosyntactic feature values only together with the relevant exponents. This means that *sits* gains the feature values 'third-person singular subject agreement', 'present tense' and 'indicative mood' only by adding -*s* (whether -*s* is inserted from the lexicon or is introduced by a rule or formula). In **realizational** theories the stem *sit* is associated with a particular set of morphosyntactic feature values ('third-person singular', and so on) and this licenses the introduction of the inflectional exponents for them (whether this is by lexical insertion or by applying a rule).

Since the distinctions are orthogonal, there are four types of theory of inflectional morphology, namely: lexical-incremental, lexical-realizational, inferential-incremental and inferential-realizational. We find examples of each, as indicated in (1).

(1)   Stump's typology of morphological theories

	lexical	inferential
incremental	Lieber (1992)	Steele (1995)
realizational	Distributed Morphology	Word and Paradigm theories, for instance: Network Morphology, Paradigm Function Morphology

Stump gives an overview of each, and more detail can be found in the sources I shall cite. An example of a lexical-incremental theory is Lieber (1992). Distributed Morphology proposed by Halle & Marantz (1993) is a lexical-realizational theory. Steele (1995) proposes an inferential-incremental theory. And Word-and-Paradigm theories of inflection (as in Matthews 1972) are of the inferential-realizational type. Stump (2001: 3–12) evaluates the four types of theory and concludes that the data point towards **inferential-realizational** theories. Stump's own preference (Paradigm Function Morphology) is of this type, as is Network Morphology (Corbett & Fraser 1993, Evans, Brown & Corbett 2002). In such theories a stem is associated with a morphosyntactic feature specification, and these license the inflected forms. The important points to note from theories like Network Morphology and Paradigm Function Morphology in terms of agreement are that the morphology is seen as realizing the feature specifications determined by syntax, and that therefore the interface between syntax and morphology is a featural one.

3.2   Means of exponence

How then is agreement expressed morphologically? We find quite a range of possibilities. In §1.4.2 I suggested that in the canonical instances agreement is realized by canonical inflectional morphology. We start with that, and then consider less canonical means.

3.2.1   Affixes

The most canonical examples involve inflectional affixes; in our first key language, Russian, these occur after the stem, hence as **suffixes**:

Russian

(2)   nov-yj   žurnal
                new-M.SG.NOM   magazine(M)[SG.NOM]
                'a new magazine'

(3)   nov-aja   knig-a
                new-F.SG.NOM   book(F)-SG.NOM
                'a new book'

(4)   nov-oe   pis′m-o
                new-N.SG.NOM   letter(N)-SG.NOM
                'a new letter'

Kayardild, our third key language (§1.5.2), is like Russian in expressing agreement by suffixes. But in many languages the affixes occur before the stem, and are thus called **prefixes**. We find this in Bantu languages like Chichewa:

Chichewa (Sam Mchombo, personal communication)

(5)   chi-patso   chi-modzi
                SG-fruit(7/8)   7-one
                'one fruit'

(6)   zi-patso   zi-wiri
                PL-fruit(7/8)   8-two
                'two fruits'

Some languages treat all agreement similarly, but others vary in their means. Several languages of the East Cushitic group have some verbs which mark subject agreement by prefixation while the majority of verbs use suffixation (Hayward & Orwin 1991).

Agreement may also be marked word-internally (indicated by '<>'):

Tsakhur (Kibrik 1999: 62; gender/number agreement is with the absolutive argument)

(7)   gₑja<p>Xi
                <III.SG>cut
                'cut'

(8)   gₑja<t>Xi
                <IV.SG>cut
                'cut'

We shall return to these examples when we consider the various ways of marking agreement in Tsakhur (§3.3.3).

There is debate about what constitutes an **infix**. Some insist an infix is material that is inserted into the root (and not just between a preverb and a root as in Tsakhur). There are clearer and less clear cases; when the only motivation for dividing the root into two parts is that the agreement markers occur there, then it is fully justified to talk of infixes. We have already met internal marking in Archi (§2.2.4); for comparable examples from Marind, of southern Irian Jaya, see Drabbe (1955: 18–20), discussed in Corbett (2000: 59–60). An intriguing final example is provided by Malagasy, where number is marked infixally, but on very few items, for instance:

Malagasy (Keenan & Polinsky 1998: 567–8)

(9) a. io   trano io   b. i\<re\>o   trano i\<re\>o
         this house this   this\<PL\> house this\<PL\>
         'this house'   'these houses'

(10) a. iny   trano iny   b. i\<re\>ny   trano i\<re\>ny
         that house that   that\<PL\> house that\<PL\>
         'that house (far)'   'those houses (far)'

Thus in agreement we see displaced information being realized right inside another word, which is as contrary to the notion of iconicity as it could be. More generally, we have seen that all the primary means of inflectional morphology are available for agreement.

3.2.2   Stem alternations

We now turn to non-canonical inflection. Stems may show minor alternations, such as stress differences, and various segmental alternations, right up to suppletion (§3.4.2). Sometimes the alternation follows the values of an agreement feature, so it is tempting to believe that the alternation is also marking agreement. For instance, the French verb *savoir* 'know' in the present tense has different stems in the singular and plural:

(11)   Stem alternation in French following a feature value

	savoir 'know'	
	singular	plural
1	sais	savons
2	sais	savez
3	sait	savent

Here the stem alternation shadows the number value. Equally we find many cases where there is no such correspondence with a morphosyntactic feature. Consider these present tense verbs in Russian, each with a consonant alternation in the stem:

(12)   Stem alternations in Russian not following a feature value

peč 'bake'				*ljubít* 'love'		
	singular	plural			singular	plural
1	pekú	pečëm	1		ljubljú	ljúbim
2	pečëš	pečëte	2		ljúbiš	ljúbite
3	pečët	pekút	3		ljúbit	ljúbjat

In the first paradigm, four cells show the mutation of *k* to *č*, as does the infinitive, while two do not. In the second, only one cell is affected out of six. In both we are dealing with morphological patterns, which accompany the marking of agreement information but which do not correspond directly to any agreement feature. The verb *ljubít'* 'love' also shows an alternation in stress, having ending stress in the first person singular and stem stress in the remaining person/number forms (while *pekú* etc. show stress on the ending). Again, this alternation does not correspond to any agreement feature. Since such alternations need not relate to agreement (as in (12)), we should be careful of assuming a significant connection when they do match an agreement feature (as in (11)).

3.2.3   Clitics

Clitics fall between full words and bound inflections, in that typically they cannot stand alone (unlike full words) but they may attach to different hosts (unlike inflections). There are various gradations between the more word-like and the more affix-like ones. Given their intermediate status, clitics may be treated as a syntactic problem, but are increasingly seen as an inflectional matter, falling within 'phrase level morphology' as in Anderson (1992: 210–23), Miller & Sag (1997) and Spencer (2000). It is generally accepted that diachronically pronouns provide a major source of agreement morphology, progressing from full pronouns, to clitics, to inflections (§9.1.1). An interesting issue is the function of particular clitics, specifically whether they function as pronouns or as agreement markers (or both); for helpful analysis see Spencer (1991: 384–90).

For us it is important that there are instances of clitics which function as obligatory agreement markers. An interesting example is Skou, which has 700 speakers, mainly in the villages Skou-Yambe, Skou-Mabu and Skou-Sai, located on the central north coast of New Guinea. It is part of the Macro-Skou family.

Skou (Donohue 1999; ue is for the high central vowel [ɯ] and u is for high back [u])
(13)   Ke   móe   ke=fue.   (*Ke móe fue.)
        3SG.M fish 3SG.M=see.3SG.M
        'He saw a fish.'

(14)   Pe   móe pe=fu.   (*Pe móe fu.)
        3SG.F fish 3SG.F= see.3SG.F
        'She saw a fish.'

Skou has strict subject-object-verb word order. The initial subject pronoun is normally present: 'speakers prefer free pronouns to be present in addition to subject clitics' (Donohue 1999: 7), though the pronoun can be dropped if it is first or second person. It may also not appear 'if the subject of the clause has already been established as a topic of discourse' (Donohue 2003a: 480). Furthermore, Donohue argues, the pronoun is not an instance of topicalization.

The clitics, marked off by '=', distinguish two numbers, three persons, and within the third person singular two genders. I gloss them as masculine and feminine (as in Donohue 2000). About one third of the verbs take only the clitic, others like *fue* 'see' have additional agreement. The latter verbs vary interestingly in how many distinctions they make; the verb *fue* 'see' in the examples given above makes a three-way distinction: third singular feminine, all plurals and the rest.

We have what appear to be clitics marking subject agreement. As the ungrammatical variants of (13) and (14) show, they are obligatory. The remaining question is then 'Are they really clitics?' Donohue (1999) gives three arguments to indicate that they are. The clitics are phonologically independent of the verb root, while subject prefixes which occur with some verbs (as in (15) though not with *fue* 'see') show a variety of alternations. Second, the clitics can attach to words of more than one syntactic category, in particular to 'adjunct nominals'. These are nouns which expand the otherwise restricted verbal lexicon; they have a fixed position adjacent to the verb. Depending on the verb, the clitic's host is either the adjunct nominal or sometimes it is the verb. Example (15) shows the verb *hùng* 'sit' and its adjunct nominal *ta* 'seating':

(15)   Títí-nì=ne   ke=ta   k-ùng   tang
        father's.elder.brother-1SG.GEN=1SG.DAT 3SG.M=seating 3SG.M-sit canoe
        'My uncle sat down in the canoe.'

Here we see the clitic on an adjunct nominal, while a verb like 'shoot', which also has an adjunct nominal, would have the verb root as host for the clitic. A third argument (Donohue 2003a: 484) is that various discourse markers can intervene between the agreement prefix and the proclitics. This suggests that we are dealing with clitics, though with clitics which are closer to inflections than to free words. These are just one of the means of marking agreement in Skou, and will be discussed again in the next section. Before leaving (15) it is worth noting that possession is marked by the dative pronoun, which is a clitic, and also with a genitive; thus Skou has 'doubling' of agreement within the noun phrase as well as in subject agreement. There can even be triple marking in the noun phrase (Mark Donohue, personal communication).

3.2.4 Multiple exponence

Morphosyntactic feature values, including those for agreement, may be realized by more than one formant. I treat this as less canonical than single exponence. In Archi we find:

Archi (Kibrik 1977a: 127–30, 320, 1994: 318–22)

(16)   **d**-aš-a-**r**-ej-**r**-u-t̄u-**r**   ł anna
         II-of.me-self-II-SUFFIX-II-SUFFIX-ADJ-II   wife
         'my own (emphatic) wife'

The initial *d-* signals gender II singular agreement. Next is a pronominal stem. Then, following Kibrik's analysis, there are two complex suffixes for forming reflexives, each with an internal agreement slot: *a-GN-u* and *ej-GN-u* (*GN* = gender/number marker). Both suffixes are used here, with the first *u* dropped before the second suffix. The final suffix *-t̄u-* derives an adjective, and brings with it an agreement slot (naturally). Thus we have a prefixed gender/number marker (the *d-*), a suffixed form (the final *-r*) and two internal forms (the other occurrences of *-r-*). The four markers are all the same, in that they mark the same person/number combination for agreement with the same controller. Agreements of this type are problematic for analyses based on the notion of functional heads, as Spencer (1992: 323–9) shows, and are strong evidence supporting realizational accounts of morphology (Stump 2001: 3–7).

Skou, discussed in the last section, marks agreement by subject clitic (all verbs), consonant alternations (most verbs), vowel changes (some verbs) and alternations of the adjunct nominal (just three verbs). The following example has all these types of marking:

Skou (Donohue 1999, discussed in Anderson 2001: 10)

(17)   Te   te=i   t-i.
         3PL   3PL=fall.PL   3PL-go.3PL
         'They fell over.'

The first word *te* is the third plural pronoun. The following *te=* is the agreeing clitic, discussed in §3.2.3. Its host *i* is the plural form of the adjunct nominal *kú*; the consonant and vowel modification in its paradigm is such that this item could be considered suppletive. Next we have the agreement prefix *t-*, which combines with *ri* the third person plural of the verb *re* 'go' to yield *ti*. These dramatic alternations make more sense when seen against the less extreme examples presented by Donohue. Thus (17) has agreement marked four times. However, the Archi example (16) is an even clearer instance of multiple exponence, since the same distinctions are drawn at each position (while the Skou markers show different syncretisms within the paradigm) and the Archi forms are phonologically more similar too.

In the Archi example (16) we saw four agreement slots, for agreement with the *same controller*, in respect of the *same features*. Four appears to be the maximum number of same-controller agreement slots. As a variant of the same-controller type, the different slots of the target may show agreement with the same controller, but with different morphological patterning; this is found in Skou, and in the Daghestanian language Khinalug (Corbett 1991: 119–23). We also find targets with more than one agreement slot, which agree with a single controller in respect of *different features*. Thus Maltese imperfective verbs agree with their subject prefixally in terms of person (and to a limited extent in gender) and suffixally in terms of number (Fabri 1993: 94). Furthermore, there are targets with more than one agreement slot, for agreement with *different controllers*, but these are not examples of multiple exponence, since different morphosyntactic specifications are being realized. Thus verbs may agree with both subject and object; for discussion of handling such cases by the use of 'layered features' see Anderson (1992: 93–100); an alternative, 'tagged features', is presented in Zwicky (1986a). Most complex is the situation in which we find different agreement slots for which different controllers compete. Under the right circumstances, agreement with a given controller may be found in more than one slot, giving multiple exponence (an interesting example is found in the Chukotko-Kamchatkan language Itelmen; see Bobaljik & Wurmbrand 2002).

3.3   Morphological prerequisites for agreement

Agreement morphology is the 'prerequisite' for agreement. If the target does not have the means to realize the agreement features, then we have no evidence for agreement. (Of course, one can claim that we have invisible agreement in examples like *she came* versus *they came*, but if all English examples were like this then there would be no evidence for agreement.) Morphological prerequisites vary from being met quite generally (for instance, any Russian verb will show number agreement) down to extremely limited instances (as we noted in §1.4.2 only one adjective can show number agreement in Kuwaa).

We start with examples where the category (part of speech) of the target is sufficient to meet the morphological prerequisites (§3.3.1). For instance, in a particular language any adjective will have the necessary means to realize agreement. Then there are instances where, in realizing one agreement feature, another feature has a role (§3.3.2). An example would be a language in which gender agreement is possible, but only together with a given number value; here the other feature (number) is the prerequisite. And then there are different types of lexical prerequisites: in some languages we cannot simply say that 'verbs agree'; instead 'some verbs agree' and the interest is in determining which. Or else, the ways in which targets of the same category show agreement may differ, another type of lexical prerequisite (§3.3.3). The notion of defectiveness fits next (§3.3.4), followed by the unusual phenomenon of 'collaborative' agreement (§3.3.5). These prerequisites are to be distinguished from 'conditions', which can come into play once the prerequisites are met. We discuss conditions in chapter 6 and the distinction between them and prerequisites is clarified in §6.3.1.

3.3.1   Category prerequisites

As we saw in §2.2, the category of the target has a major effect on agreement. Sometimes we can state morphological prerequisites at this level. For example, in Russian verbs and adjectives agree but adverbs do not. Besides the agree/not agree prerequisites there are featural prerequisites, to which we now turn.

3.3.2   Feature prerequisites

Naturally we need to specify which agreement features a particular language realizes in its morphology. But a simple list of these features can be inadequate in two ways: there can be interactions of features with target categories, and interactions between features. We consider these in turn.

First, we may say that a given language has agreement in particular features, but there may be variation among the agreement targets:

Upper Sorbian
(18)   wón je   pisa-ł
          he   be.3SG write-PST[M.SG]
          'he wrote'

Here we have periphrastic expression (§3.4.3): the auxiliary verb agrees in number and person, while the past participle agrees in number and gender. It is often the case that not all targets show all possible features.

The second reason why a simple list of features is inadequate is that the expression of one feature may depend on another feature. Earlier we saw Russian examples (2)–(4), showing agreement in gender. If we change them from singular to plural, we find that the form for each is identical:

Russian
(19)   nov-ye   žurnal-y
          new-PL   magazine(M)-PL
          'new magazines'
(20)   nov-ye   knig-i
          new-PL   book(F)-PL
          'new books'
(21)   nov-ye   pis′m-a
          new-PL   letter(N)-PL
          'new letters'

The plural adjective is *novye* 'new'. Thus gender is constrained by number in Russian: gender distinctions are found only in the singular number, they are neutralized in the plural.[1] This conforms to Greenberg's universal number 37 'A language never has more gender categories in nonsingular numbers than in the singular' (Greenberg 1963: 112). There are further universal constraints of this type (for which see Greenberg 1963, and for discussion of counter-examples see Baerman, Brown & Corbett 2005: 83, 87–90). There are also some language-specific prerequisites. Both universals and language-specific prerequisites may involve just the agreement features, or they may refer to other features too. For instance, Russian verbs show agreement in gender only when in the past tense (§4.2.1); gender is an agreement feature in Russian, while tense is not. The general issue of forms not making all the distinctions which might be expected (that is, single forms filling more than one potential cell in a paradigm) is a hot topic in morphology. It is 'syncretism', in the broad sense of the term. Its specific importance for agreement is indicated in §3.4.1 below.

Before leaving feature interactions, we should consider an important and unusual one found in Kayardild. Several (but not all) of the cases of Kayardild are what Evans calls 'verbalizing cases' (earlier 'verbal cases', 2003: 214n13). Various domains involve verbalizing case, and once an element is marked by verbalizing case, it will take agreement in tense, aspect, mood and polarity. For example, beneficiaries take the verbalizing dative case marker -maru- (originating in a verb meaning 'put' but now integrated into the case system). As a result, they then take verbal inflections for tense, aspect and mood:

Kayardild (Evans 2003: 215)
(22)   ngada   waa-jarra wangarr-ina   ngijin-maru-tharra thabuju-maru-tharra
        1SG.NOM sing-PST   song-MOD_ABL my-V_DAT-PST   brother-V_DAT-PST
        'I sang a song for my brother.'

The items bearing the verbalizing dative here show tense. Furthermore, (23) illustrates polarity (in the sense of negation):

(23)   ngada   waa-nangku wangarr-u   ngijin-maru-nangku thabuju-maru-nangku.
        1SG.NOM sing-NEG.POT song-MOD_PROP my-V_DAT-NEG.POT   brother-V_DAT-NEG.POT
        'I won't sing a song for my brother.'

We can contrast the examples of verbalizing case with the 'ordinary' cases of Kayardild, represented here by the ablative and instrumental (Evans 2003: 207):

(24)   dan-kinaba-nguni dangka-naba-nguni mirra-nguni wangal-nguni
        this-ABL-INS   man-ABL-INS   good-INS   boomerang-INS
        'with this man's boomerang'

In (24) there are no tense/aspect/mood/polarity markers. The main point is that once the case is selected, this determines whether there will be marking of tense/aspect/mood/polarity: with verbalizing cases (as in (22) and (23)) there is, with ordinary cases (as in (24)) there is not. Of course, it is unwise to label

---

[1] In the standard language, the oblique cases of oba 'both' make a single exception.

anything in Kayardild 'ordinary'. The ordinary cases in (24) show case stacking (taken up in §4.4.1). The ablative case indicates the relation of the phrase 'this man' to the head, while the instrumental indicates the relation of the larger phrase to the rest of the clause, and is marked on all elements of the larger phrase. We return in §4.5.2 to the question of whether we should recognize tense, aspect, mood and polarity as agreement features.

3.3.3 Lexical prerequisites

We have seen clear differences between word classes in the agreements they show (§2.2). For some languages the generalizations can all, or nearly all, be stated at this level. Thus for Russian verbs agree in person and number (in the non-past) and in number and gender in the past, adjectives have their agreement features (see §4.2.1), and so on. In other languages we find great differences *within* word classes, as these Macedonian adjectives illustrate:

(25)   Macedonian adjectives (Victor Friedman 1993: 266–7 and personal communication)

masculine	feminine	neuter	plural	gloss
nov	nova	novo	novi	new
	kasmetlija		kasmetlii	lucky
	taze			fresh

Typical native adjectives like *nov* 'new' distinguish three genders and two numbers. Adjectives like *kasmetlija* 'lucky' agree in number but not in gender. On the other hand, *taze* 'fresh' and adjectives like it are indeclinable, they are unable to agree. This means that we cannot necessarily say that in a given language adjectives (or whatever word class we have in mind) agree in particular features. There may be variation within the word class; in other words we need information about particular lexical items.

In Macedonian this lexical information can largely be predicted from the phonology. (Those without a full paradigm are borrowings, mainly from Turkish, and this is manifest in their morphology.) Adjectives with the stem ending in *-lij-*, like *kasmet-lij-a* 'lucky', mark number only. Those with the stem ending in a vowel are indeclinable. Those with the stem ending in a consonant typically decline. Native adjectives with the stem in a consonant must inflect for gender and number, like *nov* 'new'. However, there is a small number of borrowings which do not decline, like *super* 'super'. The Turkish borrowing *kor* 'blind' declines in some dialects and not in others.

A second example comes from Ingush. Compare two verbs, both of which have the experiencer in the dative and the stimulus in the absolutive:

Ingush (Nakh branch of Nakh-Daghestanian, Nichols 1989: 159)

(26)   suona   v-ieza   sej   vaša
        1SG.DAT I-like   my   brother(I)[ABS]
        'I like my brother'

(27)   suona   j-ieza   sej   jiša
        1SG.DAT II-like my   sister(II)[ABS]
        'I like my sister'

(28)   suona   d-ieza   yz   bier
        1SG.DAT III-like this child(III)[ABS]
        'I like this child'

(29)   suona   b-ieza   yz   jett
        1SG.DAT IV-like this cow(IV)[ABS]
        'I like this cow'

The verb -*ieza* 'like' agrees with the absolutive argument in gender and number (singular in all our examples here). Now compare *gu* 'see':

(30)   suona   gu   sej   vaša
        1SG.DAT see my   brother(I)[ABS]
        'I see my brother'

(31)   suona   gu   sej   jiša
        1SG.DAT see my   sister(II)[ABS]
        'I see my sister'

(32)   suona   gu   yz   bier
        1SG.DAT see this child(III)[ABS]
        'I see this child'

(33)   suona   gu   yz   jett
        1SG.DAT see this cow(IV)[ABS]
        'I see this cow'

This verb does not mark agreement, but the syntax is not affected. We noted in §1.4.2 that overall only around 30% of Ingush verbs show agreement. Thus we need lexical information to determine agreement here. The question is whether this information is itself predictable. It is in part: to be inflectable, a verb must be vowel initial in Ingush, but being vowel initial does not guarantee that it will inflect (Johanna Nichols, personal communication).

As we saw with Macedonian adjectives, lexical variation can be a matter not just of agreeing or not agreeing, but of differences within the targets which agree. If we look at one of our key languages, Tsakhur, we find great variety. Verb inflections are of two types, labelled strong and weak,[2] with the following agreement markers:

---

[2] 'Weak' and 'strong' are convenient labels for inflectional types which may be opposed in various ways. The terms go back at least as far as Jacob Grimm (Frans Plank, personal communication),

(34) Verb agreement in Tsakhur (Kibrik 1999: 62, 68)

		inflection set	
		strong	weak
SG	I	-r-	Ø
	II	-r-	-j-
	III	-b-	-w-
	IV	-d-	Ø
PL	I/II	-b-	-w-
	III/IV	-d-	Ø

Here 'weak' and 'strong' describes the inflections: the strong inflections are consonantal, while the weak ones are glides or have no realization. For any part of the paradigm (two numbers and four genders, §1.5.2) a given verb has one set only. Some verbs consistently use one set, while 'mixed' verbs take different forms according to aspect and mood. The majority of verbs have these markers between a fossilized preverb and the root, hence in an internal position:

(35) Illustrative strong and weak verbs in the aorist in Tsakhur

		'cut' (strong)	'throw' (weak)
SG	I	gja-r-Xi	ahu
	II	gja-r-Xi	a-j-hi
	III	gja-p-Xi	a-w-hu
	IV	gja-t-Xi	ahu
PL	I/II	gja-p-Xi	a-w-hu
	III/IV	gja-t-Xi	ahu

Agreement is with the absolutive argument (§2.3.2). The first paradigm shows instances of assimilation (these need not detain us, we just need to note that other Tsakhur paradigms which we meet will show slightly different forms). Note how both strong and weak types make three gender distinctions in the singular. There is further interesting syncretism between singular and plural markers. While neither weak nor strong verbs alone distinguish four genders, the mixed type do, since these verbs take both sets of agreements in different aspects. The distribution of verbs of different types is given in (36), from Kibrik (1999: 62):

where the notion is that to make a particular distinction weak items need an additional affix which the strong do not. However, as their use for Tsakhur shows, 'weak' and 'strong' are now used in various analogically related ways.

(36)   Types of verbal stem in Tsakhur

verb type	inflectional set	
	perfective	imperfective and potentialis
weak (50%)[3]	weak	
strong (20%)	strong	
mixed (30%)	strong	weak

Thus to determine agreement, the feature specification depends on the gender/ number of the absolutive argument, while the set of inflections to be used depends on the verb, whether it is strong or weak (and for mixed verbs it depends also on aspect and mood). As a result, the form of the inflections varies, and also the specific distinctions drawn (specifically, whether in the singular the syncretic forms are those for genders I and II or those for I and IV). This would appear problematic for analyses which involve moving morphemes from node to node, since the information to be realized depends on the type of verbal stem.

When targets have to be divided into inflectional classes, as in Tsakhur, the class into which a particular item falls may be predictable to different degrees. Moreover, the different classes may make different *distinctions*, as is the case in Tsakhur, or the distinctions may be the same but just the phonological material involved may be different (we have seen such an instance in Russian, discussed further in §4.2.2).

Finally, there are instances where particular lexical items require specific and quite idiosyncratic lexical information to be stored. Thus, as we saw in §2.4.9, in Archi some personal pronouns agree with the absolutive argument, but only when they are in specific cases. And in English the verb *be* makes idiosyncratic agreement distinctions.

3.3.4   Defectiveness

Defectiveness depends on a notion of what can be reasonably expected. An impersonal verb is not expected to have a first person singular form. Similarly an ant with six legs is fine, while a spider with seven is defective. It is not the same as uninflecting, where an item is simply morphologically inert (as are many verbs in Ingush, §3.3.3); defectiveness implies the lack of specific forms, which the lexeme might reasonably be expected to have. The Russian verb *pobedit'* 'win' has all the expected forms, apart from one:

---

[3] The number of verbs counted is no longer available.

Russian
(37)   *pobežd-u / *pobež-u / *pobedj-u
         win.PFV-1SG / win.PFV-1SG / win.PFV-1SG
         'I will win'

Part of the reason for this particular gap is that we would expect there to be a stem alternation (§3.2.2), but speakers are not confident what it should be.

3.3.5 'Collaborative' agreement

This is a curious phenomenon in which the target establishes the prerequisites for agreement. Examples have arisen in Slavonic, as a result of the loss of the dual number (for many nouns the nominative dual and genitive singular coincided). This has produced complex constructions with lower numerals in various languages. In Russian the numerals *dva* 'two', *tri* 'three' and *četyre* 'four', when themselves in the nominative, take a noun in the genitive singular. *Dva* 'two' has the feminine form *dve*:

Russian
(38)   dv-e   sosn-ý
         two-F.NOM   pine(F)-SG.GEN
         'two pines'

The numeral governs the form of the noun, requiring it to be genitive and singular (the stress in this example shows unambiguously that the noun is genitive singular). It is only because the noun is singular that there can be agreement in gender, since gender is not distinguished in the plural in Russian (this feature-based prerequisite was discussed in §3.3.2). So the genitive singular noun, required to be in that form by the numeral, in turn acts as the controller for gender agreement of the numeral, hence the term 'collaborative agreement'. For further discussion of the headedness relations here see Corbett (1993); we return to these numerals in §6.6. In this Russian example the interaction is striking. However, such examples are commonplace if one takes the view that the verb governs its subject just as it governs its other arguments. From that viewpoint examples of subject-verb agreement, like (18) for instance, are also 'collaborative', in that the verb requires its subject to be in the nominative case and then agrees with it.

3.4 Special morphological phenomena

Here we consider three morphological phenomena: syncretism, suppletion and periphrasis. All have been mentioned before, but each is of special interest for agreement.

3.4.1   Syncretism

It is common to find different morphosyntactic feature specifications which have a single realization, that is, syncretism. Informally, the morphology 'lets down' the syntax, in that it cannot provide different realizations for all the distinctions required. We saw examples in Tsakhur in §3.3.3, and there is discussion of the theoretical importance of syncretism in Baerman, Brown and Corbett (2005). Occasionally the existence of syncretism in targets, which would appear to be purely a matter of morphology, makes possible a type of agreement which would otherwise be unacceptable. We shall see an instance in §8.5.2, when we analyse gender resolution in the Bantu language Chichewa.

3.4.2   Suppletion

Suppletion is found in English examples like *go* ~ *went*, where the regular opposition present ~ past is realized by forms which are not related phonologically. We might think that this phenomenon would be restricted to what I shall call 'inherent' features (§4.2.3). However, suppletion can be involved in agreement, as we saw in §1.4.2:

Norwegian (Bokmål, Tore Nesset, personal communication)
(39)   en   lit-en   bil
          one/a   small-M.SG   car(M)[SG]
          'one small car'

(40)   to   små   bil-er
          two   small.PL   car-PL
          'two small cars'

Here we see agreement (for this particular adjective) expressed by suppletion. This is not what we expect for contextual features (§4.2.3), and it has interesting implications for what is a possible word.

3.4.3   Periphrasis

Periphrasis is the use of more than one word in a cell of an inflectional paradigm. For example, in Russian 'I write' is *ja pišu*, 'I wrote (IPFV)' is *ja pisal*, but 'I will write (IPFV)' is *ja budu pisat'*. The latter verb form *budu pisat'* is said to be periphrastic. We noted a periphrastic form in §3.3.2, and saw how the different components of the periphrastic form may mark different agreement features. However, there is a subtler issue for agreement, which has been largely unnoticed. It is generally assumed that there is a single morphosyntactic specification for a periphrastic cell of a paradigm (even if different components realize different subsets of the features). However, this is not necessarily the case, as the following example shows:

Czech (Eva Hajicová and Jarmila Panevová personal communications)

(41)   by-l-a   jste   velmi laskav-á
             be-PST-F.SG   AUX.2PL   very   kind-F.SG
             'You were very kind' (addressed to a woman)

This is a polite expression, for a single addressee. The pronoun *vy* 'you' could be included if there were stress on it, for instance for contrast (*Vy jste byla velmi laskavá*). The auxiliary verb, the clitic *jste*, is second person plural, while the past participle *by-l-a*, literally 'was', is singular. Thus the two parts of the periphrastic verb have different values for number. Further examples can be found in Comrie (1975), and agreement with honorific pronouns is discussed further in §7.7.1.

3.5   Alliterative agreement

Alliterative agreement is often called 'alliterative concord' since some of the best-known examples are in Bantu languages, and the term 'concord' is widely used in the Bantuist tradition.[4] There are two ways of thinking of alliterative agreement, first as a way of characterizing (part of) the morphology of agreement in particular languages, and second, more radically, as a claim about the whole nature of agreement systems. We examine these in turn.

3.5.1   Alliterative agreement as a characterization of morphological exponence

Alliterative agreement can be illustrated with this well-known Swahili example:

Swahili (Welmers 1973: 171)

(42)   ki-kapu   ki-kubwa ki-moja ki-li-anguka
             SG-basket(7/8)   7-large   7-one   7-PST-fall
             'One large basket fell.'

There are two characteristics of this type of morphology to be separated out:

1.   the controller has a marker which clearly indicates its featural informa-
             tion (*ki-kapu* 'basket' marks number, and since this is one of the many
             instances where inflection and gender line up, the marker indicates the
             singular of nouns in gender 7/8, which Bantuists often indicate simply
             as '7');
2.   the same agreement marker is used for agreement targets (*ki-*, the '7'
             marker, for singular agreement with gender 7/8, occurs on different
             targets, here adjective, numeral and verb).

---

[4] 'Alliterative' was first used, naturally, of prefixes, but it is now generalized to suffixes too.

Both characteristics are necessary. A language may mark the featural information of controllers clearly, but use different phonological material for marking
agreement on targets. This would not be alliterative agreement. And this is not
an 'all or nothing' classification of languages. Swahili examples are not all like
(42), so it does not have full alliterative agreement. Bantu languages typically
show a high degree of alliterative agreement, and elsewhere in the Niger-Congo
family we find even more consistent examples, such as Amo (spoken in north-
central Nigeria, Anderson 1980) and Uskade (a Lower Cross language, Connell
1987).

Conversely, languages which do not normally figure in discussions of alliterative agreement are often partly alliterative. Indo-European languages often show
alliterative agreement, at least for a part of the system:

Russian

(43)   Maš-a   čita-l-a
        Masha(F)-SG read-PST-F.SG
        'Masha was reading'

Here the same marker -a is found on controller and target. However, there are
many instances where there would be no such resemblance in Russian. English
shows highly un-alliterative agreement, where plural controllers typically have
-s (and variants), while -s in verb targets normally indicates the singular. On this
view, therefore, alliterative agreement is one end of a scale along which languages
can be measured. A language with consistent alliterative agreement would have
the values of the agreement features clearly indicated on both controller and target,
and by the same phonological material.[5]

3.5.2   Radical alliterative agreement: a claim about agreement systems

There is a more significant view of alliterative agreement, which has
been put forward with varying degrees of explicitness at different times. This
view is that agreement can match the form of the target directly to the form of
the controller. Specifically, if a subject noun phrase is headed by a noun ending in -a, the predicate will end in -a, if in -u, then in -u and so on. The data
offered are sometimes quite slender, but the claim is made more plausible by
appealing to borrowings; agreements are claimed to match new forms found in
borrowings.

If the claim could be maintained, this would make a dramatic difference to
the way in which the organization of grammar is generally conceived. Syntax is

---

[5] Note also the phenomenon of 'alliterative discord', as claimed for Lavukaleve: 'There is a deep
relationship between deictics and focus markers involving, among other things, a system of alliterative discord, a type of agreement system in which the form of a deictic in a focus construction
requires the form of the focus marker to disagree with it in its initial consonant' Terrill (2003:
15–16).

normally taken to be 'phonology-free' (Zwicky & Pullum 1983, Pullum & Zwicky 1988). That is, rules of syntax do not have access to the phonological forms of syntactic units. We do not find rules like: 'vowel-initial adjectives stand before the noun and consonant-initial stand after it'; or 'questions are formed by taking the longest word and moving it to initial position'; or 'two-syllable transitive verbs govern the genitive case'. Similarly, we do not expect an agreement rule which effectively says 'take the phonological form of the controller and match it (to a specified degree) on the target'. Of course, we may have a language in which many nouns of feminine gender end in -*a* and feminine singular adjectives end in -*a*. But the rule is framed in terms of the number and gender features. We are not surprised if some feminine nouns in this language do not end in -*a*; feminine nouns behave alike because they share a gender, not because of shared phonology.

Given the significance and generality of the claim that syntax is 'phonology free', we must take seriously the suggestion that agreement could be straightforwardly alliterative, that is, that the target would simply match the phonology of the controller. I review the instances that have been offered and conclude that the case is not yet convincing. The main discussion is in work by Dobrin, who uses the terms 'literal alliterative concord' (1995), 'alliterative agreement' (1998: 59) and 'phonological agreement' (1998: 78). The term I have used, 'radical alliterative agreement', is due to Aronoff (1998: 13).

Dobrin (1995) discusses some of the familiar instances cited as illustrating radical alliterative agreement, and considers especially the Arapeshan dialect Abu? (Torricelli family). This includes examples of semantic assignment of nouns to gender, and is not strictly alliterative. Dobrin (1998) is another interesting contribution. In particular it discusses the spontaneous development of a new *s*-gender in Arapeshan languages which, it is argued, is the direct result of copying the final segment of recent borrowed nouns. These languages have extensive gender systems, with nouns assigned to two of the genders by semantics (nouns denoting males are in one gender, those denoting females are in another), and then for the vast majority of nouns there is an implicational relationship between stem phonology and morphological class (in particular, the plural marking), and also between morphological class and gender, as shown below:

(44)   Formal assignment in Arapesh
         Stem Phonology => Morphological Class => Gender

For a Network Morphology account of the assignment system, and an implementation, see Fraser & Corbett (1997). Dobrin discusses examples from the Bukiyip dialect:

Bukiyip dialect of Arapesh (Dobrin 1998: 69)
(45)   nebebe-s-i   balus   sa-naki   Ukarumpa
         very.large-'s'-ADJ   airplane   's'-came.from   Ukarumpa
         'a very large airplane arrived from Ukarumpa'

Balus 'airplane' is a borrowing from Tok Pisin. There was previously no gender agreement in -*s*-, and a new agreeing form has been created on the basis of these nouns (indicated 'S' in the morphosyntactic gloss). Most of the available consonants were already markers for gender agreement, and so this development is consistent with that pattern. Dobrin goes on to suggest that there is a phonological default which comes into play when the normal semantic assignments, morphological assignments and morphological default have failed (1998: 73–4). Dobrin (1999) includes further interesting material, but does not answer all the questions we would like to have answered. The main problem is the plural; when nouns are in the plural, the agreement is not alliterative:

Bukiyip dialect of Arapesh (Dobrin 1998: 65)
(46)   barah-ijer . . .   wa-kana 'e   babwen . . .'
          granddaughter(IV)-PL . . . IV.PL-say 'hey grandfather . . .'
          'the granddaughters . . . said "hey grandfather . . ."'

There are various plural inflections (thus *barah-ijer* is the plural of *barah-ok^u* 'granddaughter'), but there is a single agreement marker for a particular gender in the plural. This is not alliterative agreement (though note the interesting data in Dobrin 1998: 72). The right generalization appears to be that the singular form is a good predictor (via a phonological assignment rule and gender agreement) of what the agreement form will be, but that the plurals demonstrate that we do not have an alliterative agreement system.

Aronoff (1998) starts from Dobrin's data and draws out the consequences. He treats agreement as a copying operation, with complete copying as the final default. Radical alliterative agreement emerges when forced to do so, when there is no gender available. Thus Aronoff sees radical alliterative agreement as a type of last resort, but as one which is indicative of how agreement operates (rather as does Dobrin 1998). I assess the evidence to be somewhat less strong, and I believe it is too soon to put so much weight on it.

Other possible cases of radical alliterative agreement have been suggested. These are: Wolof, but plural agreements are not alliterative (see McLaughlin 1996, 1997), Landuma (Wilson 1962: 37–8, Sumbatova 2003: 331–2) and Bainuk (Banyun) as in Sauvageot (1967). Another instance was proposed by Grinevald (2000) concerning classifiers in Movima, an isolate of Bolivia. However, the Movima data are open to other interpretations (Haude 2003). For some of these languages the data are insufficient to make a judgement. For Arapeshan languages the data are intriguing, but in my view not yet convincing. To give up a major tenet of how grammar is organized I would prefer to have more secure evidence.

For all the need for caution, the impact of phonological similarity needs to be taken seriously. Evidence from language acquisition gives another angle on the issue (see §9.3, footnote 5).

3.6 Additional syntactic effects on agreement morphology

We expect the form of agreement to be determined by syntax, in terms of the agreement elements (principally controller, target and domain). In this section we look at additional syntactic effects. We start with instances where further syntactic distinctions are realized by the morphology together with agreement (§3.6.1). Then we move to examples where, in particular syntactic circumstances, not all the possible distinctions are drawn, giving an opposition of full and reduced forms (§3.6.2). As the extreme case, the distinctions may be reduced to none, in which case we have default agreement (§3.6.3). And finally, there may be a special form, a 'neutral' form, for the instances where no distinctions are made (§3.6.4). In this section my emphasis is on the morphology, though I shall naturally pay some attention also to the syntactic conditioning of the different forms (conditions are the topic of chapter 6).

3.6.1 Further distinctions fused with agreement morphology (Hungarian objects)

It is worth reminding ourselves that other distinctions may be realized, fused together with agreement distinctions. Consider these examples:

Russian
(47)   knig-a,   **kotor-aja**   lež-it . . . .
         book(F)-SG.NOM   which-F.SG.NOM   lie-3SG
         'the book, which is lying . . .'
(48)   knig-a,   **kotor-uju**   ja   čitaj-u . . .
         book(F)-SG.NOM   which-F.SG.ACC   1SG   read-1SG
         'the book, which I am reading . . .'

In each of them, the relative pronoun agrees in gender and number with its antecedent. Its case is determined by its role in the clause, and not by agreement. However, the values for gender, number and case are all realized together in a single inflection.

There are some less obvious instances of this type of fusion. I take one which has been important in discussions of agreement, namely Hungarian. We do not expect a language to have a verb which agrees in definiteness with one of its arguments. Yet Hungarian has often been cited as a language which appears to show this (see also Abondolo 1988).[6] My first example has an intransitive verb:

---

[6] I take up here an ALT list discussion of November 1999; I will not ascribe the analyses to individuals, in case they changed their view during the debate. For an analysis within Minimalism see Bartos (1997); for discussion of competing syntactic analyses see Kiss (2002: 49–55); and for the issue of which noun phrases count as definite here see Moravcsik (2003: 404–5, 445–6).

Hungarian (Edith Moravcsik, personal communication)
(49)   Iskolá-ba   jár-nak.
           school-ILL   go-3PL
           'They go to school.'

Next we consider a transitive verb, first with an indefinite object and then with a definite one:

(50)   Egy könyv-et   olvas-nak.
           a   book-ACC   read-3PL
           'They are reading a book.'

(51)   A   könyv-et   olvas-sák.
           the book-ACC   read-3PL
           'They are reading the book.'

The verbal suffix thus differs in form when the object is definite. Three contrasting analyses have been suggested.

First analysis: Since the verbal inflection differs only in the environment of a definite object, then the inflection itself must be a fused subject (person, number) agreement and object (definiteness) agreement marker, there being no other property of the object which is referred to by the affix, such as gender or number. This may be represented schematically as:

(52)   they read-3PL.SBJ_DEF.OBJ the book
           they read-3PL.SBJ   a book

Second analysis: Such contrasts indicate that the verb agrees with its object under the condition of definiteness, that is, when the object is definite, but otherwise it does not. This does not mean that it agrees in the feature definiteness, but that agreement is possible only in the environment of definiteness. This may be represented as follows:

(53)   they read-3PL.SBJ_3SG.OBJ the book
           they read-3PL.SBJ   a book

Third analysis: Hungarian verbs do not agree with their objects, rather they take a special kind of subject agreement in the presence of 'definite' objects and then only with third person objects (except for the 1.SUBJ-2(familiar) OBJ marker -*lek*/-*lak*).

(54)   they read-3PL.SBJ (CONDITION: DEF) the book
           they read-3PL.SBJ   a book

That is, there is subject agreement which has a realization conditioned by the presence of a 'definite' object. For this discussion we note that both solution two and solution three do not require us to recognize definiteness as an agreement feature.[7] They do require us to have a condition on agreement involving definiteness. Thus recognizing agreement conditions (chapter 6) simplifies the typology of features.

The Hungarian situation is comparable to the form of the German adjective being conditioned by the presence or absence of a particular type of determiner (§3.6.2.3). We shall see another, more complex example, when we tackle Newar (§5.5.1).

3.6.2 Reduced agreement forms

Here we consider further examples where syntactic circumstances require a choice between paradigms. That is, one and the same lexical item will have more than one way of realizing a particular feature specification. It is not sufficient to specify that the syntax requires, say, third singular feminine, there is a further choice to be made. In the reduced set of inflected forms fewer distinctions will be made.

3.6.2.1 Reduced agreement in Somali

Somali verbs show two sets of inflections:

(55)   Somali past simple tense of *keen* 'bring' (Saeed 1993a: 87)

	full agreement	reduced agreement
1SG	keenay	keenáy
2SG	keentay	keenáy
3SG.M	keenay	keenáy
3SG.F	keentay	keentáy
1PL	keennay	keennáy
2PL	keenteen	keenáy
3PL	keeneen	keenáy

Note that the reduced paradigm does not represent a simple collapsing of the full paradigm. The full paradigm has just two interesting syncretisms (1SG=3SG.M and 2SG=3SG.F); in the reduced paradigm second singular and third singular feminine are different, though overall there is more syncretism and considerably fewer distinctions are made. Reduced agreement represents a second set of forms for the same target, with the same possible feature specifications. In terms of morphology, the essential point about reduced paradigms is the *existence* of two sets of forms, where in most languages we find one. The *use* of the different sets of forms is a matter of conditions, to which we return in §6.7.3.

---

[7] For another, rather complex, instance of subject agreement having different realizations according to the presence of a 'definite' object see Muna (Austronesian), as described by van den Berg (1989: 59–60).

3.6.2.2   Reduced agreement in Inari Sami

Another example of reduced agreement is found in Inari Sami (Toivonen 2003; Toivonen uses the terms 'full' and 'partial').

(56)   Inari Sami present indicative of *leδe* 'be' (Toivonen 2003)

	full agreement	reduced agreement
1SG	lam	
2SG	lah	lii
3SG	lii	
1DU	láán	
2DU	leppee	
3DU	lava	láá
1PL	lep	
2PL	leppeδ	
3PL	láá	

Here are examples:

Inari Sami (Toivonen 2003)
(57)   Meecist   lava   uábbi   já   viljá.
            forest.LOC be.3DU sister.NOM and brother.NOM
            'In the forest are my sister and brother.'

Example (57) shows full agreement. It is an instance of number resolution (§8.2).

(58)   Riddoost   láá   kyehti keeδgi.
            beach.LOC be.NON_SG.RED_AGR two   rock
            'On the beach are two rocks.'

(58) shows reduced agreement. As (56) shows, the same form is used for all persons dual and plural (the same as the third plural in full agreement). It appears that animacy is playing a role here (a point taken up in §6.3.2). With noun phrases denoting animals, both forms are found:

(59)   Kyehti poccuu ruáttáain / ryettih   meecist.
            two   reindeer ran.3DU / ran.NON_SG.RED_AGR forest.LOC
            'Two reindeer ran in the forest.'

The conditions under which reduced agreement is used are not fully understood, but Toivonen (2003) suggests that, besides the important factor of animacy, a secondary factor is specificity (non-specific noun phrases can take reduced agreement even when they denote animates).

3.6.2.3   German weak and strong adjectives

German adjectival inflections fit here, which shows that the full/reduced distinction is not restricted to verbs. The examples are like those of Somali and Inari Sami, in that for a given agreement feature specification there is more than one possible realization, according to an outside factor; one set of realizations makes fewer distinctions, hence 'full' and 'reduced' forms are appropriate terms. The traditional terms for German adjectives are 'strong' and 'weak'. They are not weak and strong like the Tsakhur verbs discussed earlier (nor indeed like German weak and strong verbs), since in these latter cases a given verb paradigm (or part of the paradigm) has only one set of forms. Besides the so-called strong and weak inflections of German adjectives, there is a third 'mixed' set of forms. This set makes fewer distinctions than the strong, but more than the weak (it is closer to the weak). We follow in part the discussion in Zwicky (1986b).

(60)   German *gut* 'good' strong paradigm (full agreement)

	SINGULAR			PLURAL
	MASCULINE	NEUTER	FEMININE	
NOMINATIVE	gut-er	gut-es	gut-e	gut-e
ACCUSATIVE	gut-en	gut-es	gut-e	gut-e
GENITIVE	gut-en	gut-en	gut-er	gut-er
DATIVE	gut-em	gut-em	gut-er	gut-en

Although sixteen cells are distinguished syntactically, extensive syncretism means that there are only five distinct forms. Now compare the mixed set:

(61)   German *gut* 'good' mixed paradigm (partially reduced agreement)

	SINGULAR			PLURAL
	MASCULINE	NEUTER	FEMININE	
NOMINATIVE	gut-er (S)	gut-es (S)	gut-e	gut-en (W)
ACCUSATIVE	gut-en	gut-es (S)	gut-e	gut-en (W)
GENITIVE	gut-en	gut-en	gut-en (W)	gut-en (W)
DATIVE	gut-en (W)	gut-en (W)	gut-en (W)	gut-en

Forms which are shared with the strong paradigm above are marked '(S)'; those shared with the weak paradigm below are marked '(W)'. The remainder (unmarked) are shared across all three sets of inflections.

(62)   German *gut* 'good' weak paradigm (reduced agreement)

	SINGULAR			PLURAL
	MASCULINE	NEUTER	FEMININE	
NOMINATIVE	gut-e	gut-e	gut-e	gut-en
ACCUSATIVE	gut-en	gut-e	gut-e	gut-en
GENITIVE	gut-en	gut-en	gut-en	gut-en
DATIVE	gut-en	gut-en	gut-en	gut-en

It is clear that the mixed paradigm in (61) is reduced with respect to the strong, and the weak paradigm (62) is further reduced. In each instance there are fewer distinct inflections (five for the strong, four for the mixed and two in the weak). However, the sets of cells which are distinguished in the strong paradigm are not simply collapsed: the weak paradigm has different forms for the feminine singular and the plural, which are identical in the strong paradigm.

(63)   Examples of the use of German weak and strong adjectives (nominative case)

	SINGULAR			PLURAL		type
	gut-er 'good	Mann man'		gut-e 'good	Männ-er men'	strong
dies-er 'this	gut-e good	Mann man'	dies-e 'these	gut-en good	Männ-er men'	weak
kein 'no	gut-er good	Mann man'	kein-e 'no	gut-en good	Männ-er men'	mixed

The paradigm to be used depends on the presence and the type of the determiner. Zwicky (1986b: 984–7) treats the choice as government, which seems right; the morphosyntactic specification is a matter of agreement, certainly for gender and number at least, but the selection of the type of paradigm represents an additional distinction, which is not a matter of agreement.

3.6.3   Default forms

Agreement may be suspended. The simplest case is that in which there is no controller with the necessary features. We usually find a default form used to meet this eventuality. Typically there is nothing remarkable in morphological terms, it is one of the normal possibilities drafted in for this extra duty. In a sense, this is the logical extension of reduced agreement, where just one form is possible.

Russian

(64)   Sveta-l-o.
        dawn-PST-N.SG
        'Day was dawning.'

In Russian we have the common choice of neuter singular as the default. Tsakhur
has a four-gender system and the singular form for gender IV is used:

Tsakhur (Kibrik 1999: 435)

(65)   bajram-i-s   mik'a-da   wo-d-un.
        Bajram-OBL-DAT   cold-ADV.IV   be-IV-ATTRIB
        'Bajram is cold.'

The choice of form to be used is considered in §5.2.1. There are other circumstances under which default forms are used (§5.2.2), extending their use beyond
what we might expect. In particular, there are instances (for instance, in Tuscan
Italian, discussed in §6.4) where an apparently viable controller does not in fact
control agreement.

3.6.4   Neutral forms

As we have just seen, languages may solve the problem of agreement
with problematic controllers by pressing one of the regular agreement forms into
service. While these forms may appear to be identical to some other form, they
are usually odd in some ways. Thus they typically appear identical to singular
markers but they lack plural counterparts (this is evident if there can be conjoined
controllers, §2.1.2, footnote 2). Moreover, certain target types may be avoided.

On the other hand, some languages have unique agreement forms, which I shall
term 'neutral' forms, just for agreement with problematic controllers. The Sele
dialect of Slovene (spoken in Sele, Carinthia, Austria) has lost the neuter gender,
even in pronouns, but some original neuter forms survive only in impersonal
predicatives:

Sele dialect of Slovene (Tom Priestly 1983: 355, 1984: 44–5, and personal
communications)

(66)   ta   wín   je   súx
        this   wine(M) be.3SG   dry[M]
        'this wine is dry'

(67)   ta   srájca   je   súx-a
        this   shirt(F) be.3SG   dry-F
        'this shirt is dry'

(68)   nòs   je   sòx
        today   be.3SG   dry.NEUTRAL
        'today it is dry'

The adjectival form in (68) is a remnant of the neuter gender. Just a few adjectives
have this third form; it is available only in uses with problematic controllers: there
are no nouns in the neuter gender.

Comparable neutral forms are found in Ukrainian (Shevelov 1963: 128–33, Blevins 2003: 492–5), in Surselvan Romansh (Haiman 1974: 130–4) and in Spanish and Portuguese, all discussed in Corbett (1991: 214–16). However, no language has yet been found with a full set of unique neutral forms: regular gender/number forms are used for some targets.[8]

Further afield we also find neutral forms in Maithili. If a verb takes a single argument, and there is one non-nominative argument, which is first or second person honorific or third person non-honorific proximate or remote, then we find non-agreement; the authors call it 'dummy agreement', and it is equivalent to our 'neutral' agreement. It is a frozen form, related to but not exactly like the third singular (Balthasar Bickel, personal communication). For example:

Maithili (Bickel, Bisang & Yādava 1999: 489):
(69)   hamrā   bhukh   lāgait   ai-ch
          1SG.DAT hunger   be(come).perceptible.IPFV.PTCP   NEUTRAL-AUX
          'I am getting hungry'

3.7   Rich agreement and strong agreement

The original basic idea of 'rich agreement' is that the shape of the agreement paradigm will allow predictions about syntax: variation in the agreement paradigm will lead to variation in the syntax. While a good deal has been written on this, there are serious problems with it and rather few remaining predictions.

'Rich agreement' was a live issue within Germanic linguistics. The main notion, worked out during the 1980s and 1990s, is that verb movement in Germanic languages is caused by rich agreement, that is by the existence of agreement paradigms showing person and number agreement; this work culminates in Rohrbacher (1999). Bobaljik (2003) outlines the development of the idea, and produces serious counter-examples. The term 'rich agreement' was also used in discussion of null subjects (pro drop), together with the alternative term 'strong agreement'. For example, Borer (1989: 78) wrote: 'In standard accounts of null subjects it is customarily assumed (following a proposal originating with Taraldsen 1980) that null-subjects are licensed by an INFL node which is – in some sense – rich enough to identify the null subject.' Similarly Jaeggli & Safir (1989: 32), in discussing 'identification' (which is required in their analysis of different types of null subject) state: 'The most common notion of identification is by rich (or what may best be called "strong") agreement, where inflectional affixes correspond to members of the conjugational paradigm.' Thus pro drop was intimately linked with agreement morphology, which was the basis of the pro-drop parameter. Problems soon emerged with this parameter. Jaeggli & Safir (1989: 27–9)

---

[8] Lithuanian has an impressive set of neutral forms (Ambrazas 1997: 134–7, 171–2, 182–3, 196–7, 203–5).

include 'rich' agreement in a very helpful discussion, and show the difficulties with it. We return to this issue in §3.8.2.

A more recent development has been to disregard morphology and to treat agreement features as weak or strong according to the syntactic result required. Thus 'weak' and 'strong' have for some become diacritics on nodes, specifying the syntactic outcome desired, rather than a reflection of morphological difference.

Rich agreement is also used in a rather different sense; thus Hawkins (2002: 138) uses it for the situation where 'the verb has verbal affixes or cliticized morphemes that index at least two argument positions in a clause'. He adds that 'This definition follows the ("head-marking") classification of Nichols (1986, 1992).' This therefore treats systems as having rich agreement where some would rather analyse them as having pronominal affixes. Hawkins argues that rich agreement in this sense will be found most frequently in verb initial languages, for parsing reasons. See Dryer (2002: 154–7) and Polinsky (2002: 188–90) for further data and discussion on this.

3.8 Pronominal affixes

Suppose a language typically has verbs with bound markers for person, number and perhaps gender. Should we assume that these are instances of agreement? Or can these be pronouns, though attached to the verb? This issue has been debated extensively by Baker (1996), Evans (1999), Mithun (2003) and Siewierska (2004b: 120–7) among others. Yet often linguists have assumed one or other answer for a particular language without supporting argument. The issues are discussed in detail in Corbett (2003b); extensive references are provided, and diagnostics for distinguishing agreement markers and pronominal affixes are proposed. Since that account is available I give only an outline here. The issues are complex, and for some readers they lie outside the main concerns of agreement; such readers may prefer to skip this section on first reading.

In terms of syntax, pronominal affixes are arguments of the verb; a verb with its pronominal affixes constitutes a full sentence, and additional noun phrases are optional. If pronominal affixes are the primary arguments, then they agree in the way that anaphoric pronouns agree (§2.2.2). I take an example from the Iroquoian language, Tuscarora:

Tuscarora (Mithun 1999: 190)
(70)   wahrakyétkaht
          wa?-hrak-etkaht-?
          FACTUAL-3SG.AGENT> 1SG.PATIENT-chase-PFV
          'He chased me.'

Here '>' indicates the combination of roles in a marker; others use '/' for this purpose. Where helpful, an orthographic first line is added in examples, distinct from the segmented second line.

In terms of morphology, pronominal affixes are bound to the verb; typically they are obligatory (for some this would be criterial). They often form portmanteaux combining marking of both core arguments (Evans 1999: 262), as here:

Tuscarora (Marianne Mithun, personal communication)
(71)   waʔkə́:tkaht
          waʔ-kə-tkaht-ʔ
          FACTUAL-1SG.AGENT>2SG.PATIENT-chase-PFV
          'I chased you.'

The 1SG.AGENT marker on its own is *-k-*, and the 2SG.PATIENT marker is *-eθa*; the form for 1SG.AGENT on 2SG.PATIENT is *-kə-*, which is not simply a combination of the two but a portmanteau marker. Forming portmanteaux is a rare possibility for clitics (as in Tagalog) and is something which is not characteristic of free pronouns.

3.8.1   The background for pronominal affixes

There are two logical extreme positions: all pronominal affixes count as agreement, or no pronominal affixes count as agreement. If we could sustain either view, we should do so, but this appears unlikely.

According to the **pure agreement** view, the presence of person/ number/gender features on the verb is a sufficient condition to say that we have verb agreement. Melčuk discusses agreement at length and states unequivocally that polypersonal verbs show 'the most common agreement' (1993: 342–3, 365–7). Some versions of this approach further assume that agreement features must have a local controller, and therefore insert the required phrases in the syntactic structure if they do not appear on the surface.

According to the opposite view, the **pure pronoun** view, once an affix can be analysed as being pronominal in nature, it is an incorporated pronoun/pronominal affix and as such does not fall within agreement. That is, agreement and pronouns are quite distinct. However, we have instances of free pronouns showing agreement (§1.4.3). Thus pronouns can be agreement targets (like verbs, adjectives and so on), and so deciding that a particular affix is pronominal does not thereby exclude it from consideration.

There are several interlocking factors here which are often not separated out. As well as the extreme cases of canonical agreement on the one hand and pronominal affixes on the other, most of the intervening territory can be filled. 'Pronominal-affix languages' are not a homogeneous group; they vary, including in ways which affect the status of their affixes. Even within a given language, pronominal affixes may not form a homogenous group (as Baker 2002: 52 points out for Ngalakgan). Since pronominal-affix languages cannot be neatly circumscribed, we should continue with our canonical approach. That is, we separate out different factors and recognize that some cases are more categorial than others. Whether incorporated pronouns are near the edge of the phenomenon of agreement or the beginning of the neighbouring phenomenon is less important than see-ing the connections and differences. And the varying factors observable with pronominal affixes overlap considerably with those found in canonical agreement systems.

In current linguistic usage many treat pronominal affixes as part of agree-ment. For example, Bickel and Nichols (forthcoming) draw a distinction between grammatical agreement and pronominal agreement, noting that the distinction has a long tradition. Their 'pronominal agreement' is what others discuss under pronominal affixes. In whatever way we analyse the phenomenon, it seems we are duty bound to include it.[9]

Given the difficulty of identifying pronominal affixes, it is tempting to have recourse to a **pronominal-argument parameter**, according to which various phe-nomena cluster together in languages with pronominal affixes. However, Austin & Bresnan (1996) show that the phenomena claimed to cluster in this parameter vary independently of each other; it follows that attempting to identify pronom-inal arguments on the basis of other co-varying characteristics of a language is unsound. We must therefore tackle them directly.

3.8.2   Criteria for pronominal affixes

The next step therefore, following our canonical approach, is to separate out the different factors.

(72)   The syntax and morphology of pronominal affixes

syntax:	non-argument	argument	
linguistic element:	'pure' agreement marker	pronominal affix	free pronoun
morphology:	inflectional form		free form

In the canonical case a pronominal affix has the syntax of an argument of the verb but the morphology of an inflection. (72) is a simplification since it presents boundaries as sharper than they are. In terms of syntax, there are instances where it may be arguable whether a given element represents an argument or does not

---

[9] The usage of Mallinson & Blake (1981: 42–6) is still influential. They treat languages like Swahili as having pronominal prefixes: 'in Swahili the verb can stand on its own to form a sentence, the pronominal prefixes on the verb functioning like unstressed pronouns'. They contrast this with Germanic languages where, they say, the verb cannot stand alone and so the agreeing elements are not pronominal. Their usage is as follows (1981: 46): 'we will use *agreement* as the super-ordinate term covering the Germanic type of verb agreement and the Swahili type. We will use the term *cross-referencing agreement* or simply *cross-referencing* for the Swahili type.' More recently, Croft uses 'agreement' as a cover term for various types of marking on the verb (2001: 139–40n3).

fill the argument slot.[10] In morphology the boundary between inflectional and free forms is occupied by clitics.[11]

(72) does capture the dual nature of pronominal affixes, sharing syntactic behaviour with pronouns (specifically with the weak pronouns, what Givón 1984: 361 calls the 'unstressed, clitic or "agreement" pronouns') and sharing morphological behaviour with other inflectional affixes, including agreement affixes.[12] However, this dissociation of function and form is not complete.

If pronominal affixes fall between agreement markers and free pronouns, we can read the central line of (72) as expressing a scale. Then we can ask what other criteria relate to this scale. We shall compare across languages, based on the primary means of expression, that is, contrasting pronominal affixes in a language where they are primary with free pronouns in a language where they are primary. Thus we are comparing typical agreement with typical pronominal affixes and with typical free pronouns (and not, for instance, pronominal affixes with free pronouns within languages which have both).

(72) is also helpful for distinguishing two types of analysis of the verbal marker when it appears together with a full noun phrase and when without. Some take a 'syntactic view' and suggest different functions for a single marker: it is a pronoun when there is no full noun phrase argument, and an agreement marker when there is a full noun phrase argument. This first position has been characteristic of those working in LFG, where particularly detailed work has been done (for instance, Bresnan 2001a: 146). Others take a 'morphological view' and suggest that if a form cannot be distinguished across environments then it should be assigned to a single category (for example, Georgopoulos' account of Palauan, 1991: 49).

The different assumptions here are worth bringing out. The **syntactic** view, at its simplest, starts from a concern to understand reference. It assumes that full noun phrases and free pronouns are the 'best' referential expressions (the best links to entities in the world). If a noun phrase or free pronoun is found, it is likely to be referential. If there is also a marker on the verb, which might otherwise function as a pronoun, then in this instance it cannot be doing so and is an agreement marker. (This preserves 'functional uniqueness' or its equivalent, at the cost of giving particular morphological markers a dual function.)[13] The **morphological** view, also at its simplest, starts from a concern to understand verbal morphology. It states that markers bound to the verb should, all things being equal, be assigned

---

[10] The obvious case concerns pro-drop phenomena; if there is, say, a marker on the verb, and there is no overt subject pronoun, different analyses might accord argument status to the absent pronoun or to the marker which is present.

[11] For an interesting account of the different possible realizations of pronouns within Optimality Theory see Bresnan (2001b).

[12] We may see (72) as representing a potential path of grammaticalization, discussed further in §9.1.1.

[13] It is natural to treat it as a 'cost' to give markers a dual function; however, Toivonen (2000) argues that there can be positive evidence to show that this is the better approach. She considers possessive markers in Finnish. The paper is of interest here not only because of its explicit defence of dual function, but also because it reminds us that the issue of 'dropping' arises within the noun phrase as well as within the clause.

to a single category. Therefore, if particular markers can function as pronouns, they *are* pronouns irrespective of other structure. Thus even if co-occurring with a full noun phrase or free pronoun, the bound marker is still a referring pronoun. (This preserves a single function for the marker, but means that the theory of pronominal binding has to be made more complex.) Various analyses take one of the different starting points for granted, and come to conflicting conclusions from similar data. A salutory example is the different labellings of the Swahili object marker, which depend on these different starting views (see Seidl & Dimitriadis 1997: 381).

Let us turn to a brief comparison of agreement markers, pronominal affixes and free pronouns using five criteria: a full account is given in Corbett (2003b).

First consider the number of **case roles** which may be indexed by the different means. In the indisputable instances of verb agreement, normally we find that just one case role can be indexed, whether the subject or the absolutive argument (§2.3.2). In languages claimed to have pronominal affixes, we typically find that these index all the main arguments (two or three), as suggested, for instance, by Mithun (1986: 197).[14] Free pronouns, on the other hand, can typically index all the case roles possible in a given language; in some instances this is a fair number (§4.4.1).

A second criterion is the **degree of referentiality**. Of the three items in (72), agreement markers are least likely to be used referentially. Nevertheless, in a language where pronouns rarely appear in argument positions one could argue that the agreement markers can have referential uses. Pronominal affixes frequently are referential. Free pronouns are normally referential, though even they may have non-referential uses, however untypical (Evans 1999: 256–7). This is a scalar criterion for analysing verbal markers: the more referential they are, the stronger the case for treating them as pronominal affixes, and the greater the restrictions on referential use, the stronger the case for treating them as agreement markers.

As discussed by Evans (1999: 256), if a marker is non-committal with respect to anaphoric or referential status, as is for example the obligatory third-person-singular agreement marker in English (which can agree with definite, indefinite and negative expressions), then it is an agreement marker. Conversely, if the marker unambiguously 'refers' to some entity then it has the status of a pronoun and is an incorporated pronoun. Non-referential use of the marker is for Evans a diagnostic of lack of full pronominal status. Evans suggests that their obligatory nature can lead to pronominal affixes no longer being able 'to encode such contrasts as referential vs non-referential, definite vs indefinite and so on' (1999: 255). Take this example from Bininj Gun-Wok (Mayali):

---

[14] Perhaps this defines a 'polysynthetic language'. Evans & Sasse (2002: 3) suggest that 'a proto-typical polysynthetic language is one in which it is possible, in a single word, to use processes of morphological composition to encode information about both the predicate and all its arguments, for all major clause types (i.e. one-, two- and three-place predicates, basic and derived), to a level of specificity allowing this word to serve alone as a free-standing utterance without reliance on context'.

Bininj Gun-Wok (Evans 1999: 265): Gun-djeihmi dialect
(73)   al-ege daluk   gaban-du-ng
          F-DEM woman   3SG>3PL-scold-NON_PST
          (a) 'That woman scolds people.'
          (b) 'That woman scolds them.'

Whereas a free pronoun, in languages like English (and in Bininj Gun-Wok), does not have the generic reading (the (a) reading) in comparable examples, this is possible for the pronominal affix. A free personal pronoun is a means of forcing a definite referential reading:

Bininj Gun-Wok (Evans 1999: 266): Gun-djeihmi dialect
(74)   al-ege daluk   gaban-du-ng   bedda
          F-DEM woman   3SG>3PL-scold-NON_PST them
          'That woman is scolding them.'

Similarly, free pronouns are typically not used with indefinite objects, while pronominal affixes can be (Evans 1999: 267):

Bininj Gun-Wok (Evans 1999: 267): Dulerayek dialect
(75)   balanda   bi-mey
          European 3SG>3SG.HIGHER_OBJ.PST-marry.PST_PFV
          (a) 'She married the white man.'
          (b) 'She married a white man.'

This view has been challenged as a general view of how pronominal affixes work. For a different view, based on a careful analysis of Central Alaskan Yup'ik and Navajo, see Mithun (2003).

A third, related criterion is the degree of **descriptive content**. In particular, how much lexical meaning is associated with each item in (72), as opposed to 'functional' or 'grammatical' meaning. We can fix the two end points of our scale. Starting this time with the personal pronouns, many have descriptive content albeit to a restricted degree. For instance, there are languages where pronouns are literally 'personal': they can be used for reference to persons only, with some other means being required for non-persons (Corbett 1991: 245–8). At the other end of our scale, we might expect that agreement markers would have no descriptive content. After all, the agreement system is a major locus of repeated grammatical information. However, we cannot simply exclude agreement markers here, as examples of semantic agreement (§5.4) demonstrate. Given our discussion of (72), we would expect pronominal affixes to occupy a middle position, between agreement markers and free pronouns, but here we are predicting rather than reporting.

The scale of (72) leads us naturally to a discussion of the **balance of information** between full nominal phrases and the three items we are discussing. We need to consider how information is distributed across stretches of discourse, including those larger than single utterances. Let us take a hearer perspective and ask what can be gained from a nominal phrase compared with agreement markers, pronominal affixes and free pronouns. At one level the answer is evident: there are potentially vast numbers of nominal expressions, while in contrast the three items under discussion are limited in number. There are evidently very substantially more possible nominal expressions than there are pronouns available. This is why anaphora works as it does, namely by introducing a referent through a nominal expression (one of the many possible) and, having established it, continuing with pronominal expressions (a choice from relatively few).

The question may be posed at a more interesting level. We may investigate the balance of information just for the features which may potentially be shared (the agreement features). Let us begin with agreement markers. In canonical agreement controller and target mark the same features, and share the same number of feature values. There are many systems which are not fully canonical in this way and, interestingly, the balance may be shifted in either direction. Consider again Russian:

Russian

(76)   ja   piš-u
          1SG.NOM   write-1SG
          'I am writing.'

Here the controller marks person and number as does the target verb. The same distinctions are made in each, an instance of canonical agreement. Now compare the past tense:

(77) a.   ja   pisa-l   b. ja   pisa-l-a
          1SG.NOM   write-PST[M.SG]   1SG.NOM   write-PST-F.SG
          'I was writing.' (man)   'I was writing.' (woman)

Both the controller and the target mark number. The controller marks person, which is not marked on the target. Conversely the target marks gender, which is not a category of first-and second-person pronouns in Russian. Here, and much more generally, we find instances where the controller makes distinctions not reflected or not fully reflected in the target, and conversely the target makes distinctions not (fully) found on the controller. In terms of cumulating information, the balance may be tilted either way, with more information coming from controller or from target. Impressionistically, the balance is roughly equal.

When we turn to pronominal affixes and free pronouns, however, there is a clear shift in favour of these two. It is rare to find (morphosyntactic) feature distinctions marked on the noun phrase which are not also found on the pronominal affixes or free pronouns (whichever the language favours). We do find the opposite: pronominal affixes and free pronouns frequently distinguish number in languages where normal noun phrases do not (this is a part of the predictions which can be drawn from the Animacy Hierarchy; see Corbett 2000: 54–66 for details). We would predict a difference between pronominal affixes and free pronouns (recall that we are comparing the major strategy *between* languages here), but the evidence is yet to be collected to support such a hypothesis.

This brings us to the last criterion showing variation across our scale, namely **multipresentation**. By this I mean the co-occurrence of elements within the same clause indexed to the same referent. In canonical agreement we find multirepresentation: we have a controller noun phrase and agreement marked on one or more targets. However, varying from language to language we find instances of unirepresentation (the interesting case being where the marker on the verb is the only overt indexation of the referent).

Variants of this type are usually discussed as 'doubling' (cf. 'multirepresentation') and 'dropping' (cf. 'unirepresentation'). I use unfamiliar terms just in this section to stress that I wish to avoid any processual reading. (There is no chance that these will replace the traditional terms.) 'Pronoun incorporation' and 'pro drop' were used originally to indicate operations on phrase structure. In constraint-based models, however, the terms are used without any implication of movement or deletion (Bresnan 2001a: 177n4). We need this neutral sense: multi-representation/doubling for us implies two or more elements, not that having one is somehow basic, for a given language; unirepresentation/dropping implies one element, without the implication that having two is basic.

Languages are sometimes classified too rigidly according to this phenomenon. Thus Russian, one of our featured languages, is generally regarded as a language in which the subject pronoun is normally present. It therefore has canonical agreement in this respect. And yet we do find instances without the pronoun.[15] Its South Slavonic relative Bulgarian is described as a pro-drop (null-subject) language, but this too is not an absolute phenomenon. Consider some hard data on the issue, from a sample of five parallel texts in five Slavonic languages (two Slavonic originals and translations, and the translations of three non-Slavonic originals), from which we have 2,000 examples for each language:

(78)   Null and overt pronominal subjects in Slavonic languages (Seo 2001: 92)

	null subject	overt subject	% overt subject
Russian	443	1557	77.9
Bulgarian	1556	444	22.2
Serbian/Croatian/Bosnian	1683	317	15.9
Czech	1829	171	8.6
Polish	1859	141	7.1

Of course there are issues to do with the use of written texts and the effect of translation. However, the basic message is clear: languages are not simply

---

[15] We also find, in colloquial Russian, examples of the pronoun 'doubling' a noun phrase; see McCoy (1998) for discussion of data earlier described by O. B. Sirotinina.

'pro drop' or not, rather there is wide variation.[16] Languages range between having pronouns typically present, right through to languages where they are typically absent. And, contrary to a widespread belief, one cannot maintain a straightforward link between inflectional explicitness and the presence or absence of subjects. Asher (1996: 115–16) points out that Tamil sentences readily have no overt subject; some attribute this to the fact that verbs are marked for person and number and (in third person singular) gender. Asher undermines this explanation by pointing to Tamil forms with no agreement (but where the subject is equally likely to be absent) and to Tamil's relative Malayalam, which does not have marking for person/number/gender on verbs, but which is as likely as Tamil to have sentences without an overt subject. There are also languages of south-east Asia lacking relevant inflectional morphology, such as Japanese and Korean, which show regular absence of independent pronouns (Huang 2000: 57–9).

Before leaving pro drop, I should mention Jelinek's influential paper (1984) on Warlpiri, where she claims that Warlpiri clitics are the arguments of the verb and that nominals are adjoined. Unlike most investigators, Jelinek takes the logical next step of discussing pro-drop phenomena (as in Spanish) in the same terms. She suggests that Spanish has 'pronominal suffixes' and that overt subjects represent nominal adjunction. The consequence of this reasoning would be to assign languages like Russian (with agreement) and Bulgarian (with pronominal suffixes, on such an analysis) to radically different types. And yet this is not convincing: when we examine the agreement systems in detail, looking at which features are involved, and going down to the specifics of instances where different feature values are possible and the conditions which influence the choice between them, we find substantial similarities between those Slavonic languages with frequent instances of pro drop and those with fewer instances (Corbett 1983).[17] Austin & Bresnan (1996) give a systematic comparison of Australian languages with regard to pro drop, and throw considerable doubt on Jelinek's analysis.

If we now turn to consider multirepresentation with regard to pronominal affixes, we again find great differences from language to language. Some show a large proportion of clauses in natural texts in which the verb's arguments are expressed solely through the verbal affixes. Mohawk represents a dramatic case: Marianne Mithun (personal communication) reports five predicates for each syntactic nominal in one sample of spoken texts.[18]

Finally, free pronouns are typically in complementary distribution with full noun phrases having the same function within the clause. Indeed theories of

---

[16] For additional statistics on Russian and Bulgarian see Dončeva (1975); for statistics on varying rates of dropping in varieties of Spanish see Cameron (1993). For references and data on pro drop varying according to person, particularly in Bislama, see Meyerhoff (2000: 113–14, 136–9), and in Romance see Heap (2000). Ariel (2000: 236–7) shows how dropping varies according to tense in Hebrew, and links this to how alliterative the markers are (§3.5.1).

[17] For discussion of the pro-drop parameter with reference to Slavonic see Franks (1995: 287–304). Franks does not adopt the 'pronominal affix' position, but rather treats all the family as showing agreement, with or without pro drop.

[18] If the count is done according to morphological form, then the ratio is much higher, since there are many instances of morphological verbs used as nominals.

pronominals often trade on the assumption that a pronoun will not be coreferential with a noun phrase within the clause. This is covered, for example, by Binding Theory or by the LFG principle of 'functional uniqueness' (Bresnan 2001a: 145, 158).

This characteristic is particularly important, and we need to ask whether we can use it to determine whether an affix is a pronominal affix or an agreement marker. There is an intuition that the (im)possibility of a free pronoun occurring in the same clause as the marker gives an indication as to the status of a verbal marker. Note that we can apply this heuristic 'in both directions': the pronoun may block the marker and the marker may block the pronoun. Consider first Macushi, a Carib language, with around 15,000 speakers in Brazil and Venezuela. In a transitive clause the absolutive argument (with no case marker) precedes the verb, and the ergative argument follows it. This order is seen too in the markers on the verb:

Macushi (Abbott 1991: 24–5, 101, discussed in Siewierska 1999: 226)
(79)   i-koneka-'pî-i-ya
          3SG-make-PST-3SG-ERG
          'He made it.'

In (79) the verb bears a prefix *i*– corresponding to the absolutive argument and a suffix -*i* corresponding to the ergative argument. We wish to ascertain the nature of these markers.

(80)   t-ekîn   era'ma-'pî paaka esa-'ya
          REFL-pet   see-PST   cow   owner-ERG
          'The owner of the cow saw his own pet.'

In (80) the verb bears no markers co-indexing the ergative or the absolutive argument. Once there is a free nominal or pronominal argument, there will be no marker on the verb:

(81)   *uurî-ya i-koneka-'pî-u-ya
          1SG-ERG   3SG-make-PST-1SG-ERG
          'I, I made it.'

These data strongly suggest that the markers in (79) are pronominal. Some would treat them as pronominal affixes; for others, the fact that the verb may appear without them (they do not appear where there is a free argument as in (80)) would make them clitics.[19]

---

[19] There are less straightforward cases. There are languages where the marker may be in complementary distribution with only full nominals and optionally co-occur with pronouns (Welsh) or conversely, where the complementary distribution is with pronouns, not lexical noun phrases (Palauan). In Kichaga the object marker must occur with free pronouns, but may or may not occur with lexical noun phrases (Bresnan & Moshi 1990: 151–2; in the LFG analysis the object marker is seen as marking grammatical agreement when it doubles the pronoun, but as an incorporated pronoun – which shows anaphoric agreement with a topic – in the non-doubling use; when there is a lexical noun phrase present this is treated as a dislocated topic, Bresnan 2001a: 151). Siewierska also remarks that there may be a split between common and proper nouns. A further factor is

The converse case is even more interesting: the marker is obligatory and it prevents the occurrence of the free pronoun. This situation is found in Ngalakgan, a language of the Gunwinyguan family spoken in southern Arnhem Land. When a verb is inflected with a first-or second-person marker, coreferential independent pronouns cannot occur in the same intonational phrase (Baker 2002: 60–1). It seems reasonable here to interpret the marker on the verb as pronominal.[20] (Independent pronouns are rare in natural speech in Ngalakgan.)

For the clear cases, then, we might suggest that if a free pronoun can co-occur without problem in the same clause, then we are dealing with agreement. And if a free pronoun is not easily possible in the same clause, then we have a pronominal affix. This test works well, but for relatively few cases. Languages like Ngalakgan are rare. Other languages allow free pronouns, but with restrictions and/or with marked effects (such as strong contrast). Once again it becomes difficult to draw the line. We have discussed this test with regard to a free pronoun, as being the clearest case. The possibility or not of a noun phrase headed by a noun occurring freely in the clause is a less clear test.[21]

A further problem with the complementary-distribution test is that when a pronoun (or a lexical noun phrase) co-occurs with a verbal marker, it may be argued that it is appositional to the verbal marker, and that the marker is the argument (whether in some cases or all cases). Often this is just stated rather than justified. One needs language-specific arguments for each case. Without them it is impossible to decide which of two coreferential items is in argument position and which is in apposition to it.

There is, however, a clear and useful test concerning multirepresentation, and one that is little discussed. It is the possibilty of multiple targets.[22] If there is more than one target within the clause (that is, if the marker in question is not unique), then we are dealing with agreement. If it is unique, then there is no prediction. This heuristic is linked to the last, since it is based on the intuition that we do not expect a pronoun to be repeated. Consider this example from Serbian/Croatian/Bosnian:

Serbian/Croatian/Bosnian
(82)   došl-a   je
          came-F.SG AUX.3SG
          'She came.'

---

word order, where a verbal marker may co-occur with a postverbal noun phrase, but not with a preverbal noun phrase (1999: 229).

[20] Third person independent pronouns are so rare that the situation is unclear. However, coreferential nouns do co-occur with the verbal marker; Baker takes this as evidence that the verbal markers act as agreement markers under those circumstances.

[21] An idea of the complex possibilities within multirepresentation and unirepresentation can be gained from Larike, a Central Moluccan language of Ambon Island, Indonesia. Laidig & Laidig (1990) describe two sets of pronominal affixes, either of which may be dropped where this is semantically and pragmatically appropriate. Larike is unusual in marking both subject and object optionally (according to the right conditions).

[22] I believed this heuristic was original, but in fact it was hinted at by Georgopoulos (1991: 56).

The fact that both elements of the verb include markers leads me to believe that we are dealing with agreement (subject pronouns are regularly absent). Conversely, if we were to argue that there is an incorporated pronoun here, then we would need arguments as to which component contained the pronoun, and which then agreed with it. This is important for us because we wish our key examples to be close to canonical agreement wherever possible. The Daghestanian examples, which have a prominent place in our account, typically show marking on several elements. Hence we must be dealing with agreement.

Let us review the five characteristics:

(83)   Agreement, pronominal affixes and free pronouns (typical instances)

	agreement marker	pronominal affix	free pronoun
case roles	1	2	all
referentiality	low	high	highest
descriptive content	low	higher	highest
balance of information (features vs those of noun phrase)	roughly equal	higher	higher
multirepresentation	normal	possible	largely excluded

Remember that we are taking typical instances here, given the variation within each type. We should also recall that we are considering only a part of agreement here, namely agreement of the verb. Allowing for that, we do see how pronominal affixes fall between undisputed agreement affixes on the one hand, and free pronouns on the other. The relative nature of these differences shows why it is difficult to frame tests to distinguish agreement markers from pronominal affixes.[23]

Part of the difficulty is the assumed, often unstated, linkages between characteristics which are in principle distinct. Languages vary in how likely they are to include all arguments: this is assumed to correlate with the presence of agreement morphology, but it can vary independently. The degree to which particular elements are bound morphologically varies from language to language, and does not automatically identify their syntactic status. And the referential status of pronouns does not necessarily translate directly from language to language.

Being able to draw a sharp analytical line between pronominal affixes and agreement is of importance only if one believes that agreement is restricted to the clause. If, as many believe, agreement reaches beyond the clause, then pronouns agree with their antecedents (see §1.4.3). On this account the difference between an agreement marker and a pronominal affix is much less significant, since the

---

[23] For discussion of tests proposed in the literature and the attendant difficulties see Siewierska (1999: 230–1).

pronominal affix is then also an agreement target. We can see this if we compare these two structures (element order is not relevant):

(84)   [pronominal affix+agreement marker]VERB
(85)   [agreement marker]VERB

For some linguists, as I noted above, the appropriate analysis would hinge on whether a full noun phrase is also present (for some the question is whether one *may* be present). For others the structure of the verb with its affixes will be uniform across constructions (that is, it has one structure irrespective of whether or not a noun phrase is present).

Let us consider the task of the hearer in each case. In (84) the hearer's task is to identify the referent of the argument of the verb. This is to be done by cumulating information from the [pronominal affix+agreement marker] with other information, possibly supplied by a noun phrase. The information may unify in a straightforward way, with varying amounts of information coming from the distinct sources, or there may be conflicting information, as when feature values are assigned in one instance by grammatical criteria and in the other by semantic criteria (§5.4). Since the amount of information provided by the [pronominal affix+agreement marker] may vary, it narrows the search to a greater or lesser degree.

If we treat (85) in the same way, then the task is essentially the same. The hearer will attempt to identify the referent of the argument of the verb. This is to be done by cumulating information from the [agreement marker] with other information, possibly supplied by a noun phrase. The information may unify in a straightforward way, with varying amounts of information coming from the distinct sources, or there may be conflicting information. Again the [agreement marker] may provide more or less information (thus a gender marker in a language with four genders may provide more information than its counterpart in a language with two genders).

Given that the tasks are essentially equivalent, we may reasonably ask whether speakers need to distinguish the two structures. There is an important point here, which picks up the earlier discussion about pro drop and its relation to agreement. We noted there that two languages may have very similar agreement systems and be pro drop (null subject) in one case and not in the other. A similar point can be made about languages with and without incorporated pronouns (pronominal affixes).[24] The agreement system need not be substantially different in the two types.[25] For this reason a canonical approach is appropriate; the insistence on

---

[24] This is a distinct case, provided one does not assume that for a language to be pro drop automatically implies it has incorporated pronouns.

[25] For example, a set of tests and arguments for distinguishing incorporated pronouns has been developed by those working within LFG, and these tests have been applied particularly to Bantu languages. Several Bantu languages have been analysed as having ambiguous subject markers but incorporated pronouns for objects. Applying this approach, Demuth & Johnson (1989) show that Setawana (a dialect of Setswana) has incorporated pronouns both as the subject marker and as the object marker. This sets Setawana apart in this

a rigid classification into languages with agreement or with pronominal affixes would limit rather than enhance future research.

3.8.3   Pronominal affixes: essential points

This is an area where the use of terms varies dramatically; some would exclude pronominal affixes from agreement, others treat them as the most interesting type of agreement. When reading the literature one should bear in mind that some writers simply assume which language or languages have pronominal affixes and rarely give criteria for identifying them. Tradition also plays an unfortunate role: languages in certain parts of the world are normally treated as having verb agreement and those in other parts as having pronominal affixes, and the distinction is not always one of substance. Moreover, given the gradient nature of the categories, there are many cases where the distinction may not be a reasonable one to draw.

It is important that not all pronominal affixes are the same. We noted that they vary from language to language, and even within languages (as in the case of Ngalakgan). They can co-exist with agreement markers, as in Lavukaleve (Terrill 2003: 244–5). There are often subject-object asymmetries, as in various Bantu languages.

We have to keep the 'big picture' in mind. The logical outcome of some views of pronominal affixes, which stress their ability to occur without a noun phrase as controller, is to put languages like Mohawk, Spanish and Bulgarian into the same type, with English and Russian in another, while we know that in most relevant respects Russian and Bulgarian belong together.

Finally, this is just one part of what agreement is about; agreement covers more than the markers on the verb and their relation to its arguments.

3.9   Conclusion

The morphology of agreement is one of the most interesting parts of inflectional morphology, precisely because it involves the realization of displaced information. All the resources of inflectional morphology are available, from the canonical right through to suppletion. It is important to allow for the diversity we find: within a part of speech we may find some items which simply do not agree, and among those that do there may be great differences in the feature values

respect from other Bantu languages investigated to date; however, Demuth & Johnson do not point to any differences in the agreement system (for instance, in the features involved).

Having or not having incorporated pronouns is part of the balance of how far the language is head marking rather than dependent marking (Nichols 1986). While various differences follow from this distinction, the agreement system need not be greatly affected. Certain agreement domains will differ. In other respects we find agreement systems with similar properties on both sides of this typological divide.

realized and in the inflectional means used. Conversely, similar morphology can express rather different phenomena. So while morphology provides the essential data for investigating agreement, we must beware of rushing to conclusions on the basis of morphology alone. It is now time to move on to the feature interface beween syntax and morphology.

4 Features

When attempting to understand and to model the complexity of natural language, researchers typically use features. This is true for the most abstract theoreticians through to the most applied computational linguists. Features are the key underpinning for linguistic description, being used to factor out common properties.[1] It is therefore natural to use them in analysing agreement. Yet we have conflicting and incompatible accounts of features left from different periods. The fact that agreement involves comparable features but in different situations (relating to controllers and to targets) makes it the ideal area for coming to a fuller understanding of features. In this chapter I concentrate on features (such as number) while in the next I look at their values (such as singular, dual, plural), and in particular at the instances where controller and target have different values.

4.1 Copying of features or unification

A sketch of the history of ideas in this area will help us to understand the current scene. In the early days of Transformational Grammar, from the late 1950s till the 1970s, agreement was treated as a straightforward issue. It was used as a test for investigating trickier topics; for instance, in analysing subject-raising, agreement was taken as a safe test to demonstrate what was the subject. Agreement itself was handled by copying feature values from one node to another (controller to target). Thus for English, in a phrase consisting of a demonstrative and a noun, the number value of the noun was copied to the demonstrative. Given a noun like *book* marked as plural, the grammar would account for phrases like *these books*. Evidence accumulated that agreement was not so simple: Morgan (1972) showed that agreement in English is far from trivial, Moravcsik (1978) showed that languages vary considerably in their agreement systems and Corbett (1979) demonstrated that there are numerous mismatches where such simple agreement rules do not work, but that these mismatches follow general patterns.

The earlier rule-based approaches, which copied features from controller to target, face problems: the controller may be absent (as in pro-drop languages) or it may be present but underspecified, something which occurs frequently with

[1] As noted in §1.3, some use 'category' where I use 'feature'; then 'feature' is used for my 'feature value'.

pronouns (Barlow 1992: 30–43; his arguments are developed in Pollard & Sag 1994: 62–7). Consider this Russian example:

Russian

(1)   Ja   sidel   / sidel-a
      1SG.NOM   sat[M.SG] / sat-F.SG
      'I was sitting' (man / woman talking)

In accounts based on a rule of feature-copying we need to say that Russian has two pronouns *ja*, one masculine and one feminine, which happen to be phonologically identical. There are many similar instances. In copying analyses such cases require every controller to be given a specification as detailed as that of the most specified potential target. This means that copying accounts involve a considerable degree of redundancy.

The 1980s saw the rise of unification-based frameworks, particularly GPSG and LFG. These were declarative rather than procedural in nature, and they held particular promise for modelling agreement systems. Unification-based accounts, where agreement can be seen as a matter of cumulating partial information from the controller and the target, have much better prospects (Shieber 1986: 21–22, Barlow 1992: 22–45). In a unification-based approach, taking the case of the woman talking in (1) above, we could have the following feature structures (the first for the pronoun and the second for the verb):

(2) $\begin{bmatrix} \text{NUMBER:} & \text{singular} \\ \text{PERSON:} & 1 \end{bmatrix} \begin{bmatrix} \text{NUMBER:} & \text{singular} \\ \text{GENDER:} & \text{feminine} \end{bmatrix}$

These feature structures can be unified, since they are compatible, to give the following structure:

(3) $\begin{bmatrix} \text{NUMBER:} & \text{singular} \\ \text{PERSON:} & 1 \\ \text{GENDER:} & \text{feminine} \end{bmatrix}$

Thus the information is cumulated from different parts of the structure. The standard reference on unification is Shieber (1986), and there is another helpful introduction in Copestake (2002); the problems with unification and the advantages of subsumption-based strategies are discussed in Blevins (forthcoming). Recall that unification handles canonical agreement well, but has problems with mismatches (§1.4.4).

However, if we represent agreement in this way we need some other means to make the asymmetric nature of agreement explicit. There is, after all, a strong intuition, captured in the controller-target terminology, that agreement is asymmetric, involving displaced information. In GPSG the asymmetry is reintroduced by the Control Agreement Principle (based on work by Keenan 1974, as discussed in §2.3.1), which specifies possible controllers and targets, and gives them different statuses (see Gazdar et al. 1985).

Since the 1990s, in Head-Driven Phrase Structure Grammar, the asymmetry is captured through 'anchoring': gender, number and person features are anchored to real-world entities through noun phrase indices, even though they may be expressed morphologically other than on the noun phrase (see Pollard & Sag 1994: 60–99, and compare Kathol 1999).[2]

In spite of the problems outlined above, some continued with copying-style analyses, particularly those working in the Government and Binding (GB) framework. In the Minimalist Program this was replaced by 'checking', which shares some characteristics with unification, but leads to deletion (or elimination) of the target feature. In Minimalism it is important to eliminate uninterpretable features (§4.2.5), while in unification-based theories this is not an issue: 'Checking reduces to deletion under matching with an active local goal and ancillary deletion of the uninterpretable feature that rendered the goal active' (Chomsky 2000: 123).[3]

From a situation where agreement was a helpful test for use when tackling more difficult problems in syntax, we have now come to the point where agreement in all its complexity is recognized as being one of the major challenges for syntax, indeed as a major test for our theories of syntax.

4.2   Feature types and their relevance for agreement

We need to establish what sorts of feature there are, and particularly which of these are involved in agreement, that is, which type of featural information can be 'displaced'.

4.2.1   Overt features versus conditions

A distinction is sometimes drawn between overt and covert features. I shall recognize only overt features as features; what are sometimes called covert features[4] in the sense of 'conditions' are rather different, as we shall see. The importance of this distinction is the desire to avoid allowing in spurious features.

To establish the (overt) agreement features I start from the agreement targets in a given language. I take the targets because without distinctions on targets there is no evidence for agreement. I establish the paradigms for the various agreement targets, which may be straightforward, but equally it can be a substantial analytical task. I then ask which features are required to identify each cell. These features are the (overt) features, and only these.

---

[2] For a different approach to the compatibility of feature specifications in agreement see Steele (1990: 90–3). And for a critique of the treatment of agreement in unification-based grammars and an account of an approach using Lambek Categorial Grammar see Bayer & Johnson (1995).

[3] For a critique of checking see Johnson & Lappin (1997: 279–83, 313–18), and for a Minimalist account using feature-matching rather than feature-checking see Radford (2004: 281–323). A survey of techniques used for treating agreement in GB and early Minimalism can be found in Belletti (2001); see also Bejar (2003).

[4] I am concerned here with the nature of features, not with overt/covert operations on features.

We begin by looking at the past tense of a Russian verb:

(4)   Past tense forms of Russian *stojat´* 'stand'

masculine	feminine	neuter	plural
stojal	stojala	stojalo	stojali

We need (at least) one feature with four values. While the morphology could work with these specifications, the interface to the syntax would be problematic. As the labels imply, we are not dealing with a single feature with four values. Rather we have one form, the plural, which can agree with noun phrases headed by nouns of all genders when plural,[5] and other forms which are used for singulars, according to gender:

(5)   Morphosyntactic feature description for the past tense forms of Russian *stojat´* 'stand'

	singular	plural
masculine	stojal	
feminine	stojala	stojali
neuter	stojalo	

Some other targets have different phonological forms but the same distinctions (the cells are the same but the forms which fill them may differ). The present tense forms are structured rather differently:

(6)   Morphosyntactic feature description for the present tense forms of Russian *stojat´* 'stand'

	singular	plural
1	stoju	stoim
2	stoiš´	stoite
3	stoit	stojat

We have already accepted the need for a number feature; these forms also require a person feature. And to specify these forms as opposed to the very different past tense forms in (5) we need a tense feature. Thus for verbs we have to recognize the following features and values:

GENDER: masculine, feminine, neuter
NUMBER: singular, plural
PERSON: 1, 2, 3
TENSE: present, past

---

[5] Thus gender is restricted to the singular; I discussed such featural restrictions in §3.3.2.

Where features and values are presented in this format (rather than in glosses) it is conventional to give the feature in upper case and the value in lower case. While these are *overt* features, they may or may not be *agreement* features. Thus TENSE on the Russian verb is not an agreement feature.

At this point we can clarify the contrast with a so-called 'covert' feature, or what I shall call a condition on agreement. When all cells are accounted for, that is to say, we have recognized sufficient features to describe each one, there may still be additional conditions on the use of the forms specified. For example, the plural form may be used rather than a singular form for some controllers, according to whether the controller precedes the target or not. That is not a feature of the paradigm. There is, of course, no morphological exponent for precedence in the paradigms above. Precedence is a condition generalizing over the possibilities described by the overt features (it affects the choice between singular *stoit* and plural *stojat*, and in the past tense the choice between all singulars and plural *stojali*). Such conditions are the topic of chapter 6.

There are, however, some instances where it is less clear at first sight whether a feature should be recognized. We might expect each feature to have a form or set of forms uniquely determined by it. This is not necessarily so. Consider first the forms of the Russian adjective. By the same reasoning as for the verb we accept a number feature.

(7)   Paradigm of the long form adjective (traditional presentation): *staryj* 'old'

	singular			plural
	masculine	feminine	neuter	
nominative	staryj	staraja	staroe	starye
accusative	as NOM / GEN	staruju	staroe	as NOM / GEN
genitive	starogo	staroj	starogo	staryx
dative	staromu	staroj	staromu	starym
instrumental	starym	staroj(u)	starym	starymi
locative	starom	staroj	starom	staryx

This traditional adjectival paradigm has many more cells than there are distinct phonological forms, owing to pervasive syncretisms. The most interesting of these concerns the accusative case, to which we return below. In addition, the masculine and neuter are identical in the oblique cases and the feminine does not distinguish the oblique cases (the adjectival instrumental inflection *-oju* is now largely limited to poetry, and I shall exclude it). Taking into account too the unexpected identity of the masculine/neuter instrumental singular with the dative plural, there are twelve distinct inflections. These syncretisms are brought out in (8):

(8)   The paradigm of the long form adjective *staryj* 'old' (showing syncretisms)

	singular			plural
	feminine	neuter	masculine	
nominative	staraja	staroe	staryj	starye
accusative	staruju		as NOM / GEN	
genitive	staroj	starogo		staryx
locative		starom		
dative		staromu		starym
instrumental	staroj(u)	starym		starymi

Thus we have to recognize the following features and values:

CASE: nominative, accusative, genitive, dative, instrumental, locative
NUMBER: singular, plural
GENDER: masculine, feminine, neuter

I leave open the question of case as an agreement feature, and return to it in §4.4.1.

Let us now look at the accusative cells. For the masculine singular and for the plural the form is identical to the genitive for animates and to the nominative for inanimates. Here animate nouns are approximately those which denote entities which can move and respire. At the boundary, insects count as animates, plants are inanimate, and there is some uncertainty over microbes. Here are some clear instances:

Russian
(9)   ja   viž-u   star-yj   dom
            1SG.NOM see-1SG old-M.INAN.SG.ACC house(M.INAN)[SG.ACC]
            'I see an old house.'

(10)   ja   viž-u   star-ogo   drug-a
            1SG.NOM see-1SG old-M.ANIM.SG.ACC friend(M.ANIM)-SG.ACC
            'I see an old friend.'

We cannot simply say that for animates the genitive case is used through the noun phrase, since nouns belonging to a different inflectional class (class II in (25) below) have a separate accusative form:

(11)   ja   viž-u   star-ogo   dedušk-u
            1SG.NOM see-1SG old-M.ANIM.SG.ACC grandfather(M.ANIM)-SG.ACC
            'I see (my) old grandfather'

Here *dedušku* is unambiguously accusative (the nominative would be *deduška* and the genitive *deduški*). For a formal account of this syncretism, which goes over paradigm boundaries, see Corbett & Fraser (1993), and for further discussion and for the typological implications see Baerman, Brown & Corbett (2005: 204–17). We have to recognize that the genders of Russian are subdivided into two subgenders: ANIMATE and INANIMATE (Corbett 1991: 161–8). Thus Russian agreement in animacy involves forms which are syncretic with another case; however, the syncretic pattern is distinctive for animates. Hence we allow an (overt) agreement feature here, namely animacy.[6]

As a different illustration we consider person in Archi (Nakh-Daghestanian). We tend to assume that languages have a person feature, but with Archi the situation is not self-evident. Archi (like some related languages) has no unique forms for agreement in person; it distinguishes four genders and two numbers:

(12)   Gender and number agreement in Archi (Kibrik 2003: 562)

gender	number	
	singular	plural
I	w-	b-
II	d- -r-	
III	b-	Ø-
IV	Ø-	

The basic prefixal agreement forms are given here (the infixal forms are the same except for <r> in gender II singular); in suffixal position gender IV has a distinctive (non-null) marker. The agreements that occur with first and second person pronouns can all also be found with third person pronouns. The singular pronouns *zon* 'I' and *un* 'you' take gender I (male human) or gender II (female human) agreements, based on the sex of the speaker or addressee respectively.[7] (Agreement markers for genders I-IV on the pronoun itself, when in an oblique case, were illustrated in §2.4.9.) In the plural there are two agreement markers, as compared with four in the singular. The marker *b-* (with an *-a-* inserted by a general rule) is for genders I and II plural (that is, for all humans), in the third person:

---

[6] Russian animacy is therefore a 'dependent target gender', that is 'a target gender consisting of a set of morphological realizations which mark agreement with members of a given agreement class by an opposition involving only syncretism (and no independent form)' (Corbett 1991: 161–8).
    Animacy also has a role in predicate agreement, where it is a condition in Russian. In Russian predicate agreement animacy does not involve distinctive use of forms, only a condition on the choice in the values of number (§6.1.2). Thus animacy plays two rather different roles in Russian.

[7] If an animal is personified, agreements with first and second person pronouns are then gender III or IV, depending on the gender (Marina Chumakina, field notes).

Archi (Aleksandr Kibrik 1972 and personal communication)

(13)   teb   ba-qIa
             they   I/II.PL-came
             'they (human) came'

Example (13) is appropriate where *teb* denotes humans; the same agreement form would be used if in place of the pronoun there were a plural noun phrase denoting humans. *Teb* 'they' can also be used with the zero plural agreement form, used for genders III and IV:

(14)   teb   Ø-qIa
             they   III/IV.PL-came
             'they (non-human) came'

This is acceptable when *teb* denotes non-humans; the same verb form would be found with plural nouns of genders III and IV. Now consider the following examples:

(15)   nen   Ø-qIa
             we.EXCL   1PL-came
             'we came'

(16)   žʷen   Ø-qIa
             you.PL 2PL-came
             'you came'

Since both pronouns denote humans, we might have expected the form **ba-qIa*, following the pattern from the singular, where just gender and number had to be taken into account. In fact, we have agreement in person, the first and second persons taking the bare stem (zero marking: Ø-). This happens to be the same as the plural for genders III and IV. The paradigm is given in (17):

(17)   Person agreement in Archi

person	number	
	sg	pl
1	gender agreement	Ø-
2	gender agreement	Ø-
3	gender agreement	gender agreement

Thus, in the plural, the marker for first and second persons is Ø-, which also serves for genders III and IV in the third person. There is no unique form for person agreement. However, we require an overt person feature to account for the use of the forms and their distribution in the paradigm. Interestingly too we need a person feature for resolution purposes; without such a feature, gender resolution would become very complex (§8.3.3). Thus we need to know the person of the absolutive argument in Archi in order to select the appropriate agreement marker for the verb, even though there is no marker which is unique to person agreement. (Further instances of pronouns which induce comparable mismatches are given in §5.6.4.)

Before leaving the overt/covert distinction, I should note that I have used 'covert' negatively, to separate off instances where the introduction of a feature would be spurious. This is the absolute use of the term 'covert', since if a feature claimed to be an agreement feature is only covert, then it should not be a feature (and henceforward I shall call it a 'condition'). 'Covert' also has a benign use, when it is used not of features per se but of their use relative to particular agreement elements. Thus nouns may be said to have 'covert gender' where there is no realization of gender on the noun itself, but where gender is overt on targets (for instance, in verb agreement), for which see Corbett (1991: 62–3). That is, there is an overt gender feature (as shown by agreement), but it is covert with respect to the particular controller.

4.2.2   Morphosyntactic versus purely morphological features

As the name implies, morphosyntactic features are those which are relevant to syntax and to morphology. Thus the feature number in the Russian examples above is relevant to syntax, since it has a role in agreement; it is also relevant to morphology, since the rules of exponence which determine the form of the adjective or verb need to refer to this feature. (The relation between the role of such features in syntax and morphology is not always straightforward, as phenomena such as syncretism and deponency show us.) Morphological features have a role only in morphology. For instance, similar to the paradigm for *stojat´* 'stand' in (6) above, Russian has a paradigm for *pisat´* 'write' and similar verbs.

(18)   Purely morphological distinction (Russian conjugation)

	conjugation 1	conjugation 2
	'write'	'stand'
1SG	pišu	stoju
2SG	pišeš´	stoiš´
3SG	pišet	stoit
1PL	pišem	stoim
2PL	pišete	stoite
3PL	pišut	stojat

These differences between the two inflectional classes (conjugations) are internal to morphology. We say that the two verbs belong to two different inflectional classes, or that they bear different morphological feature specifications,

INFLECTIONAL CLASS: 1 (*pisat'*) and INFLECTIONAL CLASS: 2 (*stojat'*). We have already met inflectional class differences when discussing, for example, the strong and weak verbs of Tsakhur in §3.3.3. In that instance the shape of the paradigm differed between the inflectional classes, while the Russian examples above make the same distinctions, and the only difference is in the phonological realization. In all these examples, the differences have no impact outside morphology.

Such morphological features can be arbitrary; they may have to be specified for individual lexical items, hence they are instances of lexical features. Alternatively they may be predictable, to varying extents, from phonological and/or semantic factors. That is, given the phonology or semantics of a given lexical item, it may be possible to assign its morphological feature by an assignment rule, rather than having to specify it in the lexicon (see Fraser & Corbett 1995 for details and for a Network Morphology implementation). Unlike morphological features, morphosyntactic features (like number in (18) and gender) are never completely arbitrary. This is true provided we take the feature and its values as a whole, though they can be arbitrary in particular uses. For instance, gender systems always have a semantic core (Corbett 1991: 8–32), though particular instances of gender can be arbitrary. Only morphosyntactic features are involved in agreement. Morphological features are not, hence the notion of 'morphology-free syntax' (see §6.3.1). An apparent counter-example is mentioned in §8.5.1.

4.2.3   Contextual versus inherent features

This distinction concerns the feature in relation to where it is realized. Following work by Anderson (1982), Booij (1994, 1996) distinguishes contextual and inherent inflection. Contextual inflection is 'that kind of inflection that is dictated by syntax' (1996: 2). Inherent inflection is 'the kind of inflection that is not required by the syntactic context, although it may have syntactic relevance' (1996: 2). This is not an absolute classification, but a classification of inflection relative to particular categories (noun, verb and so on). For our purposes, we can transfer the classification to the features involved. As an example, number is an inherent feature for nouns. It is inherent to the noun, rather than being required by the syntactic context. For the adjective, however, it is a contextual feature, since it is dictated by syntax.

Taking the features in turn, we see that for nouns and pronouns, as the typical heads of controller phrases,[8] gender is an inherent feature, as is person (for pronouns) and number. Recall that where it is important to make the distinction, I indicate inherent non-overt feature values in parentheses, for instance (F), following the Leipzig Glossing Rules. Case is a contextual feature, dictated by the syntax. For typical targets, like adjectives and verbs, the features gender, person and number are contextual (but see the discussion of verbal number in §4.3.2), as

---

[8] Pronouns are also targets (§2.2.2); in this role gender and number are contextual features.

is case (for adjectives). For the verb, tense, aspect, mood and polarity are inherent features (see also the discussion of Kayardild in §4.5.2).

Since agreement is an asymmetric relation (whether in the canonical instances or, if one takes a stricter stance, in all instances), then the clear agreement features are those that are inherent to the controller. They are contextual for the target. Thus gender, person and number are inherent features for controllers, and are evidently agreement features. Case is typically a contextual feature, and its status as an agreement feature is therefore less clear (see §4.4.1 below).

4.2.4   Direct versus indirect features

This distinction, due to Zwicky (1992), concerns how features apply across components, in particular in relation to semantics. Direct features, like number, gender, person, tense, aspect and polarity, express intrinsic content. They are 'associated directly with prototypical, or default, semantics: number with numerosity, gender with a variety of classifications of objects, person with reference to participants in the speech act, tense with times, and so on' (1992: 378). Indirect features like case, finiteness, dependence, declension 'are not so directly meaningful'; they express meanings indirectly, via other grammatical constructs, in particular, grammatical relations; thus the nominative case is associated by default with the subject grammatical relation, which is associated with the prototypical semantics of agency. This classification of features cross-cuts the others, but has an interesting consequence. The direct features of nouns and noun phrases are: gender, number and person. From one more perspective, then, these three are picked out, and they are the main agreement features (§4.3).

4.2.5   Interpretable versus non-interpretable features

This distinction is drawn in Minimalism, for instance in Chomsky (2001: 4–6). Interpretable features can be interpreted at LF (logical form). Hence number is potentially an interpretable feature, while a purely syntactic feature (like the EPP feature, which requires the auxiliary carrying it to have a subject) is uninterpretable. Thus far this is equivalent to direct versus indirect (§4.2.4). However, a feature is (un)interpretable with respect to a given element, thus number is interpretable for, say, a subject noun phrase but is uninterpretable for an agreeing verb (since it does not affect the semantic interpretation of the verb). In this regard the distinction follows the inherent/contextual distinction (§4.2.3). Thus interpretable features are those which are direct and inherent.

The distinction is important in Minimalism since uninterpretable material should not be found in LF, and so uninterpretable features must be deleted from the syntax. The uninterpretable features on a given element make up the 'probe' which seeks a 'goal', a matching set of interpretable features (Chomsky 2001: 5). For Chomsky, 'probe' is largely equivalent to 'target features' while 'goal' is 'controller features' (though probe and goal are not used of pronoun-antecedent relations). However, others allow the terms to slip and use 'probe' for target and 'goal' for controller. While the notion of uninterpretable features may seem merely to rename previous distinctions, there is a deeper problem. In instances of canonical agreement (like *Mary runs*) it is the case that the number feature on the verb adds nothing to semantic interpretation. However, in a substantial number of instances we find mismatches between controller and target (see chapter 5). In these instances target features cannot be treated as uninterpretable, which casts doubt on the validity of treating them as uninterpretable also in those instances when they do match those of the controller.

4.2.6   Structuring within features

I have listed features and their values such as these:

GENDER: masculine, feminine, neuter
NUMBER: singular, dual, plural
PERSON: 1, 2, 3

That is, the values were given as 'atomic', without any internal structuring. Some assume that features are composite, and so automatically introduce additional structuring where there are more than two values (thus a three-gender system might be analysed as neuter versus non-neuter, the latter splitting into masculine and feminine). However, we should do this only when we find linguistic justification. The attempt to import feature geometry from phonology into morphosyntax has to date failed to cover the feature values already documented (see Baerman, Brown & Corbett 2005 for discussion). There is clear evidence for structuring within number values (Corbett 2000: 38–50). For the other features there are two sorts of evidence. The first is defaults: the value selected in exceptional circumstances is of different status from the others (§3.6.3, §5.2). The second type of evidence comes from superclassing, where a subset of the values are available in given circumstances (§5.3.1).

4.3   Main agreement features ('phi features')

The three indisputable agreement features are **gender, number** and **person**. They are called phi-features in Government and Binding (GB) and Minimalism and they are the agreement features of HPSG (Pollard & Sag 1994: 67) and of LFG (Bresnan 2001a: 144–6). We consider these first, in turn, and we shall see that they are different in nature. Examples will be given of systems with more feature values than those found in the most familiar languages such as French, that is, with more than three persons, two numbers and two genders. This is important for the rest of the book, since claims about these features in the literature are often based on French-type systems, and such claims do not hold in larger systems.

4.3.1   Gender

Gender is an inherent feature of the noun. It is found on the target, say the adjective, as a consequence of its presence in the noun:

Russian
(19)   nov-yj   korabl´
         new-M.SG   ship(M)[SG]
         'a new ship'

Here the use of the masculine form *novyj* 'new' has nothing to do with the lexical meaning of the adjective, but results from the fact that the adjective is modifying a masculine noun. Compare the following:

(20)   nov-aja   lodk-a
         new-F.SG   boat(F)-SG
         'a new boat'

(21)   nov-oe   sudn-o
         new-N.SG   vessel(N)-SG
         'a new vessel'

Gender is a lexical feature for nouns in that, like the morphological features discussed earlier, its value has to be available in the lexicon. And as with other lexical features, a given lexical item normally has one value of the feature, and this value may have greater or lesser semantic justification. Unlike morphological features, gender is available for agreement. It may therefore be considered the canonical agreement feature (§1.4): it is clearly a feature of the controller, it may or may not be explicable in semantic terms (for a given controller), and hence the realization of the value for gender on the target is the canonical instance of the need for a syntactic rule of agreement.

An important issue with gender, which will recur in subsequent chapters, is that of assignment. If a speaker of Russian uses the word *kniga* 'book' or *djadja* 'uncle', how does he or she 'know' the gender? Knowing the gender is essential for making the appropriate agreements. A model of the way in which speakers allot nouns to genders is called a *gender assignment system*.

Gender assignment may depend on two sorts of information: the meaning of the noun and its form (compare the definition of agreement in §1.3). In what I shall call **strict semantic systems** the meaning of a noun is sufficient to determine its gender, for all or almost all nouns. This type is found in Dravidian languages like Kannada (Karnataka, southern India; Sridhar 1990: 198). In Kannada nouns denoting male humans are masculine, those denoting female humans are feminine. There are also deities, demons and heavenly bodies in these genders. All remaining nouns, including those denoting infants and animals, are neuter. Thus *appa* 'father' and *candra* 'moon' are masculine, *amma* 'mother' is feminine and *na:yi* 'dog' is neuter.

Many languages have **predominantly semantic assignment systems**, which do not cover the noun inventory as completely as do the system of Kannada. An example is found in Bininj Gun-Wok (introduced in §2.2.1). The semantic categories found in each gender are as follows:

(22)   The semantics of gender in the Kunwinjku dialect of Bininj Gun-Wok
         (Evans, Brown & Corbett 2002)

Masculine	Vegetable
• Male higher animates	• Plants and their products, including life-form terms
• Overall default for animates	• Sexual and excretory body parts
• Some lower animates	• Song, ceremony and custom
• Rain	• Fire (both bush and domestic)
• Compass points	• Food, vegetable and otherwise
• Most celestial bodies	• Some types of honey
• Some items used in painting	• Boats, planes and cars
• Trade items, esp. Macassan and European	• [Drink, water, well]
• Some types of honey	• [Camp nexus]
	• [Landscape features with water associations]

Feminine	Neuter
• Female higher animates	• Most parts of animals and plants
• Some lower animates	• Some parts of the landscape
• Sun	• Weather and sea
	• Time measures
	• Languages and speech
	• Country; place-based social categories

The items in square brackets represent categories which have moved into the vegetable gender from the neuter in the speech of younger speakers. The semantic assignment rules are more numerous and more complex than those of Kannada, yet they cover the nouns of the language less well. For example, lower animates are split between the masculine and feminine genders, and it is hard to be more specific; nouns denoting reptiles, birds and fish are found in both genders. There may well be principles of categorization here of which we are still unaware, but it seems likely that for some nouns there is no longer a principle for assignment still operating for current speakers.

Thus in languages with semantic assignment systems the meaning of the noun determines gender. In the strict assignment systems the rules are obvious and cover (virtually) the entire noun inventory. In the predominantly semantic systems there is a minority of exceptions; however, once the cultural setting of the language is taken into account, for some languages these exceptions have been claimed to be largely only apparent.

In some other languages, however, assignment by semantic rules would leave many nouns unassigned. In languages like Kannada the nouns not assigned by the semantic rules (the 'semantic residue') all belong to a single gender. In the languages we consider next these residue nouns are distributed over more than one gender. Here we find additional rules for assigning nouns to genders according to their form. There is a significant asymmetry: languages may base their assignment system on semantic rules, or on semantic *and* formal rules, but not just on formal rules. Formal assignment rules may in turn access two types of information: phonological and morphological. There may be combinations of such rules.

A good example of assignment depending on phonological information is provided by Qafar (an East Cushitic language of north-eastern Ethiopia and Djibouti, Parker & Hayward 1985). In Qafar semantic assignment is fairly standard: for sex-differentiable nouns, those denoting males are masculine and those denoting females are feminine. For nouns in the semantic residue, there are the following phonological assignment rules: nouns whose citation form ends in an accented vowel are feminine (for example, *karmà* 'autumn'), while all others are masculine (for example, *gilàl* 'winter', which does not end in a vowel, and *tàmu* 'taste', which does end in a vowel, but not an accented one). There are few exceptions.

The second type of formal assignment rule accesses morphological information. Here Russian is a good example. Once again for sex-differentiables nouns denoting males are masculine and those denoting females are feminine. Unlike the situation in languages like Kannada, the residue is shared between the three genders, with the neuter gender not even receiving the majority. We might think that further semantic rules would be sufficient, but this turns out to be at best highly unlikely, as the following triplets suggest:

(23)   Russian nouns belonging to the semantic residue

masculine	feminine	neuter
korabl' 'ship' cf. (19)	*lodka* 'boat' cf. (20)	*sudno* 'vessel' cf. (21)
žurnal 'magazine' cf. (25)	*gazeta* 'newspaper' cf. (25)	*pis'mo* 'letter' cf. (25)
dom 'house'	*izba* 'hut'	*zdanie* 'building'
čaj 'tea'	*voda* 'water'	*vino* 'wine'
avtomobil' 'car'	*mašina* 'car'	*taksi* 'taxi'
lokot' 'elbow'	*lodyžka* 'ankle'	*koleno* 'knee'
nerv 'nerve'	*kost'* 'bone' cf. (25)	*serdce* 'heart'
večer 'evening'	*noč'* 'night'	*utro* 'morning'
čas 'hour'	*minuta* 'minute'	*vremja* 'time'

Thus the nouns of the semantic residue are scattered across the three genders:

(24)   Gender assignment in Russian

masculine	feminine	neuter
Sex differentiables denoting males PLUS part of semantic residue	Sex differentiables denoting females PLUS part of semantic residue	Part of semantic residue

To understand how the remaining nouns are assigned, we need to look not at their meaning, but at their morphology. Russian nouns have four main inflectional classes:

(25)   Main inflectional classes in Russian (singular forms)

	I	II	III	IV
nominative	žurnal	gazeta	kost´	pis´mo
accusative	žurnal[9]	gazetu	kost´	pis´mo
genitive	žurnala	gazety	kosti	pis´ma
dative	žurnalu	gazete	kosti	pis´mu
instrumental	žurnalom	gazetoj	kost´ju	pis´mom
locative	žurnale	gazete	kosti	pis´me
gloss	'magazine'	'newspaper'	'bone'	'letter'

Given information about the inflectional class of nouns, assignment is unproblematic. Nouns in class I are masculine, those in classes II and III are feminine, and those in IV are neuter. (Further rules are required in Russian for the minor classes, such as the fourteen nouns like *vremja* 'time' and for nouns like *taksi* 'taxi' and *pal´to* 'coat' (§5.1.1), which are indeclinable and neuter.) In view of the coverage of these rules, we might be tempted to think that we could dispense with semantic assignment, since *mal´ čik* 'boy' is in class I, while *sestra* 'sister' is in class II and *mat´* 'mother' is in class III. In other words, many of the sex-differentiable nouns would be assigned to the appropriate gender by the morphological assignment rules. But there are also instances where this is not so, for instance, *djadja* 'uncle', which denotes a male but is in class II, whose nouns are typically feminine. *Djadja* 'uncle' is masculine. Nouns like this fit with the claim that we do not find languages where formal assignment is sufficient.[10]

---

[9] Since the noun is inanimate the accusative is as the nominative. If it were animate, the accusative would be as the genitive; see (10).

[10] Even in languages where formal assignment covers a large proportion of the nouns, semantic assignment rules always give a more complete system.

Of course, there are languages where assignment is more complex than these, but for languages where careful research has been undertaken, gender is always predictable from a set of assignment rules (semantic or semantic plus formal), for at least 85% of the noun inventory and usually for a substantially larger proportion than that. For more details on these assignment systems see Corbett (1991: 7–69). We return to assignment systems in §5.5.3, and in particular to 'hybrids', for which there is not a unique assignment.

We can now ask how gender systems are distributed over the world's languages. In a sample of 256 languages (Corbett 2005) there is no gender system in 144, somewhat over half. The minimal gender system has two genders, and such systems are common, with fifty examples in the sample. Three genders is around half as common (twenty-six examples), and four genders roughly half as common again (twelve languages). Larger systems with five or more genders represent a substantial minority (twenty-four languages in the sample). Fula (a Niger-Congo language) has around twenty genders, the Fuuta Jalon dialect having a particularly extensive system. Of the languages with a gender system, the majority have a system based on sex (eighty-four languages), but twenty-eight languages of the sample, notably in the Niger-Congo and Algonquian families, have systems based on animacy. And as for the type of assignment system, taking strict semantic and predominantly semantic assignment systems together, we find these in just under half the languages (fifty-three languages), while a slight majority (fifty-nine languages) had semantic and formal assignment (see Corbett 1991 for illustrations).

4.3.2   Number

Number is a lexical feature of some nouns: those which are only singular (like English *health*) or only plural (like *trousers)* impose this feature on their modifiers. Typically, however, a considerable proportion of the nouns of a given language can be associated with both (or all) numbers. Consider a straightforward example involving such a noun:

Russian
(26)   nov-ye korabl-i
          new-PL ships-PL
          'new ships'

Here the number feature appears to relate primarily to the noun; the property denoted by the adjective is not affected by the change in number.

Many languages have a third member of the number system, the dual, for two items. More complex systems may also be found, for example, with special forms for three items (the 'trial', as in Larike) or for a small but unspecified number of items (the 'paucal', as in Bayso, see §5.9); see Corbett (2000: 20–42) for examples and sources on larger number systems.

Number can be a contextual feature for verbs, in which case it is an agreement feature. However, it can also be an inherent feature, called 'verbal number', and it is important to distinguish the two (see Corbett 2000: 243–64 and references there). A striking example to make clear the difference is found in the Kartvelian language Georgian:

Georgian (Aronson 1982: 243, 406–7, Durie 1986)

(27) ivane   še-mo-vid-a   da   **da-ǰd-a**
     John[NOM]   PRV-PRV-enter-AOR.3SG and PRV-sit.SG-AOR.3SG
     'John entered and sat down.'

(28) čem-i   mšobl-eb-i   še-mo-vid-nen   da   **da-sxd-nen**
     my-AGR[11] parent-PL-NOM PRV-PRV-enter-AOR.3PL and PRV-sit.PL-AOR.3PL
     'My parents entered and sat down.'

The verb 'sit' exhibits verbal number: there are different stem forms according to whether one person sits (*da-ǰd-*), or more than one (*da-sxd-*); the verb 'enter' does not vary in this way. The verb 'sit' also agrees in number with the subject (as does 'enter'). The difference between verbal number and agreement is shown in this example with a numeral phrase:

(29) čem-i   sam-i   megobar-i   še-mo-vid-a   da   **da-sxd-a**
     my-AGR three-AGR friend.SG-NOM PRV-PRV-enter-AOR.3SG and PRV-sit.PL-AOR.3SG
     'My three friends entered and sat down'

Numerals require a singular noun (*megobari*) and numeral phrases control singular agreement (as we saw for Hungarian in §1.4.4, example (41)). We find singular agreement on both verbs. The verb 'sit', which shows verbal number according to the number of participants, has the plural verbal form *dasxd-* (there is more than one participant in the action). The same verb marks both verbal (inherent) and nominal (contextual) number, but with different values. Thus we have plural verbal number with singular agreement. For more Georgian examples, this time with transitive verbs (where the form depends on the object) see Aronson (1982: 406–7); further discussion and an account of the history of verbal number in Kartvelian languages can be found in Tuite (1998: 63–8). Diagnostics for verbal number are given in Corbett (2000: 252–7), and a further example appears in §5.1.4.

4.3.3   Person

Person is an inherent feature of the pronoun, but a contextual feature of the verb. Thus in Russian *ja beru* 'I take' *ja* 'I' is first person inherently, while *ber-u* 'take-1SG' is first person by agreement. While the first and second persons are for the speech act participants, the third person is basically what is not first and second person.

---

[11] This agreement marker (AGR) -*i* is syncretic, covering nominative singular and plural, and genitive singular and plural.

It is often assumed that noun phrases are always third person by default, but there are cases where this can be overridden:

Spanish (G. Martínez Sierra, quoted by Harmer & Norton 1957: 270)
(30)　　　¡Qué desgraciad-as　　somos las　　　mujer-es!
　　　　　how　unfortunate-F.PL　be.1PL　DEF.F.PL　woman(F)-PL
　　　　　'How unfortunate we women are!'

Here though there is a noun phrase subject we have a first person verb. A second type of noun phrase which can induce non-third person agreement is a vocative:

Czech (Sgall, Hajičová & Panevová 1986: 285)
(31)　　　Chlapč-e,　　　kter-ý　　　**jsi**　　statečn-ý,　　　zachra
　　　　　boy(M)-SG.VOC　who-M.SG.NOM　be.2SG　brave-M.SG.NOM　save.IMP
　　　　　tonouc-ího.
　　　　　drowning.person-M.ANIM.SG.ACC
　　　　　'(You) boy, who are brave, save the drowning person.'

Here the verb is second person; it is controlled by the relative pronoun, which does not overtly mark person, and the antecedent of the relative pronoun is a noun in the vocative.[12]

Further feature values are found in languages which subdivide one or more of these three persons in some way. For example, languages like Bininj Gun-Wok (Evans 2003: 262–4) subdivide the first person plural into the first person inclusive (including the hearer) and exclusive (excluding the hearer). Another type of extended system occurs when the third person is divided into proximate and obviative (for less central participants in the situation), as in Algonquian languages like Nishnaabemwin (Valentine 2001: 183–5, 623–43). For illustration of person systems see Cysouw (2003) and Siewierska (2004b), and for further exemplification of all three agreement features see Moravcsik (1978: 336–62).

4.3.4　Characteristics of the three main agreement features

The three main agreement features are all nominal, which fits with the fact that canonical controllers are nominal. They differ too. As Nichols shows, they have an interesting hierarchical relationship: gender is the one which is most prone to be marked *only* by agreement, number is quite likely to be marked only in this way, but this never occurs with person (1992: 116–62). This observation relates interestingly to a finding from a different perspective by Bybee (1985: 20–48). In a sample of fifty languages Bybee counted the inflectional features shown by verbs, and found gender agreement in 16%, number agreement in 54% and person agreement in 56%. Errors involving the different features also form an interesting pattern (§9.4.1).

---

[12] Furthermore, French predicate nominals allow relative clauses maintaining the person of the main subject; see Høybye (1944: 112) for examples.

4.4   Less clear agreement features

We now turn to two disputable agreement features. If agreement is taken to be asymmetric, in the sense that features on controllers are primary and expression on targets is secondary, it is not obvious whether case and definiteness are, as sometimes claimed, possible agreement features. I discuss them in turn.

4.4.1   Case

Traditional grammars often include agreement in case on a par with the other agreement features. Yet a closer look suggests that case is somewhat different. This issue was raised in §1.4.3, where according to criterion 14 canonical agreement is an asymmetric relation. This is the key issue for case, as can be illustrated by this phrase:

Russian

(32)   v   nov-om   avtomobil-e
          in   new-M.SG.LOC   car(M)-SG.LOC
          'in a new car'

Here the adjective and noun stand in the same case, but this covariance differs from that found with gender, number or person. We should think of this first in terms of the type of feature involved, and second in terms of the syntactic relation.

In terms of features, case is not an inherent feature of the noun: it is imposed on the noun phrase for semantic reasons or by government by some other syntactic element (in this example the preposition *v* 'in', which requires the locative case). Thus the noun and adjective are in the same case because it is imposed on both. This will not count as canonical agreement, if we take seriously the issue of asymmetry. Of course, case interacts strongly with agreement features, being realized together with them in (32), but, as we saw in §3.6.1, an item may take agreement features and case from different sources, as is arguably also true in (32).

In terms of syntactic relations, the argument runs along the same lines, provided one adopts a view of syntax which is based on the notion of constituency. If *nov-avtomobil-* is a constituent in (32), it follows that we have matching of features within the noun phrase resulting from government (rather than agreement in case). The same is true of case stacking phenomena to be discussed shortly. However, for those who accept a dependency view of syntax, a different conclusion follows. If the noun is the head of the phrase and the adjective depends on it, and both show case, then we would have agreement in case (as in Mel'čuk 1993: 329, 337). This would still be less canonical than agreement in gender, because of the difference in feature type, as just discussed. It is worth emphasizing that one's view of what counts as agreement can rest on issues which are more general (as here, the nature of syntactic relations) and which may have been decided, consciously or unconsciously, without reference to the evidence of agreement.

There is more to case, however. Even if one takes the constituency view and excludes agreement in the usual noun phrase constructions, one cannot thereby eliminate all possible instances of case agreement. There are other, rarer constructions which show agreement in case. Various constructions with predicate nominals (nouns and adjectives) come into this category. A good contender is this Polish construction:

Polish (Dziwirek 1990: 147)

(33)   Sześć   kobiet   by-ł-o   smutn-ych.
        six[NOM] woman[PL.GEN] be-PST-N.SG   sad-PL.GEN
        'Six women were sad.'

The numeral *sześć* 'six' takes a noun in the genitive plural. The verb is third singular neuter 'by default' (§3.6.3). The adjective appears to agree in number and case with the quantified noun of the subject noun phrase (alternatively, according to Dziwirek (1990: 158n16) the neuter singular adjective is found in 'informal spoken Polish'). This difficult construction suggests that agreement in case is possible, even if our view of syntax is constituency based. An HPSG analysis is given by Przepiórkowski (2001).

Similar constructions are found in some other Slavonic languages. One of the first instances of Slovene that many visitors to Slovenia would see is:

Slovene (luggage carousel at Ljubljana airport, own observation)

(34)   Veliko   kovčk-ov   in   potovalk   si   je
        many   suitcase-PL.GEN and   travel.bag [PL.GEN] REFL.DAT   be.3SG

        med   sabo   podobn-ih.
        among REFL.INS   similar-PL.GEN
        'Many suitcases and travel bags are similar to each other.'

Here the predicative adjective *podobnih* 'similar' is in the genitive plural to agree with the nouns in the subject noun phrase which are quantified by *veliko* 'many'. Thus besides the clear instances of case being shared within the noun phrase, there are more complex instances. There is covariance in case between predicate complements and their controllers, for which see Andrews (1971) on Classical Greek, Andrews (1982) on Icelandic, Timberlake (1988) on Lithuanian; Anderson (1992: 115–118) and Comrie (1995) discuss the phenomenon more generally. For the agreement of depictive secondary predicates see Schultze-Berndt & Himmelmann (2004: 81–84, 120–121). An important difference between these apparent instances of agreement in case and agreement in other features is that the case examples are restricted to a subset of the values of the case feature, while typically agreement is with all possible values of a feature.

Some languages allow more than one case to be stacked. We saw an example from Kayardild in §3.3.2; Australia is the main home of the phenomenon, and our next example comes from Western Australia:

Martuthunira (Dench 1995: 60–1)

(35)   Ngayu   nhawu-lha ngurnu   tharnta-a mirtily-marta-a thara-ngka-marta-a.
        1SG.NOM see-PST   that[ACC] euro-ACC   joey-PROP-ACC   pouch-LOC-PROP-ACC
        'I saw that euro (hill kangaroo) with a joey in (its) pouch.'

The locative relates the pouch to the joey; at the next level 'up' the joey in the pouch has the proprietive marked on both elements to link it to 'euro'. The whole phrase is then marked as accusative, being the direct object of the verb. For further examples see Dench & Evans (1988) and Plank (1995), where the term used is 'Suffixaufnahme'. For a further type of case stacking see Simpson & Bresnan (1983: 57) and Austin & Bresnan (1996: 253–4). A related construction is found in Daghestanian languages, where the form of the genitive varies according to whether its head is in the absolutive or in an oblique case (Kibrik 1995). Stacking is best attested with case, but it is also found in the Arawak language Tariana (Aikhenvald 2003: 99–101) for classifying elements which are closest to gender (from among the agreement features).[13]

We have seen that most cases of supposed case agreement are better treated as government (for those who take a constituency-based view of syntax). Agreement in case is clearly not canonical agreement (§1.4.3). However, even under this view there are some instances, particularly in predicate nominal constructions, which require us to admit the possibility of agreement in case. Systems of case can vary from minimal to extensive, for which see Blake (1994), and for interesting discussion of larger case systems see Comrie & Polinsky (1998).

4.4.2   Definiteness

Definiteness is sometimes treated as an agreement feature, since there are languages in which definiteness is marked more than once within the noun phrase. However, we may view this as a feature value being imposed on the noun phrase as a whole, which may be indicated at more than one point in the phrase. For illustration we turn to Modern Hebrew, as discussed by Wintner (2000); see this source for discussion of earlier analyses. Hebrew has a definiteness marker *ha-*, which can occur on most of the elements of the noun phrase:

Hebrew (Wintner 2000)[14]

(36)   sefer   ('exad)   / ha-sefer
        book(M)[SG]   (one.M[SG])   / DEF-book(M)[SG]
        'a book'   / 'the book'

(37)   sefer   gadol   ('exad)   / ha-sefer   ha-gadol
        book(M)[SG]   big[M.SG]   (one.M[SG])   / DEF-book(M)[SG]   DEF-big[M.SG]
        'a big book'   / 'the big book'

---

[13] For the development of classifiers into gender see §9.1.1.
[14] I am grateful to David Gil for discussion of these examples and to Yaron Matras for standardizing the transcription of the Hebrew examples used in the book.

It is arguable whether Hebrew has indefinite articles; forms like *'exad* in (36) are 'optional and not common' (Wintner 2000: 323). In (37) the definiteness marker must be on both elements of the noun phrase or on neither. In the following example, the definiteness marker is not required, but again its use must be consistent:

(38)   sefer   ze[15]   /   ha-sefer   ha-ze
          book(M)[SG] this.M.SG /   DEF-book(M)[SG] DEF-this.M.SG
          'this book'   /   'this book'

The most interesting examples for our purposes involve construct-state nouns, which are used in noun-noun constructs:

(39)   pirx-ey   ha-gan   ha-yaf-im   parx-u
          flower(M)-PL.CONSTRUCT DEF-garden(M)[SG] DEF-beautiful-M.PL bloom.PST-3PL
          'the beautiful garden flowers bloomed'

Here the phrase as a whole is to be marked as definite. The head *pirxey* 'flowers' cannot be marked as definite, since it is in the construct state, which does not allow such marking. However, the definiteness marker is found on the complement *gan* 'garden', and on the adjective, which agrees in number with *pirxey* 'flowers'. This suggests that there is a mechanism for marking definiteness multiply on the noun phrase, which is at some distance from canonical agreement (though sharing characteristics with less canonical instances of agreement). Wintner's analysis is in HPSG terms, and it is significant that he handles the definiteness marker by a different mechanism (subsumption) than that typically used for agreement, namely unification (2000: 348–50).

A definiteness marker is found in other Semitic languages, varying from language to language. A language where it is perhaps clearer that we are not dealing with agreement is Maltese (Fabri 2001). Maltese has a definiteness marker which appears first of all on nouns. It may additionally appear, for instance, on adjectives, in which case it marks the adjective as contrastive. Marking of definiteness is also found in Scandinavian languages, and in Norwegian we find the converse of Maltese: under the right circumstances (involving a possessive adjective, with the construction as in (41)) the definiteness marker appears on the adjective but not on the noun:

Norwegian (Bokmål, Torodd Kinn and Tore Nesset, personal communications)
(40)   det   ny-e   hus-et   mitt
          DEF.N.SG new.DEF.N.SG house(N)-DEF.N.SG   my.N.SG
          'my new house'
(41)   mitt   ny-e   hus
          my.N.SG   new-DEF.N.SG house(N)[INDEF]
          'my new house'

---

[15] This variant is literary and archaic according to Yaron Matras (personal communication).

For more on definiteness marking in Scandinavian languages see Delsing (1993: 113–84) and Börjars & Donohue (2000).[16] Definiteness marking is also found in the Balkan region: for definiteness in Romanian including coordinated phrases, also Bulgarian and Albanian, see Ortmann & Popescu (2000).

In the examples discussed definiteness is assigned to a noun phrase as a whole. We shall see definiteness in another guise, as a condition on agreement, in §6.7.2.

4.5   Unusual agreement features

We now turn to features which occur only infrequently as agreement features.

4.5.1   Respect

Agreement is often affected by respect or 'address', that is, the speaker's social relation and attitude to the addressee, and sometimes to third persons too. In many of the more familiar languages the effect of respect is seen indirectly on other features, usually number, sometimes person. Thus in Russian, to show respect, the speaker uses *vy* 'you (PL)' even to a single addressee; the agreements are then singular or plural, depending on the target (§7.7.1).[17] There are other languages where the existence of multiple honorifics suggests an agreement analysis, but where it is not clear that this is justified. It may be argued that each honorific is determined on pragmatic grounds (and that they agree only in the sense that they are being used in the same pragmatic circumstances).[18] However, there are languages where we need a separate feature, since there are distinct morphological forms to signal respect to the addressee.

The need for a respect feature is particularly clear when politeness can be marked at the same time as number and separately from it, as shown by the Austronesian language Muna (spoken on Muna, off the southeast coast of Sulawesi).

---

[16] Börjars & Donohue call definiteness an agreement feature. However they state (2000: 333n9) that 'the term agreement feature is just a convenient shorthand' for a feature whose domain is each word (as opposed to a feature required to occur only once in a phrase). I am taking a more restrictive view.

[17] How is this different from person in Archi (17), where we required a feature for person even though there was no unique exponent? First, there is no independent reason for needing a respect feature in Russian (while we do need a person feature for the resolution rules to operate in Archi). Second, no variability is reported for the Archi forms, whereas the Russian use of number for respect shows the variability according to target which is typical of an agreement condition. In other words, the Archi person feature leads directly to a specific realization, while for Russian respect leads to the use of the plural for some targets, the singular for others, with some uncertainty at the margin (Corbett 1983: 51–6).

[18] Thus Pollard & Sag (1994: 96–101) treat politeness in Korean in terms of agreement, while others have given alternative analyses; for instance, Choi (2003) considers the data from conjoining and argues for a pragmatic account. Boeckx & Niinuma (2004) treat Japanese honorification as agreement, while Bobaljik & Yatsushiro (forthcoming) argue against this.

The sentence 'you go' might be translated as follows; *ihintu* is a free pronoun whose inclusion would be emphatic:

(42)   Number and politeness markers in Muna (van den Berg 1989: 51, 82)

	singular	plural
neutral	ihintu o-kala	ihintu-umu o-kala-amu
polite	intaidi to-kala	intaidi-imu to-kala-amu

Here *to-* marks polite address, irrespective of number. In Bavarian German the agreement forms for polite agreement have become differentiated from the original third person forms, so that here too we need a respect feature (Simon 2003, 2004). Tamil too has a distinct form for agreement with honorifics (Schiffman 1999: 115–16); for the development of the polite forms see Rangan & Suseela (2003).

While the Muna data prove the need for a respect feature particularly clearly, the system is restricted in terms of values by comparison with the luxuriance of Maithili. We have already seen Maithili examples in connection with agreement with possessors:

Maithili (Stump & Yadav 1988)

(43)   tohar   bāp   aelthun
        your.MID_HON   father.HON   came.3_HON.2_MID_HON
        'Your (mid-honorific) father (honorific) came.'

(44)   ham   torā   beṭā-ke   dekhaliau
        I   your.NON_HON   son-OBJ   saw.1.2_NON_HON
        'I saw your (non-honorific) son.'

Details of this system can be found in Bickel, Bisang and Yādava (1999); realization of the respect feature is fully embedded in a complex verbal paradigm. In the second person there are these grades: non-honorific, mid-honorific and honorific; and in the third person we find: non-honorific, honorific and high-honorific.[19]

4.5.2   Tense, aspect, mood and polarity

We now take up the Kayardild data mentioned in §2.5.2 and discussed in §3.3.2. Recall that, besides ordinary cases, Kayardild has various verbalizing cases (Evans 2003). I will illustrate this with the verbalizing dative (V_DAT), which

---

[19] The list of agreement features would be extended further if Wh-agreement were recognized. There are two rather different phenomena which have been put forward as examples in the literature. Wh-agreement has been suggested for the Austronesian language Chamorro by Chung in various papers and in a monograph (1998). However, a plausible alternative has been offered (Donohue & Maclachlan 2000, Donohue 2003b). Second, O'Herin (2002: 249–76) presents intriguing data from Abaza, a member of the Northwest Caucasian family, with Wh-marking in the verb. There are some unanswered questions, however. It is not fully clear that we are dealing with agreement. (I am grateful to Jurij Lander for discussing Abaza and related languages.)

is used for beneficiaries; it is marked on all parts of the noun phrase with -*maru*-, and this then brings with it regular verbal inflections:

Kayardild (Evans 2003: 215)

(45)   ngada   **waa-jarra**   wangarr-ina   **ngijin-maru-tharra   thabuju-maru-tharra**
       1SG.NOM   sing-PST   song-MOD_ABL   my-V_DAT-PST   brother-V_DAT-PST
       'I sang a song for my brother.'

Items inflected for verbalizing case take the same set of markers for tense, aspect, mood and polarity as the verb; (46) illustrates polarity:

(46)   ngada   **waa-nangku**   wangarr-u   **ngijin-maru-nangku**
       1SG.NOM   sing-NEG.POT   song-MOD_PROP   my-V_DAT-NEG.POT
       thabuju-maru-nangku
       brother-V_DAT-NEG.POT
       'I won't sing a song for my brother.'

Main verbs can be nominalized (with the nominalizer -*n*-) and can then be used as predicates indicating ongoing uncompleted action; items bearing verbalizing case take the nominalized form to match:

(47)   ngada   **waa-n-da**   wangarr-inja   **ngijin-maru-n-da**
       1SG.NOM   sing-NMLZ-NOM   song-A_OBL   my-V_DAT-NMLZ-NOM
       thabuju-maru-n-d[20]
       brother-V_DAT-NMLZ-NOM
       'I am singing a song for my brother.'

However we analyse the data above, the phenomenon is clearly highly significant. The argument as to whether we have agreement in tense, aspect, mood and polarity runs parallel to that concerning case in the noun phrase (§4.4.1). If, for other reasons, one believes that case is a feature of noun phrases (the constituency approach), then marking of case on multiple items in the noun phrase is symmetrical marking, and hence not (canonical) agreement. Similarly, if one believes that tense, aspect, mood and polarity are features of the clause, then marking of these features unusually on items other than on the verb is symmetrical marking and hence not (canonical) agreement.

Conversely, in a dependency approach, it can be argued that case is primarily associated with the head of the noun phrase, and other items are marked only secondarily; this approach implies asymmetric marking and agreement within the noun phrase. And similarly, it is reasonable to argue that tense, aspect, mood and polarity are primarily features of the verb, and if marked on other items this is secondary; again we have asymmetric marking, and a very interesting instance of agreement.

The parallel goes further. With case we found less common instances where on any analysis it appeared necessary to accept asymmetric marking, and where

---

[20] Phrase-final -*a* is deleted (Nicholas Evans, personal communication).

an agreement analysis seemed best (the examples of predicate nominals showing agreement in case). Similarly, with tense, aspect, mood and polarity there is a specific construction, still in Kayardild, which suggests that these features must be recognized as potential agreement features.[21] The relevant examples consist of a 'verbal group' (Evans 2003: 215–16, 223–4):

(48)   niya   kuujuu-ja   thaa-th
        3SG.NOM swim-ACTUAL   return-ACTUAL
        'He's gone off for a swim'

A 'verbal group' has a main verb with one or two additional verbs for associated motion, adverbial quantification and aspect. They appear in fixed order in a single intonational group. The meaning may be non-compositional, as in (48); the verb *thaa-tha* 'return' indicates 'go off and V', rather than 'V and return'. The important point is that all verbs in the group must take identical values for tense, aspect, mood and polarity. We see this by taking a past tense example:

(49)   niya   kuujuu-jarra thaa-tharr
        3SG.NOM swim-PST   return-PST
        'He went off for a swim.'

The two verbs do indeed match in tense. Evans (2003: 223) stresses that (49) is appropriate when the referent went off in the past, swam in the past, but has unexpectedly not yet returned. The past on the verb 'return' is, Evans claims, the result of a rule of agreement with the head verb 'swim', and not because the past tense is independently appropriate for the return. These examples are perhaps more cogent that those with verbalizing case, but one might still argue that the verbal group is a semantic and syntactic unit, that tense is assigned to this unit (together with aspect, mood and polarity), and that there is no necessary asymmetry. Thus the argument for tense, aspect, mood and polarity as agreement features remains open; the answer will depend on the particular syntactic analysis adopted, but these features cannot be rejected as agreement features without very careful consideration. If they are included, then we need to revise the typology of controllers, domains and features. As Evans puts it:

> In many ways, Kayardild is a language with a great deal of agreement, in the familiar sense of grammatically stipulated featural compatibility between different words. But it just happens to manifest agreement by unfamiliar semantic categories, on unfamiliar targets, over unfamiliar domains, in unfamiliar directions, with unfamiliar patterns of nested multiple agreement, with unfamiliar consequences for the morphological word-class membership of the target, and with unfamiliar functions.   Evans (2003: 232)

Before leaving verbal features as agreement features we should note further intriguing cases, each deserving further study. For Shipibo-Konibo, a West Central

---

[21] For a distantly related construction in Swedish see Anward (1988).

Panoan language spoken in the area of the Ucayali River in the Peruvian Amazon, Valenzuela (1999) gives examples of place and manner adverbials which vary according to the transitivity of the verb. And in Malagasy (Keenan & Polinsky 1998: 566–7) certain locatives and prepositions show agreement in tense.

4.6   Interaction with the domain

On the simplest view, we might expect to be able to account for agreement features just as a matter of controller and target: that is, we would need to state which controllers are specified for particular features and which targets can realize particular features. However, it has been claimed, notably by Lehmann (1982), that there is also an effect of domain. He distinguishes 'case-domain agreement' or 'NP internal agreement' from 'person-domain agreement' or 'NP external agreement'. Lehmann lists the specific domains which fall under each and claims that agreement in case and in person are in complementary distribution, case agreement being found in the first domain, and person in the second (gender and number can be found in both). Problems with this view were noted in Källström (1994) and in Bickel, Bisang & Yādava (1999: 516 n6).

A clear counter-example is provided by Tundra Nenets. We had an initial look at data from this language in §2.2.6. Now we should consider a fuller set of examples, from the eastern dialect area:

Tundra Nenets (Nikolaeva 2005)

(50)   (møny)   serako / serako-myi te-myi
          1SG   white / white-1SG   reindeer-1SG
          'my white reindeer'

(51)   (pidør°)   serako / serako-r°   te-r°
          2SG   white / white-2SG   reindeer-2SG
          'your white reindeer'

In these examples the pronominal possessor may be omitted, but the marker on the noun possessum is obligatory. (With a noun possessor, as in §2.2.6, the marker on the possessum is optional.) This agreement occurs with inalienably possessed nouns only, where what is inalienable depends on the specific culture: 'reindeer', 'boat', 'sled' are inalienably possessed while 'dog', 'car' and 'house' are not (Irina Nikolaeva, personal communication). What is particularly interesting about (50) and (51) is that the modifier *serako* 'white' can optionally agree in person and number. This person agreement can co-occur with case marking:

(52)   (pidør°)   serako-m-t°   te-m-t°
          2SG   white-ACC-2SG reindeer-ACC-2SG
          'your white reindeer (ACC)'

There is an interesting asymmetry: person and number marking on the possessum is obligatory when the possessor is a pronoun, as we noted earlier, but optional when it is a noun. If there is (optional) person and number marking on the adjective, this requires marking on the noun

(53)   Wata-h   serako-da   te-da / *ti
         Wata-GEN   white-3SG   reindeer-3SG / reindeer
         'Wata's white reindeer'

Finally note that the noun phrase as a whole remains third person:

(54)   te-r°   xøya / *xøya-n°
         reindeer-2SG   leave[3SG] / leave-2SG
         'Your reindeer left.'

There are interesting conditions on the use of person agreement in Tundra Nenets, relating to the communicative function of the possessor. When the possessor takes agreement it has a marked discourse status, either comparable to that of topic or otherwise prominent in the interpretation of the noun phrase (Nikolaeva 2005; for more on the conditions involved see Nikolaeva forthcoming).

The Tundra Nenets data are a direct counter-example to Lehmann's claim (1982: 216). Nevertheless, person agreement is rare cross-linguistically within the noun phrase and common outside it.

4.7   Conclusion

Features are a key component in understanding how agreement works. The different agreement features differ substantially in their content, in the number of values they can have, in the targets where they are usually realized and in their distribution across the world's languages. And conversely, since in agreement we find the same features fulfilling different functions (on controllers and targets), agreement is one of the phenomena which can tell us most about how features function.

5   Mismatches

When a target realizes displaced information, we would expect this displaced information to match that of the controller. This matching would cover both the features (such as number and gender) and their values (say singular and neuter):

Hypothesis III: Displaced information will match that of the controller both in terms of features and of their values. (False)

Hypothesis III is met in examples of canonical agreement (§1.4). However, there are several circumstances where such matching does not occur. I shall analyse the different types of mismatch in turn.

We must first ask whether we can still talk of agreement if the controller and target do not match. Indeed, some have argued that the existence of mismatches shows that a particular phenomenon is not an instance of agreement. That line of argument is fallacious, since we find mismatches quite commonly in the least contentious agreement systems (for instance, that of Russian). We need to see examples of mismatches against the background of all the cases where we do find matching.

Some mismatches result from limitations of the morphology in a given language. Others have a deeper cause. Recall that according to Steele's definition (§1.3) agreement involves systematic covariance with a semantic or formal property of the controller. In the simplest instances there is covariance with both. Thus in phrases like *this cat* and *these cats* the demonstrative varies according to the meaning *and* the form of the controller. In less simple instances meaning and form point in opposite directions. *Committee* denotes more than one individual but is singular in form. Whether the agreement is singular or plural there is a mismatch.

In certain examples of mismatches there is a unique outcome (the agreement feature in question always has the same value), and the mismatch is based only on our expectations as linguists: it is interesting that form and meaning fail to match up in particular constructions, or it is surprising that in similar constructions the outcome in one language is different from that in another. There are other mismatches, however, which deserve greater attention. These are mismatches which involve one and the same agreement controller taking different feature values with different targets, that is, we have an inconsistent controller (§1.4.1). These controllers may permit a choice of agreements with a single target.[1] Such mismatches provide a window onto how agreement systems work, and how they change (§9.1.3). They are highly significant: while unification has great advantages for handling canonical agreement, it seems that straightforward unification is inadequate for handling mismatches. And 'checking' is inadequate since as Chomsky (1995: 309–10) puts it 'mismatch of features cancels the derivation'. Feature mismatches and the associated agreement choices are therefore of great importance for an eventual overall theory of agreement.

5.1   Unproblematic mismatches

Some mismatches are readily understood, and we deal with these first. They arise from the fact that unique forms are not available to realize particular feature specifications.

5.1.1   Restrictions on the controller

Here we consider mismatches which arise because the controller lacks forms which would guarantee matching. However, non-systematic variations in the morphology of the controller do not affect agreement. For example, the majority of Russian nouns inflect for number and case, but a substantial minority are indeclinable. Agreement with an indeclinable noun (1) is as with a declinable (2):

Russian

(1)   U   nee   by-l-o   pjat´ nov-yx   pal´to.
        at 3SG.F.GEN   be-PST-N.SG five new-PL.GEN   coat
        'She had five new coats.'

(2)   U   nee   by-l-o   pjat´ nov-yx   pojas-ov.
        at 3SG.F.GEN   be-PST-N.SG five new-PL.GEN   belt-PL.GEN
        'She had five new belts.'

We do not have obvious matching between *pal´to* 'coat' and its target, because *pal´to* is indeclinable, and cannot mark number. Yet this does not affect agreement: the adjective still agrees (is plural). This illustrates the difference between indeclinability and defectiveness (illustrated with regard to targets in §3.3.4), in that *pal´to* 'coat' has no inflections, but can still use its one form to fill any cell in the paradigm. We might say then that in instances like (1) we have matching, it is simply that the controller cannot show it. This is as we would expect given that syntax is morphology-free (§6.3.1).[2]

---

[1] They are relatively frequent in spoken language. A corpus of some 49,000 words of spoken Russian (Zemskaja & Kapanadze 1978) was scanned for examples of these three agreement choices: with conjoined noun phrases, quantified expressions and relative *kto* 'who' (with a plural antecedent) as controller. There were twenty-two examples. This means that agreement options occurred more frequently than once in 2,500 words. There were instances of other agreement choices in addition to the three included in the count.

[2] For interesting complications with indeclinables see Wechsler & Zlatić (2003: 125–52).

5.1.2 Restrictions on the target

There may be restrictions on the target which prevent full matching. These can be of different types. The most general are feature restrictions (co-occurrence restrictions) on agreement, as discussed in §3.3.2. For example, there is no person agreement in the past tense in Russian. This is a general restriction on every verb. There can be other general restrictions which limit the values of a feature (rather than ruling it out as in the Russian example). Thus Tsakhur, like several other Daghestanian languages, has four genders (I-IV in (3)). This can be demonstrated by verb agreement (here the combination of verb and auxiliary distinguishes four gender forms within the singular, unlike the paradigms given in §3.3.3):

(3)   Present tense of 'see' with postposed auxiliary in Tsakhur

	singular	plural
I	Gaʒe-wor	Gōʒe-wob
II	Gēʒe-wor	Gōʒe-wob
III	Gōʒe-wob	Gaʒe-wod
IV	Gaʒe-wod	Gaʒe-wod

We see that in the plural only a two-way distinction is drawn, and these syncretisms are again quite general. Thus these targets do show agreement, but they do not match the controller as fully in the plural as in the singular. Besides these blanket restrictions, we may also find various lexical limitations, from quite general ones based on differing inflectional classes down to idiosyncratic ones affecting individual lexical items, as discussed in §3.3.3.

5.1.3 Subset relation between values of controller and of target

We also find instances where the possible values are different between controller and target, with one being a subset of the other. In Hebrew some nouns distinguish three number values, while verbs have only two (see Corbett 2000: 95–6, 98–100 for details). There is a straightforward relation, with dual subjects patterning with plurals and taking plural predicates:

Hebrew (David Gil personal communication)
(4)   ha-yom-ayim 'avr-u   maher
       DEF-day-DU   pass.PST-3PL quickly
       'the two days passed quickly'

And in Skou (Donohue 2003a: 482) the free pronouns distinguish singular/dual/plural, while various agreement markers, including clitics, distinguish only two numbers. As in Hebrew, plural agreements are used for the dual:

Skou (Donohue 2003a: 482)

(5)   Amanè   ne=e.
        1DU.INCL 1PL =board
        'You and I boarded.'

It is important to note that the relation can also be in the other direction, that is, the target may distinguish more values than the controller. This is seen in Inari Sami:

Inari Sami (Ida Toivonen 2003 and personal communication)

(6)   Almai   kuáláást onne.
        man.SG.NOM fish[3SG] today
        'The man is fishing today.'

(7)   Alma-h   kuá'láást-ava onne.
        man-PL.NOM fish-3DU   today
        'The two men are fishing today.'

(8)   Alma-h   kuá'láást-eh onne.
        men-PL.NOM fish-3PL   today
        'The men are fishing today.'

In the light of examples like this, instances where the noun phrase does not change at all (but the predicate does) assume a new interest (see §5.8.1).

5.1.4   Features are of different types

If the features of the controller and the target do not correspond (say one has number and one has tense), then we are not dealing with agreement. This is a natural consequence. It is worth noting, however, that features may appear to correspond but actually be of different types. A good instance of this is verbal number, which operates separately from nominal number (Corbett 2000: 243–64). The point was illustrated in §4.3.2, using data from Georgian. Here we consider Yurakaré, an isolate of Bolivia. Yurakaré has a set of verbs which have different stems for verbal number, including *dele/ñeta* 'fall down':

Yurakaré (Rik van Gijn personal communication)

(9)   dele-Ø   ti-mesa[3]
        fall.down.SG-3 1SG-table
        'my table fell down'

(10)   ñeta-Ø-w   ti-mesa-w
        fall.down.PL-3-PL 1SG-table-PL
        'my tables fell down'

In (10) the plural verb *ñeta* is selected (for plural participants), and there is also plural agreement. Yurakaré has a class of nouns which are always grammatically singular, even though they can denote plural entities. One such is *sibbæ* 'house':

---

[3] Recall that we use Ø only for convenience, without giving it any theoretical status. In these Yurakaré examples the singular is implied when number is not glossed while the third person is indicated by Ø.

(11)   lætta sibbæ dele-Ø
         one   house fall.down.SG-3
         'one house fell down'

(12)   læshie sibbæ ñeta-Ø   (not *ñeta-Ø-w)
         two   house fall.down.PL-3 fall.down.PL-3-PL
         'two houses fell down'

In (12) we have the plural verb *ñeta* because there are plural participants (the stem follows the semantics), but the agreement remains singular (the form with no plural marker), because *sibbæ* 'house/houses' is always grammatically singular. This shows clearly the difference between verbal number and number agreement.

5.2   Defaults and extended use of defaults

In the examples we have considered so far, forms are not available to realize particular feature specifications, and so a mismatch is inevitable and unproblematic. We now move to more interesting examples. When we arrange inflectional forms in paradigms, this suggests that they all have the same status. In some respects they do, in others they do not. In particular, some may have uses beyond those implied by their feature specification. That is, there is evidence for structuring, with particular specifications having special status. This is true for agreement features, and for features more generally (Corbett 2000: 38–50). In analysing this structuring I shall talk in terms of defaults, rather than the related notion of markedness. The reason for preferring 'default' is that defaults are language specific, while 'marked' is used by many linguists with the implication that marked values are universal. The latter is incorrect for our purposes: masculine is usually the default in two-gender systems, but sometimes the feminine is the default, and in the semantically similar four-gender systems of Archi and Lak, gender IV is the default in Archi, and gender III in Lak.[4]

A danger is that we may look only at binary systems (with two genders and two numbers), which is like investigating harmony by looking only at music with two parts. It is easy to be misled when finding phenomena involving the same value in a two-value feature; this may not be significant, since chance alone will produce such overlaps in a two-valued system. When we look at larger systems, the complexity of the relations between feature values becomes more apparent. Thus in the three-gender system of Russian in one sense the default is the masculine: it has the largest number of nouns, and attracts the largest number of borrowings. But it is the default only for nominals. For items typically outside the gender system (clauses, interjections and so on) the default is the neuter (Fraser & Corbett 1995).

---

[4] The default choice in Lak is motivated by the syncretism of the gender IV and gender II agreements in the singular; avoiding this syncretism appears to be the reason for bypassing gender IV and using gender III (Corbett (1991: 206–8, Aleksandr Kibrik, personal communication).

How can we say that there is more than one default? We can distinguish 'normal case default' and 'exceptional case default' (Fraser & Corbett 1997). The first is the general case, which applies normally, and the second is a last resort. Let us take an analogy. Jane and Fred work for a firm based in London. Jane is the personnel manager and works in the office in London. Sometimes she attends meetings at the firm's other office in Newcastle. By default, then, Jane works in the office in London. Fred is a salesman. He normally spends Mondays in the south of England, Tuesdays in Wales, and so on. If, however, an appointment is cancelled or his car is unservicable or there is a department meeting, he goes to the office in London. On Fridays he often plays golf, but when it rains he goes to the office. By default, Fred also works in the office in London.

The two cases are different. Jane is 'normally' at the office, Fred is not. And yet at a higher level of abstraction it is true to say that the office is the default workplace for both. It is these two types of default, both reasonable uses of the term, which have led to the differences in usage in the literature. The first type, the normal case default, accounts for the cases when 'everything goes right' (as in Jane working in the office). The second type, the exceptional case default, applies when the normal system breaks down, when 'something goes wrong' (as in Fred working in the office).[5] There is a common conceptual core running through both usages of the term 'default': the default is the last thing you get to. One form of default is concerned with typicality, the other with exceptionality. It is therefore particularly important that conceptual and terminological confusion be avoided by proper definition of terms. One of the payoffs of working in a formally explicit framework, such as Network Morphology where this distinction was worked out, is that it lays bare the differences between these otherwise confusable notions.

Normal case defaults cause few problems for agreement (as for instance nouns assigned to gender by the normal rules, §4.3.1). Exceptional case defaults are more tricky. We consider them in §5.2.1; we next look at extensions beyond their expected use in §5.2.2, and these lead to interesting mismatches; finally we look at a special type of extension, namely evasive use, in §5.2.3.

5.2.1   Exceptional case defaults

Defaults were considered in terms of morphology in §3.6.3, with examples from Russian and Tsakhur. As a reminder, here is a more interesting Tsakhur example:

Tsakhur (Kibrik 1999: 367)

(13)   insan$_j$-ē   zer-i-s   iIXīX-a   wo-d
        man(I)-ERG   cow(III)-OBL-DAT   IV.SG.hit-IMPV   be-IV.SG
        'a man is hitting a cow'

The Tsakhur verb 'hit' takes an argument in the ergative (agent), one in the dative (patient) and one in the absolutive (instrument). Recall that in Tsakhur the verb

---

[5] This has affinities with the OT notion TETU (the emergence of the default).

agrees with the absolute argument (§2.3.2). There is no absolutive argument, no instrument, in (13) and so the verb cannot agree; it therefore takes the exceptional case default, which in Tsakhur is gender IV singular.

In Russian, as we noted in §3.6.3, the exceptional case default form usually looks like the neuter singular (see Blevins 2000 for discussion of such forms). It is used when there is no agreement controller, when the controller is a clause or infinitive phrase and so on. It is reasonable therefore to invoke a default here. The circumstances are, roughly speaking, all those where agreement is not controlled by a canonical noun phrase (one headed by a noun or pronoun). This can be seen as things going wrong (agreement is normally controlled by a canonical noun phrase) and so we have an exceptional case default. While in Russian the form is usually identical to the neuter singular, occasionally it has a special form, the 'neutral' form, one specially reserved for use as the default (for instance, the pronoun *èto* 'this' is used rather than *ono* 'it' for antecedents that are not genuinely neuter singulars). Clearly then the differences are less striking in Russian than in the languages cited in §3.6.4.

A clear case of the default form having special properties is found in Romanian, where it varies according to the particular agreement target (see §5.8.2 for the gender system). This results in a remarkable type of mismatch.

Romanian (data from Donka Farkas, in Corbett 1991: 213–14, and Mara van Schaik-Rădulescu, personal communication)

(14) e evident că a venit
      is clear[M.SG] that has come
      'it is clear that s/he came'

Here we have a clause as subject (some might prefer to say there is no subject); the predicative adjective, which has to mark agreement, is masculine (the feminine *evidentă* is unacceptable). The next example includes attributive modifiers for a non-word:

(15) un bum puternic
      INDEF.M.SG "boom" strong[M.SG]
      'a loud boom'

Here *un* 'a' is again masculine. Moving to other targets, the relative pronoun has a special 'neutral' form (*ceea ce*). The demonstrative is the most interesting for our purposes:

(16) ast-a e uluitor
      this-F.SG is amazing[M.SG]
      'this is amazing'

Here *asta* denotes a situation, not a specific object. While it is morphologically feminine, its predicate is masculine. Thus *asta* is a special neutral form, since it controls a different agreement from the *asta* which can stand for a noun of feminine gender. This leads to an unusual mismatch.

5.2.2   Extension in use of the default ('pancake sentences')

The use of default forms is extended in an interesting way, beyond where they are needed. They can be used when the controller is an apparently straightforward noun phrase. We find examples in English, but the phenomenon is found more luxuriantly in Scandinavian languages (Faarlund 1977; for extensive discussion see Källström 1993: 188–246, also Enger 2004). This is the example which gives the construction its name:

Norwegian (Bokmål/Nynorsk, Faarlund 1977: 240)
(17)   Pannekake-r   er   god-t.
           pancake-PL   COP   good-N.SG
           'Pancakes is good.' ('Eating pancakes is good.')

Though there is a plural noun phrase in (17), we do not find plural agreement. (Note that the verb does not agree, so it is the predicate adjective which is of interest.) The adjective uses the default form, when it is apparently not needed, suggesting that there is additional information available. The sentence indicates that it is what goes with pancakes (the eating of them) that is good.[6] The mismatch is even clearer in these Swedish examples:

Swedish (Källström 1993: 277)
(18)   Ny-a   hyresgäst-er är   ängslig-a.
           new-PL   tenant-PL   COP   anxious-PL
           'New tenants are anxious.'

(19)   Ny-a   hyresgäst-er är   ängslig-t.
           new-PL   tenant-PL   COP   anxious-N.SG
           'Having new tenants makes one anxious.'

The agreement in (18) is what we might have expected, with the predicative adjective matching the plural subject. In (19) we have default agreement of the predicate adjective, though the attributive adjective *nya* 'new' agrees normally. These different agreements in the different syntactic positions indicate that the construction conforms to the Agreement Hierarchy, a point taken up in §7.4.3.

5.2.3   Evasive uses

A rather specific use of a default is to avoid a problematic choice. Thus Polish has an 'evasive' neuter (Gotteri 1984, following Doroszewski). It

---

[6] This example shows a striking mismatch in gender:

Norwegian (Nynorsk, Faarlund 1977: 251)
(i)   Ein ny   utanriksminister ville ikkje vere så dum-t.
        a   new foreign.secretary would not   be   so stupid-N.SG
        'A new foreign secretary would not be a bad idea.'

The singular adjective distinguishes neuter and common. The neuter gender form here suggests that having a new foreign secretary would not be a bad idea. The common form *dum* 'stupid' would agree with the subject noun phrase to give an unkinder reading.

is used in limited circumstances when the masculine-feminine choice is hard to resolve. Consider this example:

Polish (Weiss 1993: 77)

(20)   Jedn-o   z   małżonk-ów   obję-ł-o   prawn-ą
         one-N.SG   from   spouse-PL.GEN   obtain-PST-N.SG   legal-F.SG.ACC

         opiek-ę   nad   dzieć-mi.
         care(F)-SG.ACC   over   child-PL.INS

         'One of the couple obtained custody of the children.'

Małżonkowie is masculine personal plural and means 'husband and wife'. Yet the evasive neuter is used, in *jedno* 'one' and the agreeing verb. This avoids the evident disadvantages of using masculine or feminine.

5.3   Partial agreement

We have seen examples where instead of agreement we have a default form; that is, rather than full agreement there is no agreement. There are also various possible outcomes, which fall between these two end points. There are two types of partial agreement. In superclassing (§5.3.1), within a particular feature, the full distinctions in terms of values are not made, but there is partial agreement in values. The second type, partial agreement in features, is found when, of the agreement features in play, at least one is matched fully while another is not (§5.3.2). These instances of partial agreement have often not been carefully distinguished from similar phenomena, so for each I give the relevant comparisons.

5.3.1   Superclassing (partial agreement in values)

In the more familiar instances we have a single default, in the sense that there is either a full array of values (for agreement with canonical controllers) or there is a default (typically using a form equivalent to that of one of the values, but sometimes a unique neutral form). But there is a half-way-house, which Evans (1997: 127–40) describes as 'superclassing' in his account of Bininj Gun-Wok (Mayali). In superclassing some but not all of the available distinctions are drawn. (As an analogy, it is as though, in answer to the question 'Did you go to London, New York, Melbourne or Tokyo?' one could answer 'to the northern hemisphere', thus giving just a part of the information.)

Superclassing is also found in Jingulu, a non-Pama-Nyungan language of the Northern Territory of Australia (Pensalfini 2003). Like Bininj Gun-Wok, Jingulu has four genders: masculine, feminine, neuter and vegetable. Assignment of nouns to genders is largely a matter of semantics: nouns denoting male animates are masculine, those denoting female animates are feminine, edible plants are vegetable and the residue neuter. However, there are additional principles and some 'leaks'. Adjectives agree in gender as follows:

Jingulu (Pensalfini 2003: 160–1, 164–7)

(21)   Lalija   darra-nga-ju **jamurriyak-a.**
        tea(M)   eat-1SG-do   cooled-M
        'I'm drinking cold tea.'

(22)   Wijbirri-rni   **jalyamingk-irni.**
        white.person-F new-F
        'The white girl is new-born.'

(23)   Miringmi-rni   darra-nga-yi **bardakurr-imi.**
        gum(VEG)-FOC   eat-1SG-FUT   good-VEG
        'I'll eat the sweet gum.'

(24)   Jami-rna   dimana-rni   laja-ardu **ngamulu** lanbu.
        that.M-FOC horse(M)-ERG carry-go   big.N   load(N)
        'That horse is carrying a big load.'

However, sometimes we find less than full agreement, as in these examples:

(25)   Ngamulirni **jalyamungk-a** binjiya-ju, birnmirrini.
        girl(F)   young-M   grow-do   prepubescent.girl
        'That little girl is growing up into a big girl.'

(26)   **Jama**-rni nyanyalu-ngkujku, darrangku kirdkilyaku.
        that(M)-FOC   leaf-HAVING.N   tree.N   bent.N
        'That bent tree is leafy.'

(27)   **ngininiki** barndumi   *or* **ngimaniki** barndumi
        this(N)   lower.back(VEG)   this(VEG)   lower.back(VEG)
        'this lower back'   'this lower back'
                                         (offered by speaker as alternatives)

According to Pensalfini, these examples are typical of those where we do not find full agreement: masculine may be used for feminine, neuter may be used for vegetable, and masculine can be used for both the latter genders. We may represent this situation as in (28):

(28)   Gender superclassing in Jingula

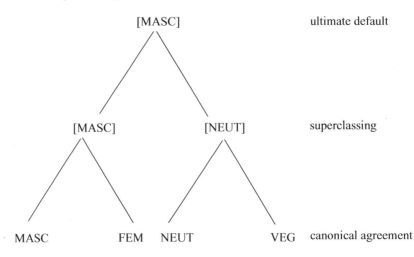

At the lowest level we have full (canonical) agreement. Then at a level up we have superclassing, where only some of the potential distinctions are drawn. And at the top level we have the ultimate default, the masculine in this system.

I have represented this superclassing in a way familiar from number systems, where in larger systems it is sometimes possible to disregard some of the possible divisions (Corbett 2000: 42–8). With number, agreement may or may not be involved. In our discussion here we are, of course, focussing on agreement, and Jingulu indeed allows superclassing for number. It has singular, dual and plural, and full agreement is possible. But the following types of example are also found (Pensalfini 2003: 173–4):

(29) **Nyama-baji** imimikin-bili-rni-rni   ardalakbi-wurru-ju.
       DEM-PL   old.woman-ANIM.DU-F-ERG   hot-3PL-do
       'The two old women feel hot.'

(30) Kunyirrirni dij **bila-nya-mi**   kandirri!
       2DU.ERG   PRV divide-2SG-IRR[7] bread
       'You two cut up the bread.'

(31) **Nginda**-rni ngaja-mi jurliji-rdarra diyim **ka-rdu**!
       DEM(M)-FOC   see-IRR bird-PL   fly   3SG-go
       'Look at all the birds flying!'

We see that the plural may be used for the dual, as in (29), that is, we have superclassing of dual and plural, and that the singular may be used as an overall default (in (30) and (31)). We may represent this as follows:

(32)   Number superclassing in Jingulu

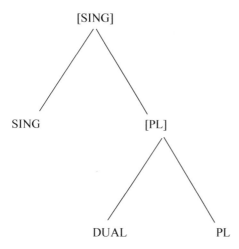

Singular is the ultimate default here. The singular~plural opposition represents superclassing of dual and plural, while canonical agreement differentiates the three values. The term 'superclassing' is used specifically of agreement

---

[7] *Bil-* has a range of meanings; together with the adverbial preverb *dij* it means divide (Rob Pensalfini, personal communication).

phenomena; it is one aspect of the more general structuring of feature values seen particularly in 'facultative' number (Corbett 2000: 42–50).

It is worth pausing to see how this interesting phenomenon differs from other types of reduced differentiation of feature values. It differs from syncretism (§3.4.1) in that syncretism does not give a choice of forms. The Tsakhur situation (example (3)), where genders are collapsed in the plural, comes within syncretism broadly understood. In other examples syncretism can be purely morphological, combining unrelated cells of the paradigm, which is not the case for superclassing. We must also distinguish superclassing from reduced agreement (§3.6.2). The latter is used under other (non-agreement) conditions, and the reduced paradigm makes fewer distinctions than the full paradigm. However, this does not translate neatly into a description of features and values as is the case with superclassing. Furthermore, the use of reduced paradigms is not optional. Similarly, the subset relations described in §5.1.3 involved no choice of forms, unlike superclassing.

5.3.2   Partial agreement in features

In this type of partial agreement there is agreement in respect of at least one feature, but not in respect of a second. We shall discuss the case of Miya in detail in §6.1.1. Meanwhile I take a celebrated example, that of Arabic, in its different varieties. A good deal has been written on this (including Hallmann 2000; LeTourneau 2003).[8] I take my examples from Chekili (2004):

Modern Standard Arabic (Chekili 2004: 35)

(33)   l-ʔawlaad-u   xaraj-uu   (not: *xaraj-a)
        DEF-boys-NOM   went.out-3PL.M   went.out-3SG.M
        'the boys went out'

(34)   l-banaat-u   xaraj-na   (not: *xaraj-at)
        DEF-girls-NOM went.out-3PL.F   went.out-3SG.F
        'the girls went out'

(35)   xaraj-a   l-ʔawlaad-u   (not: *xaraj-uu)
        went.out-3SG.M DEF-boys-NOM   went.out-3PL.M
        'the boys went out'

(36)   xaraj-at   l-banaat-u   (not: *xaraj-na)
        went.out-3SG.F DEF-girls-NOM   went.out-3PL.F
        'the girls went out'

All the examples cited involve nouns denoting humans (for other types, and for other varieties of Arabic, there are additional complications).[9] Examples (33) and (34), with the subject preceding the predicate, show full agreement. When the controller does not precede the target, as in (35) and (36), we get (in Modern Standard Arabic) partial agreement, agreement in gender but not in number. In §6.5 we shall see examples of precedence as a condition on agreement; in Modern

---

[8] LeTourneau (2003) calls it 'impoverished' agreement.
[9] Gulf Arabic shows four different systems plus a further variant (Holes 1990: 155–6).

Standard Arabic it is an absolute, since the order subject-predicate is required to make possible full agreement with plural noun phrases. With the reverse order we get partial agreement rather than the default, since only one feature is affected.

5.4 Syntactic and semantic agreement

We continue moving up to more serious mismatches, and will now discuss controllers which induce more than one type of agreement. I shall use the well-established terms **syntactic** and **semantic** agreement. In the most straightforward cases syntactic agreement (sometimes called 'agreement *ad formam*', 'formal agreement' or 'grammatical agreement') is agreement consistent with the form of the controller (*the committee* has *decided*). Semantic agreement (or 'agreement *ad sensum*', 'notional agreement', 'logical agreement' or 'synesis') is agreement consistent with its meaning (*the committee* have *decided*).[10] The distinction between syntactic and semantic agreement links to Steele's definition (§1.3) in that the covariance involves a 'semantic or formal property' of the controller.

The terms syntactic and semantic agreement are used only when there is a potential choice. In many instances formal and semantic properties of the controller coincide and so agreement is both syntactically and semantically justified, as in:

(37)   Mary has decided . . .

Here the singular verb is consistent both with an individual 'decider' and with a singular subject noun phrase. I use the labels 'syntactic agreement' and 'semantic agreement' only when a mismatch gives rise to a potential choice. This is shown in Figure 5.1.

Consider a further instance of semantic agreement, this time from the Talitsk dialect of Russian (Bogdanov 1968). In this dialect a plural verb can be used with a singular noun phrase, to indicate reference to a person or persons besides the one indicated directly. That is to say, we have an 'associative' construction, but it is indicated not by a marker on the nominal, but by plural agreement:

Russian (Talitsk dialect, Bogdanov 1968)
(38)   **moj**   brat   tam   toža   **žy-ľ-i**[11]
            my[M.SG]   brother(M)[SG]   there   also   live-PST-PL
            'my brother and his family also lived there'

The plural agreement is found in the verbal predicate, but not in the noun phrase, and so we have different agreements according to the target. We say that the verb shows semantic agreement, since the plural here matches the meaning but not the form of the controller.

---

[10] In Semitic linguistics the terms 'strict' and 'deflected' are used (Ferguson 1989: 9), in a potentially confusing way, since 'strict' is according to meaning and 'deflected' is according to form.

[11] Bogdanov's transcription has been transliterated here and in chapter 7. Note that the associative construction in this dialect is distinct from honorific usage.

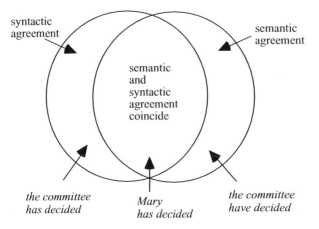

Figure 5.1   *Syntactic and semantic agreement*

Why then do we need the term 'semantic agreement'? Could we not just refer to 'plural agreement' in examples like (38)? The point is that different features may be involved, not just number. Furthermore, in different constructions different values of the same feature may be instances of semantic agreement: in the example just discussed, plural represents semantic agreement, while with honorific (polite) plural pronouns the singular represents semantic agreement (§7.7.1). Syntactic and semantic agreement are thus cover terms to describe contrasting agreement possibilities. In the simplest cases syntactic agreement is based ultimately on lexical properties of a noun, typically but not always determined by its formal properties. Semantic agreement is consistent with properties of the referent.[12] We need the terms only when there is a mismatch between the two.

It is important to stress that semantic and syntactic agreement are not labels we can attach to agreements in isolation. They are relative terms to be used of different agreement possibilities. I use 'semantic agreement' of the agreement which has greater semantic justification. In some instances, where there is a meaning-meaning mismatch, the choice will be between two agreements, each of which has some semantic justification, and I shall use 'semantic agreement' of the choice whose feature values more closely matches the referent. (For such instances, 'pragmatic agreement' would be appropriate, but this would be less good for some other types; on balance, it is better to retain the traditional terms here.)

As we shall see in chapter 7, there are drastic constraints on the distribution of syntactic and semantic agreement, which are generalizations over different

---

[12] When discussing gender, Dahl (2000) suggests 'lexical' and 'referential' gender would be preferable terms, since nouns may have a lexical gender which is not clearly linked to a formal property. This is a useful clarification for hybrids involving gender, but the broader terms, the traditional syntactic and semantic gender, are worth retaining because the opposition we are tackling goes beyond individual lexemes to include different agreements based on constructional mismatches (§7.4).

features and their values, imposed, for example, by the Agreement Hierarchy. In addition to the more straightforward instances of agreement according to different values of a feature, the syntactic-semantic contrast may cover: default agreement versus specified (semantic plural) agreement with quantified subjects (§5.5.2); instances where more than one feature is involved (Serbian/Croatian/Bosnian *d(j)eca* 'children', with feminine singular versus neuter plural versus masculine plural, Corbett 1983: 76–88); agreement with one conjunct versus agreement with all conjuncts (§7.4.1); and even a variant on the latter where agreement with one conjunct involves default agreement, as in Qafar (Corbett 2000: 203–5).

5.4.1 Recognizing syntactic and semantic agreement

To recap, then, a distinction of syntactic versus semantic agreement implies a situation where generally there is matching, but with deviations. These mismatches depend on particular types of controller, but also on the target, since if all targets show the same features for the same controller, then there is no reason to distinguish syntactic and semantic agreement. The minimal requirement is that one target should show a different feature value (for the same controller in respect of the same feature) as compared to a second target. The difference may be that the value is simply different, or that there is a choice for at least one target which is not identical to that found with the second. These possibilities are represented in abstract form in (39):

(39)   Situations where syntactic and semantic agreement must be recognized

controller	feature value marked on target 1 (e.g. the attributive adjective)	feature value marked on target 2 (e.g. the predicate verb)	comment
type 1	A	A	no syntactic/semantic agreement split
type 2	A	B	semantic agreement for one value
type 3	A	A or B	semantic agreement for one value
type 4	(A) or B	A or (B)	semantic agreement for one value
type 5	A or B	A or B	homonymous controllers

In (39), '( )' indicates a restricted or less common option. We discuss each of the five types in turn.

Type 1: normal. Examples of type 1 (as in *this apple tastes good*) may have semantically justified agreement forms, but they are not instances of semantic agreement, since all targets behave alike (all have singular agreement).

Type 2: Talitsk Russian. In example (38) above we saw both singular and plural agreement with a given controller. Singular represents syntactic agreement (the noun is singular), and plural represents the form with greater semantic justification (semantic agreement), since the referent is plural.

Type 3: committee-type nouns. Consider these English examples:

(40)   this committee has decided . . .
(41)   this committee have decided . . . (*these committee . . .)

Here there is a choice in the predicate, but not within the noun phrase (while in the previous examples there was no choice). Here again the plural represents semantic agreement; unlike in type 2, the use of semantic agreement is optional.

Type 4: Russian nouns denoting professions, like vrač *'doctor'.* Russian has a considerable number of nouns for professions, with the morphology typical of a masculine noun, but able to denote a male or a female. They have interesting agreements:

Russian (Kitajgorodskaja 1976, Corbett 1991: 231–2)
(42)   Ivanov-a   –   xoroš-ij   / xoroš-aja   vrač.
         Ivanov(F)-SG.NOM good-M.SG.NOM / good-F.SG.NOM doctor[SG.NOM]
         'Ivanova is a good doctor.'

A substantial questionnaire investigation was carried out during the 1960s, when the great majority of Russian doctors were women. To ensure that the referent is a woman, the surname *Ivanova* was included. Both syntactic (masculine) and semantic (feminine) agreements were reported, with a minority (16.9%, of the 3,835 who responded to this question) opting for semantic agreement. Contrast that with agreement in the predicate (it was stated that the doctor was a woman):

(43)   Vrač   priše-l   / priš-l-a.
         doctor[SG.NOM] come-PST [M.SG] / PST-F.SG
         'The (woman) doctor came.'

Here many more speakers, 51.7% of 3,806 respondents, chose semantic agreement. For both questions a minority chose neither option, which means that the overall proportion for semantic agreement is somewhat higher than 51.7%. Note then that it is not just a question of there being two forms available. At this point the important result is the marked difference between the use of the possibilities in two different targets. We shall discuss the data in more detail, with other targets, in §7.2.3. Here then we have specially interesting instance of syntactic versus semantic agreement.

Type 5: homonyms. In our final type there are two (or more) possible agreements, but these are fully determined by the semantics, and are the same across the different targets. We have two (or more) separate but related lexical items. For example, in Archi *misgin* 'poor person' takes masculine agreement when a male is referred to and feminine when a female is referred to; it also has the evasive use of gender IV singular (§5.2.3), when the sex is not known or not important (Kibrik 1972: 126). Type 5 therefore represents two (or more) instances of type 1, with the instances being equally justified in semantic terms.

Why do we treat type 1 as normal? To justify this we need the notion of **consistent agreement pattern,** which was mentioned in §1.4.1, criterion 3, and discussed particularly with regard to gender in Corbett (1991: 176–81). Examples like *apple* are consistent controllers, that is, they have a consistent agreement pattern. There are two factors involved. The first is that *apple* is one of the vast majority of nouns: they take agreeing forms like *this* and also take forms like *tastes*. That is what it means to be singular in English. (And similarly for the plural.) The second point is that these are the nouns for which we can give absolute rules: whatever the target, nouns of this type require singular agreeing forms (or plural, when they are plural). For others, like *committee*, if we ask what their number is, the response is 'who's asking?' If it is an attributive modifier which needs to know, then *committee* is unambiguously singular. If it is a predicate verb, then there is no such simple answer.

We might be tempted to give *committee* a special value of the number feature, say 'collective'. However, that will not work. 'Collective' would not be a value like singular and plural, first because the effect of this value would be different for different targets, and second because the frequency of the different actual values, singular and plural in verbal predicates, is specific to *committee*. Nouns like *team* and *government* behave slightly differently, so each would require its own specific number value (§7.2.4). Such nouns are indeed special, behaving similarly in general (for instance, all taking singular agreement of attributive modifiers) but varying as to the frequency of choices where a choice is available. This shows why we should therefore treat type 1, rather than these type 5 examples, as showing canonical agreement.

For simplicity I have restricted myself to comparing just two targets here; there can be more involved, as we shall see in chapter 7, where we consider the Agreement Hierarchy and the Predicate Hierarchy.

5.4.2   Sources of syntactic versus semantic agreement

Agreement mismatches can depend on various possible types of controller. We can find a considerable selection by looking at just a couple of languages:

(44)   Types of controllers which induce agreement mismatches

controller type	example
unique or virtually unique lexical item	Serbian/Croatian/Bosnian *deca* 'children'
set of semantically similar lexical items	English *committee*-type nouns
lexically restricted construction	masculine nouns quantified by numeral 'two', 'three' or 'four' in Serbian/Croatian/Bosnian
construction	conjoined noun phrases

There are lexical items which induce agreement choices, which are so few that they have to be listed. An example is Serbian/Croatian/Bosnian *deca* 'children' and *braća* 'brothers', which denote a plurality but have the form of a singular noun (for this complex story see Corbett 1983: 76–86; Wechsler & Zlatić 2000: 816–21). But there can also be large sets of such items, for instance British English nouns like *committee* (§7.2.4). Then there are constructions which are lexically restricted; this is clear for the Serbian/Croatian/Bosnian example involving numerals, discussed in §7.2.1. There are also more open-ended quantified expressions. Finally, there are construction types whose structure invokes agreement options, but which appear not to be lexically restricted, such as conjoined noun phrases (§5.7). Even here, however, we find that the noun phrases which are conjoined tend to be headed by noun phrases of the same type, for instance they tend to be all animate or all inanimate. The classification in (44) can be refined, including more gradations of types. The conclusion to be drawn is that controllers which allow agreement choices range all the way from unique lexical items to open-ended constructions; they are indeed pervasive.

5.5   Sources of mismatches

Having seen examples of different types, we should step back to gain perspective on the possibilities. There are mismatches where controller and target do not match as we might expect. As we examine these we must bear in mind that such mismatches may or may not lead to the particularly interesting types of mismatch we have just discussed, namely those where a given controller takes different agreements with different targets. (A way of thinking of these is that they have target-target mismatches.) At a general level, mismatches have basically two sources: meaning-meaning mismatches or form-meaning mismatches. I analyse each in turn, and then consider the special case of hybrid nouns.

5.5.1   Meaning-meaning mismatches

These involve different conceptualizations, in the broadest sense, to include pragmatics as well as semantics. For example, Levinson (1983: 71–2) points out that when answering the phone in English you say 'this is Joe Bloggs' or 'Joe Bloggs is speaking' with third person verb agreement, 'in contrast in Tamil we would have to say on the telephone the equivalent of *Joe Bloggs am speaking* with first person verb agreement':

Tamil

(45)   Mohan   peecur-een
       Mohan (man's name)   speak.PRS-1SG
       'Mohan speaking' (literally 'Mohan am speaking')

Bhuvana Narasimhan (personal communication) found several comparable examples in a mother's input to her child (age 1;3), for instance:

(46)   ammaa   edo   paNNaa   por-een
       mother something   do   go.PRS-1SG
       'mother is going to do something' (literally 'am')

There were examples of the use of the third singular, though these were fewer:

(47)   maamma   iru-kk-aaL-aa   paarU
       mother   be-PRS-3SG.F-Q   see.IMP
       'see, is mother there?'

Here the third singular is used, even though it is the mother speaking (and thus comparable to the English construction). We have a mismatch between a name and its pragmatic use, normally treated in opposite ways in Tamil and English.

An interesting type of mismatch, which we might call 'dreaming agreement', is found in Yawuru, a member of the Nyulnyulan family (non-Pama-Nyungan) of the west Kimberley region of Australia, as discussed in Hosokawa (1996).[13] Hosokawa stresses the importance of the culture-specific notion of identity for certain Yawuru constructions, including agreement. There are special constructions for body parts, and these are extended for further types of identity. In example (48), a normal intransitive construction, the verbal prefix takes the third singular form to agree with the subject:

Yawuru (Hosokawa 1996: 185)

(48)   kamba   dyurru   i-ndira-rn   yanban-gadya
       that   snake[ABS]   3SG-go-IPFV   south-INTENS
       'The snake went on southwards.'

However, suppose the snake is the *rayi*, the conceptional dreaming[14] of the addressee, then the verbal marker is in the second person, which might be seen

---

[13] I am grateful to Nicholas Evans for bringing this research to my attention.

[14] Hosokawa explains as follows: (1996: 190n33): 'The Yawuru word *rayi* "dreaming" can refer to various different kinds of "dreamings" (totems) that a person holds, such as personal dreamings (usually conceptional), inherited family dreaming(s), local dreaming (associated with one's birth place) or clan dreaming(s). It most commonly refers to one's conceptional dreaming, usually a plant or an animal that has either come up in the parent's dream, or has made a special kind of encounter with the parent(s), before the person was born. The same word *rayi* also functions as an adjective "secret, hidden" and as a preverb "hiding something, making something secret".'

as reflecting the identity of the person and their dreaming:

(49)   kamba dyurru   mi-ndira-rn   yanban-gadya
         that   snake[ABS]   2SG-go-IPFV   south-INTENS
         'The snake (which is your dreaming) went on southwards.'

Here there is a mismatch between the normal status of the referent and its significance for this addressee.

A further interesting mismatch is seen in this English example (Herb Clark,
cited in Barlow 1992: 227):

(50)   I'm parked on the hill. (My car is parked on the hill.)
(51)   *I is parked on the hill.

The impossibility of (51) suggests at first sight that any semantic/pragmatic analysis of agreement is doomed. However, in an article full of surprising and witty
examples, Nunberg (1996) argues that examples like (50) involve 'predicate transfer', so that what is special about such examples concerns the property 'parked
on the hill' (a suggestion adopted in Pollard & Sag 1994: 85–6; see further
discussion in Ward 2004). Nunberg suggests that the subject in sentences like
(50) refers to the speaker, and that 'the transfer involves the predicate' (1996:
111), so that 'being parked on the hill' is mapped onto the property 'having
a car parked on the hill'. Thus (50) and (51) are not so problematic as was
first believed. The data are interesting, and as Nunberg points out there is variability across languages as to what agreements are possible with some types of
transfer.

Finally in this section we note an unusual mismatch in Newar. There is
an opposition of 'conjunct' and 'disjunct' forms, marking evidentiality in the
verb. The use of conjunct forms involves volition, which leads to an interaction with the person feature (for a careful account see Hargreaves ms., and
for the development of the category see DeLancey 1992). Specifically in the
Dolakha dialect, however, there is a system of person and number agreement
which shares some of the characteristics of the Newar conjunct/disjunct system, and this gives rise to mismatches. There are occasional examples of this
type:

Dolakha Newar (Carol Genetti 1994: 107 and personal communication)
(52)   ji=ŋ   sir-eu   ji   chana   nāpa tuŋ   sir-i
         1SG.ABS=EMPH   die-3FUT   1SG.ABS   2SG.GEN   with TOP   die-FUT[1]
         'I will die. I will die with you.'

The first verb is marked as third person. It has a first person subject and is a
non-control verb, that is a verb which need not have a volitional instigator. Such a
verb can take third person agreement if the first person is acting non-volitionally.
Genetti (1994: 107) provides the following context. A girl considers what will
become of her after the death of a magical goat. In the first clause she implies that
her death is certain, and not a matter of her volition. In the second, the reading

is volitional: she decides to die along with the goat, and not be left alone. The mismatch in the first clause is striking, and Genetti gives further comparable examples, though this usage is rare in Dolakha Newar. We shall meet further meaning-meaning mismatches in chapter 7, for instance, the interesting neuter-feminine contrast of Konkani (§7.3.1).

5.5.2   Form-meaning mismatches

We have already seen various examples of form-meaning mismatches. Take, for instance, these examples from §1.4.4:

Russian
(53)   Voš-l-o   pjat´   devušek.
        come.in-PST-N.SG   five[NOM]   girl[PL.GEN]
        'Five girls came in.'

(54)   Voš-l-i   pjat´   devušek.
        come.in-PST-PL   five[NOM]   girl[PL.GEN]
        'Five girls came in.'

The noun phrase consists of a numeral in the nominative case, and a phrase (represented by a single noun in our examples) in the genitive plural. The form of the numeral is most like that of the singular of a particular class of nouns.[15] Hence the form of the numeral and its meaning do not match. The genitive plural noun might appear to be a possible controller, but subjects in Russian must be in the nominative to control agreement (§6.8).[16] This mismatch leads to an agreement choice: the default form can be used as in (53), or we may find semantic agreement (plural), as in (54). The conditions influencing such choices include animacy (§6.1.2), precedence (§6.1.3) and individuation (§6.5.2).

5.5.3   Lexical hybrids

These are important in our story and deserve special attention here. They are items which control different agreements for different targets. They are relatively plentiful for gender and number, while for person there are few available targets and so mismatches between targets are hard to find.

We begin with gender. According to the gender assignment rules (§4.3.1), nouns in Russian are assigned to gender by their meaning if sex-differentiable and by their form otherwise. The first three examples in (55) are therefore as expected:

[15] It is like the *kost´* type in chapter 4, example (25), but has an anomalous stress pattern for that type.

[16] The fact that the noun is morphologically plural is not important, since if instead we have *tri devuški* 'three girls', where the noun is genitive singular (as can be shown by stress for some nouns), the two agreements as in (53) and (54) are still possible, though the arithmetically smaller numerals favour the plural (§7.4.2 and §9.1.5).

(55)   Russian gender

	meaning	form	agreement
mal'čik 'boy'	A	A	A
djadja 'uncle'	A	B	A
stul 'chair'	–	A	A
vrač '(woman) doctor'	A/B	A	A/B hybrid

A = masculine, B = feminine (I use 'A' and 'B' for comparison
with number in (56) below)

For *mal'čik* 'boy' the meaning is sufficient to assign the noun to the masculine
gender; its form (morphology) would redundantly lead to the same outcome. For
djadja 'uncle' meaning and form lead to opposite outcomes, but the meaning
is what counts and the noun is masculine. In the case of *stul* 'chair' there is no
assignment based on its meaning (it is not sex-differentiable), but it is masculine
according to its form. What then of *vrač* '(woman) doctor'? While the other
nouns are normal nouns taking consistent agreements, *vrač* '(woman) doctor' is
a hybrid, taking both masculine and feminine agreements, with the proportions
varying according to the target (see (42) and (43) above). Its meaning appears to
require it to be feminine, its form suggests masculine. But if semantic assignment
wins out over formal assignment, why is it not simply feminine, as a converse of
djadja 'uncle'? First note that *vrač* can also be used of a male doctor, in which
case all the agreements are masculine. Moreover, masculine forms tend to be
used in Russian for reference to humans where sex is not distinguished. Thus
vrač when referring to a woman can be conceptualized in two ways: as a doctor
and as a woman. The semantics do not therefore point unambiguously to the
feminine; there is a meaning-meaning mismatch (hence the A/B in the meaning
column). Given this, we do not have a straightforward outcome as with *djadja*
'uncle'. Both masculine and feminine agreements are possible, depending on the
target.

To show that this is not a parochial situation in Russian, let us look at number
in English:

(56)   English number

	meaning	form	agreement
apple	A	A	A
mathematics, maths	A	B	A
flour, grain	–	A	A
committee	A/B	A	A/B hybrid

A = singular, B = plural

The first three examples are clear-cut, and are analogous to Russian, except that here number is involved. With *committee*, which takes singular and plural agreements according to the target ((40)–(41)), we might think that it were simply a question of singular form with plural meaning. But then we might expect it to behave like *mathematics*, and take the form appropriate to its meaning. Again, we have the form *committees* showing that *committee* is not a simple plural. Rather, again, a committee can be conceptualized in two ways, in terms of the group or in terms of the individuals. It is this meaning-meaning mismatch (indicated A/B again) which makes it a hybrid.

Given this, there are some who would claim that agreement is simply a matter of semantics (§1.2), and would suggest that *committee* is singular if conceptualized one way and plural if another. Alternative conceptualizations may well be the source of the alternatives, but this is not sufficient to handle the agreements, for three reasons: first, the agreements vary according to the target (and if *committee* were simply plural when conceptualized in terms of the individuals, then *these committee* should be acceptable); second, there are huge differences between the different varieties of English; and third, textual examples of predicate agreement usually follow the likely conceptualization, but they do not always do so (Levin 2001: 151–5). Recall that, even if a choice is considered to be an instance of a meaning-meaning mismatch, we retain the term 'semantic agreement' for the agreement which has greater semantic justification.

5.6   Occurrence and non-occurrence of agreement choices

We have identified the sources of mismatches. Yet, given the environment for a mismatch, there may or may not be consequences for agreement. Sometimes it is surprising that apparent mismatches do not have consequences for agreement.

5.6.1   Personification in Tsez

A striking example where a potential mismatch has no effect on agreement is provided by Tsez, as described by Polinsky & Comrie (1999). Tsez has four genders, comprising: I, male humans; II, female humans and some inanimates; III, animals and some inanimates; IV the residue. Suppose an animal is personified; we might expect this to create a mismatch, involving the gender for a person of the appropriate sex and that for animals. The situation arises in a story about a hen and a rooster, who are married, and fall out when the rooster has an affair with a frog. The sex of each character is quite clear. Consider these examples:

Tsez (Polinsky & Comrie 1999: 115–16)

(57)   sasaq   di   b-ik'-a   yoɫ.
        tomorrow 1SG   III-go-INF be.PRS
        'Tomorrow I (the hen speaking) will go.'

(58)   ɫu   mi   nediy   b-od-ā?
        who.ERG 2SG   thus   III-do-PST.WITNESSED.Q
        'Who treated you (addressing the frog) thus?'

We see that the agreements are in gender III; the absolutive argument, with which the verb agrees, is first person (in (57)) and second person (in (58)). The rooster is clearly personified as a male human, but nevertheless in (59) we find the distal demonstrative stem for classes II-IV(*neɫo-*) and not the gender I form (*nesi-*):

(59)   onoč-ā   ħukmu   b-oy-no
        hen(III)-ERG   decision(III)[ABS]   III-do-PST.UNWITNESSED

        neɫo-ɫ   xiz-āz   b-oq-a.
        that.III–CONT behind-DIST III-begin-INF.

        'The hen decided to set out after him (= the rooster).'

This is so contrary to our expectations that even doing the glossing is difficult in English. Tsez demonstrates that, even though we can identify the situations when mismatches are likely, we cannot be sure that they will indeed occur.

5.6.2   Hungarian numeral phrases

In Hungarian, as we saw in §1.4.4, numerals require the noun to stand in the singular. This gives a potential mismatch of form (singular) and meaning (plural). However, the verb agreement is as follows:

Hungarian (Edith Moravcsik, personal communication)

(60)   Tíz mókus   szalad.
        ten   squirrel[SG] run[3SG]
        'Ten squirrels are running.'

Without the numeral, plural forms would be used:

(61)   Mókus-ok   szalad-nak.
        squirrel-PL run-3PL
        '(Some) squirrels are running.'

Again we find no agreement choice here.

5.6.3   Generics in English

A further instance where a type of agreement is excluded, even though it might be expected on semantic grounds, was pointed out by Perlmutter (1972: 245):

(62)   *The hedgehog are becoming extinct.

One might argue that the plural verb is excluded because *the hedgehog* refers to a kind here and that the singular verb is required because reference is to one kind. However, bare plurals like *hedgehogs* can also be used to refer to a kind; if (62) could be explained on semantic grounds then we would expect **hedgehogs is becoming extinct* (using *hedgehogs* to refer to a kind) but this is of course excluded. One or other of the sentences is a problem for a semantic account of the agreements.

5.6.4   Pronouns with unexpected feature specifications

In some languages pronouns take particular agreements not in terms of their expected agreement features, but simply as pronouns. Thus Jarawara, a language of the Arawá family spoken in southern Amazonia, has two genders:

Jarawara (Arawá family, Dixon 2000: 494, 497)
(63)   Okomobi tafa-ka
          Okomobi eat-DECL.M
          'Okomobi (a man) is eating'
(64)   Manira tafa-ke
          Manira eat-DECL.F
          'Manira (a woman) is eating'

Pronouns take feminine agreement, the unmarked gender, irrespective of their own specification:

(65)   ee   tafa-ke
          1INCL   eat-DECL.F
          'We (inclusive) are eating'

Moreover, if a noun is inalienably possessed, and the possessor is a pronoun, there will be feminine agreement (Dixon 2000: 489–90).

   A comparable situation is found in Burmeso, a Papuan language with no known relatives; the first person singular takes feminine agreement and the second person takes masculine agreement (Donohue 2000: 345).

5.6.5   Cross-linguistic variation

In §5.5.1 we noted instances in which Tamil has semantically justified agreement, while English in similar circumstances does not. This serves to make the obvious point that there is cross-linguistic variation in this area: given a particular type of potential mismatch, different languages show different outcomes. The contrast between English and Tamil is striking, since normally English favours semantic agreement, yet on this occasion excludes it. While English, and particularly British English, does indeed allow semantic agreement in situations which for closely related languages like German would be quite impossible, there are languages where agreement is even more open to semantic and pragmatic factors. Good examples are found in Tibeto-Burman (Bickel 2000 talks of 'associative agreement' in these languages) and in the Gunwinyguan language Ngalakgan (Baker 2002); the latter is particularly interesting for the differences between targets: only agreement of verbs with their arguments shows semantic effects, not the agreements of nominal modifiers. This is a pattern conforming to the Agreement Hierarchy (§7.1).

5.7   A predictable mismatch: conjoined noun phrases

Conjoined singular noun phrases typically produce a mismatch. Consider phrases like *Jane and Fred* or *a passport and a visa*. An agreement target cannot match both the form and the meaning of such phrases, since they contain singular forms and yet the meaning is of a plurality.[17] Conjoined noun phrases are therefore particularly interesting. It is time to set out the basic options. There may be agreement with all/both of the conjoined phrases (66), or with just one (67):

Russian (Graudina, Ickovič & Katlinskaja 1976: 31)

(66)   prepodava-l-i-s´   matematik-a   i   fizik-a
         taught-PST-PL-REFL   mathematics(F)-SG   and physics(F)-SG
         'mathematics and physics were taught'

(67)   prepodava-l-a-s´   matematik-a   i   fizik-a
         taught-PST-F.SG-REFL   mathematics(F)-SG   and physics(F)-SG
         'mathematics and physics were (literally 'was') taught'

There are various conditions on the option, in different languages, and these are discussed in chapter 6, specifically in §6.1.2 and §6.1.4. A major factor is the particular domain; here we we shall concentrate on subject-predicate agreement[18] (we compare other domains in §7.4.1). If agreement is with all the conjuncts taken together, then the appropriate feature value must be computed (plural in (66)); we discuss the resolution principles involved in chapter 8.

Where agreement is with just one conjunct, we need to establish which one is involved. In (67) we cannot tell, since both conjuncts are feminine singular. The following is more helpful:

---

[17] A mismatch is likely, but not inevitable. If we had *passports and visas*, each of the conjuncts and the whole phrase would be plural, and there would be no mismatch. In a gender language, however, the plural noun phrases could be of different genders, and so there could again be a mismatch. I analyse singulars in this section, but we must bear in mind that problems, and the need for resolution, can arise with plurals too.

[18] For examples of agreement of the preposition with the nearest conjunct in Welsh, and for discussion of possible approaches to the general issue of nearest conjunct agreement in LFG, see Sadler (2003).

Russian (from Vojnovič, *Putëm vzaimnoj perepiski* 1979)
(68) **by-l-a**   u nego   ešče **gitar-a**   i
      be-PST-FEM.SG at 3SG.M.GEN also guitar(F)-SG.NOM and

      samoučitel´   k   nej
      manual(M)[SG.NOM] to 3SG.FEM.DAT

      'he also had a guitar and a manual for it'

Clearly agreement is with *gitara* 'guitar'. Masculine singular agreement (*byl) is
excluded here. But still, what principle determines which noun phrase controls
agreement? Is it the nearest, or the first? With this word order the nearest and
the first coincide, but examples with subject-verb order indicate that the normal
situation is for agreement to be with the nearest. Our key language, Russian, does
not show this particularly convincingly, since with subject-verb order in such
examples the plural is strongly preferred.[19] Let us instead look at examples from
a language where the situation is clear:

Swahili (Bokamba 1985: 45): agreement with the nearer conjunct (normal)
(69) ki-ti   na   **m-guu**   wa[20] meza   **u-me-vunjika**
      SG-chair(7/8) and SG-leg(3/4) of   table 3-PRF-broken
      'the chair and the leg of the table are broken'

The gender system of Swahili makes it evident that the nearer conjunct is being
agreed with, the one headed by *mguu* 'leg', a gender 3/4 noun. The verb is in
the singular, agreeing just with this conjunct in form (and so not matching the
meaning, since the chair is also broken). Reversing the order of constituents brings
a change of agreement:

(70) m-guu   wa meza na   **ki-ti**   **ki-me-vunjika**
      SG-leg(3/4) of table and SG-chair(7/8) 7-PRF-broken
      'the leg of the table and the chair are broken'

Thus agreement in these two examples is just with the nearer conjunct. There is
an alternative, agreement with all conjuncts, but that requires gender resolution
(to which we return in §8.3.4).[21]

---

[19] Corbett (1983: 98) cites an example from Solženicyn, but such examples with nouns of different genders where agreement is unambiguously with the nearest preceding conjunct tend to
be avoided. Examples are found in Russian dialects (Corbett 1983: 119, 134n9). An intriguing
example is from the nineteenth century:

(i)   Russian (Gercen, cited in Vinogradov & Istrina 1954: 492)
          . . . ja   i   ešče odin iz   nas   mož-et id-ti   domoj . . .
          1SG.NOM and still one from 1PL.GEN can-3SG go-INFIN home
          '. . . I and one more of us can go home . . .'

Here there is agreement with the nearer preceding conjunct; this is surprising, as we shall see
(§6.1.4), since both conjuncts are animate and person resolution does not occur.
[20] This is the associative marker *-a*, with prefix *u-* (*w-* before a vowel) agreeing with *mguu* 'leg'
(gender 3/4 singular). *Meza* 'table' is a gender 9/10 noun, with no prefix, and the same form for
singular and plural.
[21] Resolution is obligatory if the preceding conjuncts denote humans, according to Marten (2005:
527, 528n1).

Where agreement is with one conjunct, agreement with the nearest is the normal situation (though it may be avoided in some circumstances). This is such an unwelcome conclusion for proponents of some models of syntax that the data are ignored. However, this is how things are; there are data for many languages, including: Albanian (Morgan 1984; Pullum 1984), Bagwalal (Kibrik 2001: 478), Dzamba (Bokamba 1985: 45), Latin (Kühner & Stegmann 1955: 44, 49–50), Marathi (Pandharipande 1997: 448), Ndebele (Moosally 1998: 87–9, 96–7), Serbian/Croatian/Bosnian (Megaard 1976; Corbett 1983: 17–18 for plural conjuncts), Slovene (Lenček 1972: 58n11), Spanish (Steinberg & Caskey 1988) and Tsez (Polinsky 2002: 195); for the interesting complications of Qafar see Hayward & Corbett (1988). Moreover, the theoretical significance of the data needs to be drawn out. Agreement with the nearest conjunct, which may be first or last in the set of conjuncts, shows that linear order rather than syntactic structure is involved. In that case more general cognitive processes are involved, and we should perhaps be looking to psychologists, who have demonstrated the importance of first and last positions in lists in other domains.

In addition, a few languages do also allow agreement with the distant first conjunct (as noted in §2.4.2):

Slovene (Lenček 1972: 59) Agreement with the distant first conjunct (rare)

(71)   **groz-a**   in   strah   **je**   **prevze-l-a**
        horror(F)-SG.NOM and   fear(M)-SG.NOM AUX.3SG   seize-PST-F.SG

        vs-o   vas
        whole-F.SG.ACC   village(F)[SG.ACC]

        'Horror and fear seized the whole village.'

This is a rare possibility, which is found as a less common variant of the equivalent of (70) above. Other languages known to allow distant first conjunct agreement (while preferring agreement with the nearest conjunct) are Latin and Serbian/Croatian/Bosnian (sources for both are given in §2.4.2). Agreement with the distant last conjunct is never found; that is, we do not find examples like (68) but with agreement with the last conjunct following the target (masculine agreement in (68)).

Having sorted out the main options, we shall return to conjoined noun phrases in each of the next three chapters. It is perhaps worth noting that these constructions need particular care (and indeed that there are some highly unsatisfactory analyses in the literature). One has always to ask whether a particular form could arise from agreement with all conjuncts (given the language's resolution rules), or whether it is uniquely from agreement with one conjunct.

5.8   Informative mismatches

While our focus has been on the existence of mismatches, we should remember that in mismatches the agreement may provide information not available elsewhere. We consider such cases here. They fit well with the characterization of agreement as 'information in the wrong place'.

5.8.1 Agreement provides the only information

In §5.1.3 I analysed examples where the target makes more distinctions than the controller. What then if the controller makes no distinctions? The situation arises in Walman, a Torricelli language (thanks to Lea Brown and Matthew Dryer for the examples and for discussion of their significance):

Walman
(72)   Pelen n-aikiri.
             dog   M.SG-barked
             'The male dog barked.'

(73)   Pelen w-aikiri.
             dog   F.SG-barked
             'The female dog barked.'

(74)   Pelen l-aikiri.
             dog   DIMIN.SG-barked
             'The small dog barked.'

(75)   Pelen y-aikiri.
             dog   PL-barked
             'The dogs barked.'

In Walman number is not normally marked on the noun phrase (only a few nouns denoting humans have a plural form). It is therefore not like the Russian case discussed in §5.1.1. Yet the number involved is nominal number: in (75) there must be more than one dog, but not necessarily more than one barking event (§5.1.4). And there are some *pluralia tantum* nouns which require the plural form of the verb. Clearly, then, we have an interesting mismatch. Can we say it is an instance of agreement? One position is that Walman represents the logical extension of Inari Sami (§5.1.3). According to the 'slippery slope' type of argument, if Inari Sami, with three distinctions of the target compared with two of the controller, shows agreement, then so does Walman. The difference, of course, is that Walman typically shows not only few distinctions in the controller, but also typically no distinctions. If we go down this route, then it is certainly a non-canonical instance, since the controller does not show overt expression of agreement features (§1.4.1, criterion 2).[22]

---

[22] There is still the issue of whether the markers are instances of verbal agreement or are pronominal affixes (§3.8), for which further investigation is needed. Whatever the outcome, the original interesting mismatch remains, at least for those who treat pronouns as agreement targets.

5.8.2   Agreement supplies missing participants

Consider this example from the West Slavonic language Lower Sorbian:

Lower Sorbian (Stone 1993: 663 citing Janaš 1984: 171–2):
(76)   Smej   z   nan-om   šach   gra-ł-ej.
         AUX.1DU with father-SG.INS   chess[SG.ACC] play-PST-DU
         'Father and I played chess.'

The natural reading is that there are two players, with one participant, the speaker, being indicated only by the agreement on the auxiliary. For examples and references on these 'verb coded' or 'inclusory' constructions see Corbett (2000: 232–3) and Lichtenberk (2000: 24–7). If the subject pronoun were included, we could have *mej z nanom* 'we (dual) with father', that is, 'father and I'. We saw a further instance of agreement supplying missing participants in the Talitsk Russian example (38), which is an associative construction.

5.8.3   Agreement identifies participants

There are also instances where the participants are identified by a noun phrase, but only the agreement makes clear which person they are. We saw a Spanish example in §4.3.3; here is a comparable one from Bulgarian:

Bulgarian (Osenova 2003: 665, see also Norman 2001)
(77)   Deca-ta   otid-oxme   v gradina-ta.
         children-DEF   go-AOR.1PL to garden-DEF
         'We children went to the garden.'

The noun phrase is present in the clause, but it is the agreement which identifies the children as including the speaker. The second person plural verb *otidoxte* would indicate 'you children'.

5.9   Target features

We expect that the feature values of the target will be structured along the same lines as those of the controller. There are various subset relations, as we saw in §5.1.3. However, we also need 'target features', which mark displaced (controller) information according to the system of the target. That is, the values of the target features are structured rather differently from those of the controller. Bayso provides a striking example. Bayso is a Cushitic language, but separated from the main Cushitic area. It is spoken in Ethiopia, on Gidicco, an island in Lake Abaya and in some villages on the shores of the lake. Agreement targets such as verbs distinguish singular and plural and in the singular they also distinguish masculine and feminine. These traditional labels can be justified if we look at the personal pronouns, where there is a three-way system (Figure 5.2).

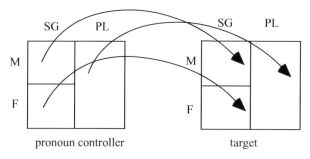

Figure 5.2   *Mapping for pronoun controllers in Bayso*

The simple mapping with the pronoun justifies the values given for the target features. We now turn to Bayso nouns, which distinguish four number values: general (where the number is not specified), singular (for one), paucal (two up to around six) and plural (more than the paucal). The agreements are as follows:

Bayso (Hayward 1979 and personal communications, Corbett & Hayward 1987, Corbett 2000: 181–3)

	lúban 'lion' M			kimbír 'bird' F	
(78)	lúban	hudure	(79)	kimbír	hudurte
	lion[GENERAL]	slept.M.SG		bird[GENERAL]	slept.F.SG
	'lion(s) slept' (one or more)			'bird(s) slept' (one or more)	
(80)	lubán-titi	hudure	(81)	kimbír-titi	hudurte
	lion-SG	slept.M.SG		bird-SG	slept.F.SG
	'a single/particular lion slept'			'a single/particular bird slept'	
(82)	luban-jaa	**hudureene**	(83)	kimbir-jaa	**hudureene**
	lion-PAUCAL	slept.PL		bird-PAUCAL	slept.PL
	'a few lions slept'			'a few birds slept'	
(84)	luban-jool	**hudure**	(85)	kimbir-jool	**hudure**
	lion-PL	slept.M.SG		bird-PL	slept.M.SG
	'lions slept'			'birds slept'	

The mapping between the two in typical instances is as follows:

(86)

controller	target
general	singular (also agreement in gender)
singular	singular (also agreement in gender)
paucal	plural
plural	masculine singular

The main point is that the mapping is not simple. If we map the controller and target forms for masculine nouns (examples (78), (80), (82) and (84)) we obtain the picture in Figure 5.3.

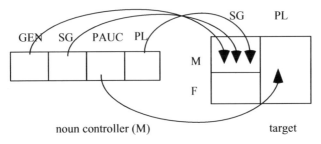

Figure 5.3   *Mapping for masculine nouns in Bayso*

Here the feature systems do not correspond. Recall that the target forms labelled 'plural' are those used for agreement with plural pronouns. With feminine nouns (examples (79), (81), (83) and (85)) the mapping is more complex (Figure 5.4).

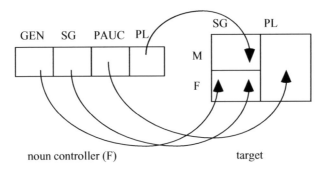

Figure 5.4   *Mapping for feminine nouns in Bayso*

Here again the feature systems do not correspond. However we label the cells, it is clear that the feature of number operates differently for controller and target in Bayso.[23] Other languages where noun phrases headed by pronouns differ from those headed by nouns in their agreements include Jarawara and Burmeso (§5.6.4) and English dialects with the Northern Subject Rule (Godfrey & Tagliamonte 1999; Pietsch 2005). Thus while controller and target features typically match, there are clear instances where they do not, and these require us to recognize the need for target features.

---

[23] There are worse cases, since Bayso is more regular than some of its relatives:

> Languages such as Arbore and Rendille have clearly preserved a good many features of the Proto-Omo-Tana system. Bayso, however, has undergone a number of changes. Taken collectively these changes have conspired towards creating a comparatively regular system.
>
> (Corbett & Hayward 1987: 25)

Of course, what counts as regular in Cushitic may not strike others as regular.

5.10   Conclusion

Mismatches are common. We have seen the circumstances under which they occur, and how they may (but need not) lead to agreement choices. I shall analyse the severe constraints on the resulting choices in chapter 7. We cannot therefore dismiss mismatches. They are central to understanding agreement. Indeed they show us more about how agreement works than thousands of 'vanilla' examples. Yet they are problematic for theories of syntax, in particular theories based on copying of features.

6   Conditions

We have analysed the main determinants of agreement: the controller, the target, the domain and the agreement features. We might think that given an adequate account of these four elements we would have a full description of agreement.

Hypothesis IV: A full description of controllers, targets, domains and features constitutes a complete account of agreement. (false)

Often these four elements are sufficient, but we also find many examples where there is something else at work, and these other factors I shall call 'conditions'.[1] The point is that agreement may be determined in part by factors which are not themselves realized directly in agreement. For instance, agreement in number with conjoined noun phrases often depends partly on the animacy of the noun phrases. But there may be no direct realization of animacy. Another important factor which works in this way is precedence. Some treat such conditions as covert features; thus noun phrases are marked as +animate or −animate. Yet this obscures the important difference between conditions and genuine agreement features (see §4.2.1).

Conditions can have an absolute effect, making one agreement outcome obligatory or impossible. Frequently, however, they are relative, just favouring a particular outcome, and so conditions are often linked to agreement choices. We first look at some examples of both types (§6.1). From these I will highlight the main characteristics of conditions and discuss why we need to recognize conditions as the fifth element in my account (§6.2). I give a typology of conditions (§6.3) and then concentrate on the factors which overlap with conditions (§6.4). I discuss in turn thematic role and animacy (§6.5), grammatical relation and case (§6.6) and communicative function and precedence (§6.7). I consider the morphological consequences in (§6.8), before concluding (§6.9).

6.1   Examples of conditions

We examine two examples, one from Miya which is an absolute condition and one from Russian which is a relative condition on an agreement choice.

[1] It might be argued that controllers, targets, domains and features are all conditions on agreement. In a sense this is true, but I reserve the term 'condition' for factors which are in addition to these four. Furthermore, there is the basic requirement that the target must be able to show agreement; the morphological factors which guarantee this I have called 'prerequisites' (§3.3), discussed further in §6.3.1.

6.1.1   An absolute condition in Miya

The West Chadic language Miya of Nigeria has an interesting condition on number agreement. The domains are clear, the target has the relevant forms, the controller even marks number overtly. Number is an agreement feature (with the values singular and plural), yet there is not always agreement in number; this is determined by an agreement condition. It is relevant that Miya also has gender: nouns denoting males are masculine, those denoting females are feminine, and non-sex differentiables are found in both genders. There are many different agreement targets, and these have three agreement forms: masculine singular, feminine singular and plural. We can see this with a demonstrative (Schuh 1989, 1998: 193n6, 197–8, 243–4):[2]

(1)   The demonstrative 'this' in Miya[3]

	singular	plural
masculine	nákən	níykin
feminine	tákən	

For number marking there is an animacy distinction: animate nouns are those which denote 'all humans, most, if not all, domestic animals and fowl, and some large wild animals'. Nouns denoting large wild animals are the 'grey area', and the remaining nouns are inanimate (Schuh 1989: 175). Animate nouns *must* be marked for plurality when appropriate:

Miya (Schuh 1998)
(2) a.   təvam   tsə́r   b. *'ám   tsər
         woman.PL two   woman.SG two
         'two women'   'two women'

For inanimates, on the other hand, marking is optional:

(3) a.   zə̀kiy-áyàw vaatlə   b. zə̀kiy   vaatlə
         stone-PL   five   stone[SG] five
         'five stones'   'five stones'

Animate plural nouns take plural agreements:

(4) a.   níykin dzáfə   b. níykin təmakwìy
         this.PL man.PL   this.PL sheep.PL
         'these men'   'these sheep'

Inanimate nouns, even if marked as plural, do not take plural agreement. This is not because agreement fails. Agreement still occurs, as shown by the fact that such nouns take agreement, but according to their gender in the singular:

---

[2] The basic analysis was given in Schuh (1989); the presentation of forms differs slightly in Schuh (1998) and we follow the later version here.

[3] ` indicates low tone, and ´ high tone; tl is a lateral fricative, and ə is a high central vowel.

(5)   nákən   víyayúw-awàw
        this.M.SG   fireplace(M)-PL
        'these fireplaces'

(6)   tákən   tlərkáy-ayàw
        this.F.SG   calabash(F)-PL
        'these calabashes'

Marking of number is obligatory for animate nouns but optional for inanimates. Agreement in number with animates is obligatory, plural agreement with inanimates is impossible. The important point is that agreement with inanimate plurals does occur, but in gender and not in number.[4] Although all the elements required for number agreement appear to be in place, number agreement does not occur. Thus agreement in number is determined by animacy, which is not an agreement feature in Miya. It is a condition on controllers, which generalizes over the different controllers (masculine and feminine) and the agreement of several different targets, and over both controllers and targets in different domains.

There are ways in which we might try to avoid this conclusion (if we believed conditions were unnecessary). The first is to try to locate all the difficulty in the morphology. The target forms I have labelled 'plural' could be analysed as 'animate plural'. The problem is that the masculine singular target forms would then have to be treated as 'masculine animate singular', 'masculine inanimate singular' and 'masculine inanimate plural' (and the feminines similarly). Moreover, we would still need access to a covert feature of animacy on the noun in order to handle these agreements. Once we introduce covert features (complicating the feature inventory) we have the equivalent of conditions. The second approach, a development of this, is to simplify the target feature specifications further, and claim they involve one category only (say gender), with the values 'masculine', 'feminine' and 'animate'. But then we have to determine which nouns are 'animate', and it is of course those which are animate and plural. Thus this account requires a feature calculation in terms of the covert feature 'number' (which is not an agreement feature in this approach). It is then very similar in terms of complexity to the account originally given, since that account had number as an agreement feature with a condition based on animacy, and the latter is not an agreement feature in Miya.

Thus Miya can show partial agreement (agreement in gender but not in number), as we saw earlier for Modern Standard Arabic (§5.3.2). The interesting difference is in the conditions. In Arabic the condition on full agreement is precedence

---

[4] What makes Miya so interesting is the examples where, for an inanimate, plural is marked on the controller and there is agreement in gender, but the form is singular. Less surprising is the situation in languages where the controller need not be marked for particular distinctions, and the target simply matches. Thus in Ndjébbana (a non-Pama-Nyungan language of Arnhem Land, Australia), number distinctions are not made for non-humans in many circumstances. As in Miya, gender is distinguished only in the singular. When the singular form is used for a clearly plural referent, there is still agreement in gender (McKay 2000: 192–3). Unlike Miya, however, we now have matching of controller and target: both are singular, even though the referent is plural.

(full agreement occurs when the controller precedes the target). In Miya the condition on full agreement is animacy (full agreement occurs when the controller is animate).

6.1.2   A relative condition in Russian

While the Miya condition is absolute, Russian shows a condition (also based on animacy) which is a relative one. Consider these examples:

Russian (Švedova 1980: 244)

(7)   Ogorči-l-i-s´/ ogorči-l-sja   brat   i   sestra.
         upset-PST-PL-REFL / upset-PST[M.SG]-REFL brother and sister
         'Brother and sister became upset.'

(8)   V èt-om   by-l-i / by-l   sv-oj
         in this-SG.LOC be-PST-PL / be-PST[M.SG]   REFL-M.SG.NOM

         rasčet   i   xitrost́.
         calculation(M)-SG.NOM and cunning(F)-SG.NOM

         'In this there was its own calculation and cunning.'

Recall from §5.7 that in conjoined structures agreement may in principle be with all conjuncts or with the nearest conjunct. In both (7) and (8) both possibilites are available, and the different gender of the conjuncts makes clear that agreement is indeed with the nearest. Both possibilities are found; however, they are not equally likely. One condition is the animacy of the controller: plural agreement is more likely with animate controllers than with inanimates. That is, the plural is more likely in (7) than in (8). This is shown in my count of Russian literary texts of the period 1930–79 (Corbett 1983: 105–35):

(9)   Predicate agreement with conjoined noun phrases in Russian:
         the effect of animacy[5]

animate		inanimate	
N	% PL	N	%PL
204	93	181	49

The data strongly suggest that animacy acts as a condition on agreement with conjoined noun phrases in Russian. This condition generalizes to other controllers; for example, quantified expressions in Russian are similarly affected (Corbett 1983: 142–52), and we return to animacy in §6.5. However, it is not the only condition operating in (7) and (8), and so the figures in (9) do not apply directly to them. We see why in the next section.

---

[5] For details of the corpus see Corbett (1983: 106, 128, 130). Besides noun phrases headed by nouns denoting humans, the 'animate' figure includes phrases headed by 'corporate' nouns such as *pravitel´stvo* 'government', and nouns denoting animals – a small minority of the textual examples.

6.1.3   Precedence as an absolute or relative condition

Precedence is a clear example of a condition, since there is no agreement form for precedence (though some would treat different word orders as constituting different domains). In the next examples the effect of the condition is seen in the distribution of singular and plural agreement. For conjoined noun phrases in Moroccan Arabic agreement with the nearer conjunct is possible, but only when the controller does not precede the target verb:

Moroccan Arabic (Aoun & Benmamoun 1999: 177–8)
(10)   ža / žaw   Omar w   Karim
          came.3SG.M /came.3PL Omar and Karim
          'Omar and Karim came'

Here the singular is possible, as is the plural verb. When the controller precedes, however, only plural agreement is possible. Thus the condition is *absolute*:

(11)   Omar w   Karim žaw / *ža
          Omar and Karim came.3PL./ came.3SG.M
          'Omar and Karim came'

For further discussion, including other varieties of Arabic, see Mohammad (2000: 109–45). Such examples are sometimes discussed as illustrating 'agreement asymmetry'.[6]

Precedence acts as a *relative* condition on agreement with Russian conjoined noun phrases. In (12) the data are again taken from the same literary texts (1930–1979) as in (9) above.

(12)   Predicate agreement with conjoined noun phrases in Russian:
          the effect of precedence

controller preceding		controller following	
N	% PL	N	%PL
182	95	203	53

Here we see a clear effect of precedence. Controllers preceding the target are more likely to take plural (semantic) agreement than those following. This condition also generalizes to other controllers, including quantified expressions (Corbett 1983: 149–52).

---

[6] Sometimes when precedence operates as an absolute or near absolute condition (such that only controllers not preceding the target allow agreement with the nearest conjunct) researchers talk of 'first conjunct agreement'. This is potentially misleading, since it is the position nearest to the target which is important, not being first, as is demonstrated by those languages which allow agreement with the nearest conjunct even when the controller precedes (§5.7). The related issues of distance and adjacency are considered in §7.7.4.

6.1.4   The interaction of conditions

We have seen that animacy and precedence both act as conditions on agreement. We have seen this specifically with regard to conjoined noun phrases in Russian (see (9) and (12)). Since these two conditions are independent, we can cross-classify for them:

(13)   Predicate agreement with conjoined noun phrases in Russian:
            the effect of animacy and precedence[7]

subject type	animate		inanimate	
word order	N	% PL	N	%PL
subject-predicate	115	100	67	85
predicate-subject	89	84	114	28

Both conditions exert a major influence on the agreement form selected. The plural, semantically agreeing form is more likely if the subject is animate and if it precedes the predicate. With both conditions exerting an influence, the likelihood of semantic agreement is greatest,[8] with neither factor it is lowest, and with just one it falls between. Returning to our examples (7) and (8), we see that the plural in sentences like (7) is found 85% of the time, while in (8) the plural is found only 28% of the time. Switching the word order to subject-predicate would increase the likelihood of plural agreement for both types. Patterns like that in (13), but with different relative weight for the two conditions, have been found in other languages (Corbett 2000: 201).[9]

6.2   Characteristics of conditions

In a sense, controllers, targets and domains work together to condition agreement feature values. However, I reserve the term '(agreement) condition' for regularities stated on subclasses of controllers, targets and domains. Conditions have the following characteristics:

Conditions generalize over different items. Conditions generalize over agreement rules by referring to a subclass of the controllers, targets or domains. For instance,

---

[7] Details of the corpus of literary works are again in Corbett (1983: 106, 128, 130).

[8] The 100% figure for plural agreement with animate conjuncts preceding the predicate is replicated in other counts of standard Russian (though not of Russian dialects, Corbett 1983: 119). Certainly examples of the singular are extremely rare. However, a nineteenth-century example is cited, in §5.7 footnote 19, somewhat as a curiosity. This may lead us to be cautious about claims for absolute conditions in languages for which there is not yet a long tradition of linguists looking out for counter-examples to generally accepted rules, as there is with Russian.

[9] Complex conditions, including precedence, are involved in the agreement of the participle in Romance; for luxuriant detail on this issue in Romance dialects see Loporcaro (1998). The loss of this agreement is considered by Smith (1995).

a condition on controllers which refers to animacy has the effect of separating the subclass of controllers denoting animates from other controllers. Thus conditions can always be restated by splitting controllers, targets or domains. We shall now see why the 'splitting' approach misses generalizations. The animacy condition on Russian conjoined noun phrases (§6.1.2) applies equally well to quantified phrases (thus, all other things being equal, in Russian we are more likely to find plural, that is semantic, predicate agreement with the animate controller *pjat´ devušek* 'five girls' than with the inanimate *pjat´ knig* 'five books'). We could split the controllers into four, essentially writing the condition into the controller:

1.   animate conjoined noun phrases
2.   inanimate conjoined noun phrases
3.   animate quantified phrases
4.   inanimate quantified phrases

Instead it is more revealing to 'factor out' the conditions. We have two types of controller:

1.   conjoined noun phrases
2.   quantified phrases

and a condition based on animacy which applies to both.

In fact, to handle the regularity of (13) we would need to subdivide again, into 'animate-controllers-preceding the target', 'animate-controllers-not preceding the target', and so on. Instead, we have a condition on precedence, applying to two types of controller. The essential point here is that conditions generalize over agreement rules. This generalizing gives us conditions on controllers, on targets and on domains.[10]

Conditions are realized indirectly in agreement. Conditions are 'at one remove' from agreement feature values. In other words, conditions are not of the form: 'in a given situation use the feminine singular'. Rather they refer to using semantic agreement (which generalizes, say, over values of gender and number), to agreeing with one potential controller rather than another (as in Dargi, §6.5), to failing to agree (and so using the default agreement, §6.7.2). Thus conditions generalize over controllers, targets and domains, and their effect is stated as a generalization over features. This is one reason why in §4.2.1 I was careful to distinguish overt

---

[10] Domains figure more prominently in the next chapter. Since we have conditions on controllers, targets and domains, we should ask why are there no conditions on features. Agreement features and their values are precisely what a study of agreement has to account for. It is true that we can subclassify features, but in order to motivate the subclassification of features, we also have to subclassify controllers, targets or domains. It is the subclassification of controllers, targets or domains which is the condition, and this condition helps towards the goal of specifying agreement features. However, as Jonathan Bobaljik points out (personal communication), within Minimalism distinctions between valued and unvalued features, or active and inactive, where the status of the feature specification can be changed in the course of a derivation, might give rise to conditions on agreement features.

features, which are directly reflected in agreement, from conditions, which are not.

Conditions are non-canonical. Conditions are 'non-canonical' (§1.4.5, criterion 20) in that it is more canonical to have no conditions. They often apply to non-canonical situations (for instance, where there is an agreement choice), and so we shall see further effects of conditions when we discuss agreement choices in chapter 7.

Conditions have a consistent effect. Conditions are even more general than implied so far, since they have the interesting property of pointing to the same outcome. If we merely listed four controller types as above, there would be no requirement for animate conjoined noun phrases and animate quantified expressions to behave similarly. However, our animacy condition will apply in the same way to each (the outcome may not be identical, but the effect of the condition will always be in the same direction, favouring semantic agreement).

Moreover, this holds cross-linguistically. It is not just that animacy favours semantic agreement in the constructions mentioned in Russian. Rather, whenever it has an effect it will be in that direction (no language, I predict, has a condition where animacy favours syntactic agreement, which would be the opposite of what we find in Russian). We see a similar effect in Miya as in Russian. In other words, conditions are language-level statements of typological regularities (in this case the Animacy Hierarchy, discussed further in §6.3.2). For a given language the regularity may be reflected in an absolute or a relative condition.

6.3 Typology

There are conditions on controllers, on targets and on domains (§6.2). We can also think of conditions in terms of the linguistic level at which they apply (§6.3.1), and then in §6.3.2 we have an initial discussion of hierarchies.

6.3.1 Linguistic level

Conditions can be classified in terms of the linguistic 'level' involved. Several apparent conditions are not conditions on agreement in the sense of this chapter, but rather 'prerequisites' for agreement to be possible at all (examples were given in §3.3). The essential difference is that prerequisites specify what is necessary for agreement (for instance, only vowel initial verbs can show agreement in Ingush, §3.3.3), while conditions affect the use of an agreement form where the prerequisites are met (for example, conjoined noun phrases are more likely to show semantic agreement in Russian if they refer to animates than if they refer to inanimates, §6.1.2).

Let us consider the possible levels in turn. At the phonological level we find various prerequisites. Targets may require a particular phonological shape in order to be able to agree. The verbs of Ingush fit this description (though we might argue that being vowel-initial in Ingush is really a phonological predictor for a morphological prerequisite). In contrast to prerequisites, we would not expect to find real phonological conditions on agreement, because syntax is generally held to be 'phonology free' (§3.5.2). There are several apparent examples, but to date these are all better analysed in other ways. For instance, in the Cushitic language Qafar verbs when singular have two forms, and a superficial examination suggests that one form is used when the subject is headed by a noun whose citation form ends in an accented vowel (like *karmà* 'autumn') and the other verbal agreement form in all other instances. This generalization would cover a large proportion of the instances. However, looking more closely we see that when the subject noun phrase is headed by *abbà* 'father' we do not find the predicted form. A better analysis is that we have a gender system, and nouns are assigned to gender either by meaning (as in the case of sex-differentiables like *abbà* 'father') and by phonological form in the remainder (§4.3.1). Qafar is unusual in that almost all of the sex-differentiable nouns are also regular in terms of phonological assignment. Hence this apparent phonological condition hides a second step: phonological form has an important role in gender assignment, and gender is an agreement feature.[11]

For the morphological level, we may say that the different sorts of prerequisite (§3.3) boil down to having the morphology which allows the target to agree. In contrast, we do not expect to find genuine morphological conditions on agreement, because of the principle of 'morphology-free syntax' (Zwicky 1996: 301). Syntax can have access to morphosyntactic features, such as number and gender, but not to the way in which these are realized morphologically (thus no access to purely morphological features, like the features for inflectional class). A counter-example has been suggested, involving gender resolution in Serbian/Croatian/Bosnian. This is mentioned in §8.4.1, with a reference to an analysis suggesting that it does not in fact contravene the notion of morphology-free syntax.

Real conditions on agreement involve the 'higher' linguistic levels. There are clear examples of conditions at the syntactic level, for example based on word order (§6.1.3). Other conditions are (lexical-)semantic in nature, for instance involving animacy (§6.1.1 and §6.1.2). And then there are pragmatic conditions, as we shall see in §6.7 and in §6.9.

6.3.2   Hierarchies (illustrated from animacy)

We start from simple conditions, identified in a single language. For example, in Russian conjoined noun phrases denoting animates are more likely

---

[11] Another interesting issue is the Spanish definite article, which has the singular forms *el* (masculine) and *la* (feminine). However, before feminine nouns with an initial stressed *a*, the form is *el*, as in *el agua* 'the water', where *agua* is feminine. There has been considerable debate about the significance of these data (Plank 1984, Posner 1985, Harris 1987). Janda & Varela-García (1991) show that the data are more variable than was generally thought. The details of the use of the *el* form have yet to be fully established, but they are to be treated as 'shape conditions', which govern 'the allowable shapes of particular sequences of adjacent words' (Pullum & Zwicky 1988: 263).

to take semantic (plural) agreement than are inanimates. This condition has the effect of subdividing a set of controllers into two. We then establish that this condition applies cross-linguistically, in that whenever animacy operates as an agreement condition, higher animacy will favour agreement with a greater degree of semantic justification. This is a typological generalization.

The final step is to say that conditions can be chained together to form hierarchies. Thus for animacy we have so far considered animate versus inanimate. However, agreement with German conjoined noun phrases provides evidence for two conditions (Findreng 1976: 145, 165–6, 197):

1.   conjoined noun phrases referring to animates are more likely to take semantic agreement than are those referring to inanimates;
2.   conjoined noun phrases referring to concrete inanimates are more likely to take semantic agreement than are those referring to abstract inanimates.

We can chain these together to give the following Animacy Hierarchy:

(14)   animate > concrete inanimate > abstract inanimate

We then have the condition that the higher the conjoined noun phrases are on the Animacy Hierarchy, the greater the likelihood of semantic agreement. Thus hierarchies are generalizations over the subtypes to which conditions refer.

Other examples allow us to split 'animate' into 'human' and 'other animate', as in Inari Sami (§3.6.2.2, Toivonen 2003) and in Cairene Arabic (Belnap 1999: 174), and so we can chain these sub-conditions into our hierarchy:

(15)   human > other animate > concrete inanimate > abstract inanimate

The Animacy Hierarchy may be extended further, with the top positions, above 'human', being first person, second person and third person. (Some linguists separate these off as the Person Hierarchy.) This will be relevant when we come to Dargi in §6.5.

Hierarchies such as the Animacy Hierarchy may be justified from agreement evidence; it may be, in the best case, that they have independent justification from other phenomena. The Animacy Hierarchy has a good deal of support; however, the agreement evidence is stronger than, for example, number marking (Corbett 2000: 66–9). Where there is support from different sources this can make it hard to pull different factors apart, as will become plain in the next section. We return to hierarchies, notably the Agreement Hierarchy and the Predicate Hierarchy, in the next chapter.

6.4   Factors which overlap with agreement conditions

There are various factors which may determine agreement, or sometimes only influence it. These can overlap in misleading ways, offering the researcher every opportunity to jump to the wrong conclusion. They can be seen from different perspectives: conditions are an essential part of an account of agreement and, from another perspective, agreement is one means of expressing topicality, definiteness and so on. An important point to bear in mind is that those concerned with information structure typically concentrate on the clause, but the agreement conditions found there may well apply in other agreement domains too (thus precedence may apply within the noun phrase as well as within the clause).

To investigate these factors, a helpful start is the mappings for the 'regular active transitive construction' (Polinsky 1995: 360):

thematic roles:	agent	theme
grammatical relations:	subject	direct object
communicative functions:	topic	focus

The clause can be seen as having 'three distinct levels of representation, namely: the meaning of the clause, represented by thematic roles and verbal semantics, and the form of the clause represented by grammatical relations, on the one hand, and by communicative functions on the other'. (Polinsky 1995: 360). In the canonical case all three line up:

(16)   The farmer is planting potatoes.

Here *the farmer* is the agent in semantic terms; it is also the grammatical subject, and is presented as being what the sentence is about, that is, the topic. So far we have seen mainly examples in which the controller of the verb is determined by grammatical relations (§2.3.3).[12] However, as we shall see, a full typology of agreement shows that languages may require access to information of all three types. Some very relevant data are provided by Nocentini (1999). In Standard Italian the subject controls agreement, even if it lacks several other characteristics of subjecthood:

Standard Italian (Nocentini 1999: 316, Pierluigi Cuzzolin, personal communication)
(17)   Arriv-ano   i   prim-i   turist-i.
         Arrive-3PL DEF.M.PL   first-M.PL tourist(M)-PL
         'The first tourists are arriving.'

This is a poor instance of a subject: it does not precede the verb, is not the topic and it does not fill the thematic role of agent. Nevertheless, it still controls agreement; this situation is familiar from other Indo-European languages. By contrast, in spoken Tuscan Italian the conditions for controlling agreement are much stricter. The subject must precede the verb and must be topical. Here is one which fails to qualify as a full controller:

---

[12] Thus a relation such as subject-predicate within the clause has been taken as the domain. If we need additional information, such as whether the subject is also the topic, I have treated that as a condition. Others take another level as basic. The general point would still hold: in the canonical situation we can state the domain in terms of just one role; if more information is required we are dealing with a condition.

Spoken Tuscan Italian (Nocentini 1999: 319, 321)

(18)   Mi   manc-a   cinque bollin-i   per arriv-are a   venti.
          1SG.DAT   lack-3SG   five   coupon(M)-PL   to   get-INF   to twenty.
          'I need five coupons to get to twenty.'

Standard Italian would have plural *mancano* 'lack', but since the subject does not precede the verb, in spoken Tuscan Italian we find the default agreement form. Now consider an example where the subject does precede:

(19)   Quant-i   bollin-i   ti   manc-a   per arriv-are a   venti?
          How.many-M.PL coupon(M)-PL 2SG.DAT lack-3SG to   get-INF   to twenty?
          'How many coupons do you need to get to twenty?'

Here we have the necessary word order, but still no agreement; this is because the subject is focus and not topic. Only when all the conditions are fulfilled do we find agreement:

(20)   I   bollin-i   manc-ano ancora.
          DEF.M.PL   coupon(M)-PL   lack-3PL   still
          'The coupons are still missing.'

Thus, in spoken Tuscan Italian just being the subject is not sufficient to be the agreement controller; the subject must also meet two conditions: it must fulfil the right communicative function and it must precede the target in order to control agreement.[13]

As noted earlier, there is considerable overlap between particular conditions. Some of the notions are quite slippery and others are easier to investigate. For example, topic and precedence are linked (many languages put topics early in the clause) and precedence lends itself readily to objective investigation. So let us look at the linkages in turn.

The thematic role of agent is linked to animacy. In: *The farmer is planting potatoes*, the agent (*the farmer*) is animate, and that is a typical linkage. Languages vary according to their readiness to allow the agent role to be filled by items low on the Animacy Hierarchy. We look further at agent and animacy in §6.5.

In our example *the farmer* is also the subject. Though case is barely reflected in English, we may note that if we substitute a pronoun, it would be *he* rather than *him*. Particularly in languages with richer case morphology, the question then arises whether the verb agrees with the subject (thus according to grammatical relations) or with the noun phrase in the nominative case (according to case). In many instances the two coincide, but we shall see that they can be separated and each can play a role (§6.6).

The noun phrase *the farmer* is also the topic of the sentence, what it is about. While in English topic and subject typically coincide, in many languages they are more independent of each other, as we saw in the spoken Tuscan examples above, where being topic is important for agreement. Being topic often correlates

---

[13] For partly comparable conditions in Sardinian see Bentley (2004).

with word order (§6.1.3) and with definiteness, both of which figure in accounts of agreement. We consider these overlaps in §6.7.

6.5   Thematic role and animacy

We are now ready to tackle some interesting data from the Nakh-Daghestanian language Dargi (Chirag dialect).[14] Dargi (or Dargwa) has ergative-absolutive case marking. Transitive subjects stand in the ergative and objects in the absolutive. The verb can agree with both:

Dargi (Chirag dialect, Kibrik 2003: 272–5)
(21)   dīc̄e   ʕu   r-iqan-da
        1SG.ERG 2SG.II.ABS II.SG-lead-1
        'I lead you (woman)'

There are three genders, and assignment is straightforward: male humans are assigned to gender I, female humans to II, and the residue are in III. The suffix -*da* in (21) is first person, but does not distinguish number.

(22)   dīc̄e   it   r-iqan-da
        1SG.ERG 3SG.II.ABS II.SG-lead-1
        'I lead her'

(23)   ʕīc̄e   du   r-iqan-de
        2SG.ERG 1SG.II.ABS II.SG-lead-2SG
        'you lead me (woman)'

(24)   ʕīc̄e   it   r-iqan-de
        2SG.ERG 3SG.II.ABS II.SG-lead-2SG
        'you lead her'

So far, the system seems relatively straightforward. The gender/number prefixed agreement seems to be controlled by the absolutive argument (here the transitive object) and the personal suffixed agreement is controlled by the ergative argument (subject). When we look at further data we see that the situation is more complex:

(25)   it-e   du   r-iqan-da
        3SG-ERG 1SG.II.ABS II.SG-lead-1
        'he/she leads me (woman)'

(26)   it-e   ʕu   r-iqan-de
        3SG-ERG 2SG.II.ABS II.SG-lead-2SG
        'he/she leads you (woman)'

(27)   it-e   ruše   r-iqle
        3SG-ERG girl.SG.II.ABS II.SG-lead
        'he/she leads the girl'

---

[14] For the slightly different but equally interesting situation in Akusha Dargi see van den Berg (1999).

There is no person agreement in example (27). From these examples it looks as though the person agreement needs complex alternative specifications: thus *-da* marks first person agent in (21); it also functions in further examples (not given here) as the subject of intransitives. But (25) shows that it can also mark the first person patient (theme). And *-de* is similarly split. Kibrik suggests an alternative, namely that *-da* is used for first person agreement and *-de* for second person agreement.

We can then have these conditions on person (suffixed) agreement:

1. if one argument only is first or second person, agreement is with that;
2. if both arguments are first and second person, agreement is with the agent.

The first condition accounts for examples (22), (24), (25) and (26), the second accounts for examples (21) and (23). In (27) there is no first or second person argument and so there is no person agreement (the verb also has an irregular stem).[15]

In Dargi then, person agreement is controlled by different noun phrases according to person *and* according to the configuration of thematic roles. Let us take these in turn. First, there is a simple hierarchical condition, in that first and second persons outrank third person. (For instances of more complex hierarchies with similar functions see Kibrik 2003.) We can treat this as a separate person hierarchy or as the top section of the Animacy Hierarchy (as discussed in §6.3.2). Such examples, where the agreement controller is determined according to position on a hierarchy, is sometimes termed 'hierarchical agreement' (Siewierska 1996).[16] And second, where both potential controllers are high enough on the animacy/person hierarchy, the competition between them is determined by which is the agent. Both conditions are absolute conditions.

Looking at agreement in Dargi as a whole, the transitive verb agrees with the absolutive noun phrase in number and gender, as we expect in a Daghestanian language. There is also innovative person agreement; this depends upon

---

[15] The attentive reader may ask why we should not state the condition in terms of case instead of thematic role; in other words, the second condition could refer to ergative case instead of agency. Consider this example (Kibrik 2003: 485):

(i)   dami   ʕu   čarʀₒan-da
        1SG-DAT   2SG.II.ABS understand-1
        'I understand you (woman)'

Here we have an argument in the dative (since it is a verb of perception). This requires us to extend the second condition to include experiencer as well as agent, perhaps making the condition refer to the highest argument on the thematic hierarchy. Stating the condition to refer to dative case would be unsatisfactory, given other uses of the dative, which do not induce agreement. Once auxiliary verbs are included, the situation becomes more complex, and then it appears we need reference both to thematic roles and to case (see Kibrik 2003: 485–8).

Elsewhere in Daghestanian languages agenthood is a condition on person agreement in Lak (Kazenin 1999). Further afield a clear example is provided by Guarani, a Tupi-Guarani language of Paraguay (Velázquez-Castillo 1991).

[16] For complex interaction of conditions, based on hierarchies, see Tsunoda's (1981) analysis of the Australian language Djaru; here agreeing clitics are involved.

the configuration; the condition involves both the person and the thematic role (agent).

We noted earlier that agents are typically animate, and animacy is a common condition on agreement; we investigate this further in §6.5.1. Then we look at the related factor of individuation (§6.5.2), which also relates to the agent role.[17]

6.5.1   Animacy

We have already considered animacy in terms of the Animacy Hierarchy (§6.3.2). Indeed animacy has a wide range of effects, varying in different languages: see Comrie (1989b: 185–200) and Minkoff (2000). And we have established that, while animacy is linked to agency, it can be a condition on agreement independent of the thematic role of agent. We saw this in Miya (§6.1.1), where animacy operates as a condition within the noun phrase as well as within the clause. Its role as a condition is particularly clear in the following Turkish examples:

Turkish (Jaklin Kornfilt, personal communications for data and judgements)

(28)   Namzet-ler   oda-ya   bir-er   bir-er   gel-sin-ler / gel-sin.
         candidate-PL   room-DAT   one-by   one-by   come-OPT-3PL / come-OPT[3SG]
         'The candidates should come into the room one by one.'

In (28) the verb may agree (third plural) or it may not, in which case it stands in the third singular (default) form. The conditions are particularly interesting. First, the choice exists only if there is an overt subject. If there is no subject, then singular agreement can only be understood as implying a singular subject, however clear the extralinguistic situation:

(29)   Namzet-ler-e   söyle,   oda-ya   bir-er   bir-er
         candidate-PL-DAT   tell-IMP   room-DAT   one-by   one-by

         gel-sin-ler / *gel-sin.
         come-OPT-3PL / come-OPT[3SG]

         'Tell the candidates that they should come into the room one by one.'

Under the natural interpretation where it is the candidates who are to come into the room, singular (default) agreement is unacceptable. There is a syntactic requirement for this agreement that there should be an overt subject in the same clause.

---

[17] In the canonical instance agent, subject and topic line up (§6.4). Each can be a condition favouring agreement. The other overlapping factors (theme, direct object and focus) have a lesser place in a typology of agreement, but we note some intriguing pointers here for further work. Consider the direct object in the transitive construction. In ergative-absolutive systems (as in Tsakhur) it is the controller of choice (§2.3.2). There are interesting connections with the features involved. In Tsakhur, as in several related languages, the absolutive argument controls agreement in gender and number, but not in person. We discussed the limited nature of person agreement in Archi in §4.2.1. In Dargi we see the rise of new person agreement, not working by the old system, but conditioned in part by the agent. For more on the rise of person agreement in Daghestanian languages, see Helmbrecht (1996).

Suppose this condition is met, as in (28). Then both options are fully acceptable for subjects denoting humans, while with inanimates the default form is normal:

(30)   Top-lar masa-dan yer-e   yuvarlan-dI   / *yuvarlan-dI-lar.
         ball-PL table-ABL floor-DAT roll-PST[3SG] / roll-PST-3PL
         'The balls rolled from the table (down) to the floor.'

Non-human animates come in the middle, giving a version of the familiar hierarchy:[18]

(31)   human > other animate > inanimate

One further effect is of interest, namely comparison with an example with conjoined noun phrases:

(32)   Ali-yle Oya oda-ya   gel-sin-ler / gel-sin.
         Ali-and Oya room-DAT come-OPT-PL / come-OPT
         'Ali and Oya should come into the room.'

Here both types of agreement are possible, but with the plural now rather better, as compared with (28) where they were equally acceptable.[19]

6.5.2   Individuation

There is also a link between the role of agent and the notion of individuation (and the latter, of course, relates to animacy in that we individuate animates more readily than inanimates). Recall that the meaning of the clause is seen through thematic roles and verbal semantics (§6.4), and the link between these two can be found in agreement. Specifically, if we consider agreement with conjoined noun phrases in subject position in Russian, we find that agreement in number depends in part on the semantics of the clause. The more agent-like the subject is (as evidenced by the semantic type of the predicate) the more likely is plural agreement. An activity predicate (which is likely to indicate an agentive subject) makes plural agreement more likely, as shown in a corpus of literary and dialect Russian (Corbett 1983: 112–13, 120–2).

Here we consider rather different data which confirm that conclusion. Robblee reports that predicates form a hierarchy of individuation, which she motivates from other phenomena as well as agreement. There are three main classes, each split into two subclasses; the reader is referred to Robblee (1993a) for justification of these, but the examples in (33) give an indication of membership. Class I predicates have an undergoer as their argument; class II also have an undergoer argument

---

[18] The different versions of the hierarchy found in the literature are not always significantly different: sometimes a researcher does not check for a particular distinction such as human versus other animate, and the data might or might not have given evidence for the distinction.

[19] I have taken Turkish to illustrate the effect of animacy, but it is in fact a good exemplar of other conditions too. Schroeder (1999: 111–25) argues that, besides animacy, the topical status of the controller, its role as agent and the degree to which the referents are individuated all affect agreement.

but the predicate additionally has a manner constituent, lacking in class I. Class III predicates have an agent argument. The six subtypes represent increasing degrees of inherent individuation of the predicate.

> A predicate of low inherent individuation may be attributed to and thus occurs with many more kinds of arguments than a predicate of high individuation. For instance, the predicate *byt′* 'be' regularly occurs with subject noun phrases that are abstract, and also with those that are concrete. In contrast, only noun phrases denoting concrete objects normally occur as the subject of the stative predicate *krasnet′* 'redden [intrans.]'.   (Robblee 1993b: 425)

How is this hierarchy of predicates relevant to agreement? Robblee took a corpus of Russian prose (1976 to 1988). She extracted instances of predicate agreement with quantified noun phrases including either a numeral or one of *neskol′ko* 'several', *malo* 'few' or *nemalo* 'several, more than a few', which in principle allow singular or plural agreement (§1.4.4). The results are given in (33)

(33)   Semantic (plural) predicate agreement with quantified noun phrases according to predicate type in Russian (from Robblee 1993b: 428)

	N		% plural	
Subtype Ia *byt′* 'be'	76		7	
Subtype Ib, e.g. *proizojti* 'occur'	47		11	
CLASS I ('inversion') subtotal		123		8
Subtype IIa, e.g. *stojat′* 'stand'	122		46	
Subtype IIb, e.g. *krasnet′* 'redden'	38		58	
CLASS II ('intransitive') subtotal		160		49
Subtype IIIa, e.g. *rabotat′* 'work'	13		69	
Subtype IIIb, e.g. *udarit′* 'hit'	77		90	
CLASS III ('agentive') subtotal		90		87
TOTAL		373		45

The results are clear; semantic (plural) agreement is least common with *byt′* and successively more common with more individuated predicates.

The effect of the predicate is substantiated convincingly. However, we need to disentangle the different factors at work. Thus Robblee's class I comprises predicates with an undergoer argument. Among other properties, these predicates are more likely to appear in predicate-subject structures than are other predicates; and predicate-subject word order disfavours semantic agreement (as we saw in §6.1.2; it is true for agreement with quantified noun phrases (Corbett 1983: 149–52) as it is with conjoined noun phrases). It would be helpful, therefore, to have a count in which the factor of word order is held constant, in order to isolate the effect of the predicate type. Robblee provides this in a later paper; she takes the same 373 examples as in (33) and cross-classifies her three main predicate types with word order.

(34)   Semantic (plural) predicate agreement with quantified noun phrases
       according to word order and predicate type in Russian (from Robblee 1997:
       235)

	subject-predicate word order		predicate-subject word order		TOTAL	
	N	% PL	N	% PL	N	% PL
CLASS I ('inversion')	13	15	110	7	123	8
CLASS II ('intransitive')	43	63	117	44	160	49
CLASS III ('agentive')	55	96	35	71	90	87
TOTAL	111	74	262	32	373	45

Thus of the class I predicates, of the thirteen found with subject-predicate word
order, 15% had plural agreement. Plural agreement is more likely with subject-
predicate order (15%) than with predicate-subject (7%), and the same is true for
each class of predicate (63% versus 44%, and 96% versus 71%). But equally, if
we keep the word order constant and consider the class of predicate (comparing down the columns) then we see that plural is least likely with 'inversion'
predicates, more so with other intransitives and most likely with agentives. Here
then we have clear evidence that this hierarchy has an effect independent of word
order.[20]

We conclude that agency (as here investigated through predicate type) is relevant to agreement in that it can affect the values of the agreement features
expressed on the target. A qualification is required here, since for some researchers
the use of a default form (for instance the neuter singular in Russian) can be taken
as a sign that there is no agreement. Hence the discussion about agreement with
quantified expressions would, for some, be recast as a contrast between agreement (shown by the plural) and no agreement (shown by the neuter singular).
However, this would not affect the claim that thematic roles are relevant since
the other evidence alluded to earlier in this section (in Corbett 1983: 112–13,
120–2) involves conjoined noun phrases, where the agreement options are: full
agreement with the nearest conjunct, or plural agreement.

---

[20] We should ask how this hierarchy relates to Comrie's Predicate Hierarchy (1975). Robblee's
Predicate Hierarchy of Individuation provides a cross-cutting classification, as becomes clear
when we consider non-verbal predicates. A few of these, such as *vidno* 'visible', are in class
Ib (Robblee 1993a: 216), while the majority are lower on the hierarchy (1993a: 230). Overall,
predicative nouns and adjectives would be more individuating than transitive verbs, therefore
the most individuating in the Predicate Hierarchy of Individuation (Karen Robblee, personal
communication). In Comrie's Predicate Hierarchy, which has a syntactic and morphological basis,
verbs and non-verbs are fully separated. Thus Robblee's hierarchy can be seen as a factor ranging
over the predicate types defined in Comrie's hierarchy. It would be of great interest to know
more about the interactions between the two, in particular to know more about how adjectives
behave in structures which allow agreement choices. It is established that, when other factors are
held constant, adjectives favour semantic agreement by comparison with verbs (Corbett 1983:
163–70).

6.6   Grammatical relations and case

We now ask how far grammatical relations allow us to determine how agreement operates in different languages. Suppose we can establish the grammatical relations in a particular construction according to other criteria (for instance according to the criteria of Keenan (1976), that is, controlling reflexives, being the target for promotion, being the missing argument for imperatives, and so on, as discussed in Comrie 1989b: 104–23).[21] Can we then straightforwardly determine how agreement will operate? Is Blake right to suggest that 'Agreement is normally on the basis of grammatical relations . . .' (1994: 140)?

We might expect that if we appeal to grammatical relations we shall not also need to refer to case. Indeed the Relational Grammar literature stressed the importance of instances where the controller was of the 'right' grammatical relation but the 'wrong' case (quirky case) and still controlled agreement (§2.3.3). However, there are also clear instances demonstrating the need to refer to case as well as to grammatical relations for specifying agreement. These are of two types, one concerning controllers and the other concerning agreement choices.

First, in terms of the controller, we find instances, as in Russian, where a noun phrase in the right grammatical relation (subject) but not in the right case (nominative) cannot control agreement. The subject in Russian can arguably be in different cases (for criteria for subject see Testelec (2001: 325–6)). To control agreement it has to be in the nominative:

Russian

(35)   Mož-et byt́, kogda u menja   **bud-et**   sv-oj
        may-3SG be.INF when at 1SG.GEN be.FUT-3SG   REFL-M.SG.NOM

        milliard   dollar-ov,   ja . . .[22]
        milliard(M)[SG.NOM] dollar-PL.GEN 1SG.NOM

        'Maybe, when I have my (own) milliard dollars, I . . .'

Here in the Russian possessive construction the possessor phrase (*u menja*, literally 'at me') is subject-like in that it controls reflexivization (including *svoj* 'one's own'), but it does not control agreement. The verb is not first person but third. Moreover, a noun phrase which is not the subject for reflexivization purposes but which is in the nominative can control agreement. Agreement is with the 'possessed' noun phrase *svoj milliard dollarov* 'my own milliard dollars'.

A comparable interesting situation is found in Hindi/Urdu, as described in Butt (2001), following Mohanan (1994: 102–6). Agreement is as follows:

---

[21] Criteria can differ substantially from researcher to researcher, and so comparison of different claims is often difficult. For analysis of oblique subjects see Moore & Perlmutter (2000) and Perlmutter & Moore (2002) on Russian, discussed by Sigurðsson (2002) with interesting comparisons with Icelandic.

[22] Viktor Dorenko, *Bandity s bol´šoj dorogi*, Moscow, ÈKSMO, 1996, p. 245.

1.   if the subject is in the nominative, the verb agrees with it;
2.   otherwise, if the object is in the nominative, the verb agrees with that;
3.   otherwise the verb shows default agreement (masculine singular).

These conditions can be seen operating in the following examples:

Hindi/Urdu (Butt 2001)

(36)   **adnan**   gari   **cala-ta**   hɛ
        Adnan(M)[NOM]   car(F)[NOM]   drive-IPFV.M.SG   AUX.PRS.3SG
        'Adnan drives a car.'

(37)   nadya=ne / adnan=ne   **gari**   **cala-yi**   hɛ
        Nadya(F)=ERG / Adnan(M)=ERG   car(F)[NOM]   drive-PFV.F.SG   AUX.PRS.3SG
        'Nadya / Adnan has driven a car.'

(38)   nadya=ne   gari=ko   **cala=ya**   hɛ
        Nadya(F)=ERG   car(F)=ACC   drive-PFV.M.SG   AUX.PRS.3SG
        'Nadya has driven the car.'

Thus in different configurations agreement depends in part on case. For other comparable examples in Indo-Aryan see Bickel & Yādava (2000) and Bickel (2003: 711–16); for discussion of Inari Sami see Toivonen (2003), and for Icelandic see Sigurðsson (1996, 2002) and Boeckx (2000). Note the regularity that when the noun phrase in the 'right' grammatical relation has its controlling potential usurped by another, that noun phrase is typically in the 'right' case: this is true of the instances just discussed, of back agreement (§2.4.4), and of long-distance agreement (§6.7.1).

A second type of evidence showing that we need access to case as well as to grammatical relations to account for agreement involves agreement choices. We find instances where a modifier in the 'right' (nominative) case outweighs all other factors which may determine the feature value. The examples are again from Russian and concern determiners and adjectives within quantified expressions. Agreement with quantified expressions in Russian is highly complex, with numerous conditions having an influence, which leads to differences in speaker judgements. One regularity, however, takes precedence over all others, namely that if there is a plural modifier in the nominative case, then plural agreement is guaranteed. A striking instance is found with the numerals *dva/dve* 'two', *tri* 'three' and *četyre* 'four'. These numerals when themselves in the nominative (or in the accusative which is identical to the nominative for inanimates) take a noun in the genitive singular (§3.3.5). Predicate agreement can in principle be in the default neuter singular form or can be in the plural:

Russian (judgements of Marina Chumakina)

(39)   Na stol-e   leža-l-o   / leža-l-i   četyre   knig-i.
        on table-SG.LOC   lie-PST-N.SG / lie-PST-PL   four[NOM]   book(F)-SG.GEN
        'On the table lay four books.' ('There were four books on the table.')

An attributive adjective in a phrase like *četyre knigi* 'four books' can be nominative plural or genitive plural; in the modern language this choice is largely restricted to occurrences with feminine nouns (with masculines and neuters the genitive plural is overwhelmingly preferred). There are other factors in play (if the numeral is in the accusative, though identical in form to the nominative, this favours genitive of the adjective, and the higher the numeral the more likely the genitive, that is, four > three > two); for these see Corbett (1993). Given a feminine noun like *kniga* 'book', an attributive adjective can be nominative plural or genitive plural:

(40)   četyre   bol´š-ie   /   bol´š-ix   knig-i
         four[NOM]   large-PL.NOM /   large-PL.GEN book(F)-SG.GEN
         'four large books'

Some speakers claim that there is a slight difference in meaning, but it is very hard to pin down, and the fact that the existence of a choice depends on the gender of the noun makes this a minor distinction at best.

    If we put together phrases including an attributive modifier and a predicate we might expect four possibilities. Suprun (1957: 76–7) investigated a corpus of literary texts. He found 236 relevant examples, and an interesting effect: of the four outcomes one might theoretically expect, one is excluded:

(41)   Constructions with 'two', 'three' and 'four' in Russian

attributive modifier	predicate agreement	example
genitive plural	neuter singular	(42) below
nominative plural	plural	(43) below
genitive plural	plural	(44) below
nominative plural	neuter singular	(45) below: EXCLUDED

I examined a larger corpus of 415 examples, from literary texts 1970–80, and confirmed Suprun's observation. This observation is also confirmed by work with consultants. Speakers have varying preferences for the three attested types of example (Marina Chumakina accepts all three):

(42)   Na stol-e   **leža-l-o**   četyre   **bol´š-ix**   knig-i.
         on table-SG.LOC   lie-PST-N.SG   four[NOM]   large-PL.GEN   book(F)-SG.GEN
         'On the table lay four large books.'

(43)   Na stol-e   **leža-l-i**   četyre   **bol´š-ie**   knig-i.
         on table-SG.LOC   lie-PST-PL   four[NOM]   large-PL.NOM   book(F)-SG.GEN
         'On the table lay four large books.'

(44)   Na stol-e   **leža-l-i**   četyre   **bol´š-ix**   knig-i.
         on table-SG.LOC   lie-PST-PL   four[NOM]   large-PL.GEN   book(F)-SG.GEN
         'On the table lay four large books.'

The fourth combination is unacceptable:

(45) *Na stol-e   **leža-l-o**   četyre   **boľš-ie**   knig-i.
      on   table-SG.LOC lie-PST-N.SG four[NOM] large-PL.NOM book(F)-SG.GEN
      'On the table lay four large books.'

The judgements are clear about (45); if there is a nominative plural modifier, then the predicate must be plural (and this is a much more robust effect than any claim about meaning differences). Within a set of complex conditions, this one effect is clear-cut. We find this both in the corpus studies and in speakers' judgements. Again the condition involves the nominative case.

I conclude that a full typology of agreement needs reference both to grammatical relations and to case.

6.7   Communicative function and precedence

My goal is to account for the agreement systems found in the world's languages. From that perspective, communicative (or discourse) functions fit in as conditions on agreement. From the perspective of someone trying primarily to understand information structure, agreement is one means out of several. The different perspectives have led linguists to investigate and to measure different aspects of the data, but we are beginning to see the connections between the different approaches. A full account of agreement certainly needs to include communicative functions (a useful overview of research and terms used can be found in Nikolaeva (2001: 3–9) and more detail in Lambrecht & Michaelis (1998)).

6.7.1   Topic

The 'topic' is a 'referent which a proposition is construed to be about in a given discourse situation . . .' (Lambrecht & Michaelis 1998: 494). We consider first a clear instance of topic functioning as a condition on agreement. We have already observed the interesting phenomenon of long-distance agreement in Tsez (§1.4.2, §2.4.7). It is now time to investigate the conditions for the different agreements. Recall that this example is as we might expect:

Tsez: normal agreement (Polinsky & Comrie 1999: 116–17)
(46)   eni-r   [už-ā   magalu   b-āc'-ru-łi]
        mother(II)-DAT boy(I)-ERG bread(III)[ABS] III-eat-PST_PTCP-NMLZ[ABS]

        r-iy-xo.
        IV-know-PRS

        'The mother knows that the boy ate the bread.'

The matrix verb *r-iy-xo* 'know' shows gender IV agreement; this is the default, which results because its absolutive argument is the bracketed complement. The type of example which we have yet to explain is this one:

Tsez: long-distance agreement

(47)   eni-r   [už-ā   magalu   b-āc'-ru-ɬi]   **b-iy-xo.**
        mother(II)-DAT   boy(I)-ERG   bread(III)[ABS]   III-eat-PST_PTCP-NMLZ[ABS]   III-know-PRS
        'The mother knows that the boy ate the bread.'

In (47) the matrix verb *b-iy-xo* 'know' shows gender III agreement, agreeing with the nominal *magalu* 'bread', which is inside the complement. This latter type of agreement is conditioned by topicality. It occurs when 'the referent of the absolutive noun phrase is the main internal topic of the embedded clause' (Polinsky & Comrie 1999: 122).

Polinsky & Comrie produce convincing evidence for their analysis. First, if the absolutive argument of the embedded clause is overtly marked as focus (thus it cannot be topic) then long-distance agreement is impossible:

(48)   eni-r   [už-ā   magalu-kin
        mother(II)-DAT   boy(I)-ERG   bread(III)[ABS]-FOC
        b-āc'-ru-ɬi]   **r-iy-xo / *b-iy-xo.**
        II-eat-PST.PTCP-NMLZ[ABS]   IV-know-PRS / III-know-PRS
        'The mother knows that the boy ate BREAD.'

Since *-kin* marks *magalu* 'bread' as focus, this latter cannot be the topic. A second focus marker (*-x*) has the same effect.

Tsez also has overt topic marking, for which it uses the particles *-n(o)* (regular topic) and *-gon* (contrastive topic). If one of these marks the absolutive argument in the embedded clause, showing it unambiguously to be topic, then long-distance agreement is obligatory:

(49)   eni-r   [už-ā   t'ek'-gon   t'et'r-āsi
        mother(II)-DAT   boy(I)-ERG   book(II)[ABS]-TOPIC   read-RES
        yāɬ-ru-ɬi]   **y-iy-xo / *r-iy-xo.**
        be-PST.PTCP-NMLZ   II-know-PRS / IV-know-PRS
        'The mother knows that, as for the book, the boy is reading it.'

Conversely, if some other element is marked overtly as topic, then the absolutive cannot control long-distance agreement:

(50)   eni-r   [už-ā-n   t'ek'   t'et'r-āsi
        mother(II)-DAT   boy(I)-ERG-TOPIC   book(II)[ABS]   read-RES
        yā-ru-ɬi]   **r-iy-xo / *y-iy-xo.**
        be-PST.PTCP-NMLZ   IV-know-PRS / II-know-PRS
        'The mother knows that, as for the boy, he is reading a book.'

The evidence is strong, supporting the claim that long-distance agreement is conditioned by topicality. While I have treated it as a condition, Polinsky (2003) treats the distinction as exhibiting two different structures. And as noted earlier, from a different perspective one could see long-distance agreement as an indicator of the topic of the embedded clause. Other languages show similar constructions;

while the conditions differ somewhat from language to language, it is suggested that long-distance agreement is determined by the communicative function of the controller (Polinsky & Potsdam 1999).

A second example of the effect of topicality is provided by Khanty (Ostyak), a Uralic language with some 13,000 speakers in western Siberia. The effect of communicative function is on object agreement. The basic effect can be seen in these examples (for more data see Nikolaeva 1999):

Khanty (Nikolaeva 2001: 16)

(51)   ma tam kala:ŋ   we:l-s-əm
           I   this reindeer kill-PST-1SG
           'I killed this reindeer.'

(52)   ma tam kala:ŋ   we:l-s-Ø-e:m
           I   this reindeer kill-PST-SG.OBJ-1SG
           'I killed this reindeer.'

(53)   ma tam kala:ŋ   we:l-sə-l-a:m
           I   this reindeer kill-PST-PL.OBJ-1SG
           'I killed these reindeer.'

(54)   ma tam kala:ŋ   we:l-sə-ŋil-a:m
           I   this reindeer kill-PST-DU.OBJ-1SG
           'I killed these (two) reindeer.'

In (51) there is just subject agreement, while in (52)–(54) there is agreement with the object too. Note that the realization of subject agreement is also affected by the presence of object agreement, as shown by the contrast of (51) and (52). In one sense, then, Khanty has optional object agreement. However, there are conditions on it. When the object is the focus, then object agreement is not possible. The type of object which controls agreement has some topic properties. For instance, it is specific. In fact Nikolaeva (2001) argues that it expresses a secondary topic (the subject being systematically associated with the primary topic). A secondary topic is: 'An entity such that the utterance is construed to be ABOUT the relationship between it and the primary topic.' (Nikolaeva 2001: 26; see that source for examples). Thus in Khanty the occurrence of object agreement is conditioned by communicative function.

Tsez and Khanty provide clear instances of topic as a condition. But topicality also overlaps with other factors which have a major impact on agreement. First, there is a preference (stronger or weaker in different languages) for the topic to be the subject (and of course the subject is a typical controller). Moreover, in many languages, including the Slavonic languages, topics tend to occur early in the utterance. For such languages we can use word order as a good indicator of communicative function, given a sufficient corpus (compare Nichols, Rappaport & Timberlake 1980, and commentary in Corbett 1983: 137, 154, 175). There is evidence of this type from different Slavonic languages. Part of the evidence, comparing controllers which precede and follow their target in Russian texts, was given in §6.1.3. These data can be taken indirectly as counts of controllers which are topics versus those which are not. The full range of evidence involves quantified expressions, conjoined noun phrases and comitative phrases (Corbett 1983: 107–50 passim). To give another part of the evidence: Sand examined a large corpus of various Serbian/Croatian/Bosnian texts of the 1960s. The largest controller type investigated was the numerals from *pet* 'five' upwards. For these (55) has been drawn up from Sand's data (1971: 73–5):

(55)   The effect of precedence on agreement with quantified expressions (involving *pet* 'five' and above) in Serbian/Croatian/Bosnian

	singular	plural	percent plural
subject-predicate	249	61	20
predicate-subject	830	21	2

Clearly subject-predicate word order is more likely to produce plural agreement than is predicate-subject order. We see that the more topic-like the subject (as reflected in word order) the more likely is plural agreement. Thus we see that the *value* of the agreement features is influenced by the communicative function of the controller, while in Tsez topicality determined which noun phrase was to be the controller; in Khanty it determined whether or not there would be agreement with the object, and in Tundra Nenets it determines whether there is person agreement (§4.6, Nikolaeva 2005, forthcoming).

Though precedence and topicality are related, they are not identical. On the one hand, topics do not always precede. And on the other, precedence is a wider condition, in that it applies to other domains (for instance, within the noun phrase) and not just within the clause, and so it cannot be seen just as an indicator of topic. For instance, in Spanish, with conjoined noun phrases precedence has a dramatic effect on the possibilities for verb agreement (resolution is normal in subject-verb clauses, while agreement with the nearer conjunct is marginally possible in verb-subject clauses), and it is also a major factor within the noun phrase (attributive modifiers following the head may show number resolution or agreement with the nearer conjunct while those which precede must agree with the nearer conjunct (Camacho 2003: 95–8, 111–13, 127–30)). Another example involves agreement with mass nouns in the Lena dialect of Spanish, see Hualde (1992) and Corbett (2000: 124–6). For further instances of the effect of precedence see Bakker (2005). The related questions of adjacency and distance are discussed in §7.7.4.

Topicality is also linked to definiteness, to which we now turn.

6.7.2   Definiteness and specificity

We have already encountered the role of definiteness in discussion of Macedonian object clitics (§1.4.2) and of the different agreement forms in Hungarian (§3.6.1). We now turn to data which provide a fine illustration of the combined effect of several conditions, including definiteness and specificity.

The language is Rural Palestinian Arabic, as spoken in rural communities in the northern West Bank (Hoyt 2002). The following alternative agreements are possible:

Rural Palestian Arabic (Frederick Hoyt 2002: 111 and personal communication)[23]

(56)   **bæka** / **bæku**   fi: χams ɪzlæːm   fɪ-d-daːr
        be.PFV.3SG.M / be.PFV.3PL.M EXPLETIVE five man(M).PL in-DEF-house
        'There was / were five men in the house.'

Hoyt provides details of the conditions on these agreements. Default agreement (the third singular masculine) can be found most frequently with the verb 'be', but also with other intransitive and passive verbs in existential sentences (compare the verbs discussed in §6.5.2). Then precedence has a role. As in other forms of Arabic, if the controller precedes, there is full agreement; the default agreement option is available only where the controller follows the target (§5.3.2). Next, and most relevantly, if the subject is definite (even if following the target), it must take full agreement (Hoyt 2000: 24):

(57)   **bæːkyɛ** / *bæːki   hanæːk **marat**   ɪḥmad   ɪd-dabbæːč
        be.ACT_PTCP.F.SG / be.ACT_PTCP.M.SG there wife.F.SG Ahmad DEF-Dabbak
        'Ahmad the Dabbak's wife was there.'

Thus it is indefinites which can take default agreement. Within the indefinites we may further divide between specific indefinites, that is those where the speaker can identify the referent but the addressee cannot, and the non-specific indefinites. There are subtle effects here (see Hoyt (2002)), with more specific subjects being more likely to take full agreement. For comparable data on Armenian see Sigler (1992).

6.7.3   Focus

The focus is the 'semantic component of a pragmatically structured proposition whereby the assertion differs from the presupposition.' (Lambrecht 1994: 213).[24] Linguists often indicate its distinctive intonation with capitals, as in *The farmer is planting POTATOES*. If the subject is the focus, that makes it 'less subject-like' (since the expected linkage is subject and topic) and it may no longer be able to control verb agreement. Following earlier work by Lambrecht and others, Lambrecht & Polinsky (1997: 190) distinguish three major focus categories.

In the first, the subject, or some other argument, is in focus; the predicate is within the presupposition:

---

[23] The transcription is according to the Americanist tradition.

[24] We should note that focus may be indicated by an agreeing marker; we saw this in Tsakhur, which uses the copula in this way (§2.2.9, see also Kibrik 1999: 582–609). Marking focus by various cleft constructions is a historical source of agreement, particularly of ergative-absolutive agreement. The interaction of focus and agreement in Daghestanian languages is discussed by Harris (2002: 228–34) and Kazenin (2002).

(58)   ARGUMENT FOCUS:
        Context sentence: Why didn't she come to work today?
        Sentence: *Her SON is responsible.*

Second, in predicate focus, the reverse holds; the predicate is in focus while the subject (and possibly other material) comes within the presupposition:

(59)   PREDICATE FOCUS:
        Context sentence: Why didn't she come to work today?
        Sentence: *Her son had an ACCIDENT.*

And third, in sentence focus, both subject and predicate are in focus. There is no bi-partite pragmatic structure:

(60)   SENTENCE FOCUS:
        Context sentence: Why didn't she come to work today?
        Sentence: *Her SON is sick.*

The one of special interest is the last. In the sentence-focus construction, sometimes called 'thetic', both subject and predicate are in focus. There is no pragmatic presupposition attached to the subject nor to the predicate. The 'problem' is to distinguish such constructions from the second type, that with predicate focus. The difference is that in sentence focus constructions there is no nominal topic constituent. To ensure that, it makes sense to 'detopicalize' the nominal constituent. Since the prime candidate for topic is the subject, we find various devices for detopicalizing the subject, and Lambrecht & Polinsky show that it can be given different properties normally associated with the object, such as non-nominative case marking. Another device is the lack of agreement in some languages.

An illustration of this is found in various Bantu languages in Locative Inversion constructions. Example (61) is from the Bantu language, Kinyarwanda; it has predicate focus structure (PF) and shows normal subject-verb agreement (though there is continuing debate as to the status of the verbal marker):

Kinyarwanda (Lambrecht & Polinsky 1997: 202)
(61)   aba-shyitsi   ba-ra-riríimbir-a   mu gi-sagára   (PF)
        PL-guest(1/2)   2-PRS-sing-IPFV   in SG-village(7/8)
        'The guests are singing in the village.'

In the comparable sentence with sentence focus (SF), the verb has locative gender (gender 16) agreement.

(62)   ha-ra-riríimbir-a   aba-shyitsi   mu gi-sagára   (SF)
        16-PRES-sing-IPFV   PL-guest(1/2)   in SG-village(7/8)
        'There are guests singing in the village.'

The lack of subject agreement with *aba-shyitsi* 'guests' shows that the latter is a less than full subject; in particular it is not also the topic.

In most of the examples provided by Lambrecht & Polinsky, this 'suspended' verb agreement, as they call it, is found with syntactic inversion. However, they claim it can occur on its own, and give these Russian examples (1997: 202):

Russian

(63) pjat′   fil′m-ov   pojavi-l-i-s′   na   èkran-ax   (PF)
      five[NOM] movie-PL.GEN appear-PST-PL-REFL on   screen-PL.LOC
      '(The) five movies were RELEASED.'

(64) pjat′   fil′m-ov   pojavi-l-o-s′   na   èkran-ax   (SF)
      five[NOM] movie-PL.GEN appear-PST-N.SG-REFL on   screen-PL.LOC
      'Five MOVIES were released.' / 'There were five MOVIES released.'

Here the choice is between semantic agreement (plural) in (63), where there is predicate focus (and a normal topic), and default agreement (neuter singular) in (64), where there is sentence focus and hence no topic.

At first sight this ties in perfectly with the conditions I have proposed. I showed how animate subjects and those with precedence relative to the target are more likely to take plural agreement. One could reasonably argue that these two conditions are more likely to apply for topics than for non-topics. Yet there is more going on than the simple link like this would suggest. First note that the agreement option is available in Russian only for certain controllers, namely those which invoke agreement mismatches. The latter are a relatively restricted set of the possible noun phrases which could appear in sentence focus constructions. And second, the mismatches and their distribution fit into a bigger picture, involving other domains besides subject-predicate agreement. Thus the conjoined noun phrases which adhere to the conditions we have been discussing are also constrained by the Agreement Hierarchy (§7.1).

The approach of Lambrecht & Polinsky fits particularly well in one way. We noted that conditions always point in one direction cross-linguistically. This is true here, in that controllers which are also topic will always be more likely to control agreement (and to control semantic agreement) than non-topics (compare §9.1.1).

Focus is also the condition which determines when we have full and when reduced agreement in Somali (see §3.6.2.1 for the forms). There is an overt focus marker, which makes the situation clear. In (65), the focus is on *aníga* 'me':

Somali (John Saeed 1993b: 73 and personal communication)

(65) Baabuurrá-dii aníga   ayà=y   i   dhaaf-een.
      truck.PL-DEF 1SG.NON_NOM FOC=3PL 1SG.OBJ pass.PST-3PL
      'The trucks passed ME / It was ME that the trucks passed.'

Here we find full agreement of the verb, with the subject (there is also a subject clitic hosted by the focus marker). Contrast this with an example where the subject is the focus:

(66)   Baabuurrá-díi ayàa i   dhaaf-áy.
        truck.PL-DEF FOC 1SG.OBJ pass.PST-3PL.RED_AGR
        'THE TRUCKS passed me / It was THE TRUCKS that passed me.'

Since the focus is on the subject, we find 'reduced agreement'. The subject still controls the agreement, but since it is the focus, it controls less full agreement than in (65). For further discussion of focus marking in Somali see Saeed (1999: 230–40) and Mereu (1999). A second condition under which reduced agreement occurs is in relative clauses, where the head is also the subject of the relative clause (Saeed 1993b: 73).

6.8   Morphological consequences

The reason we need to appeal to conditions is because they affect agreement, as we see in the agreement forms. In some instances a condition makes one or other normal agreement form more likely (say the singular or plural with singular conjoined noun phrases, as in §6.1.2). But in other instances conditions determine full or partial agreement (as in Somali, §6.7.3) or indeed whether a particular controller can control agreement or not (as in Dargi, §6.5). In the latter case some may say that there is no agreement, others say rather that there is a default agreement form. Thus there are various instances where agreement is potentially available but does not appear: there is a controller with feature specification, but the target does not match it. There may instead be a default form (§3.6.3, §5.2.1), or sometimes there is 'reduced agreement' (§3.6.2), in which not all of the normal distinctions are made.[25] In all of these, the lack of agreement requires an explanation; the grammar would be simpler, in a sense, if there were agreement. In such instances the term 'anti-agreement' is sometimes used. It has had a chequered career; it figures large in Steele (1990), and there is helpful discussion in Lapointe (1996: 376–9). Its short career has seen various usages (some like den Dikken (1999) use it just to indicate feature mismatches), and these are so divergent that the term is best avoided.

6.9   Conclusion

We have seen that we do indeed need to include conditions in a typology of agreement systems. They are the most challenging of the five elements, since they concern the areas where agreement systems interface with other factors. Indeed the very need for a condition is an indication that a particular type

---

[25] Ackema & Neeleman (2003) discuss another instance of reduced agreement (which they call 'agreement weakening') in Dutch, where the paradigms differ just in the form of the second person singular, and they suggest that the condition involves the target preceding the controller and both being in the same prosodic domain.

of agreement is non-canonical (§1.4.5). Conditions can overlap, so that disentangling them may require careful analysis. It is important to keep in mind that the overlap is often not a full one. A clear instance is animacy, which frequently acts as a condition on agreement. It overlaps with the thematic role of agent, but it can have a role as a condition beyond that, as the Miya data demonstrate. Particular overlaps and tendencies may crystallize into absolute conditions in individual languages; for instance, precedence operates as a relative condition in many languages, while in different varieties of Arabic it has become an absolute condition. We now turn to agreement choices, and here conditions have an important role.

7   The Agreement Hierarchy

We have already seen many instances of agreement options. Indeed there is such variety that we might wonder if we are faced with anarchy. In this chapter I continue to isolate and analyse in turn the factors which have an influence. We shall see that there are constraints on agreement options, which limit the distribution of syntactic and semantic agreement (§5.4). The constraints are powerful, typically outweighing the conditions of the last chapter. In particular, the Agreement Hierarchy sets the main constraints; the other constraints which we will consider typically fall within positions of the hierarchy.

The Agreement Hierarchy refers to domains. My strategy will therefore be to keep the controller constant, that is I shall take a given controller and observe what happens in different domains. For this we need controllers whose feature specification varies according to 'who's asking' (§5.4.1). These controllers include both lexical hybrids and constructional mismatches.

A good deal of evidence supporting the Agreement Hierarchy, from many languages, has accumulated over the years (Corbett 1979, 1983: 8–41, 1987: 318–22, 1991: 225–60, 2000: 188–92; Cornish 1986: 203–11; Barlow 1991, 1992: 136–7; see Wechsler & Zlatić 2003: 83–94 for discussion). I shall therefore concentrate on some of the most graphic examples, while providing an outline of other data in the summary tables in §7.3.1 and §7.3.2.

7.1   The Agreement Hierarchy as a constraint on agreement patterns

The agreement mismatches we discussed in §5.4 and §5.5 are extremely varied, yet we can identify clear patterns. Let us look again at nouns like *committee* in British English:

(1) a.   The committee has decided.   b. The committee have decided.

Committee is not uniquely singular or plural: we find both possibilities in the predicate (in British English and, as we shall see, more frequently in some other varieties than the speakers sometimes realize). However, it is not simply that *committee* is singular or plural. In a different agreement domain there is no choice:

(2) a.   this committee   b. *these committee

Thus agreement with this controller varies according to the domain. There are further domains to consider:

(3) a.   The committee, which has decided . . .   b.   The committee, who have decided . . .
(4) a.   The committee . . . . It . . .   b.   The committee . . . . They . . .

With such controllers, syntactic (singular) or semantic (plural) agreement is possible for all agreement targets, except attributive modifiers, where only syntactic agreement is acceptable. There is a large number of theoretical possibilities: could we find an example like *committee* but which took semantic agreement in attributive position and syntactic agreement elsewhere? Or one which took syntactic agreement as in (2a) and (4a) but semantic agreement as in (1b) and (3b)? These and many other possibilities are not found. They are excluded by the Agreement Hierarchy:

(5)   The Agreement Hierarchy (Corbett 1979)

attributive > predicate > relative pronoun > personal pronoun

These four positions represent successively less canonical agreement (§1.4.3).[1] The Agreement Hierarchy constrains possible agreement patterns as follows:

> For any controller that permits alternative agreements, as we move rightwards along the Agreement Hierarchy, the likelihood of agreement with greater semantic justification will increase monotonically (that is, with no intervening decrease).

This claim is a linking of conditions, a chaining together of typological generalizations (§6.3.2). Thus semantic agreement is as likely or more likely in the predicate as compared with attributive position; and then semantic agreement is as likely or more likely in the relative pronoun as in the predicate, and so on. This covers the situation with British English *committee*, and it rules out the hypothetical patterns we discussed.

7.2   Representative data

I illustrate the Agreement Hierarchy with four sets of data. The first is a rather odd, parochial construction, which nevertheless provides a particularly clear illustration of the Agreement Hierarchy, backed up by clear-cut statistics. The second is another unusual construction, which has figured earlier in the book.

---

[1] For consistency I use the '>' sign to represent decreasing canonicity. With it goes greater likelihood of semantic agreement, which could equally be indicated with '<'. Either makes good sense; what is important here is the relative places of the four positions. Note also that the relative pronoun position is the least important, since many languages do not build relative clauses with a pronoun.

The third shows massive variation, with a good deal of relevant evidence available. And the fourth can be investigated in large corpora and provides a thorough test of the Agreement Hierarchy. (Later, in §7.8, I tackle a very general construction, conjoined noun phrases, which shows considerable optionality and the interaction of several other factors.)

7.2.1   Phrases with lower numerals in Serbian/Croatian/Bosnian ▨

We start with quantified expressions in Serbian/Croatian/Bosnian, consisting of a lower numeral ('two', 'three', 'four') or *oba* 'both' and a masculine noun of the first inflectional class. The noun itself stands in a special form, a survival of the dual number which is synchronically a genitive singular. Attributive modifiers must take the ending -*a* (and so show alliterative agreement, §3.5.1) This form too is a remnant of the dual number;[2] there are arguments for analysing it synchronically as a neuter plural (Corbett 1983: 13–14, 89–92); here I will label it as 'remnant'. It represents agreement according to form (syntactic agreement):

Serbian/Croatian/Bosnian

(6)   dv-a   dobr-a   brat-a
       two-M.NOM good-REMNANT brother(M)-SG.GEN
       'two good brothers'

In the predicate the remnant form is again found, but so is the masculine plural form, the one we might have expected:

(7)   on-a   dv-a   brat-a   su
       that-REMNANT two-M.NOM brother(M)-SG.GEN AUX.3PL
       nesta-l-a / nesta-l-i
       disappear-PST-REMNANT / disappear-PST-M.PL
       'those two brothers have disappeared'

The relative pronoun is also found in both forms:

(8)   dv-a   brat-a   koj-a / koj-i . . .   On-i . . .
       two-M.NOM brother(M)-SG.GEN who-REMNANT / who-M.PL . . . 3-M.PL . . .
       'two brothers who . . . They . . .'

The personal pronoun must stand in the masculine plural form *oni* (**ona* is unacceptable).[3] The remnant form represents syntactic agreement, determined by formal factors, while the masculine plural is an instance of semantic agreement (the influence of meaning is evident). We find syntactic agreement in attributive position, both types of agreement occur in the predicate and the relative pronoun, and only semantic agreement is found with the personal pronoun. We have statistical data on the distribution of forms in the two relevant domains, collected before

---

[2] Recall that the loss of the dual led to 'collaborative agreement' in Russian (§3.3.5).
[3] This pronoun is identical in a few forms with the demonstrative *onaj* 'that' (as in (7)); this is not significant for our examples.

my claim about the Agreement Hierarchy was first made. The figures are derived from Sand (1971: 55–6, 63), who surveyed texts mainly from Serbian and had a large proportion of newspapers in her sample. There is a second survey, by Leko (2000), which specifically tests the validity of the Agreement Hierarchy. This uses the Oslo Corpus of Bosnian texts from the 1990s (around 1.5 million words).

(9)   Semantic agreement (per cent) with lower numerals in Serbian/Croatian/Bosnian

	attributive	predicate	relative pronoun	personal pronoun
Sand (1971) Serbian texts	[0%]	18% (N=376)	62% (N=32)	[100%]
Leko (2000) Bosnian texts	1% (N=507)[4]	42% (N=259)	56% (N=52)	100% (N=18)

I give the percentage of masculine plural forms (semantic agreement) from the total of plural forms (the masculine plural and the remnant forms).[5] For completeness (9) also includes, in '[ ]', the positions where Sand gives no data, since there is essentially no choice. The number of personal pronouns in Leko's count is small because subject pronouns are typically dropped. The shading is intended to give an impression of the likelihood of semantic agreement.[6]

This is a convincingly clear picture. Each successive cell in the table shows a monotonic increase in the likelihood of agreement with greater semantic justification. The two corpora differ in various ways, and the actual percentages naturally vary, but the pattern is the same.

7.2.2 Associative agreement in Russian (Talitsk dialect)

We should consider again this interesting construction which was used for illustration in §5.4:

Russian (Talitsk dialect, Bogdanov 1968)
(10)   **moj**   brat   tam   toža   ž̌y-l̕-i
          my[M.SG]   brother(M)[SG] there also   live-PST-PL
          'my brother and his family also lived there'

Here the plural verb indicates the associative construction: it is not just 'my brother' who lives there, but also associated people, his family. The plural

---

[4] Leko records six plural attributive modifiers but these are of the frozen modifier *nekih* 'some', which is genitive plural, and not strictly relevant (2000: 268).

[5] The predicate may occasionally also be singular, as is much more common with higher numerals (compare the data in §6.7.1); I omit four such examples from Leko's figures, for comparability with Sand's count.

[6] This idea for clarifying the presentation is developed from Wechsler & Zlatić (2003: 85–6).

agreement of the verb represents semantic agreement; in attributive position we find singular (syntactic) agreement. No examples of relative pronouns are given by Bogdanov; however, the personal pronoun in this construction is plural (Bogdanov 1968: 71):

(11)   Pra   Kuz′m-u   my   šypka ab′is′n′i-t′ toža n′e mož-ym,
        About Kuz′m-ACC 1PL.NOM much explain-INF also NEG can-1PL

        paš′imu   on′i   n′e   p′iš-ut   vam.
        why   3PL.NOM NEG write-3PL 2PL.DAT

        'About Kuz′ma we also can't explain much, why they don't write to you.'

Again the distribution shown in (10) and (11) conforms to the constraint of the Agreement Hierarchy: we find syntactic agreement in attributive position, and semantic agreement in the other positions for which we have information.

7.2.3   Russian *vrač* '(woman) doctor' and similar nouns

Russian nouns which have the form of a masculine noun and can be used for females, like *vrač* '(woman) doctor', have an important place in our story. In §5.4.1 they were the illustration of a particular type of hybrid controller. We return to them, since they show a choice for each position on the hierarchy (if only marginal for the personal pronoun). These hybrids can take both masculine (syntactic) and feminine (semantic) agreements (or 'lexical' and 'referential' gender, see chapter 5, n 12). We noted that we have some detailed information from a questionnaire survey of usage in the 1960s. For instance, speakers were asked to choose from these alternatives:

Russian (Kitajgorodskaja 1976; Corbett 1983: 30–9)
(12)   Ivanov-a   –   xoroš-ij   / xoroš-aja   vrač
        Ivanov(F)-SG.NOM good-M.SG.NOM / good-F.SG.NOM doctor[SG.NOM]
        'Ivanova is a good doctor'

Having the female name *Ivanova* makes it clear that the doctor is a woman. There were 3,835 respondents for this question, and 16.9% chose the feminine form. Some were undecided; the figure is not provided, but from other responses we may infer that 5–10% did not give a positive response, still leaving those choosing the feminine (semantic) form as a clear minority. Respondents were also asked about this sentence (they were told that a woman doctor was intended):

(13)   vrač   priše-l   / priš-l-a
        doctor[SG.NOM] come-PST [M.SG] / PST-F.SG
        'the (woman) doctor came'

From 3,806 replies, 51.7% chose the feminine here. Since just under 10% of the replies were undecided, there is a clear majority for the feminine. We thus find a choice in both positions. In accord with the Agreement Hierarchy, the likelihood of semantic agreement is considerably higher in the predicate, the position to the right. Now a self-reporting questionnaire is a poor way to investigate this issue; the use of the feminine form is likely to have been considerably under-reported because of the belief that the feminine is 'incorrect'. However, the difference between the two sentence types is so substantial that it is unlikely to be illusory. Furthermore, the survey data were broken down according to age, education, profession and area of longest stay, and in each category there was a clear difference in the responses, always with semantic agreement higher in (13) than in (12).

Other target types were not included in the questionnaire. There are some data from elsewhere for the relative pronoun. Janko-Trinickaja (1966: 193–4) studied women's journals of the 1920s and reports that feminine (semantic) agreement of the relative pronoun is found with nouns like *vrač* 'doctor' more frequently than it is found in the predicate. (Of the six examples with relative pronouns which she cites, five have feminine agreement.) As for the personal pronoun, the feminine *ona* is usual, but (linguistic) consultants say that in certain settings the masculine *on* 'he' is possible. This may seem unlikely, and yet I can vouch for it. On Red Square in May 1988 a woman was organizing guided tours round the Kremlin. Having gathered sufficient people she said:

Russian (own field notes, Red Square 1988)

(14)　　　Èkskursovod　　pered　vami.　　**On**　　　podnja-l　　　ruk-u.
　　　　　Guide[SG.NOM]　before　2PL.INST　3[M.SG.NOM]　raise-PST[M.SG]　hand-SG.ACC
　　　　　'Your guide is in front of you. She (literally 'he') has lifted (her) hand.'

The guide was a woman. This confirms that with such nouns we find a choice of agreement at all four positions on the Agreement Hierarchy. There is a monotonic increase in the likelihood of semantic agreement as we move from left to right, as required by the Agreement Hierarchy.

7.2.4　　English *committee* nouns

With these nouns there is dramatic variation, a good deal of data, and a perfect fit with the constraints of the Agreement Hierarchy. Statistical information on American, British and New Zealand English was reviewed in Corbett (2000: 188–90). That picture is confirmed and extended by more recent research (Levin 2001), done specifically with the Agreement Hierarchy in mind, so we shall concentrate on this more recent evidence. Levin's investigation is the single most rigorous test of the Agreement Hierarchy since it was proposed.

Levin investigated sizable corpora, checking for twenty-six nouns (2001: 50), which we call '*committee* nouns'.[7] First we look at text counts of three newspapers,

---

[7] To deal with the failure of the relative pronoun to mark number, Levin examined his substantial data and confirmed that singular verbs are normally found with *which* and plural with *who*. He then counted relative pronouns as singular or plural in this way, rather then establishing their number each time from the verb. Since relative *that* allows greater choice he included predicates of *that* within the predicate count. These decisions blur the picture a little, but Levin gives explicit information to allow others to recalculate and reinterpret his results (2001: 32–3, 55–60).

the *New York Times* (*NYT*), the *Sydney Morning Herald* (*SMH*) and *The Independent* (published in Great Britain), all sampled for 1995:

(15)   *Committee* nouns in written American English, Australian English and British English (Levin 2001: 108)

	verb		relative pronoun		personal pronoun	
	N	% plural	N	% plural	N	% plural
NYT	3,233	3	702	24	1,383	32
SMH	2,106	10	498	26	746	39
Independent	2,943	23	710	41	1,094	56

There is a substantial amount of information here for the three positions on the Agreement Hierarchy where there is a potential choice (recall that in attributive position we find 0% semantic agreement for these controllers). For each sample, there is striking evidence of a monotonic increase in semantic agreement as we move rightwards along the hierarchy. There are considerable differences between the varieties, with American English having the fewest examples of semantic agreement, though there are some; British English, as expected, has most, with Australian English in between.

We can now compare with the spoken language. Here Levin sampled the Longman Spoken American Corpus (LSAC), which has five million words, and the ten-million word section of the British National Corpus (BNC) devoted to spoken language (he did not have a corpus of spoken Australian English):

(16)   *Committee* nouns in spoken American English and British English (Levin 2001: 109)

	verb		relative pronoun		personal pronoun	
	N	% plural	N	% plural	N	% plural
LSAC	524	9	43	74	239	94
BNC	2,086	32	277	58	607	72

Again the data provide solid support for the Agreement Hierarchy: semantic agreement increases monotonically, in both samples. Both samples show considerably higher rates of semantic agreement than in the respective written language samples in (15). These data also show that the behaviour of the pronoun fits into the pattern of the other targets, and is not to be separated off as a different phenomenon.

Sometimes when assessing evidence relevant to the Agreement Hierarchy we have to group items together in order to have sufficient examples on which to base any claim. With Levin's investigation there is sufficient data for us to consider individual lexical items. We can see the behaviour of four individual lexical items as controllers:

(17) Predicate agreement with different lexical items in different varieties of English

	American NYT		Australian SMH		New Zealand DOM/EVP		American LSAC		British CBA		British Independent		British BNC	
	N	%pl	N	%pl	N	%pl	N	%pl	N	%pl	N	%pl	N	%pl
government	191	0	345	0	100	0	27	4	3,282	4	365	5	383	18
committee	149	0	123	5	100	1	27	4	281	9	137	9	104	26
team	154	1	161	7	100	7	28	11	656	32	145	37	97	37
family	162	4	118	16	100	41	117	5	848	40	173	37	102	43

Note: data from *NYT, SMH*, LSAC, *Independent* and BNC are from Levin (2001: 166–169); data on New Zealand English, from the newspapers *Dominion* and *Evening Post*, are from Hundt (1998: 82), who counted 100 examples for each item; CBA indicates data from the British English component of the Cobuild Bank of English, about five million words from newpapers, magazines and ephemera, also including some spoken language (Depraetere 2003: 110–11).

There are considerable differences between the varieties, and between written and spoken language.[8] But it is also striking that the different lexical items take semantic agreement to widely differing degrees. And yet, where there is sufficient data available on all the targets (as provided in Levin 2001: 165–9), there is a remarkable degree of fit with the Agreement Hierarchy. It is therefore possible to test fully the claim that the Agreement Hierarchy constrains 'any controller that permits alternative agreements' (this was largely the case with Russian nouns like *vrač* 'doctor', but Levin's data are even fuller). We return to *committee* nouns when we discuss 'real distance' in §7.7.4.

7.3 Overview of evidence: lexical hybrids

Having looked at four representative sets of data in detail, I will now review other evidence more quickly, starting with lexical hybrids. We have already looked at two important examples, Russian *vrač* '(woman) doctor' and English *committee*. These illustrate gender and number in turn, and we shall consider further examples according to the feature involved.[9] My account will be brief, since fuller descriptions are available elsewhere (as will be indicated). I shall pick examples to give a sense of the range of data covered by the Agreement Hierarchy.

[8] And even between types of subject matter. In the witty *Football Lexicon* there is the example *Newcastle were lucky* with the comment: 'There is no surer way of betraying an ignorance of football than that of using a singular instead' (Leigh & Woodhouse 2004: 167). A computational perspective on the lexical semantics of these nouns is provided by Copestake (1995).

[9] We find mismatches in person (§5.5.1), but typically these involve a single domain and so are not relevant for the Agreement Hierarchy.

7.3.1   Gender

We noted in §1.4.4 that gender is the canonical agreement feature, and we discussed it further in §4.3.1. Gender often gives rise to lexical mismatches, because of conflicting principles of assignment. These may be restricted to relatively few nouns (for instance 'child' and related nouns to be discussed in this section) or they may be substantial in number (as with the Russian nouns for profession discussed in §7.2.3). Gender provides a good deal of relevant data. The evidence that was available and given in detail in Corbett (1991: 225–60) is given briefly here, together with some new data.

Words for children, particularly for girls, are often hybrid nouns. The German *Mädchen* 'girl' is regularly cited to illustrate the Agreement Hierarchy. It takes neuter agreement of the attributive modifier, neuter agreement of the relative pronoun, but with some examples of feminine agreement too, and neuter or feminine with the personal pronoun. A similar but clearer example, since it shows agreement at all positions on the Agreement Hierarchy, is Serbian/Croatian/Bosnian *d(j)evojče* 'girl, lass'. Leko (2000) constructed this example of the expected forms (as well as giving more complex examples from a corpus):

Serbian/Croatian/Bosnian (Bosnian variant: Leko 2000: 263)
(18)   **T-o**   djevojč-e   **koj-e**   plač-e   je   **doš-l-o**   juče,
        That-N.SG   girl-SG   who-N.SG   cry-3SG   AUX.3SG   come-PST-N.SG   yesterday,

        ali   sam   **ga**   / **je**[10]   već   zavoli-o.
        but   AUX.1SG   3SG.N.ACC   /3SG.F.ACC   already   like-PST-M.SG

        'That girl who is crying arrived yesterday, and yet I already like (have started to like) her.'

This example includes an instance of each of the Agreement Hierarchy positions. Each shows syntactic agreement (neuter singular), and only in the personal pronoun is semantic agreement available as an alternative to syntactic agreement.

Titles often give mismatches. For example, with French titles, some of which are now obsolete, the agreements are rather surprising. Many titles used of men take feminine agreement, following their form, for instance:

French (Cocteau, quoted by Grevisse 1964: 314)
(19)   Votre Éminence est   trop   bonne
        Your eminence COP.3SG too   good.F.SG
        'Your Eminence is too kind.'

Éminence 'eminence' (like similar titles) is established as a noun, and by the normal assignment rules it is feminine. This gender is maintained when the noun is used as a title, in all positions on the Agreement Hierarchy. Only the personal

---

[10]   The first *je* in the example is a verbal clitic. This one is an object clitic, occurring later in the clitic cluster than *sam*, the verbal clitic.

pronoun admits the masculine, and then less frequently than the feminine (syntactically agreeing) form (Grevisse 1964: 314, 405–6; Corbett 1991: 226–7). We return to French titles in §7.6.2. Another instance where semantic agreement is available only in the personal pronoun (and even then as an alternative to syntactic agreement) is Chichewa diminutives (Corbett 1991: 248–50).

Returning to titles, we find that in Spanish too they take feminine agreement in attributive position:

Spanish (John England, personal communication)
(20)   Su   Majestad Suprem-a
         his[SG]   majesty   supreme-F.SG
         'His Supreme Majesty'

Unlike French, in all other positions the masculine is used (Corbett 1991: 230).

A rather different situation is found in Konkani (an Indo-Aryan language of the Indian west coast), which has developed an interesting set of semantic assignment rules for gender. Neuter agreements are used for nouns denoting females who are young, or young relative to the speaker. Some hybrid nouns take neuter and feminine agreements. When a young or relatively younger female is referred to, the use of the neuter represents the agreement with greater semantic justification in the new gender system. In appropriate circumstances the hybrid *awoy* 'mother' takes neuter agreements for all targets, except attributive modifiers, where the feminine is used:

Konkani (Miranda 1975: 211)
(21)   jɔnič-i   awoy   ayl-ɛ̃
         John.POSS-F.SG   mother(F) came-N.SG
         'John's mother came.'

The possessive adjective in (21) shows syntactic (feminine) agreement and the verbal predicate (like other agreeing targets) shows semantic agreement.

So far in this section we have looked at examples where only one target has allowed a choice of forms. At this point Russian *vrač* '(woman) doctor' (§7.2.3) fits into the picture; this readily takes semantic agreement in more positions. We next move to two examples which are also more complex, this time because the agreement choice is found only when the controller is plural. Thus Serbian/Croatian/Bosnian nouns like *gazda* 'landlord, master, boss' denote males, but are declined according to a pattern which includes mainly feminine nouns. In the singular the semantic criterion overrides the morphological, as expected, and masculine agreements are found. But when the noun is plural, feminine (syntactic) and masculine (semantic) agreements are found. The following examples are from the newspaper *Oslobođenje*, typically from the sports section (and involving male football teams):

Serbian/Croatian/Bosnian (Marković 1954: 95–6)

(22)   Sarajlij-e   su   **nadigra-l-e**   sv-og
            Sarajevan-PL.NOM   AUX.3PL   defeat-PST-F.PL   REFL-ANIM.M.SG.ACC

            protivnik-a
            opponent(ANIM.M)-SG.ACC

            'the Sarajevans defeated their opponent'

Example (22) shows syntactic agreement. Semantic (masculine plural) agreement of the predicate is also possible:

(23)   Sarajlij-e   su   **dominira-l-i**   teren-om
            Sarajevan-PL.NOM   AUX.3PL   dominate-PST-M.PL   pitch-SG.INS

            'the Sarajevans dominated the pitch'

In attributive position we can find syntactic agreement:

(24)   Ov-im   svoj-im   rad-om   **naš-e**
            this-M.SG.INS   REFL-M.SG.INS   work(M)-SG.INS   our-F.PL.NOM

            zanatlij-e   su   **dokaza-l-i**
            artisan-PL.NOM   AUX.3PL   prove-PST-M.PL

            'By this work of theirs our artisans proved . . .'

Example (24) is particularly interesting in that it also shows semantic agreement of the predicate, demonstrating again that hybrids can control different agreements at the same time. The attributive can also, if less commonly, show semantic agreement:

(25)   **mnog-i**   Sarajlij-e
            many-M.PL   Sarajevan-PL.NOM
            'many Sarajevans'

Information on the relative frequency of the options depends on small samples (see Corbett 1983: 14–17): in attributive position feminine (syntactic) agreement occurs in over half the instances. The samples indicate that in the predicate the masculine is the more common. The relative pronoun also allows both agreements; it favours semantic agreement and does so to a greater extent than the predicate. Limited data on the personal pronoun suggest that it is normally masculine (semantic agreement). Again we have a pattern which fully conforms to the Agreement Hierarchy. Though the data are patchy, these nouns are worth noting because they provide valuable evidence on other phenomena below (namely stacking (§7.7.2) and parallelism (§7.7.3)), and since the agreement choice involved occurs in the plural only.

This restriction to the plural is shared by another interesting phenomenon, this time in Polish. Polish has a complex gender system, with three genders in the singular, roughly comparable to those of Russian (§4.3.1), but in the plural there is a split into masculine personal and all others. Thus *Polak* 'Pole' has a plural form involving consonant alternation *Polacy*, and takes masculine personal agreements (for example *mil-i Polacy* 'nice-M.PERS.PL Poles'), while *Polka* 'Polish woman' has the plural *Polki* and, like all remaining types of noun, takes non-masculine-personal agreements (for example *mił-e Polki* 'nice-NON_M.PERS.PL Polish women'). There are some hybrid nouns: *łajdaki* 'scoundrels, wretches', is a plural of *łajdak*, showing non-masculine personal morphology, despite denoting male humans. This form takes non-masculine personal agreements in attributive position:

Polish

(26)   T-e   łajdak-i   ... On-i ...
          this.NON_M.PERS.PL.NOM   wretch-PL.NOM   ... 3-M.PERS.PL
          'those wretches ... They ...'

The personal pronoun is masculine personal (*oni*). For the other two positions, there is considerable variation among speakers (and different lexical items in the group behave somewhat differently). Rothstein (1980: 85–6) found both forms possible in the predicate, while in the relative pronoun the masculine personal form predominates. This is fully consistent with the Agreement Hierarchy. I record this pattern below, while bearing in mind that speakers vary greatly.

I review the evidence in summary form, reordered according to the readiness with which semantic agreement occurs:

(27)   The Agreement Hierarchy: evidence from gender agreement

	attributive	predicate	relative pronoun	personal pronoun
French titles	f	f	f	f / (M)
Chichewa diminutive for human	class 12	class 12	class 12	class 12/ (CLASS 1)
Serbian/Croatian/Bosnian *d(j)evojče* 'girl'	n	n	n	n / F
Polish *łajdaki* 'wretches'	non_m.pers	non_m.pers / M.PERS	M.PERS	M.PERS
Spanish titles	f	M	M	M
Konkani young females	f	N	no data	N
Russian *vrač* 'doctor' (§7.2.3)	m / (F)	m / F	(m) / F	(m) / F
Serbian/Croatian/Bosnian *gazde* 'bosses'	f / (M)	(f) / M	((f)) / M	M

Notes: 1. lower case indicates syntactic agreement, and upper case SEMANTIC AGREEMENT
2. parentheses indicate a less frequent variant
3. where I did not cover all the cells of the table, the full data are in Corbett (1991: 226–36)

The picture is clear. We have hybrid controllers of very different types, and their agreement patterns all conform to the Agreement Hierarchy. Table 7.1 gives sources of additional evidence.

Table 7.1 *The Agreement Hierarchy: additional evidence from gender*

language	controller	source
Bulgarian	personal names	Mladenova (2001: 39–41)
Bulgarian	titles	Osenova (2003: 666)
Czech	*děvče* 'girl' (colloquial)	Vanek (1970: 87–8; Corbett (1983: 11–12)
Dutch	diminutives like *jongetje* 'little boy'	Tasmowski & Verluyten (1985: 352–3)
French	*ministre* 'minister'	Boel (1976: 66–7)
French	*sentinelle* 'sentry, guard'	Tasmowski & Verluyten (1985: 353), Cornish (1986: 160–1)
German	*Mädchen* 'girl"	Corbett (1991: 228), Zubin & Köpcke (2005)
German	*Person* 'person', *Waise* 'orphan'	Zubin & Köpcke (2005)
Greek	*koritsi* 'girl'	Valiouli (1997)
Icelandic	professions	Grönberg (2002: 166–9)
Landuma	non-human animates	Wilson (1962: 28–9), Corbett (1991: 229–30)
Lavukaleve	*ruima* 'old man'	Terrill (2003: 142–4)
Old English	*bearn* 'child', *cild* 'child'	Curzan (2003: 62–4)
Polish	*ofiara* 'victim'	Herbert & Nykiel-Herbert (1986: 66–7)
Polish	titles	Corbett (1983: 23)
Russian	*značiteľnoe lico* 'important person' (usage of Gogolʹ)	Corbett (1981)
Russian	titles	Corbett (1983: 23–4)
Serbian/Croatian/ Bosnian	personal names	Mladenova (2001: 39–41)
Swedish	*barn* 'child'	Källström (1993: 263–5)
Swedish	*statsråd* 'member of the government'	Andersson (2000: 553–4)

Note: Some sources do not give information on all four hierarchy positions.

7.3.2   Number

For examples involving number let us first look at Russian *para* when meaning 'couple, man and woman'. In the following example (used in §2.2.2 to illustrate agreement of the relative pronoun) we find singular agreement of the attributive adjective, predicate and relative pronoun:

Russian (Bunin, *Gospodin iz San-Francisko* 'The Man from San Francisco')

(28)   . . . **by-l-a   izjaščn-aja   vljublenn-aja**   par-a,
          be-PST-F.SG elegant-F.SG.NOM loving-F.SG.NOM couple(F)-SG.NOM

          za   **kotor-oj**   vs-e   s   ljubopytstv-om sledi-l-i
          after which-F.SG.INS all-PL.NOM with curiosity-SG.INS follow-PST-PL

          'there was an elegant loving couple, who everyone watched with curiosity . . .'

Further reference with the personal pronoun is with the plural *oni* 'they' (Corbett 1983: 12–13). This means that we find semantic agreement with this hybrid just on the extreme right of the hierarchy.

We have already discussed *committee* nouns, with their different pattern of agreement, but which belong here as hybrids in number. We review the evidence in (29).

(29)   The Agreement Hierarchy: distribution of number agreement

	attributive	Predicate	relative pronoun	personal pronoun
Russian *para* 'couple'	sg	sg	sg	PL
English *committee* (§7.2.4)	sg	sg / (PL) (PL 9%)	(sg) / PL (PL 74%)	(sg) / PL (PL 94%)

Notes: for *committee* nouns I take the figures for spoken American English from (16) above

Table 7.2 *The Agreement Hierarchy: additional evidence from number*

language	controller	source
Old Russian (11th–14th centuries)	collectives	Igartua (2004)
Spanish (Lena dialect)	mass nouns	Hualde (1992), Corbett (2000: 124–6, 192–3n13)
Spanish	collectives	Nuessel (1984)
Old Church Slavonic	collectives	Huntley (1989: 24–5)
Samoan	collectives (like *aiga* 'family')	Mosel & Hovdhaugen (1992: 91, 443)
Serbian/Croatian/ Bosnian	collectives (like *unučad* 'grandchildren')	Wechsler & Zlatić (2003: 75–6): gender also affected
Serbian/Croatian/ Bosnian	*d(j)eca* 'children'	Corbett (1983: 76–88): gender also affected

Note: not all sources give information on all four hierarchy positions

These examples fit the requirements of the Agreement Hierarchy. Compared with the variety of evidence from gender, number seems not such a rich source. Our examples in (29) and most of those in Table 7.2, could all be called 'collectives' in the broadest sense. However, these are common, both as types cross-linguistically and as tokens in texts. Furthermore, the number feature figures more prominently in constructional mismatches (§7.4) than in lexical hybrids (the converse of the picture with gender). This makes good sense since, the number feature typically corresponds to its semantic base more closely than does gender.

7.4   Overview of evidence: constructional mismatches

In the previous section the mismatches could be pinned on particular lexical items. We now look at instances where they arise from a construction. The opposition of syntactic and semantic agreement in these cases may again be realized in terms of gender and/or number, but there are other possibilities, as we shall see.

7.4.1   Conjoined noun phrases

As we established in §5.7, with conjoined noun phrases the possibilities are agreement with one conjunct (normally the nearest), which is syntactic agreement, or agreement with all the conjuncts. The latter involves resolution, to determine the feature values, and represents semantic agreement. Our key language Russian is particularly helpful here. Take this significant example:

Russian (Černov, Introduction to Smol'janinov, *Sredi morennyx xolmov*)
(30)   **Èt-a**   vyskatel'nost,   samokritičnost'   tože
         This-F.SG.NOM   exactingness(F)[SG.NOM]   self-criticalness(F)[SG.NOM]   also

         raspolagal-i   k   nemu.
         disposed-PL   to   3SG.M.DAT

         'This exactingness and self-criticalness also disposed me favourably towards him.'

The attributive modifier is singular, agreeing with the nearer conjunct. The predicate is plural, showing agreement with both conjuncts (number resolution has applied). The fact that we find singular agreement and plural agreement with the same controller is significant. If we were to try to account for the singular agreement of the attributive modifier by treating the coordinate phrases as unbalanced,[11] then we could not naturally account for the plural agreement of the predicate.

---

[11] Such analyses treat the conjunction as the head, with the conjuncts having different status as specifier and complement, as, for instance, in Johannessen (1996); there is helpful critical commentary in Borsley (2005).

I have already established that the predicate can be singular or plural (§5.7). What is particularly interesting about Russian is that the attributive modifier can also be plural, that is, we have resolution (representing semantic agreement) within the noun phrase:

Russian (Solženicyn *Rakovyj korpus* 'Cancer Ward')

(31)   A   **èt-i**   brat   i   sestr-a   skaza-l-i:
          but this-PL.NOM brother(M)[SG.NOM] and sister(F)-SG.NOM say-PST-PL

          poduma-em.
          think-1PL

          'But this brother and sister said: Let's think.'

Examples like (31), with a plural attributive, are easier to find if the controller is animate (§6.1.2). Taking all examples (inanimates as well as animates) in attributive position the singular is more likely.[12] A sample of literary prose was scanned,[13] and these were the results:

(32)   Number agreement with Russian conjoined noun

attributive	predicate	relative pronoun	personal pronoun
sg / (PL)	(sg) / PL	((sg)) / PL	PL
(PL 12% N=34)	(PL 70% N=230)	(PL 100% N=10)	(PL 100% N=10)

Semantic agreement is possible but less likely in attributive position. In the predicate the plural is more likely, but there is a sizable minority of examples of the singular. In the other two positions our small corpus suggests that there is semantic agreement. In fact, wider investigation shows that the relative pronoun takes syntactic (singular) agreement in a small minority of instances (see Corbett 1983: 73–4, 159). Examples of singular personal pronouns occur, but are vanishingly rare. Thus we have another pattern in accord with the Agreement Hierarchy, including the unusual possibility of plural agreement in attributive position with conjoined noun phrases. The examples here have involved only number, but there are languages where gender too is involved. Note too that comitative phrases (*Ivan s Mašej* 'Ivan with Masha') behave broadly similarly in Russian with respect to agreement, except that overall they show lower proportions of semantic agreement.

---

[12] See King & Dalrymple (2004) for an attempt to address the issue within Lexical-Functional Grammar, and Dalrymple & Nikolaeva (2004) for interesting data on Finnish, Hindi and Nenets. Another language which allows number resolution within the noun phrase is Archi (Kibrik 1994: 343).

[13] Works by Amal'rik, Nabokov and Vojnovič, details in Corbett (1983: 106, 158).

7.4.2 Syntactic head versus semantic head in complex noun phrases

In a phrase like *the house of my best friends* the head of the phrase is *the house*, both syntactically and semantically (the whole phrase refers to an object and not to a set of people). We therefore expect agreement to be singular. However, there are various types of phrase with apparently similar structure where the headedness relations are not so clear; thus *a mountain of a man* is a man rather than a mountain, and *a peach of an example* is not very edible. In such instances agreement choices may arise. When they do, these choices are constrained by the Agreement Hierarchy:

French (Hulk & Tellier 1999: 183)

(33)   **Ton**   phénomène   de fille   est   bien   **distrait-e.**
        your.M.SG   phenomenon(M)   of   daughter(F)   COP.3SG   quite   absent-minded-FEM.SG
        'That amazing daughter of yours is quite absent-minded.'

In this example it is clear that reference is to a person, not to a thing: the semantic head is *fille* 'daughter'. Now consider the syntax. The attributive modifier is *ton* 'your', which is masculine singular, agreeing with the syntactic head (**ta* (F) is not acceptable). The predicate on the other hand agrees with *fille* 'daughter'; agreement with the syntactic head (**distrait* (M)) is unacceptable. This is the beginning of a familiar pattern. We should ask what happens in other domains:

French (consultant)

(34)   Ton   phénomène   de fille,   avec **laquelle**
        your.M.SG   phenomenon(M)   of   daughter(F)   with   REL.F.SG

        je   viens   de parl-er . . .   **Elle** . . .
        1SG   come.1SG   of   speak-INF . . .   3SG.FEM . . .

        'That amazing daughter of yours, with whom I have just been speaking . . . She . . .'

The relative pronoun agrees with the semantic head, as does the personal pronoun (the masculine forms **lequel* and **il* are not acceptable). Thus we find a pattern of syntactic agreement in attributive position and semantic agreement elsewhere, a pattern fully in accord with the Agreement Hierarchy. There are complications concerning animacy, there are instances of lexicalization, languages vary of course, but it appears that these constructions are constrained by the Agreement Hierarchy. Hulk & Tellier (1999) discuss comparable examples (primarily agreement of the predicate) in French, Italian and Spanish, and the French and Spanish constructions are analysed further in Casillas Martínez (2003).

There are several types of related construction, in which the balance between syntactic and semantic head can differ. There are numerous quantified expressions (*a bag of . . . a couple of . . .* and so on), which in different languages give rise to agreement choices (see, for instance, Veselovská (2001) on Czech). Numerals can be more or less noun-like, and so more or less likely to control agreement. There is an interesting regularity that, for the simple numerals, the larger the cardinality, the more noun-like they are (see Corbett 2000: 213–18, and §9.1.5). If the syntactic head loses its head-like properties, we have constructions like *this sort of people* (§2.4.6).

Finally we should note that the possibility for the 'wrong' part of a complex noun phrase to control agreement in such constructions, together with the influence of linear order, can lead to cases of 'attraction' in ordinary complex noun phrases, for instance:

George Bush (Washington, 23 January 2004)
(35)   . . . the illiteracy level of our children are appalling.

Attraction is discussed by den Dikken (2001); we return to psycholinguists' interest in attraction in §9.4.2.

7.4.3   Default form versus agreement

In §5.2.2 we met examples of 'pancake sentences':

Norwegian (Bokmål/Nynorsk, Faarlund 1977: 240)
(36)   Pannekake-r   er   **god-t.**
            pancake-PL   COP   good-N.SG
            'Pancakes is good.' ('Eating pancakes is good.')

There is a mismatch, in that we have a noun phrase which has an agreement feature (number) available, and yet the default form (neuter singular) is used. (This links to the last section, in that we have what looks like a simple noun phrase, but it is treated as a complex one.) As we noted in §5.2.2, based on Swedish examples, different targets do not behave alike. We can see this in a comparable Norwegian sentence:

Norwegian (Bokmål, Enger 2004: 20)
(37)   **Nystekt-e**   pannekake-r   er   **god-t**.
            new.fried-PL   pancake-PL   COP   good-N.SG
            'Newly-fried pancakes is good.' ('Eating newly-fried pancakes is good.')

We need to ask what would happen with a relative pronoun, an issue not discussed in the literature. Though the relative pronoun does not inflect, we can infer its feature specification from a predicate adjective in the relative clause:

Norwegian (Bokmål, Hans-Olav Enger, personal communication)
(38)   Narkotika,   **som**   er   **grusom-t**   for   både   misbrukere   og
            Narcotic(M)[SG], which   COP   awful-N.SG   for   both   addicts   and

            pårørende,   **de-t**   skulle   aldri   vært   oppfunnet.
            relatives.spouses, it-N.SG   should   never   been   invented

            'Drugs, which is awful for both addicts and those close to them, – it should never have been invented.'

Here we see that the relative pronoun controls neuter agreement on *grusomt* 'awful', and so, we infer, has a default specification. The mismatch is in gender, since the noun phrase is masculine singular. The example illustrates the personal pronoun as well, also neuter. We therefore have gender/number agreement in attributive position, and the use of the default in the other hierarchy positions. Thus this interesting construction is an unusual illustration of conformity with the Agreement Hierarchy.

7.4.4   Schematic view of constructional mismatches

Here we put together the data from constructional mismatches, including those we discussed as representative data and the examples from §7.4.

(39)   The Agreement Hierarchy: evidence from constructional mismatches

	attributive	predicate	relative pronoun	personal pronoun
Russian conjoined noun phrases (§7.4.1)	sg / (PL) (PL 14%)	(sg) / PL (PL 71%)	(sg) / PL	((sg)) / PL
Serbian/Croatian/Bosnian lower numeral phrases (§7.2.1)	remnant	remnant / (M.PL) (M.PL 18%)	(remnant) / M.PL (M.PL 62%)	M.PL
French complex noun phrases (§7.4.2)	syntactic head	SEMANTIC HEAD	SEMANTIC HEAD	SEMANTIC HEAD
Norwegian agreement vs. default (§7.4.3)	agreement	DEFAULT	DEFAULT	DEFAULT
Associatives (Talitsk Russian) (§7.2.2)	sg	PL	no data	PL

Note: as earlier, lower case indicates syntactic agreement, and upper case SEMANTIC AGREEMENT; parentheses indicate a less frequent variant.

These rather different constructions all conform to the Agreement Hierarchy. There is a little additional evidence from two further sources. First, from Qafar conjoined noun phrases, where there is a choice between default agreement (the surprising outcome when agreement is with the nearer conjunct) or resolution (Hayward & Corbett 1988: 275; Corbett 2000: 203–6). And second from Russian expressions of respect (Corbett 1983: 24–5), as introduced in §1.2 example (11).

7.5   Roles of the Agreement Hierarchy

In its basic role of constraining agreement options, the Agreement Hierarchy covers a good deal of disparate data. In addition, however, it has additional roles; as with other hierarchies, having different functions makes the case for the hierarchy more convincing.

7.5.1 Constraining agreement choices

We have seen remarkably varied agreement choices, and yet there is a clear pattern, namely a monotonic increase in the likelihood of semantic agreement along the hierarchy. Thus the Agreement Hierarchy constrains the distribution of agreement choices. This holds for different types of controller, from lexical hybrids through to various constructional mismatches. It interacts with resolution (discussed in chapter 8) since resolution produces semantically agreeing forms. It extends even to the idiosyncratic use of a given controller by a single author (Corbett 1981). It generalizes over different features, especially number and gender, and also over more abstract notions such as agreement with one conjunct or all conjuncts. It generalizes over instances where there is a sharp cut-off at a particular position on the hierarchy (as with English *committee*, where semantic agreement is absolutely excluded in attributive position) and where there are gradual transitions, as between predicate and relative pronoun in the Serbian/Croatian/Bosnian construction discussed in §7.2.1. It covers a wide range of different languages (though this range is partly limited by the need for very detailed studies, which are not available for many languages). The Agreement Hierarchy also covers the varying data of varieties of a language, as we saw for the varieties of English in §7.4.2, and it covers sociolinguistic variation (Corbett 1983: 30–9). It is a path for linguistic change, as shown, for instance, in the gender systems of various Bantu languages (Wald 1975; Corbett 1991: 248–59). Finally Kirby (1999: 92–6) discusses the place of the Agreement Hierarchy in the emergence of language universals.

7.5.2 Constraining possible targets (of possessive adjectives)

The Agreement Hierarchy also has a different role, in determining possible targets of agreement, as can be seen in the following Slavonic data. In §2.1.4 we considered possessive adjectives as unusual agreement controllers:

Upper Sorbian (Faßke 1981: 385):
(40) To je **naš-eho** wučerj-ow-a zahrodk-a.
      That be.3SG our-M.SG.GEN teacher(M)-POSS-F.SG.NOM garden(F)-SG.NOM
      'That is our teacher's garden.'

The adjective *wučerj-ow-* 'teacher's', formed from *wučer* 'teacher', controls the agreement of the adjective *naš* 'our'. The latter is masculine singular, agreeing with the adjective, not with *zahrodka* 'garden', the head of the noun phrase. This is unusual behaviour both within Slavonic and beyond it. This is not the only possible target type here, since example (40) can continue:

(41)   **Wón**   wjele w njej   dźěła.
        3[M.SG.NOM] a.lot in 3SG.FEM.LOC work[3SG]
        'He [our teacher] works in it a lot.'

The agreement of the personal pronoun *wón* is controlled by the possessive adjective phrase (realizing the antecedent phrase *naš wučer* 'our teacher'). This is less remarkable; it is possible in all the Slavonic languages. There are also examples of the possessive adjective controlling the relative pronoun:

Upper Sorbian (Lötzsch 1965: 378; for more examples see Faßke 1981: 385)
(42)   ... Wićaz-ow-y   hłós,   **kotryž**   je   zastupi-ł
        Wićaz-POSS-M.SG.ACC voice(M)[SG.ACC], who.M.SG.NOM AUX.3SG go.in-PST[M.SG]
        '... Wićaz's voice, who has gone in'

The relative pronoun *kotryž* is masculine singular; the full context shows that its antecedent is *Wićaz*, the noun underlying the possessive adjective, and not *hłós* (which is also masculine singular); for contemporary speakers, however, there are various problems with relative pronouns (Eduard Werner, personal communication).

For the possessive adjective to be able to control an attributive modifier (as in (40)) is highly unusual, and the construction appears to be in decline. Apart from Upper Sorbian, only Slovak has this (and to a very limited extent). It is more common to have control of the relative pronoun (as in (42)). Control of the anaphoric pronoun (as in (41)) is found in all the languages (apart from some limitations in Polish). This is made clear in (43).

(43)   Control possibilities of the possessive adjective

	attributive	relative pronoun	personal pronoun
East Slavonic			
Russian	□	□	■
Russian (19th Century)	□	◪	■
Old Russian	◪	■	■
Belarusian	□	□	■
Ukrainian	□	□	■
South Slavonic			
Bulgarian	□	□	■
Macedonian	□	■	■
Slovene	□	◪	■
Serbian/Croatian/Bosnian	□	◪	■
Old Church Slavonic	□	■	■
West Slavonic			
Polish	□	□	◪
Czech	□	◪	■
Slovak	◪	◪	■
Lower Sorbian	□	■	■
Upper Sorbian	■	■	■

There is therefore an implicational hierarchy of possible targets for the possessive adjective:

(44)   The Control Hierarchy

> attributive > relative pronoun > personal pronoun

As we move rightward along the Control Hierarchy (44), the likelihood of control by the possessive adjective will increase monotonically. This control hierarchy can be subsumed under the Agreement Hierarchy. It is identical to it, except that the predicate is omitted, for reasons discussed in Corbett (1987: 320–1). The hierarchy has a rather different role here. While the Agreement Hierarchy is concerned with situations where agreement is required, but where there is a choice, the Control Hierarchy is concerned with the possibility of controlling an element whose very presence is optional. The Control Hierarchy consists of those elements of the Agreement Hierarchy which are optional.

Finally it is worth noting that back agreement (§2.4.4) in Latin is controlled by the Agreement Hierarchy, being excluded in attributive position, possible in the predicate, frequent with the relative pronoun and obligatory with the personal pronoun (Corbett 1979: 205–6).

7.6   Implications of the Agreement Hierarchy

The Agreement Hierarchy has some interesting implications. It highlights the gradient nature of agreement choices, which is challenging for syntactic theory, particularly since a single controller can control different feature values on different targets at the same time. Examples of this are: (10), (21), (24), (30), (33), (34), (37), (46), (60) and (61). It helps us to understand the syntax of relative pronouns: if the relative pronoun is simply an element of the noun phrase, we would expect it to be structurally closer to the head noun phrase than the predicate is, and yet the evidence of the Agreement Hierarchy points in the other direction. Two points deserve closer consideration. The first is that personal pronouns are in some senses integrated into the agreement system (§7.6.1). The second is that splitting agreement into two types does not solve the problem posed by agreement choices (§7.6.2).

7.6.1   The status of personal pronouns

The Agreement Hierarchy constrains agreement choices for personal pronouns, just as it does with other targets. Moreover, the diachronic development of agreement choices makes no sharp distinction between personal pronouns and other agreement targets (Corbett 1991: 248–59). These are additional arguments why personal pronouns should be treated as agreement targets (§1.4.3, §2.2.2). We have already noted that they frequently realize the same features as other targets;

they are also subject to resolution in the same way (§8.5.3). Barlow (1992: 134–52) reviews relevant research at greater length and concludes that there are no good grounds for distinguishing between agreement and antecedent-anaphora relations. Of course, this is not to say that pronouns are 'just' agreement. Their distribution and their control by antecedents are separate issues. But they are also a part of what a theory of agreement must account for. Thus controller and pronoun constitute a domain of agreement (one of the least canonical domains). For interesting discussion see Wechsler & Zlatić (2003: 197–225). The argument for including pronouns as agreement targets will be reinforced in the next section.

7.6.2   Splitting agreement: no solution to the problem of choices

When attempting to account for agreement choices, a common first move is to split agreement into two different phenomena. Barlow (1992: 134) makes the point that those who would draw a major boundary within the domains of agreement, do so at different points. This in itself suggests that the evidence for a particular major boundary is weak.

One suggested boundary is between noun-phrase internal and noun-phrase external agreement. Setting such a boundary gives the wrong predictions for the data we have already examined. Relative pronouns are noun-phrase internal; but they do not, as would be predicted by such a boundary, pattern with attributive modifiers, as opposed to noun-phrase external agreement in the form of predicate agreement. As we noted earlier, the data show that relative pronouns are 'further away' in terms of the Agreement Hierarchy than are predicate agreement targets.

A second place where one might draw a boundary is between sentence internal and sentence external agreement. This has little merit, since personal pronouns occur both within the sentence and beyond it, without a clear-cut distinction (but see Levin 2001: 101 for frequency effects).

The most popular contender is local agreement versus anaphoric agreement. As Barlow says: 'This distinction is widely held – though rarely discussed' (1992: 139–40). Somewhat different accounts of such a distinction can be found in Bresnan & Mchombo (1987; taken up by Bresnan 2001a: 150–60) and in Zwicky (1987); see Barlow (1992: 139–52) for discussion of both. For Bresnan & Mchombo the distinction is important for investigating the status of markers on verbs, whether they are pronominal affixes or agreement markers in given languages (§3.8). The local-anaphoric distinction may be drawn differently for different languages, but even then it does not allow us to account for the agreement options laid out earlier. That is, local versus anaphoric agreement is a division of agreement into two types, differing according to the researcher, but it does not directly tell us how syntactic and semantic agreement will be distributed. For comparable distinctions in HPSG see Pollard & Sag (1994: 61–99),

Kathol (1999) and, for the most developed account, Wechsler & Zlatić (2003: 8–30).

Whichever way we attempt to split agreement into two phenomena, we do not thereby solve the problem of the distribution of agreement options. First, the boundary between local and anaphoric would have to be at different places in different languages. Even then the dividing line between where syntactic agreement and semantic agreement are found in a given language is not necessarily clear-cut, since we often find syntactic and semantic agreement as alternatives for a given agreement target (see §7.2.1, §7.2.3 and §7.2.4). Most importantly, agreement choices can be found at the extreme positions of the Agreement Hierarchy. Attributive modifiers must surely come within the domain of local agreement, if such a distinction is drawn, and yet we can find semantic agreement here (see (12)). On the other hand, the personal pronoun would be expected to fall under anaphoric agreement, and yet syntactic agreement can be found here (see (18)). I conclude that there are no good grounds for dividing agreement domains into two.

It is worth dwelling on the point about the personal pronoun, and illustrating it further, since this supports the conclusion of §7.6.1, namely that there is no principled way to distinguish the agreement variation of the pronoun from that of other targets. A telling instance comes from French, particularly earlier French, which used various titles (§7.3.1). The following example would be normal, according to Grevisse (1964: 405–6):

French (Voltaire, quoted by Grevisse 1964: 406)

(45) Votre   Majesté   part-ir-a   quand **elle**   voudr-a.
      2PL.POSS majesty(F) leave-FUT-3SG when   3SG.F   wish.FUT-3SG
      'Your Majesty will leave when he (literally 'she') wishes.'

The feminine pronoun is used, even though the king is addressed. Examples with a masculine pronoun also occur, but the feminine was more common. This shows that syntactic agreement is possible, and in this instance actually preferred, even for the personal pronoun.[14]

And finally, it is not clear that 'splitting' analyses are tackling the problem in terms of the right grammatical component. The constraints we have been discussing, in particular the Agreement Hierarchy, are violable at the 'sentence level'.[15] The Agreement Hierarchy does not necessarily rule out specific sentences, as this Serbian/Croatian/Bosnian example with a lower numeral (§7.2.1) shows:

---

[14] A more recent example of the use of syntactic agreement in the personal pronoun in French is provided by Gregory Stump, who points out (personal communication) that in the Jean Cocteau film *La belle et la bête* the beast – the male lead – is consistently referred to with the feminine pronoun *elle* 'she', since *bête* 'beast' is feminine.

[15] These constraints may also operate as a sentence-level constraint (Corbett 1983: 60–9), in which case the choice of form of one target is determined in part by the choice of form for another, but this is relatively unusual.

Serbian/Croatian/Bosnian (*Politika* 9.XII.1969, from Sand 1971: 63–5)

(46)   Dv-a   tim-a,   **koj-a**   se   nalaz-e   u   donj-em
two-M.NOM team(M) -REMNANT, which-REMNANT REFL find-3PL in lower-M.SG.LOC

del-u   tabel-e,   Radnički i   Olimpija, u   Kragujevc-u   na
part(M)-SG.LOC table-GEN.SG, Radnički and Olimpija, in Kragujevac-SG.LOC on

tešk-om   teren-u   **igra-l-i**   **su**   prljavo i   nesportski.
difficult-M.SG.LOC pitch(M)-SG.LOC played-PST-M.PL AUX.3PL dirtily and unsportingly

'Two teams, which find themselves in the lower part of the (league) table, Radnički and Olimpija, on a difficult pitch in Kragujevac played dirtily and unsportingly.'

Here we have semantic agreement of the predicate, but syntactic agreement of the relative pronoun. Though this is possible in individual sentences, this combination would not be possible generally (that is, throughout a corpus). Overall, the likelihood of agreement with greater semantic justification must be greater with the relative pronoun than with the predicate. That is the case with this type of controller in Serbian/Croatian/Bosnian (as the data in (9) demonstrate), but instances like (46) are not excluded.

7.7   Further constraints

We turn to additional constraints, which operate within the different agreement domains specified by the Agreement Hierarchy.

7.7.1   The Predicate Hierarchy

The Predicate Hierarchy (Comrie 1975) preceded the Agreement Hierarchy and partly inspired it. I shall suggest that it can be thought of as a sub-hierarchy of the Agreement Hierarchy.[16] Comrie showed how honorific plural pronouns may take singular or plural agreement, but that this variation is not random. He cited data from Slavonic languages (Polish dialects, Russian, Serbian/Croatian/Bosnian and Czech, for which see also §3.4.3), from Romance (French, Italian and Romanian) and from Modern Greek.

We will start from Bulgarian data. The pronoun *Vie* is the normal second person plural pronoun, but it can also be used politely of a single addressee. These are the agreements:

(47)   Bulgarian (Katina Bontcheva, personal communication)
Vie ste   razbra-l-i   vsičko.
you AUX.2PL understand-PST-PL everything
'You have understood everything.'

---

[16] A further sub-hierarchy, for the attributive position, has been suggested by Cornish (1986: 203–11), based on French data.
    There is also evidence that if at any position on the Agreement Hierarchy there is a difference between direct and oblique cases, the direct will favour semantic agreement (Corbett 1983: 84–8).

Even though one individual is addressed, the agreement of the auxiliary ('be') and of the past active participle is plural (syntactic agreement). Now contrast these examples:

(48)   Vie   ste   ljuboznatelen   / ljuboznateln-a.
         you COP.2PL inquisitive[M.SG] / inquisitive-F.SG
         'You are inquisitive.'

(49)   Vie   ste   poet.
         you COP.2PL poet (M)[SG] ...
         'You are a poet.'

In these examples the adjectival and nominal predicates show semantic agreement (singular in number, since there is one addressee, with the adjective being masculine or feminine according to the addressee).[17] These are the forms which descriptions of Bulgarian lead us to expect. However, the real picture is more interesting. A corpus of literary texts (about 400,000 words) reveals some variability; the instances where there is believed to be none are again given in '[ ]':

(50)   Semantic agreement (%) with honorific *Vie* 'you' in Bulgarian
         (Dončeva-Mareva 1978)

finite verb	active participle	adjective	noun
[0%]	4% (N=167)	97% (N=163)	[100%]

These data fit well with Comrie's analysis. He proposed what we may call the 'Predicate Hierarchy':

(51)   The Predicate Hierarchy

> verb > participle > adjective > noun

Reformulating Comrie's proposal, the constraint is:

> For any controller that permits alternative agreements, as we move rightwards along the Predicate Hierarchy, the likelihood of agreement with greater semantic justification will increase monotonically (that is, with no intervening decrease).

The Bulgarian data conform to this constraint.

One of our key languages, Russian, provides interesting support. As in Bulgarian, the main verb is plural with honorific *vy* 'you'; unlike in Bulgarian, the

[17] Wechsler & Zlatić (2003: 98–9) argue that the agreements with polite pronouns cannot be treated as semantic versus syntactic agreement, because the distribution of agreement options is different from that found with other controllers (they use French for illustration). However, we find several languages with different types of mismatch (for example, Serbian/Croatian/Bosnian *d(j)evojče* 'girl' and phrases with a lower numeral), and these do not all behave alike; it is therefore fully appropriate to treat the agreements with polite pronouns as being a further instance of semantic versus syntactic agreeement.

former past active participle appears in Russian without an auxiliary (§4.2.1), but it is again plural:

Russian

(52) a. Vy   plač-ete.   b. Vy   plaka-l-i.
        2PL.NOM   cry-2PL   2PL.NOM   cry-PST-PL
        'You are crying.'   'You were crying.'

The predicate noun is singular:

(53)   Vy   – poèt.
        2PL.NOM   poet[SG.NOM]
        'You are a poet.'

Some Russian adjectives have two possible forms, the 'short form', which is more verb-like, and is now restricted to predicate position, and the 'long form', more noun-like, which can appear in the predicate and in attributive position. As a target for honorific *vy* 'you', the agreements are normally as follows:

(54)   Vy   bol´n-y.
        2PL.NOM   ill-(SHORT FORM)PL
        'You are ill.' (one person addressed politely)

(55)   Vy   segodnja očen´ zadumčiv-aja.
        2PL.NOM   today   very   thoughtful-(LONG FORM)F.SG.NOM
        'You are very thoughtful today.' (one woman addressed politely)

Here the agreements differ according to whether we have a short form or long form adjective. The short form shows syntactic agreement and the long form semantic. This split within the adjectives highlights the gradient nature of the Predicate Hierarchy. While the agreements given above are those normally found, there is additional variation. In (56) there are combined figures from four different sources, not all of which included all positions in the count; this means that while the percentage figures can be taken as indicative, the totals for each category cannot be compared (see Corbett 1983: 53 for the sources):

(56)   Semantic agreement with honorific *vy* in Russian

| | active | short-form | long-form | |
finite verb	participle	adjective	adjective	noun
[0%]	0% (N=350)	3% (N=145)	89% (N=37)	100% (N=13)

Following Comrie (1975), I gathered data on all the Slavonic languages, adding Slovak, Lower Sorbian, Upper Sorbian, Macedonian, Slovene, Ukrainian and Belarusian to those already discussed; the data are in Corbett (2000: 194) and all conform to the Predicate Hierarchy. There are other controllers too, in addition to honorific pronouns, which are relevant, for instance, conjoined noun phrases. Data from such controllers lead us to ask how the Agreement Hierarchy and the

Predicate Hierarchy relate to each other. An obvious idea is to try expanding the Agreement Hierarchy by splitting the predicate position:

(57)
Expanded Agreement Hierarchy (invalid)
attributive > [verb > participle > adjective > noun] > relative pronoun > personal pronoun

Here the different predicates (within '[ ]') are fitted into the original predicate position. This is the wrong solution, since the predicate noun almost always shows semantically justified forms (Corbett 1983: 169–72), and to a greater degree than does the relative pronoun. We might try excluding the predicate nominal as being totally determined by semantics, and so being 'out of range' as an agreement target. However, there are rare examples which show that it is potentially an agreement target (Comrie 1975: 410–11; Corbett 1983: 169: 172; Corbett & Mtenje 1987: 9–10n3). This was found in nineteenth-century Russian, in the speech of the less educated:

(58)   Russian (Čexov, *Xolodnaja krov´* 1887; in Vinogradov & Istrina 1954: 520)
           Izmennik-i vy,   čto   li?
           traitor-PL   2PL   that   Q
           'Are you a traitor then?' (addressed to a single person)

If the predicate nominal is an agreement target, albeit a rare one, how do the hierarchies fit together? The Predicate Hierarchy is a genuine sub-hierarchy, and the relation may be diagrammed as follows:

(59)   The Agreement and Predicate Hierarchies

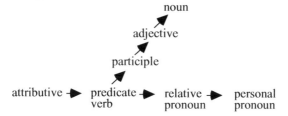

The claim for the monotonic increase in semantic agreement then applies to each link of the combined hierarchies.[18] For the evidence in favour of this solution, see Corbett (1983: 87–8 on Serbian/Croatian/Bosnian *deca* 'children', 89–92 on lower numerals, 163–74 on Russian conjoined noun phrases and on relative *kto* 'who') and Leko (2000: 271–7) on Serbian/Croatian/Bosnian lower numerals.[19] We return to the Predicate Hierarchy when we discuss interactions in §7.8.

---

[18] And specifically, semantic agreement will be more likely for predicate nouns than for predicate adjectives, and so on, but there is no direct claim about the relative frequency for predicate nouns as compared with relative pronouns.

[19] This result shows that I have weighted the odds against the Agreement Hierarchy in some of the counts presented, in those instances where I included various predicates and not just the verbal predicate in my comparisons. The effect of the Agreement Hierarchy is so robust that this does not normally give any problems (in general, the non-verbal predicates are relatively much less frequent, and so including them has a small effect).

7.7.2   Stacking

There are constructions in which a target and controller form a unit which then takes a further target of the same type, to give a structure of the sort [target [target controller]]. Recall from §7.3.1 that Serbian/Croatian/Bosnian nouns like *gazda* 'boss', when in the plural, permit both masculine and feminine modifiers. If we find stacked modifiers, usually both take the same form. This is not always so:

Serbian/Croatian/Bosnian (Marković 1954: 95; see p. 96 for a further example)
(60)   [**ov-i**   [**privatn-e**   zanatlij-e]]
        this-M.PL.NOM   private-F.PL.NOM   artisan-PL.NOM
        'these private artisans'

In (60) both agreement possibilities are found together. This is unusual: according to Leko (1986: 216) many speakers would not accept this combination, but would have *ov-e* 'this-F.PL'. Those who do accept different forms in stacked modifiers have them as in (60), with the form with greater semantic justification, the masculine, further from the controller (we do not find the reverse: **ove privatni zanatlije*). The constraint is as follows:

> If stacked targets show different agreements, the target further from the controller will show the form with greater semantic justification.

This contraint applies to different positions on the Agreement Hierarchy, though primarily to the attributive position. For examples of different agreements with stacked attributive modifiers in Chichewa and in Russian see Corbett (1991: 239–40; 1983: 70–1), and for stacked relative pronouns also in Russian see Corbett (1983: 73–4).

7.7.3   Parallelism

Two targets are said to be parallel when they fill the same syntactic slot in relation to the same controller. Usually we find the same agreement for both, but not always:

Serbian/Croatian/Bosnian (Oslobodenje 27.2.1953, quoted by Marković 1954: 96)
(61)   Sarajlij-e   **su**   **igral-e**   bolje   i   gotovo potpuno
        Sarajevan-PL.NOM   AUX.3PL   played-F.PL   better   and almost completely

        dominiral-i   teren-om.
        dominated-M.PL   field-SG.INS
        'The Sarajevans played better and dominated the field almost completely.'

The two verbal predicates are parallel. The controller of both is *Sarajlije* 'Sarajevans', another noun like *gazde* 'bosses'. The nearer target shows syntactic agreement while the further shows semantic agreement. This is not simply an instance of pro drop, since the second verb has no auxiliary. The following constraint applies:

> If parallel targets show different agreements, then the further target will show semantic agreement.

This constraint ranges over different target types; for further examples of predicates and an example of relative pronouns see Corbett (1983: 71–4). An alternative way of looking at parallel targets is to say that they are minimally stacked, and so this constraint is a sub-case of that in the previous section.

These latter two constraints operate at sentence level; they refer to the simultaneous presence of two targets. They are linked to a more general corpus level regularity which is the effect of 'real' distance.

7.7.4   'Real' distance

We have seen one effect of distance in the question of agreement with the nearest conjunct (§5.7). We shall see another effect in that the distance between controller and target can have an effect on agreement choices. That too is a relative effect. We should first ask whether strict adjacency can affect agreement. In other words, can it matter whether or not controller and target are strictly adjacent? There are general shape effects (discussed in §6.3.1, footnote 11), which are known as a special case. Otherwise, there are some interesting claims, but it seems that strict adjacency is probably not a factor in agreement. Perhaps the most interesting candidate is the 'Northern Subject Rule'. An excellent account of the extensive literature can be found in Godfrey & Tagliamonte (1999), and Pietsch (2005) provides a detailed study. The appearance of -s on English verbs (for different persons and numbers) is affected by this rule, which goes back to Old Northumbrian English and operates in many dialects, including some transplanted to North America (see, for instance, Hazen 2000). According to the rule, the verb takes -s unless it immediately follows a personal pronoun. Its effect is seen in: *I grow potatoes and sells them*, and *tractors runs away* (Godfrey & Tagliamonte 1999: 108). The rule distinguishes subject type (pronoun versus other) and concerns adjacency. We should note that these are influences on the appearance of -s, not categorial rules, and that there are various other influences, including person and number, and some other influences which have little to do with agreement. We are definitely not dealing here with a categorial agreement rule based on adjacency (see also Börjars & Chapman 1998, and for Belfast English see Henry 1995: 16–44).

So let us turn to an example of real distance. In this example, the familiar *committee* nouns, the distance between controller and pronoun target is counted in words:

(62)   Agreement of personal pronouns with noun phrases headed by *committee*
        nouns in written American English, Australian English and British English
        according to distance in words (Levin 2001: 98)

	0–4		5–9		1–14		15+	
	N	% plural	N	% plural	N	% plural	N	% plural
NYT	739	19	398	39	144	51	102	69
SMH	431	26	211	49	64	64	40	82
Independent	624	47	290	66	113	72	67	82

As the distance between controller and target increases, so does the likelihood of
semantic agreement. The data from the spoken corpora are not quite so 'perfect',
because of threshold effects: over longer distances the proportion for semantic
agreement is very high.

Data on real distance are available for Cairene Arabic, for the choice of agreement forms for plural nouns, namely feminine singular and plural (Belnap 1999:
174). Belnap's data show a clear effect of distance, but he does not separate out
the different controller types, so the data are not quite as convincing as those of
Levin.

7.8   Interactions

To see how these different factors interact, one of our key languages,
Russian, proves particularly helpful. In many respects its agreement system is
canonical. However, it also allows many agreement choices, which permit us to
see the conflicting factors at work. Let us return to this example from §5.7:

Russian (Graudina, Ickovič & Katlinskaja 1976: 31)
(63)   prepodava-l-a-s′   matematik-a   i   fizik-a
        taught-PST-F.SG-REFL mathematics(F)-SG and physics(F)-SG
        'mathematics and physics were (literally 'was') taught'

In such examples both singular and plural agreement are possible. If we keep
the controller constant and consider different domains, we know from §7.4.1
that in attributive position the likelihood of semantic agreement decreases (to
14%), while in the positions to the right it is higher (100% in our corpus, though
singular relative pronouns are found occasionally, and even personal pronouns
exceptionally).

Now consider the controller. The particular type in (63) does not favour plural
agreement. We know that, if the controller is animate rather than inanimate, this
will increase the likelihood of semantic agreement (§6.1.2); there is evidence

that this is true in attributive position too (Corbett 1983: 160). In the remaining positions, where the plural is in any case overwhelmingly favoured, having an animate controller guarantees a plural target. Moreover, if the controller precedes the target, this will increase the likelihood of semantic agreement (§6.1.3). This is easiest to demonstrate for the predicate, but there is some evidence for the effect obtaining within the noun phrase too (Corbett 1983: 161). As we saw in §6.1.4, in the predicate, having a controller which is animate and which precedes the target always leads to a plural verb in our corpus.

If within the predicate we look at the effect of the Predicate Hierarchy, we find that semantic agreement does increase as we move up this hierarchy; however, the effect is hard to detect because it is masked by the counter-effect of Robblee's predicate types (§6.5.2). There is relevant data in Corbett (1983: 166–70).

Beyond all this, there are stylistic differences: in similar sentence types different individuals have slightly different distributions of agreement, and there is a marked difference between the standard language and dialects; moreover, the situation has changed somewhat over the last two centuries (Corbett 1983: 105–30). Nevertheless, within all this variety the constraints of the Agreement Hierarchy are observed, and they prove more powerful than the other factors discussed.

7.9 Conclusion

We have surveyed many instances of agreement choices and seen a good deal of evidence consistent with the Agreement Hierarchy. This hierarchy constrains the agreement patterns found with lexical hybrids (involving gender and number) and those invoked by constructional mismatches. We noted that the Agreement Hierarchy has other roles, and considered its implications, particularly for personal pronouns as agreement targets. We also examined further constraints, and the interactions of other factors with the hierarchy. At several points we noted that resolved forms are instances of semantic agreement. It is now time to look at resolution in more detail.

8 Resolution

We have seen how important conjoined noun phrases are for understanding agreement. Agreement may in principle be with one conjunct or with all. Here we are concerned with the instances where agreement is with all conjuncts, and so where resolution rules determine the appropriate feature specification. For example, in Slovene if a masculine singular and a feminine singular are conjoined, it is resolution in gender and number which specifies the form of the target, say the past active participle, as masculine dual:[1]

Slovene (Derganc 2003: 174)

(1)   Oče   in   mati   **sta**   me   **obiska-l-a**.
            father(M)[SG] and mother(F)[SG] AUX.3DU 1SG.ACC visit-PST-M.DU
            '(My) father and mother visited me.'

As we would expect, resolution can operate to resolve clashes of values (as with gender in this example). However, it can also operate when conjuncts share feature values (singular number in (1)), and the result here is the dual. Example (2) shows that resolution can be required when conjuncts share the same gender value:

Lenček (1972: 60)

(2)   T-o   drev-o   in   gnezd-o   na njem   mi
            that-N.SG tree(N)-SG and nest(N)-SG on 3SG.N.LOC 1SG.DAT

            bosta   **ostal-a**   v   spomin-u.
            AUX.FUT.3DU remain-M.DU in memory-SG.LOC
            'That tree and the nest on it will remain in my mind.'

Though both conjuncts are neuter, gender resolution specifies masculine agreement (as we shall see later). I retain the established term 'resolution rule', due to Givón (1970), even though these rules do not only resolve clashes. They operate when agreement is with all conjuncts, irrespective of whether the feature specifications clash. To do so they require access to the feature values of all of the individual conjuncts. 'Rule' too is no longer a good term in all frameworks: we are dealing with 'patterns of feature computation'.

Examples like (2) are central to understanding resolution. We might have expected that conjoining neuter with neuter would give neuter agreement, but

---

[1] To allow the reader to concentrate on the essentials, noun phrases can be assumed to be nominative in Slovene and absolutive in Godoberi and Tsakhur, unless otherwise specified.

this is definitely not the case. This is worth stressing, since some writers pass over like conjuncts in silence as though the rule is obvious, while Slovene and similar languages show that it is not. Furthermore, the data of Slovene have eluded formal description in accounts like that of Dalrymple & Kaplan (2000). Slovene is also important because it has a dual, and this additional number value is useful when investigating the interaction of resolution systems. As we shall see, gender resolution is the same in the plural and the dual.

We must remember that resolution is generally not obligatory; instead, agreement is often with one conjunct only, and so resolution is not involved. We saw examples in §5.7 (generally the alternative is for agreement to be controlled by the nearest conjunct, and just occasionally by the first). There are some poor analyses in the literature, where researchers do not keep in mind the possibility that the controller may be one conjunct or all. We saw in §§6.1.2–6.1.4 the conditions on the choice. We have also noted (§2.1.2) that defective controllers, such as clauses, infinitive phrases, sometimes numeral phrases, take default agreement, whether this is a normal form or a special neutral form (§§3.6.3–3.6.4); where conjoining is possible, the result is still outside the main agreement system, and a default form results (see Corbett & Mtenje 1987: 15 and Corbett 1991: 212 for Chichewa examples). For the rest of this chapter we shall consider just those examples where, whatever the conditions operating in the particular language, agreement is with all conjuncts, and so resolution is called into play. This means that there is some computation of the agreement form requiring reference to the heads of at least two noun phrases. Resolution produces examples which are non-canonical (§1.4.4) and the result of resolution follows the same pattern as other instances of semantic agreement (§7.4.1).

The readiness with which conjoining is employed varies dramatically across languages: English is at one end of the typological extreme in allowing coordination easily. When investigating resolution, we discover that some combinations of noun phrases in coordinate structures are unlikely, and so we have to be ingenious when eliciting examples and somewhat suspicious of the results obtained. There are many instances where particular combinations of noun phrases are avoided, typically when they are semantically different.[2] There are cases where resolution cannot offer an acceptable outcome (and so there is agreement with one conjunct or some different strategy is employed).

Resolution rules are required for all possible combinations within person, number and gender. The rules for person (§8.1) and number (8.2) are relatively straightforward, while those for gender (§8.3) show remarkable diversity. After examining four significant examples, we look more quickly at some further systems (§8.4).

---

[2] We have to distinguish examples that need imagination in finding a context from those which are linguistically awkward. Conjoining *Mary* and *rose* seems unlikely; but in the context where Mary had long been upset that she never received letters or parcels, and one day was given a rose, to her delight, one might say *Mary and her rose were talked about for days*. Here the issue was to find the right context: the conjoining and agreement are then fine. In some other languages, even if there is a plausible context there are constraints on conjoining semantically unlike noun phrases where agreement is required (see the discussion at the end of §8.3.3).

As we look at some of the data, it may help to bear the following questions in mind. I ask how resolution relates to each of the five elements of agreement (§1.3) and how they interact with each other:

1.   How does resolution relate to *controllers*?
2.   How does resolution relate to *targets*?
3.   How does resolution relate to *domains*?
4.   How does resolution relate to *features*?
5.   How does resolution relate to *conditions*?
6.   How do the different types of resolution interact with each other? (What is the relation between person, number and gender resolution?)

We shall review these issues in §8.5, before considering the motivation behind resolution systems in §8.6.

8.1   Person

Person resolution typically follows the semantics of the person feature. For personal pronouns there is the following hierarchy:

Person Hierarchy (Zwicky 1977: 718)
(3)   1 > 2 > 3

For a group including the speaker we use the first person pronoun, if the speaker is not included but the addressee is, we use the second person, and failing both of those we use the third person. Resolution works similarly. First we have conjuncts including a first person, and indeed we find a first person verb:

Slovene (Priestly 1993: 433–434)
(4)   Jaz   in   Tone   sva   priš-l-a.
             1SG and Tone(M) AUX.1DU arrive-PST-M.DU
             'I and Tone have arrived.'

In the absence of a first person, a second person determines the agreement:

(5)   Ti,   Tone   in   Tomo   ste   priš-l-i.
             2SG Tone(M) and Tomo(M) AUX.2PL arrive-PST-M.PL
             'You, Tone and Tomo have arrived.'

Examples with third person conjuncts only have been seen already, in (1) and (2). The rules, which apply generally, and not just to Slovene, may be stated as follows:

(a)   If the conjuncts include a first person, agreement will be first person.
(b)   Otherwise, if the conjuncts include a second person, agreement will be second person.
(c)   The default situation is that agreement is third person.

There are various ways of writing the rules, which are simply a restatement of the Person Hierarchy in (3). They apply generally, but it is important to remember that person resolution may well not be obligatory. In Czech, for instance, if the controller follows the target, agreement can be with the nearest conjunct, even when this means that person resolution will not occur (see Panevová & Petkevič 1997: 327–9).

The coordinate structure may also be avoided by special pronominal coordination constructions (Corbett 2000: 231–3). So in Slovene, besides *Tone in jaz* 'Tone and I', we find *midva s Tonetom* literally 'we two with Tone'; both involve just two individuals, and the verb will be in the dual. Since Slovene is a pro-drop language, a third possibility is simply *s Tonetom* (and first person dual verb), again meaning 'Tone and I' (Derganc 2003: 169), the verb coded construction.

Person resolution is often seen as unproblematic, but it has been known for some time that there are complications. Findreng (1976: 81–4, 385–8) showed that in German there are examples which do not follow the person hierarchy. He gives examples both from texts and from work with consultants. To understand these instances we must first check on the plural paradigm of the German verb:

(6)   Plural paradigm of German *bringen* 'to bring'

1 plural	wir bringen
2 plural	ihr bringt
3 plural	sie bringen

The first and third plural forms are syncretic. The problem instances are those where we find this plural form when we would have expected the second plural, as in:

German (Findreng 1976: 83)

(7)   ... wenn du   und dein-e   Schwester   ein-e   tüchtig-e
       If   2SG   and 2SG.POSS-F.SG   sister(F)[SG]   INDF-F.SG   good-F.SG

       Portion   mehr bekomm-en **werd-en,** ...
       portion(F)[SG]   more get-INF   will-PL

       '... if you and your sister will get a good portion more ...'

The form *werden* can be analysed as first or third plural; in either case it is not the expected second plural. The form is assumed to be third plural (and in French, where exceptions are also found, it is third person forms which occur, Grevisse 1964: 741-2n 1). It is hard to understand what is going on, though there are some indicators. First, coordinations involving personal pronouns are often summarized by the appropriate pronoun (cf. English *you and I, we* . . .); this summarizing pronoun in German is the one expected according to the hierarchy, and then agreement with it is normal. The unexpected cases arise when there is no such summarizing pronoun. Second, it is clear that in German the form in *-en* is the major plural form: it appears that the less frequent second plural form is being partly squeezed out.

The German problem and the related issue of reflexive pronouns in Dutch are taken up by the psycholinguists Timmermans, Schriefers, Dijkstra & Haverkort (2004). They confirm that in experimental conditions German speakers often produce the third plural form in examples similar to (7). Indeed, around half of their sixty consultants gave the third person form consistently, and most of the remainder varied between second plural and third plural.[3] Thus person resolution is not quite as simple as grammars often imply.

8.2   Number

Number resolution also follows the semantics of the number feature fairly transparently. In earlier chapters we saw examples of conjoined noun phrases taking plural agreement in languages like Russian. More complex systems require correspondingly expanded rules, for example for Slovene we need rules equivalent to the following:[4]

(a)   If there are two conjuncts only, both singular, then agreement will be dual.
(b)   In all other cases agreement will be plural.

Given two singular conjuncts, the resolved form is the dual in Slovene, as in examples (1) and (2) above (and in Inari Sami, §3.6.2.2). With dual and singular conjoined we have the plural, by rule (b):

Slovene (Priestly 1993: 433)
(8)   Dv-e   telet-i   in   en-o   žrebe   so   bi-l-i   zunaj.
            two-N calf(N)-DU and one-N.SG foal(N)[SG] AUX.3PL be-PST-M.PL outside
            'Two calves and a foal were outside.'

Similarly with more than two singulars:

Slovene (Lenček 1972: 61)
(9)   Marin-a,   Mart-a   in   Marjanc-a   so   prizadevn-e.
            Marina(F)-SG Marta(F)-SG and Marjanca(F)-SG COP.3PL assiduous-F.PL
            'Marina, Marta and Marjanca are assiduous.'

---

[3] For the Dutch experiment they used the form of the reflexive pronoun, since in Dutch the plural forms of the verb are identical. However, Jenny Audring points out (personal communication) that the third person reflexive is often overgeneralized, independently of coordination, as in:

(i)   jullie hebb-en zich   vergist
            2PL   have-PL REFL.3 deceive.PST.PRT
            'You were mistaken.'

Thus the resolution problem can be seen as a part of an overall move towards generalization of the third person in the plural.

[4] Again I give the rules in this format for simplicity; instead we could treat the second as the default and the first as the more specific case which overrides the other. These rules are superceded in §8.5.4.

In languages like Russian, where there is no dual, the first rule is not required. Number resolution thus matches the semantics of the number feature.[5]

8.3   Gender

Gender resolution is varied and interesting. We shall look first at four significantly different cases here (there are many more examples than can be accommodated here; see Corbett 1991: 269–306; 2003a and references there for more data). I shall draw interim conclusions based on these four languages, and then in §8.4 look at other languages more briefly.

8.3.1   Slovene

Our featured language, Russian, proved very interesting for the question of whether resolution applies or not, and showed a good deal about the conditions involved (§§6.1.2–6.1.4) and the constraining effect of the Agreement Hierarchy (§7.4.1, §7.8). However, when resolution occurs, the results in Russian are of no great interest: person resolution is as normal, though special pronominal coordination is more likely; number involves only the plural; and there is no gender resolution, since genders are not differentiated in the plural. For these reasons we will look instead at Slovene, which is in many ways similar to Russian, but with the added interest here of having a dual, and of having gender distinctions in the dual and plural. We can illustrate this with a past active participle:

(10) Predicate agreement forms in Slovene (past active participle of *biti* 'be')

	singular	dual	plural
masculine	bil	bila	bili
feminine	bila	bili	bile
neuter	bilo	bili	bila

There are various syncretisms here, but these are resolved by the auxiliary verb (also 'be'), which marks person and number.

In terms of gender resolution, as we saw in (1), a masculine conjoined with a feminine takes a masculine predicate. The masculine also results from conjoining masculine and neuter:

---

[5] As Nicholas Evans points out (personal communication), another feature for which resolution can be needed is the harmonic/disharmonic opposition within kinship dyads, as in Dalabon (Alpher 1982).

Slovene (Lenček 1972: 60)

(11)   Tonček   in   t-o   dekletc-e   sta   prizadevn-a.
        Tonček(M)[SG] and that-N.SG little.girl(N)-SG COP.3DU assiduous-M.DU
        'Tonček and that little girl are assiduous.'

When a feminine and a neuter are conjoined, the masculine is still found:

Slovene (Priestly 1993: 433)

(12)   Milk-a   in   njen-o   tele   sta   bi-l-a   zunaj.
        Milka(F)-SG and her-N.SG calf(N)[SG] AUX.3DU be-PST-M.DU outside
        'Milka and her calf were outside.'

Slovene (Lenček 1972: 60)

(13)   T-a   streh-a   in   gnezd-o   na njej   mi
        that-F.SG roof(F)-SG and nest(N)-SG on 3SG.F.LOC 1SG.DAT
          bosta   ostal-a   v   spomin-u.
          AUX.FUT.3DU Remain-M.DU   in memory-SG.LOC
        'That roof and the nest on it will remain in my mind.'

We have already seen the interesting result of conjoining neuter singulars (2), namely the masculine. The way in which the feminine (syncretic with neuter) dual form can result from resolution is if two feminines are conjoined:

Slovene (Priestly 1993: 433)

(14)   Milk-a   in   njen-a   mačka   sta   bi-l-i   zunaj.
        Milka(F)-SG and her-F.SG cat(F)-SG be.DU be-PST-F.DU outside
        'Milka and her cat were outside.'

Gender resolution operates as follows:

(a)   If all conjuncts are feminine, then agreement is feminine.
(b)   Otherwise agreement is masculine.

Number resolution determines when the dual and when the plural form are to be found. As this is so, the rules just given will also account for gender resolution when the plural results. Thus in (8) above all the conjuncts are neuter, but the masculine plural form is required. Again, the feminine is possible only if all the conjuncts are feminine, as in (14). This means that gender resolution in Slovene operates in the same way, whether the resolved number is dual or plural. Equally there is no difference for the different persons. Note that in the rules as given there is no recourse to semantic factors; the syntactic gender appears to be a sufficient determining factor. Thus (12) and (13) have conjoined feminine and neuter, with masculine as the resolved form; it seems not to matter that in (12) there is an animate feminine and an inanimate in (13). I will modify this view in §8.6.

    Slovene's closest relative, Serbian/Croatian/Bosnian, works in a comparable way; it has no dual, but it has interesting complications, to which we shall return

(§8.5.1 and §8.5.2). Gender resolution like that in Slovene can operate for a two-gender system. Thus in French, which has only masculine and feminine, if only feminines are conjoined there is feminine agreement, and otherwise masculine. Such systems are common; they include Italian, Spanish, Latvian, Hindi, Punjabi and Modern Hebrew (see Corbett 2003a: 308 for sources).[6]

8.3.2 Godoberi

We find a somewhat different resolution system in Godoberi, a member of the Andic subgroup of Daghestanian languages, which has some 2,500 speakers in the Botlikh area of Daghestan. The data are from Kibrik, Tatevosov & Eulenberg (1996: 156–9), based on fieldwork with about five speakers. There are three genders in Godoberi: masculine (for nouns denoting male humans), feminine (for female humans) and neuter (for non-humans). In the plural, however, there are only two agreement forms, the human (for masculines and feminines) and the neuter.

(15)　　　The gender system of Godoberi[7]

	singular		plural
masculine	w-		
		b-	human
feminine	j-		
neuter	b-	r-	neuter

Forms in *b-* used for human plurals are often homonymous with the marker for the neuter singular; however, human plural and neuter singular are sometimes distinct, as in the case of the verb 'be'.

When all conjuncts refer to male humans, the resolved form is the human form (see Kibrik, Tatevosov & Eulenberg 1996: 156–9 and Corbett 2003a: 296–7 for the possibilities of agreement with a single conjunct):

Godoberi (Kibrik, Tatevosov & Eulenberg 1996: 156–9)
(16)　　　ima-la　　　　　waša-la　　　　b-aʔa
　　　　　father(M)[SG]-and　son(M)[SG]-and　HUM.PL-arrived
　　　　　'The father and the son arrived.'

Note that the conjunction is added to each conjunct. When all conjuncts refer to female humans, the human agreement form is again used:

---

[6] Early Germanic had an interesting set of rules, preserved in Old High German and Middle High German, and indeed in Modern Icelandic, according to which if all conjuncts were masculine, then masculine agreements were used, if all feminine, then feminine, and in all other cases neuter (Askedal 1973). For Icelandic see Friðjónsson (1989: 18–19), with thanks to Joan Maling for this reference, and Corbett (1991: 283).

[7] For showing the target gender forms (the agreement forms) I choose whichever format is clearer for the given language.

(17)   ila-la   jaši-la   b-aʔa
        mother(F)[SG]-and daughter(F)[SG]-and HUM.PL-arrived
        'The mother and the daughter arrived.'

When there are masculine and feminine conjuncts, again we find the human plural form:

(18)   ima-la   ila-la   b-aʔa
        father(M)-and mother(F)-and HUM.PL-arrived
        'Father and mother arrived.'

When all conjuncts are neuter, then neuter agreement is found:

(19)   hamaXi-la   X̄∘ani-la   r-aʔa
        donkey(N)[SG]-and horse(N)[SG]-and N.PL-arrived
        'The donkey and the horse arrived.'

In this example we find the neuter plural. Thus with any combination of noun phrases denoting humans the human plural form is used, and for noun phrases denoting non-humans the neuter plural. The remaining possibility is the conjoining of a masculine or feminine with a neuter (like $X_∘aji$ 'dog'):

(20)   wacī-la   X∘aji-la   *b-aʔa
        boy(M)[SG]-and dog(N)[SG]-and HUM.PL-arrived
        'The boy and the dog arrived.'

For some speakers, including the one Kibrik found most reliable, there was no acceptable form of agreement with conjoined noun phrases of this type. Instead the comitative construction, with the subordinate noun phrase marked by the comitative case, was the required alternative:

(21)   wacī   X∘aji-łaɫi   w-aʔa.
        boy(M)[SG] dog(N)[SG]-COM M.SG-arrived
        'The boy arrived with the dog.'

Thus the system is entirely based on semantics:

(a)   If all conjuncts refer to humans the human form is used.
(b)   If all conjuncts refer to non-humans the neuter form is used.

We do not need to specify that the agreements will be plural, since that will result from number resolution. The rules as given do not allow for the combining of humans and non-humans; an alternative construction, the comitative, must be used. (See discussion of the Tsakhur example (29) for discussion of the reason.) However, some speakers, besides accepting the comitative construction, also allow sentences like (20) above, with human plural agreement (not with neuter plural agreement). They have a more permissive form of resolution, allowing this possibility:

(c)   If the conjuncts are semantically mixed, the comitative construction is
         preferable; if gender resolution is forced, the form will be as for humans.

The fact that resolution is clearly based on semantics here is hardly surprising since the gender of nouns in Godoberi is intimately linked with their meaning. In being firmly based on semantics, Godoberi's resolution rules are comparable to those found in some other Daghestanian languages, such as Bagwalal (Kibrik 2001: 475–8), in the Nakh language Tsova-Tush (Corbett 2003a: 300–1) and in the Dravidian languages Tamil and Telugu (Corbett 1991: 269–71). We now move on to languages where meaning and gender are not so tightly linked.

8.3.3   Tsakhur

Our featured language Tsakhur proves particularly helpful in understanding resolution. As we noted in §1.5.2, Tsakhur has four genders. Nouns denoting male humans are assigned to gender I and those denoting female humans to gender II. Most of the remaining animates are assigned to gender III; just a few, however, are in gender IV. Inanimates are distributed between genders III and IV. There is a small number of significant exceptional nouns, such as *kul$_j$fat* 'child', which does not fit into any of the genders as given above. In the singular it takes gender IV agreements, but in the plural it takes I/II. There are just two agreements in the plural, one for genders I and II and one for III and IV (§3.3.3). The examples and judgements given are based on fieldwork with ten consultants (details of the response of each to each example are given in Corbett 1999b: 409–11).

When nouns from genders I and II are combined, whether the same or mixed, we find the I/II plural agreement form:

Tsakhur (Corbett 1999b)
(22) jed-i: jiš   Xa: wobummɨ
      mother(II)[SG]-and daughter(II)[SG] at.home be.I/II.PL
      'Mother and daughter are at home.'

(23) dak-i: jed$_j$ Xa: wobummɨ
      father(I)[SG]-and mother(II)[SG] at.home be.I/II.PL
      'Father and mother are at home.'

Similarly for genders III and IV, whether the nouns are animate or inanimate:

(24) t'ot'-i: kabaj   Xa: wodummɨ
      fly(III)[SG]-and butterfly(IV)[SG] at.home be.III/IV.PL
      'The fly and the butterfly are at home.'

(25) q'uq'-i: niše   Xa: wodummɨ
      egg(III)[SG]-and cheese(IV)[SG] at.home be.III/IV.PL
      'The egg and the cheese are at home.'

However, if we take conjuncts headed by nouns from I or II and from III or IV, then the result is less than fully acceptable

(26) dak-i: balkan   Xa: ??wobummɨ/ *wodummɨ
      father(I)[SG]-and horse(III)[SG] at.home ??be.I/II.PL / *be.III/IV.PL
      'Father and the horse are at home.'

(27)   gade-ji: kabaj   Xa: ??wobummɨ/??wodummɨ
         boy(I)[SG]-and butterfly(IV)[SG] at.home ??be.I /II.PL /??be.III/IV.PL
         'The boy and the butterfly are at home.'

So far we might suppose that resolution should refer to the syntactic genders of the nouns. The next example shows that that is not the best approach for Tsakhur:

(28)   jed-i: kulⱼfat Xa: wobummɨ
         mother(II)[SG]-and child[SG] at.home be.I /II.PL
         'Mother and child are at home.'

Recall that *kulⱼfat* is exceptional, since in the singular it takes gender IV agreement, but in the plural it takes I/II. It looks as though we might also need an exceptional resolution rule for it. However, this is not the case. Resolution can be as follows:

(a)   If all conjuncts refer to humans, then agreement is gender I/II.
(b)   If no conjuncts refer to humans, then agreement is gender III/IV.
(c)   If the conjuncts are semantically mixed, an alternative construction is preferred.

This approach allows us to have a simple set of resolution rules, and of a type which is also widely attested cross-linguistically. (The rules are numbered only for convenience; there is no necessary ordering.)

Archi has gender resolution rules like those just given for Tsakhur (Kibrik 1977b: 186–7; Corbett 1991: 271–3), provided that a person feature is recognized (§4.2.1), so that person resolution takes care of conjuncts with first and second person pronouns. Otherwise the statement of resolution becomes very complex.[8] In both languages a small number of examples argue for preferring semantic gender resolution rather than syntactic.

Tsakhur also allows us to tackle the issue of whether the sentences which are unacceptable (or disfavoured) are problematic because of the fact of conjoining unlike conjuncts, or because of the presence of agreement. We can see which is the key factor with the following example:

(29)   gade-j-k'le-ji: balkan-ɨ-k'le   jedⱼ   Ge:ʒe-wo-r
         boy-OBL.SG-AFF-and horse-OBL.SG-AFF woman(II)[SG] see.II-AUX-II
         'The boy and the horse see the woman.'

With verbs of perception the experiencer noun phrase stands in the affective case (AFF), which attaches to the oblique stem. The object stands in the absolutive case, and the verb agrees with it, hence the verb in (29) has the agreement markers for gender II singular, agreeing with *jedⱼ* 'woman'. This sentence, in which human and non-human are conjoined, presented no problem (though not as many speakers

---

[8] Compare Kibrik, Kodzasov, Olovjannikova & Samedov (1977a: 63–4), Kibrik (1977b: 186–7) and Corbett (1991: 127–8, 271–3).

were asked as with the conjoining cases). This is because nothing agrees with the conjoined noun phrases. Hence it is agreement which causes the difficulty in examples like (26) and (27) and not the mere fact of conjoining semantically unlike noun phrases. Aleksandr Kibrik informs me (personal communication) that the same argument holds for Godoberi.

8.3.4   Luganda

Semantic resolution has been found in many Bantu languages. These usually have several genders, which correspond to semantic classifications only partially: nouns of the 1/2 gender are human (animate in some languages), but not all nouns denoting humans belong to the 1/2 gender. For gender resolution, the important thing is typically whether a noun phrase refers to a human or a non-human, irrespective of gender. This point is illustrated by Luganda data due to Givón:

Luganda (Givón 1970: 253–4; 1971: 38–9)
(30)   omu-kazi,   es-sajja   ne   olu-ana   ba-alabwa
         SG-woman(1/2) SG-fat.man(5/6) and SG-thin.child(11/10) 2-were.seen
         'The woman, the fat man and the thin child were seen.'

Recall that Bantu genders are given labels such as '1/2', which means 'takes class 1 agreements when singular and class 2 when plural'. Odd numbers usually indicate a singular and even numbers typically indicate a plural marker (but not always: 12 is a singular in example (31)). The resolved form for conjoined nouns denoting humans is the class 2 marker – the one used for agreement with plural nouns of the 1/2 gender. In (30) only one of the conjuncts belongs to that gender. In (31) none of the conjuncts belongs to the 1/2 gender, but as all refer to humans the resolved form is again the class 2 form:

(31)   ek-kazi,   aka-ana   ne   olu-sajja   ba-alabwa
         SG-fat.woman(5/6) SG-small.child(12/14) and SG-tall.man(11/10) 2-were.seen
         'The fat woman, the small child and the tall man were seen.'

Example (31) demonstrates that the use of the gender 1/2 plural form for resolution is motivated by semantic considerations. If none of the conjuncts refers to a human, then agreement takes the class 8 form:

(32)   en-te,   omu-su,   eki-be   ne   ely-ato   bi-alabwa
         SG-cow(9/10) SG-wild.cat (3/4) SG-jackal(7/8) and SG-canoe(5/6) 8-were.seen
         'The cow, the wild cat, the jackal and the canoe were seen.'

Conjoining noun phrases denoting a human and a non-human produces an unnatural result:

(33)   ? omu-sajja ne   em-bwa-ye   bi-agwa
         SG-man(1/2) and SG-dog(9/10)-his 8-fell
         'The man and his dog fell down.'

While (33) is unnatural, if instead the class 2 (human plural) form is used, an unacceptable sentence results:

(34)   *omu-sajja   ne   em-bwa-ye   ba-agwa
        SG-man(1/2)   and   SG-dog(9/10)-his   2-fell
        'The man and his dog fell down.'

The preferred alternative (as in Godoberi) is the comitative construction:

(35)   omu-sajja   y-agwa   ne   em-bwa-ye
        SG-man(1/2)   1-fell   with   SG-dog(9/10)-his
        'The man fell down with his dog.'

In Luganda, and widely in Bantu, the conjunction glossed 'and' also means 'with' (its earlier meaning). As a result, the distinction between coordinate and comitative constructions is not always clear-cut,[9] and in practical terms great care must be taken in work with speakers. Example (35) has a simple subject, with which the verb can agree fully (in the singular), and the problem of resolution is avoided. Resolution can be stated as follows (there is no necessary ordering here):

(a)   If all the conjuncts are semantically human, agreement is gender 1/2.
(b)   If none of the conjuncts is semantically human, agreement is gender 7/8.
(c)   If the conjuncts are semantically mixed, the comitative construction
       is preferable; if gender resolution is forced, the form will be as for
       non-humans.[10]

In these rules I specify the gender of the target as, for example, 1/2. This allows easy comparison with the sources quoted and with other languages for which I have given a gender value like 'masculine' as the resolved form. The point is that it is number resolution which determines that the plural will be used, hence the 2 form in Luganda (or the masculine plural, if masculine is determined by gender resolution).

In almost all the Bantu languages investigated we find evidence for semantic resolution based on the human/non-human distinction (see Corbett 1991: 275–6 for sources on ChiBemba, Dzamba,[11] Likila, Lingala, Luvale, Tswana, Xhosa and Zulu, and Moosally 1998 for Ndebele). Frequently there are problems, however. Judgements may be uncertain with particular sentence types, as already indicated, and it is important to bear in mind the possibility of comitative constructions and cases of agreement with the nearest conjunct. Corbett & Mtenje (1987) undertook a detailed analysis of Chichewa and considered some of the trickier instances which are often ignored. We should also mention Swahili, in order to complete the discussion of the examples given in §5.7. Swahili makes an animate/inanimate rather than human/non-human distinction, so there is a resolved form for animates,

---

[9] See Mithun (1988) and Stassen (2003) on 'and' and 'with' constructions.
[10] This is the opposite solution to that of Godoberi.
[11] Dzamba is spoken in the Bomongo administrative zone in the northwest of the Democratic Republic of Congo (Eyamba Bokamba, personal communication).

and one for inanimates. Our examples in §5.7 had inanimate conjuncts, and the resolved form is as follows:

Swahili (Bokamba 1985: 44)
(36)   ki-ti   na   m-guu   wa meza vi-me-vunjika
        SG-chair(7/8) and SG-leg(3/4) of table 8-PRF-broken
        'The chair and the leg of the table are broken.'

Given the large gender systems of Bantu languages, we might have expected numerous complex resolution rules. Typically, however, resolution rules are few and fairly simple. In part this is because the genders of the conjuncts need not be represented in the resolved form (see (31)), as indeed we saw earlier with Slovene (example (2)).

8.4   Further gender resolution systems

To give a more rounded picture of resolution, I will consider three more complex systems quite briefly, outlining the system and giving references to the sources of relevant data.

8.4.1   Polish

Polish, a West Slavonic language, has an interesting system, in which there is considerable inter-speaker variation. The possibilities for predicate agreement are given in (37).

(37)   Predicate agreement in Polish (past tense of *być* 'be')

		singular	plural
masculine	personal	był	byli
	non-personal		były
feminine		była	
neuter		było	

Polish has three forms for gender agreement in the singular; in the plural there is a division into masculine personal (abbreviated 'M.PERS') and the remainder. The masculine personal gender value is marked distinctively on targets like the past of *być* by a consonant mutation. It comprises nouns which are of masculine gender and which denote humans: it does not coincide completely with the semantic criterion of male human, but its relation to semantics is much closer than that of the genders in the singular.

When in conjoined structures none of the conjuncts is headed by a masculine personal noun, then the non-masculine personal/feminine/neuter form is found:

Polish (Rothstein 1993: 732–733)
(38)   Basia   i   Marysia   przyniosł-y   sałat-ę .
        Basia(F) and Marysia(F) brought-NON_M.PERS.PL salad-SG.ACC
        'Basia and Marysia brought a salad.'

If a masculine personal noun heads one of the conjuncts, then the masculine personal form is found:

(39)   Janek   i   Marysia   przynieśl-i   ciastk-a.
        Janek(M) and Marysia(F) brought-M.PERS.PL pastry-PL.ACC
        'Janek and Marysia brought pastries.'

The basic resolution rules are as follows:

(a)   If at least one conjunct refers to a male human, agreement is masculine personal;
(b)   otherwise agreement is non-masculine personal.

However, there are several interesting complications (see Corbett 1991: 284–7 for data and sources). For most speakers the combination of a female human and a masculine non-human animate requires masculine personal agreement. This form is also the majority choice when just masculine non-human animates are conjoined. And for some speakers a noun phrase referring to a female human conjoined with a masculine inanimate can result in a masculine personal form. Polish thus has mixed resolution, with some surprising outcomes, which deserve further study.

8.4.2   Latin

Latin has three genders, differentiated in the singular and the plural. Often agreement with the nearest conjunct is preferred, but when resolution occurs, the situation is as follows (Kühner & Stegmann 1955: 44–52). Conjuncts of the same syntactic gender take agreeing forms of that gender. When conjuncts are of different genders, then the resolved form depends on whether the noun phrases refer to humans or not. For humans the masculine is used and for non-humans the neuter. When humans and non-humans are conjoined agreement is usually with the nearest conjunct, but resolution is possible and the neuter plural is found. Here, then, there is clearly a semantic principle at work.

8.4.3   Romanian

Romanian has an unusual gender system. It has two sets of agreements (target genders) in the singular and the plural. However, a substantial number of nouns are in the neuter gender, taking masculine agreement in the singular and feminine in the plural (see Corbett 1991: 150–2 for discussion and for some of the extensive literature). The resolution system is also of interest, though it must be said that the situation is somewhat confused, and certain combinations tend to be avoided. It is established, however, that animates and inanimates are treated somewhat differently.

For *animate* conjuncts, if all conjuncts denote females, feminine agreement is used; for other combinations of conjuncts masculine agreement is found. On the other hand, for *inanimate* conjuncts, if all conjuncts are masculine, the masculine is used; otherwise the feminine. For data and references see Corbett (1991: 288–90), Farkaş & Zec (1995), Moosally (1998: 110–16) and Maurice (2001: 237–8). This then is another example of a mixed system.

8.5   Characteristics of resolution systems

Having looked at a range of examples, we shall now take stock, and see how far we can answer our initial questions. We already have the data we need to answer some of them, for others we need to examine further languages.

8.5.1   How does resolution relate to controllers?

The interesting issue here is the information to which resolution has access. We have seen instances where resolution has access to the normal syntactic features of the controller, like any other agreement rule, as in Slovene (§8.3.1). We have also observed access to semantic information, as in Luganda (§8.3.4). In this respect resolution is like assignment (§4.3.1), a point to which we return in §8.6 below. It has been claimed in the literature that resolution can also have access to morphological features, namely the inflectional class of the nouns heading the conjuncts. The data, from Serbian/Croatian/Bosnian, are discussed in Corbett (1991: 299–303), where it is shown that a different analysis is preferable, and hence that this potential counter-example to the principle of morphology-free syntax (§6.3.1) is not actually a counter-example.

In some languages there are different sorts of controller, not just conjoined phrases, for which resolution may apply. However, information about these differences does not affect the result of resolution. For example, some languages have a comitative construction where (unlike those we have seen earlier as ways of avoiding resolution) agreement is possible with the complex head; for this reason they are sometimes called quasi-comitatives. When this is the case, resolution in comitative constructions will always be as in conjoined constructions. An instance of a comitative construction which allows agreement with both noun phrases (resolution) is found in Polish. This language has complex resolution (§8.4.1), but the basic rule is that conjuncts including a male human conjunct require male human plural agreement, while others require non-male human agreement. Now consider these comitatives:

Polish (Dyła 1988: 386)

(40)   Jurek   z   Janki-em   poszl-i   na spacer.
    Jurek(M) with Janek(M)-INS went-M.PERS.PL for walk[ACC.SG]
    'Jurek and Janek went for a walk.'

(41)   Ewa   z   Janki-em   poszl-i   na spacer.
    Ewa(F) with Janek(M)-INS went-M.PERS.PL for walk[ACC.SG]
    'Ewa and Janek went for a walk.'

(42)   Ewa   z   Mari-ą   poszł-y   na spacer.
    Ewa(F) with Maria(F)-INS went-NON_M.PERS.PL for walk[ACC.SG]
    'Ewa and Maria went for a walk.'

Resolution applies to give the same results as it does with conjoined expressions. Similarly, the special pronominal coordination constructions discussed in §8.1 have the values which would result from resolution. Thus the type of controller for which resolution applies does not affect the resolved form. There could not be a language which was like Polish but differed in having a rule that the resolved form for comitatives only was the non-masculine personal plural whenever at least one conjunct was feminine. However, the likelihood of resolution as opposed to agreement with just one element (the head noun phrase in this instance) does depend on the construction. Resolution is more likely with ordinary coordination than with comitatives.[12] And with disjunction the same rules apply, though there tends to be greater uncertainty (see Findreng 1976: 251–5 on German, and Peterson 1986 on English).

8.5.2   How does resolution relate to targets?

The relation to targets is essentially 'business as usual'. The feature specifications to be realized are not specific to resolution, but are found in other agreement rules. Moreover, resolution rules are no more sensitive to the target than are other rules; that is, the result of resolution cannot depend, for instance, on the part of speech of the target (see §8.5.3 for domains). There could not be a language like Slovene, except that mixed conjuncts required masculine agreement on determiners but feminine on adjectives.

There is an apparent complication here, which has an interesting solution. Serbian/Croatian/Bosnian has gender resolution similar in the main to that of Slovene. The feminine is employed if all conjuncts are feminine, the masculine under all other circumstances. Now consider this example:

Serbian/Croatian/Bosnian (Andrić, *Travnička Hronika*)

(43)   ... t-a   sećanj-a   i   razmatranj-a   sve   su   više
    this-N.PL memory(N)-PL and reflection(N)-PL all AUX.3PL more

    ustupa-l-a   mesto   nov-im   utisc-ima ...
    yield-PST-N.PL place-SG.ACC new.PL.DAT impression.PL.DAT

    'those memories and reflections gave way more and more to new impressions'

---

[12] This is true provided similar noun phrases are involved; comitative expressions are more likely with animates than with inanimates.

The assignment rules as we had them would predict masculine plural. However, that is not what we find in texts, and speakers reject it. In a way this is not surprising: the verb agrees completely with each conjunct, and resolution could not 'improve' on the form given. But this will not do as an answer, because we have seen plenty of instances where the conjuncts have the same feature values, and yet resolution operates. Something which distinguishes this example is that the conjuncts are plural, and hence there is no need for number resolution.

Since the problem is only in the plural, it still appears that we require a special rule referring to 'neuter plural' (if all conjuncts are neuter plural, agreement is neuter plural). This is precisely the sort of rule I have claimed resolution never needs. But we are in danger of being misled just because Serbian/Croatian/Bosnian has so few genders. The other instances where examples like (43) could arise (all masculine conjuncts or all feminine conjuncts) are potentially accounted for by the resolution rules. That is, if all conjuncts are feminine plural, our previous rule would account for feminine resolution, but so would a general rule (if all conjuncts are plural and of the same gender, that form is used). As so often, to see which is the right way to go we need to look at larger systems. Consider Chichewa (for details see Corbett & Mtenje 1987 and Corbett 1991: 276–8):

(44)   The target gender (agreement) forms of Chichewa

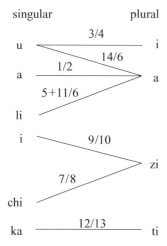

Chichewa has ten genders, indicated along the connecting lines in (44), which we refer to by the agreements they take in the singular and plural (the three locative genders are omitted in (44)). For instance, 7/8 is a gender which includes a wide variety of inanimate nouns. The basic resolution rules are as in Luganda, so that when noun phrases which do not refer to humans are conjoined, the general rule requires that the agreeing verbal predicate will be in the plural of gender 7/8, shown by the prefixal marker zi- (irrespective of whether the head nouns belong to that gender or not). However, there is an interesting class of apparent exceptions:

Chichewa (Corbett & Mtenje 1987)[13]

(45)   ma-lalanje   ndi ma-samba   a-ku-bvunda
          PL-orange(5/6) and PL-leaf(5/6) 6-PRS.rot
          'The oranges and leaves are rotting.'

Here we find noun phrases headed by nouns of the same gender, both plural, and the verb takes the same plural form. This was found fully acceptable, though it is not the form which would be predicted by the rule given. Now consider phrases headed by non-human plural nouns which are of different genders, but whose subject agreement forms happen to coincide:

(46)   a-mphaka ndi ma-lalanje   a-li   uko
          PL-cat(1/2) and PL-orange(5/6) AGR-be there
          'The cats and the oranges are there.'

The gender/number marker (AGR) on the verb (a-) is that corresponding to the plural both of gender 1/2 and of gender 5/6, as shown in (44). (The form zi-, which would be predicted by the usual rules, is a possible alternative.) The regularity here is that if noun phrases headed by plural nouns which would take the same target gender form are conjoined, then that target gender form will be the preferred form. The agreement form is determined, at least in part, by the fact that particular markers are syncretic (as mentioned in §3.4.1). If the forms did not happen to be syncretic, then the regular rule would apply.

Thus the Serbian/Croatian/Bosnian example is part of a much more general phenomenon. Where we have *plural* noun phrases (for which number resolution can add nothing) which would independently take the same agreement form, that form will be available for agreement (whether obligatorily or as an alternative). This is a general phenomenon which covers (43) above and shows that we do not need to refer specifically to neuter plural conjuncts but to target forms which are identical (including when that identity is due to syncretism).

8.5.3   How does resolution relate to domains?

Resolution is construction independent; for example, it does not differ for agreement of the verbal predicate within the clause domain, as opposed to agreement of the relative pronoun with its antecedent. Thus information about the domain cannot be part of resolution.[14] What *does* differ is the likelihood of resolution as compared with agreement with the nearest conjunct. Resolution is a particular case of semantic agreement. The distribution of resolution (semantic agreement) versus agreement with the nearest conjunct (syntactic agreement) is therefore constrained by the Agreement Hierarchy, as we saw in §7.4.1. The larger the domain, the more likely resolution becomes.

---

[13] Note that the plural prefix on nouns is *ma-* for the plural of gender 5/6 while the agreement marker is *a-*. Chichewa does not have fully alliterative agreement.

[14] For an account of the combination of number and person resolution with complementizer agreement see van Koppen (2005).

8.5.4   How does resolution relate to features?

For person and number the answer here is relatively easy. The person and number values required by resolution match the semantics of the feature in question. Thus first person is used for reference to a group including the speaker, as with English *we*. If we conjoin *I* and *she/he/you/they* we arrive at just such a group. Similarly the plural is used in English to refer to more than one, as in *the pets*. Then *Douglas* (the dog), *Cathy* (the cat) and *Godwyn* (the goldfish) form such a group, so it makes sense that we say *Douglas, Cathy and Godwyn need feeding*. And in a language like Slovene the dual is used for two, and therefore also for two singular conjoined noun phrases.

Gender is more challenging. In many instances gender has no direct semantic import. However, in the instances where it does we see a similar correspondence (Corbett 1983: 201–2). Take Serbian/Croatian/Bosnian, where just as in Slovene conjoining masculine with feminine is resolved as masculine. What happens outside resolution? There are instances like *amerikanci* 'Americans', which can be used of male and female Americans together; such forms take masculine plural agreements. (Similarly in French, Italian and so on.) Thus the semantics of the masculine gender in these languages includes reference to groups including males as well as to groups consisting only of males. To the extent that it is possible, then, gender resolution follows the semantics of the gender feature (Corbett 1991: 292). We return to this issue in §8.6.

8.5.5   How does resolution relate to conditions?

There are various agreement conditions which determine whether or not there will be resolution, as opposed to agreement with the nearest conjunct (§§6.1.2–6.1.4). Given that agreement is to be with all conjuncts, resolution determines the appropriate resolved form. Resolution differs from conditions in that resolution takes a set of controller feature values and computes a feature specification for the target, while conditions operate at one remove (§6.2).

8.5.6   How do the different types of resolution interact with each other?

The relation between person, number and gender resolution is very interesting. On the one hand they are fully independent. That is, there are no rules of the type 'if there is a second person feminine conjunct . . .' or 'if there is a neuter dual conjunct . . .' Person resolution needs to refer only to person, number to number and gender to gender. The examples in §8.5.2 need reference to identical realizations, not to the feature values which are realized. We might therefore think that person, number and gender resolution are completely independent of each other. However, while they are independent in their formulation, they are not independent in their operation. They operate as a set or not at all.

Agreement may be with one conjunct or with all conjuncts; if the latter, that is, if resolution operates, then all applicable resolution rules must operate.[15] While most of my examples have involved singular conjuncts, resolution can operate for plural conjuncts too.[16]

8.6   Motivation

We now have the pointers for a better understanding of how resolution works, and can benefit from new work by Wechsler & Zlatić (2003). We have established that resolved forms are instances of semantic agreement. Therefore instances of resolution (rather than agreement with the nearest conjunct) conform to the Agreement Hierarchy. Person and number resolution basically follow the semantics of the feature in question (though person resolution is problematic in a few languages, particularly in German). Gender, not surprisingly, is harder.

In earlier work I suggested a typology of gender resolution according to whether it worked on a syntactic or a semantic principle (see, for example, Corbett 1991: 269–84). In languages like Slovene (§8.3.1) it appeared that resolution needed access only to syntactic gender, the rules being just the same for animates and inanimates; this is the syntactic type of gender resolution. In languages like Godoberi (§8.3.2), Tsakhur (§8.3.3) and Luganda (§8.3.4) gender resolution requires access to semantic information. This is hardly surprising for Godoberi, but with the larger gender system of Luganda it means that the syntactic gender of the conjuncts is often 'ignored' by resolution. There are a couple of weak points in this typology. There are languages of the mixed type (as discussed in §8.4). More important, though, the typology applies just to gender resolution; it is surprising that gender resolution should be so distinctive, given its peripheral nature. In answer to this I suggested (Corbett 2003a, a paper submitted in 1994 but somewhat delayed in publication) that a language's type of gender resolution depends on its type of gender assignment.

Recall from §4.3.1 that gender assignment may depend purely on semantic information; this is what we find in languages like Godoberi and in Tamil. Then there are languages like Tsakhur, where semantic information is key, but where there is a minority of nouns which cannot be assigned to gender in this way. Then we find languages where semantic assignment leaves many nouns unassigned, and for these formal information is required too. This may be morphological information, as in languages like Russian and Slovene, or phonological information, as in French. There are no languages with only formal gender assignment:

---

[15] One way of thinking of the German exception to person resolution in §8.1 is to say that number resolution has operated but not person resolution. But this does not get us very far. It seems rather that the 1/3 plural form is becoming a default plural form.

[16] This can be seen by the effect of person or more often gender resolution. See, for example, Mohammad (1988) on Arabic, Steinberg & Caskey (1988) on Spanish, and Corbett (1983: 209–11) on Serbian/Croatian/Bosnian. While the resolution rules are the same, resolution is less likely to operate than with singulars, since the target will be marked as plural in any case.

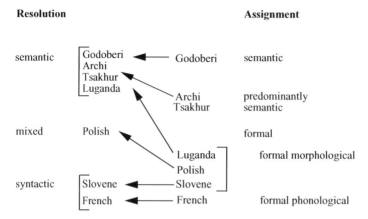

Resolution   **Assignment**

Figure 8.1   *The relation between resolution and assignment (Corbett 2003a: 318)*

gender always has a semantic core. Suggested correlations with gender resolution are given in Figure 8.1.

The regularity is that gender resolution is never determined by semantic considerations to a lesser degree than is gender assignment. This suggests that gender resolution tends to favour semantic resolution, an idea that was on the right track. Moreover, it makes the typology of resolution dependent on the typology of assignment, which seems right. After all, gender assignment is central to the gender system: first, since any language with a gender system has a gender assignment system; and second, since gender assignment is frequently invoked (whenever a noun heads an agreement controller which determines gender agreement). Conversely, gender resolution is peripheral: first, since many gender languages do not have it, the most common reason being that gender is not distinguished in the plural (as, for example, in German and Russian); and second, it is invoked only for a small number of constructions (coordinate constructions and some quasi-comitative constructions).

While it was a step forward, this account still left the relation between assignment and resolution rather vague. Meanwhile, there were more formal analyses. The attempt by Dalrymple & Kaplan (2000) failed to accommodate languages like Slovene and Serbian/Croatian/Bosnian (Wechsler & Zlatić 2003: 174–5). Wechsler & Zlatić (2003: 171–95) also gave an alternative formal account. They made the interesting suggestion that across languages *animate* noun phrases are subject to semantic resolution, while *inanimates* are subject to syntactic resolution. In all languages, even those like Slovene, Serbian/Croatian/Bosnian and French, gender resolution is semantically driven, they suggest. A key piece of evidence concerns the behaviour of hybrid nouns (§5.5.3) in coordinate structures. They cite Farkaş & Zec (1995) for this; in fact the observation had been made earlier by Megaard (1976: 95), though its significance was not recognized then. Of the evidence cited by Wechsler & Zlatić, perhaps the most convincing is from French. It concerns hybrids like *sentinelle* 'sentry' (mentioned in Table 7.1). Its agreements, except sometimes of the personal pronoun, are claimed to be feminine, even though reference is normally to a male. How then will *sentinelle* behave if conjoined with a feminine? Recall that in French resolution is as in Slovene and similar languages: the feminine is found if all conjuncts are feminine, and otherwise the masculine. Wechsler & Zlatić give these judgements, adding that there is 'cross-speaker variation':

French (Wechsler & Zlatić 2003: 177)

(47)   La   sentinelle et   sa   femme ont
          DEF.F.SG   sentry   and   3SG.POSS.F.SG wife(F) have.3PL

          été   pris   / *pris-es
          be.PST.PTCP take.PST.PTCP.PASS[M][17] / take.PST.PTCP.PASS-F.PL

          en   otage.
          in   hostage

          'The sentry and his wife have been taken hostage.'

Wechsler & Zlatić state that *la sentinelle* 'the sentry' normally takes feminine agreement in the predicate. If the resolution rule applies to syntactic gender, we would expect feminine agreement in (47). Hence they argue, even in languages like French and Slovene we still need to recognize the need for semantic gender resolution.

Wechsler & Zlatić acknowledge Farkaş & Zec (1995), who cite comparable Romanian data. However, since it is already established that Romanian has a mixed resolution system (§8.4.3), their example though suggestive does not prove the point Wechsler & Zlatić want to make.[18] It is already covered by the resolution rules in Corbett (1991: 289). The Serbian/Croatian/Bosnian data of Megaard (1976: 95) and Wechsler & Zlatić (2003: 179) are also not quite convincing, since it is known that Serbian/Croatian/Bosnian sometimes uses semantic resolution (Corbett 1991: 299–303). Hence I take the French data to be the most convincing. Once the point from French is accepted, these other examples provide useful support.

The proposal of Wechsler & Zlatić (2003: 177) based on these data is that animate noun phrases are subject to semantic resolution, and inanimate to syntactic resolution. The general system of resolution is then like that proposed for Romanian (§8.4.3). Given the system found in languages like Godoberi, we might rethink their suggestion as follows: resolution *must* be based in part on semantic criteria; it may additionally be based on syntactic criteria. This then gives us two pleasing effects. First, gender resolution is more like person and number resolution. Second, gender resolution directly reflects gender assignment, since gender assignment is always based on semantic criteria, which may or may not be supplemented by formal criteria (§4.3.1). I therefore propose this scheme:

---

[17] In this instance the form does not distinguish masculine singular and masculine plural. The finite verb shows it is plural.

[18] Moosally (1998: 111n1) could not replicate the judgements with the Romanian speaker she worked with.

(48)   The relations between gender assignment and gender resolution

	assignment	←resolution
semantic criteria	1. essential	2. essential (if there is resolution)
↑ formal criteria	3. possible	4. possible

This is to be read as follows:

cell 1.   Any language which has a gender system must have gender assignment, and this must include semantic criteria (all gender systems have a semantic core).

cell 2.   A language with a gender system may or may not also need gender resolution rules. Thus gender resolution implies gender assignment. Those languages that do require gender resolution must have semantic resolution.

cell 3.   Languages which have gender assignment (with obligatorily semantic criteria) may additionally require formal gender assignment (as in the case of Russian, French, Slovene, Luganda among others).

cell 4.   Languages with semantic and formal gender assignment which require gender resolution must have semantic resolution, but they may also require formal (= syntactic) gender resolution: Slovene does, while Luganda does not. Thus formal gender resolution implies formal gender assignment.

In terms of implications: a language with gender resolution must have gender assignment (but the reverse does not hold). Thus Russian and German do not need gender resolution, since agreement does not distinguish genders in the plural, while Slovene and Tsakhur do need gender resolution. Formal assignment rules imply semantic assignment rules (but not the reverse), and formal resolution implies semantic resolution (but not the reverse). Of the components in (48), a language may have: 1, 1+2, 1+3, 1+2+3, or 1+2+3+4.

What does this approach to gender resolution mean for the languages we have analysed? For Godoberi, Tsakhur and Luganda the analysis remains as before. They have semantic resolution. For languages like Slovene, however, the difference is the suggestion that these too have semantic resolution, including:

(a)   If all conjuncts refer to female humans, agreement is feminine.
(b)   If all conjuncts refer to humans, whether all male or of mixed sexes, agreement is masculine.

The rules for all other nouns are 'piggy-backed' on these semantic rules: (a) is the basis for a rule that feminine conjuncts will take feminine agreement, (b) is the basis for a rule giving masculine in other cases; see Wechsler & Zlatić (2003: 183–7) for a technical way of doing this. This account works more easily for Slovene and French than for languages like Romanian, which require additional machinery. That is, they require rules which are not based on the semantic ones.

Yet this seems reasonable: we know that gender varies considerably from language to language, and Romanian has a genuinely unusual system.

We can take the idea of Wechsler & Zlatić further. We need not divide the resolution rules according to animacy as they suggest.[19] We can simply say that semantic resolution must refer to *whatever the semantic gender assignment rules of the language refer to*. This solution is more elegant, in that it makes the connection with assignment complete. There are also some instances where it gives a different (and correct) prediction. For instance, in Godoberi and Tamil the rules need to refer not to animates, but to humans, since non-human animates behave differently from humans for agreement purposes in these languages. In Algonquian languages like Ojibwa, on the other hand, reference to animacy is what is required.[20] Thus assignment and resolution run in parallel, and semantic resolution can refer to a semantic property only if there is a semantic assignment rule referring to it.

Surely the results cannot be so clear-cut? We are dealing with hybrids after all. The French data evoke differing judgements, as Wechsler & Zlatić (2003: 194–5) make clear. Data from Greek too need further investigation, since data on hybrids do not fit neatly here (Michalopoulou 1994: 76–91). However, there does seem to be a general effect that hybrids show a 'semantic shift' for resolution purposes. That is, if we have a hybrid which takes syntactic agreement at a given point on the Agreement Hierarchy (we have been looking mainly at the predicate), under resolution we may well find that it is treated in terms of its semantic value. This is worth illustrating once more:

Serbian/Croatian/Bosnian (Popović 1991: 47)

(49)   Zar   ste   se   Vi   i   Mira   posvada-l-e?
         Really AUX.2PL REFL   2PL   and   Mira(F) quarrel-PST-F.PL
         'Have you (one woman) and Mira really quarreled?'

In Serbian/Croatian/Bosnian, honorific *Vi* 'you' takes masculine plural agreement of the active participle.[21] In this example *Vi* is being used of a woman. When conjoined, it is the semantic value which counts: (49) is treated as the conjoining of two noun phrases referring to females, and not as the conjunction of masculine and feminine (which would lead to masculine agreement).[22]

---

[19] Stephen Wechsler informs me (person communication) that the split is a matter of the particular data presented, and that the intention was in general along the lines of the thinking here, except that the role given here to gender assignment is treated differently by Wechsler & Zlatić. See also Wechsler (forthcoming).

[20] Ojibwa provides a small amount of evidence in support of the Wechsler & Zlatić account (see Corbett 1991: 304–5).

[21] It conforms to the Predicate Hierarchy (§7.7.1) in taking the masculine plural in all positions except for the predicate noun; besides the masculine plural, some examples of singular predicate adjectives, in the appropriate gender, are also found (Corbett 1983: 49; Popović 1991).

[22] This example shows why I have avoided the term 'pragmatic agreement', since here pragmatic agreement to show respect is overridden; reference to two females requires feminine agreement in such examples.

In a nutshell, gender resolution follows the language's gender assignment system closely.[23] This account covers more of the data than before, and more elegantly. However, relying on hybrids for crucial evidence also means that the judgements are less clear-cut, and there is still much to be understood about the more difficult systems.

8.7 Conclusion

Conjoined structures are in a way marginal, and yet they are of key importance for understanding agreement. Where resolution is called into play, person and number are relatively straightforward. Here resolution typically follows the semantics of the features. Taking the evidence of hybrids, I concluded that gender resolution too is based on the semantics of gender, to the extent that this is possible. The way to capture that result is to make gender resolution directly dependent on the particular language's system of gender assignment. This is a good step forward, but for certain languages it leaves plenty of work to be done, since some examples are typically avoided by speakers and judgements are variable. We need to continue combining careful work with consultants and work on corpora.

---

[23] To put it slightly differently, assignment has to be able to handle nonce items and new borrowings as well as established nouns; resolution can be seen as the part of it which deals with conjoined structures (Matthew Baerman, personal communication). For assigning feature values to conjoined structures, semantic factors always weigh at least as heavily as they do with established lexical items.

9   Other perspectives

While the main perspective of the book is syntactic and typological, it is worth considering four further questions: How does agreement arise and change? What does agreement do? How do children acquire it? And what can psycholinguistic research tell us about it? In this way the final chapter offers prospects as well as a conclusion.[1]

9.1   Diachrony

An important view of agreement systems is provided by the ways in which they develop. The rise and fall of agreement systems are understood in outline. However, the detail is far from clear. A good deal of what we know is by inference from current patterns and recent change, and in telling the story I can often refer back to data I have analysed earlier in the book. We shall also look at less dramatic changes which involve interesting shifts within existing agreement systems.

9.1.1   The rise of agreement systems

It has long been accepted that pronouns provide a major source of agreement morphology, progressing from full pronouns, to clitics, to inflections along a well-established grammaticalization path, as discussed, for instance, by Givón (1976), Bynon (1992) and Corbett (1995b).[2] Two different changes are

---

[1] Another perspective is provided by signed languages. Researchers of various signed languages refer to 'agreement' for the system according to which referents may be assigned to a location in space, and referred to by subsequent indicating (by pointing or gaze). The analogy is interesting, but the phenomenon seems to me to be sufficiently different to require study in its own terms, rather than being treated as a type of agreement. It does not exhibit the systematic covariance required of agreement (§1.3). Interesting references on this topic include: Cormier, Wechsler & Meier (1999), Meir (2002) and Aronoff, Meir & Sandler (2005); the latter includes a defence of the use of 'agreement' (treating the system in signed languages as similar to radical alliterative agreement, §3.5.2) and gives further references in support.
   An entry point into work giving the perspective of Natural Language Processing is provided by Barbu, Evans & Mitkov (2002), who show the difficulties for automatic anaphor resolution caused by pronouns whose feature specifications do not match those of their antecedents.
[2] The idea of a pronominal origin is an old one; see Ariel (2000: 198–9) for sources, going back to 1798. For Givón's more recent thoughts see (2001: 420–6).

involved: free independent words change in form to become clitics and finally obligatory bound inflections, and referential pronouns change in function to become agreement markers. The formal and functional changes do not necessarily run in parallel. We noted in §3.2.3 that a clitic can function as an agreement marker, and we saw in §3.8 how pronouns can be obligatorily bound to the verb and yet retain their pronominal function (as pronominal affixes, Mithun 1991). Progress down these paths can be swift or slow: the intermediate points are not inherently unstable. The main evidence for this account is from renewal. We see agreement systems being renewed by the development of free pronouns to clitics, and clitics to agreement affixes, and we take this as an indication of how agreement systems are born. Of course, we would like to see pristine examples too, but these are not easy to find.

Let us begin with the formal part of the development. Givón (1976: 68) says that agreement arises exclusively from anaphoric pronouns (schematically, *the man, he arrived* develops into *the man he-arrived*). Givón cites examples like this:

Swahili (Givón 1976: 157)
(1)   ki-kopo   ki-li-vunjika
        SG-cup(7/8) 7-PST-break
        'The cup broke.'

He states that the origin of the agreement marker as a pronoun is established beyond doubt for Bantu, and suggests that if the noun phrase is omitted such markers function as pronouns (showing their older function). This, of course, takes us back to the issues of whether to give the morphology two functions (as Givón suggests) or to suggest that the marker has a single pronominal function (issues we discussed in §3.8.2).

Renewal provides good, if indirect, evidence for a pronominal origin of agreement systems; that is, new agreement markers are added on top of an existing system. We have already seen a clear instance of this in Skou (§3.2.4). Donohue (2003a) gives an interesting picture of successive waves of cliticization, which give a complex system in the modern language. Different verbs behave differently; consider this illuminating pattern of pronoun and verb:

(2)   Skou (Donohue 2003a: 482): the verb *e* 'go east, ascend'

	singular		plural	
1	nì	nì=e	ne	ne=n-e
2	mè	mè=m-e	e	e=e
3 masculine	ke	ke=ke-e	te	te=t-e
3 feminine	pe	pe=p-e		

Here we can see the new wave of cliticized agreement markers, which look exactly like the corresponding pronoun. Indeed, at the early stages of the development of agreement markers we would expect to find alliterative agreement (§3.5.1). But inside the cliticized markers this verb also shows an older marker, in many cells of the paradigm. This marker clearly reveals its pronominal origin, but is no longer fully regular. There is more: in §3.2.3 we saw examples of the verb *fue* 'see', which, in addition to a cliticized marker, shows agreement by vowel alternation, a pattern which Donohue explains in terms of older suffixal object agreement (2003a: 495–7). Skou indeed shows successive waves of new agreement markers (we saw an example marking agreement four times in §3.2.4). Recall too that Skou displays important characteristics of canonical systems: in particular, as we noted in §3.2.3, the subject pronoun is normally present (that is, the third person pronouns are regularly included and first and second person pronouns are present more often than not, Mark Donohue, personal communication).

Of course, it would be nice to see the start of an agreement system where none existed before. This is a tall order. Mark Donohue (personal communication) offers this example. Palu'e, an Austronesian language spoken on Flores, Indonesia, has no agreement system, nor do any of its close relatives have agreement (Palu'e may have had agreement in the distant past, but there has been a clear break without agreement). Currently it has this clitic:

Palu'e (Mark Donohue, personal communication)

(3)   Ak=pana
         1SG=go
         'I went'

Ak= is available only for a nominative argument, and it is part of the same phonological word as the verb. This one clitic appears to be the very first step towards building an agreement system. In origin *ak=* is clearly related to the free pronoun:

(4)   Aku pana
         1SG go
         'I went'

Note, however, that *ak=* cannot occur together with any free pronoun:

(5)   *Aku ak=pana
         1SG   1SG=go
         'I went'

Thus Palu'e has a long way to go, if it is to join languages like Russian or Skou, both in extending the paradigm and in allowing pronouns to co-occur with the marker on the verb. A language which is also at an early stage, but rather more advanced than Palu'e, is the Melanesian Creole Bislama, for which see Meyerhoff (2000).

Why do we get precisely *verb* agreement in this way? The simple answer may well be right, namely that clauses typically have a verb, and whatever the rules are in the particular language for clitic placement, the verb is likely to qualify as a possible host or the only host. While verb agreement is very common, we can see the rise of other types too. For example, in §2.2.7 we saw innovative complementizer agreement. Complementizer agreement itself is new in Germanic, but it has arisen within an existing agreement system. Weiß (2005) provides a survey of its intricacies in different dialects. Our key language Tsakhur is also significant here. We saw in §2.2.8 evidence of how its particles take with them an agreement slot; this can create new agreement targets.

How can we relate this story to the specific nature of the morphology of agreement? The clitics in Skou appear to attach straightforwardly according to their syntactic position: subject pronouns precede the verb, and so when they attach as clitics the result is prefixes. This is how Givón (1976) suggests such markers arise. However, this is not always so; today's morphology is not always yesterday's syntax, as Comrie (1980) demonstrates. Using data from Mongolian languages such as Buryat, he shows that the current agreement markers are not positioned according to the old word order. For recent discussion of this general issue, with Spanish as a case-study, see Enrique-Arias (2002), and for a Minimalist perspective, looking particularly at Italian dialects and at Welsh, see Roberts & Roussou (2003: 175–92).

What is the mechanism that triggers the functional change that gives rise to verb agreement? As we saw earlier, Givón suggested topic-shifting constructions as the source, and the renewal of agreement in non-standard French via this route adds plausibility to this scenario (Lambrecht 1981). Various problems have been raised with this account (see Corbett 1995b for discussion). In particular, it is not a convincing source when agreement arises initially in first and second persons, since topic-shifting is not common with these persons.[3] This issue is discussed in Ariel (2000), who proposes an additional mechanism. It is known that more accessible entities receive less substantial coding. Thus zero coding may be used for highly accessible entities (as in: *Freda came in and Ø sat down*), while full noun phrases may be required to introduce entities which are not otherwise accessible for the hearer. Agreement is a less substantial means of coding than pronouns. And the first and second persons refer to highly accessible entities. Putting these points together, Ariel suggests that we should therefore expect pronouns to be reduced, via clitics, to agreement markers precisely for first and second persons. She presents this as a mechanism complementary to topic-shifting, the latter being more plausible as a source for third person agreement. For discussion see Siewierska (2004a, 2004b: 261–8), and for a Minimalist view see Fuß (2005).

There are many systems whose current stage of development is difficult to establish. In various languages the formal means available (pronouns, clitics,

---

[3] See Siewierska (2004b: 148–51) for languages with agreement marking in some but not all persons.

agreement) are used for different functions, balanced against each other in different ways. For instance, we noted in §3.8.2, footnote 16, that the relative load of overt pronouns and agreement varies according to factors such as person. Indeed the whole discussion of pronominal affixes in §3.8.2 may be seen as an attempt to grapple with intermediate (but not therefore unstable) systems. My approach has been to situate these systems at different points on a scale calibrated outwards from canonical agreement. Nascent systems like that of Palu'e are at a distant extreme, and they may move closer to canonical over time. They may never come very close, since canonical systems are rare.

There has been work on the development of agreement in different language families; see Butt (forthcoming) on Punjabi, and on Indo-Aryan more generally; for the long controversy on the development of agreement in Tibeto-Burman languages see DeLancey (1989), van Driem (1991, 1993, 1995), LaPolla (1992), Sun (1995) and Nishi (1995); for Daghestanian see Helmbrecht (1996), Harris (2002) and Schultze (2004); for Kartvelian see Tuite (1998); and for Omotic see Hayward (1998).

We must also ask about the development of agreement within the noun phrase. Givón suggested it develops from verb agreement, but gave less evidence for this part of the story. A different source was suggested by Greenberg (1978), offering evidence from Daly languages of north Australia that general classifiers are a possible source. This is made more plausible by Reid's (1997) account of Ngan'gityemerri (Daly family), a language we met in §1.4.2. According to Reid, Ngan'gityemerri shows agreement for fifteen genders. Nine are distinguished by bound agreement markers, but six have (optional) freeform generics/classifiers:

Ngan'gityemerri (Reid 1997: 177)
(6)   (tyin)   gan'gan   (tyin)   kinyi
        WOOMERA fish.spear.woomera WOOMERA this
        'this fish spear-type woomera'

Tyin is the freeform generic for woomeras (sticks designed for throwing various spears). In its first use in (6) it is analogous to a classifier. In its second use it is more like an agreement marker. At first sight we might think the language has two different gender systems, but this is not the case, since in some genders there is a generic available in addition to a marker on the noun and to a bound agreement marker. Moreover, while the use of the generic is optional, so too is agreement. Ngan'gityemerri provides a clear view of the rise of gender systems and of agreement systems. Reid (1997: 211–12) charts the likely development from freeform generic to bound agreement marker, in a system in which the generics are still feeding the gender system

A comparable system, with a large inventory of classifiers showing some agreement-like behaviour, is that of Miraña (a Witotoan language of the Colombian Amazon), as described in Seifart (2004).

Miraña (Seifart 2004: 229)

(7)   ó-dì   íʰkà-:bà   tsà-:bà   múhùː-:bà   ʔúɓìː-:bà
      1SG-POSS   be-CLF   one-CLF   big.SUBORDINATE-CLF   basket-CLF
      'I have one big basket.'

The form -:bà 'deep container' is one of over fifty specific markers, which relate mainly to shape ('tube', 'two-dimensional flexible object' and so on). For about a dozen the noun origin is relatively clear: for instance -:bà 'deep container' comes from bánè:bà 'deep pool'. In addition there are some 30 'repeaters' used in full, or reduced, which function both as free nouns and like the other markers we are discussing. They have the same meaning in both uses, and they indicate the source of the other markers. There is a further set of six general markers (masculine and feminine singular and dual, animate plural, and inanimate), which gives an exhaustive classification of the nouns. (This is another instance of superclassing, see §5.3.1.)

Note how the marker occurs on the noun, which is typical; it can also appear on other sentence elements, such as on predicates and on pronouns. For some targets the presence of a marker is obligatory. Seifart shows how such markers are used for reference tracking. We can therefore see a language which, on the basis of a system of classifiers, has just developed (non-canonical) agreement.

9.1.2   Agreement in a mixed language: Michif

In presenting the clearest examples, there is a danger of implying that systems are always clean and neat. However, given the right circumstances, truly weird systems can arise. Take, for instance, the agreement system of Michif. Michif arose in Canada by the early nineteenth century from the intermarriage of French speaking men (fur traders) and Cree speaking women. In outline, the men brought French nouns and the women contributed verbs from Cree, an Algonquian language (Bakker & Papen 1997, Bakker 1997). The result is a remarkable agreement system. The noun phrase looks rather like French: the definite article agrees in gender: *lu* M.SG, *la* F.SG and *li* PL. Adjectives also agree, but only when they precede the noun in the noun phrase:

Michif (Peter Bakker 1997: 106–7, and personal communication)

(8)   æ̃   gru   sarpã
      INDF.ART.M.SG   big[M]   snake(M)
      'a big snake'

(9)   la   gru-s   tãt
      DEF.ART.F.SG   big-F   tent(F)
      'the big tent'

When following the noun they do not agree:

(10) la   mæ̃zũ   blã
      DEF.ART.F.SG   house(F)   white[M]
      'the white house'

Demonstratives are from Cree (apart from some frozen expressions), and they preserve a three-way distinction in distance: near, intermediate and distant. In Cree they agree in animacy and number with the noun, and this is carried over into Michif, but in Michif they co-occur with the article. This means that within the noun phrase there is agreement both in French-like gender (masculine/feminine) and Cree-like gender (animate/inanimate, where animates are those denoting humans, animals and some inanimates too, see Corbett 1991: 22 and references there). Here are some examples:

Michif (Bakker 1997: 109):

(11)   awa   lu   garsū
         this.near.ANIM.SG   DEF.ART.M.SG   boy
         'this boy'

(12)   awa   la   fij
         this.near.ANIM.SG   DEF.ART.F.SG   girl
         'this girl'

(13)   ana   lu   nur
         that.intermediate.ANIM.SG   DEF.ART.M.SG   bear
         'that bear'

(14)   u:ma   lu   papji
         this.near.INAN.SG   DEF.ART.M.SG   paper
         'this paper'

(15)   anɪma   la   mæ̃zū
         that.intermediate.INAN.SG   DEF.ART.F.SG   house
         'that house'

(16)   ne:ma   lu   šã̄
         that.distant.INAN.SG   DEF.ART.M.SG   field
         'that field'

The verb in Michif agrees in the animate/inanimate gender of Cree, and the less predictable assignments of nouns to gender are preserved (Bakker 1997: 99). The Michif verb also maintains agreement in obviation; obviation may be marked on the noun, but even when it is not, the verb still shows agreement (Bakker 1997: 89). Thus the specific situation which brought about the mixed language Michif produced a remarkable mixed agreement system, including cross-cutting agreement in animacy and in French-style gender within the noun phrase. (For the partly analogous situation in Mba languages see Corbett 1991: 184–8.)

9.1.3   Change within agreement systems

Fully established agreement systems are liable to change. We saw in §5.5 that there are various mismatches which are likely to produce agreement options. These are a source of change. Such change is typically constrained by the Agreement Hierarchy (attributive > predicate > relative pronoun > personal pronoun). Changes favouring forms with greater semantic justification proceed from the right of the hierarchy. Given that personal pronouns can occur at various distances from the potential controller, there are likely to be examples where a pronoun may be used deictically (and so take the form justified by semantics) but where the hearer may construe it as controlled by the antecedent. For many nouns this leads to no effect, but where there is a potential mismatch, this can lead to the development of a hybrid. The data indicate that this has happened, for example, with Russian words like *vrač* 'doctor', which though they can denote a female remain formally like masculines (§5.4.1, §7.2.3). The personal pronoun is now normally feminine (though the masculine is not completely excluded), the relative almost always feminine; the feminine (semantic form) is also common in the predicate, though the masculine is also found, and the feminine is beginning to make headway even in attributive position (though here the masculine is the more likely). The rise of the animate gender in various Bantu languages is carefully documented by Wald (1975), and this too has spread from the right of the hierarchy. A development which appears to have moved along the hierarchy in the opposite direction is found in some southern Polish dialects (Zaręba 1984–85). Hypochoristics and patronymics used for girls and unmarried women (like *Zusię* 'Zusia') follow a declension whose nouns are usually neuter. Neuter agreements, induced this time by the form, have spread right the way along the hierarchy so that girls and unmarried women are referred to with neuter pronouns, and they use the first singular pronoun with neuter agreements to refer to themselves. In these dialects the effect is considerable; the meaning of the genders has been changed (as has happened, in a different way, in Konkani, see §7.3.1)). The feminine is now for married females, the neuter for unmarried females (both genders also include inanimates). Thus agreement fluctuations with constructions or particular lexical items may remain as minor irregularities, but they may spread to give rise to more significant changes, as in the Polish dialects just discussed.

9.1.4   Finer-grained changes in agreement systems

While agreement options are often found with the constructions and lexical items of the types listed in §5.5, the choice is severely constrained. From the point of view of the agreement controller, controllers denoting animates and those preceding the target are more likely to take agreement forms with a higher degree of semantic justification than those which denote inanimates and/or follow the controller. One possibility for change is that the importance of animacy and precedence relative to each other may vary over time. Consider the data on agreement with conjoined noun phrases in Figure 9.1, based on a corpus of Russian prose works of the nineteenth and twentieth centuries (details in Corbett 1983: 127–32). We have established that animate controllers favour semantic agreement (§6.1.2) as do controllers preceding the target (§6.1.3). When both factors point in the same direction, in every example in the corpus the semantic (plural) form

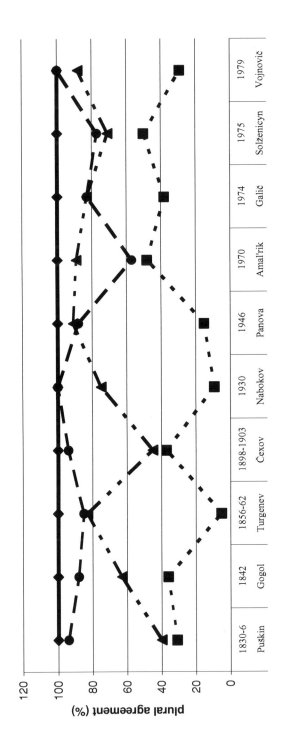

Figure 9.1   *Conjoined noun phrases in Russian: diachronic and stylistic variation*

is used. In the converse case, when inanimate conjuncts follow the target, for each author at each period, we find the lowest proportion of semantic agreement. However, the actual proportion varies quite substantially according to the author.

Most interesting in Figure 9.1 are the examples where we find one factor favouring semantic agreement, but not both. Here we typically find an in-between situation. Note, however, that in the Nabokov text the 'right' word order (subject-predicate) is sufficient to give semantic agreement. More generally, for some authors the word order has the greater effect, while for others it is animacy. Overall, in the nineteenth century word order outweighed animacy, while in the twentieth century, summing over the different authors, the effect of the two factors is almost identical. The subtle change, then, is that these two factors have moved to having equal influence.[4]

9.1.5   'There and back' changes

It is tempting to think, given the examples usually cited, that change inevitably means movement from an initial state to a predictable final state. We may come to expect that that is how change must be. Our key language Russian shows that this is not the only scenario. Consider the data in Table 9.1.

Table 9.1 *Predicate agreement with quantified subjects in Russian: 18th–20th centuries (percentage of plural agreement)*

	18th century		19th century		20th century	
Quantifier	N	%pl	N	%pl	N	%pl
'two', 'three', 'four'	412	87	411	87	856	83
'five' to 'ten'	53	64	156	53	220	50
collectives (e.g. *dvoe* 'two')	66	62	105	78	290	88
complex numbers (e.g. *dvadcat´* '20')	74	35	133	47	168	39
compound numbers (e.g. *sorok pjat´* '45')	69	35	143	50	97	41
neskol´ko 'a few'	133	21	290	48	215	36

These data (derived from Suprun 1969: 185, 188) show that the particular quantifier involved has a major influence on the form of predicate agreement, as noted in §7.4.2. What is of special interest here is the change in the agreement options over time. Table 9.1 shows that if we consider phrases quantified by complex numerals, compound numerals or *neskol´ko* 'a few', we find a rise in plural agreement from the eighteenth to the nineteenth century, and a drop again from the nineteenth to the twentieth century. Thus the change for these quantifiers moves in favour of semantic agreement and then back in favour of syntactic agreement.

---

[4] For an account of changes involving rather different agreement options, this time in the development of Arabic, see Belnap & Gee (1994) and Belnap (1999).

This suggests a model of the tide ebbing and flowing, rather than a unidirectional view of linguistic change.

9.1.6   The loss of agreement

'Agreement systems meet their predictable demise via phonological attrition much like other bound affixes' (Givón 1976: 172). Yet systems in decline still show interesting patterns. I shall give just a few examples. Marchese (1988) gives data on nine Kru languages. Agreement within the noun phrase is being lost while being preserved outside it. Within the noun phrase adjectives lose agreement in these languages before determiners, and adjectives preserve agreement in number longer than agreement in gender. Priestly (1983: 343–6) provides an interesting comparison: he is concerned with the gender agreement in Indo-European and shows how it is usually preserved best in the pronoun and less well in the adjective. Even at the level of the loss of a single agreement opposition within a particular target type there may be a great deal going on. In a detailed study Naro (1981) shows how the loss of verb agreement in spoken Brazilian Portuguese starts from a low-level phonetic rule, which makes third singular and third plural identical for one class of verbs, but that then non-agreement diffuses through the system, mainly in environments where the change is least noticeable in surface form. Ferguson (1996) gives an overview of the contrasting paths of the loss of agreement in English and Swedish, and Roberts (1985) links the loss of agreement of the modals with syntactic developments. Of course, partial loss of an agreement system may be accompanied by renewal, or remnant agreement forms may gain other functions (as in Iwaidja, Ilgar and Garig, Iwaidjan languages of north-western Arnhem land, Evans 2000: 116–18).

9.2   The functions of agreement

In some languages agreement has a very substantial presence, showing distinctive morphological realization on a wide range of targets, which occur frequently. This is the case in languages like Russian, and even more so in Tsakhur. We might expect therefore to find an equally solidly established function for agreement. In fact, suggestions about the function of agreement tend to be partially convincing for specific languages, but to be less convincing when a wider range of languages is examined. Agreement often appears to involve a lot of effort for a questionable payoff.

Levin (2001: 21–7) points to three main suggestions for the function of agreement, all of which appear several times in the literature. The first is that agreement provides **redundancy**: information is repeated and this facilitates the hearer's task. As we have seen, agreement systems vary dramatically; as we get closer to canonical systems, so the degree of redundancy increases. However, most systems are far from canonical, which suggests that if providing redundancy is one function of agreement, it is not the main function. The other suggested functions are partly complementary to the first. A second view of agreement is that it contributes substantially to **reference tracking**, allowing the hearer to keep track of the different referents in a discourse. The agreement features, particularly gender and number, facilitate reference tracking (particularly if anaphoric pronouns are included within the agreement targets, recall §2.2.2 and §7.6.1). There seems to be some truth in this; on the other hand, when we recall the exuberant marking of gender and number on various targets within a single clause in Tsakhur (as in §2.2.5 and §2.2.9), it is difficult to see each instance as contributing to reference tracking. The third suggested function is a syntactic one, **marking constituency**; agreement is claimed to indicate which elements are constituents, even when they are separated. On the face of it this sounds plausible. Yet we saw instances in Tsakhur where it was hard to fathom why the agreement domains were as they were; for instance, the restrictive particle agrees not with the constituent to which it applies but with the absolutive argument (§2.2.9). Furthermore, German noun phrases are marked by agreement, but remain intact: if agreement performs the function of marking their constituency, it does not do so sufficiently well to allow scrambling. There is some evidence for a link between word-order flexibility and agreement. Siewierska (1998: 505–8) investigated a sample of 171 languages and concluded that, while having agreement does not allow us to predict that a language will have flexible word order, the lack of agreement is a good predictor that a language will not have flexible word order. Conversely, rigid word order does not allow us to predict the lack of agreement, but flexible word order is a good predictor that a language has agreement.

We saw other possible functions of agreement when we examined agreement choices, as with, for instance, *committee* nouns. It is suggested that the agreement options permit expression of different perspectives: a committee may be viewed as an entity (singular agreement) or as a set of individuals (plural agreement). The problem is that the putative function is arbitrarily limited in its scope. The suggested function for English is available only if *committee* is in subject position and the verb is in the present tense (compare the discussion of agreement as a possible reflection of focus in Russian discussed in §6.7.3, where this is available only for a limited set of controllers). Given that the evidence for each of the proposed functions is not fully convincing, it appears unlikely that agreement is to be explained in terms of a single function. Rather, it has different combinations of functions in different languages.

9.3   Child language acquisition

It is difficult enough to show that the child has acquired a feature such as number. It is harder still to show acquisition of part of an agreement system. So it is not surprising that as yet there is no clear picture of how children acquire agreement systems. The systems they have to acquire vary considerably, from those like Russian and Tsakhur, where most utterances provide evidence about the agreement system, to the typological rarity of English, where the child has relatively little evidence to go on (and the distribution of -s is potentially confusing). Ingham (1998) reports on Sophie, who at age 2;9 rarely used verb agreement in English, even though by 2;5 to 2;6 she already showed clear command of agreement within the noun phrase.

Keeney & Wolfe (1972) investigated the acquisition of agreement by forty-six American children aged 3;0 to 4;11. They recorded the children's spontaneous speech and conducted imitation and comprehension tests. In spontaneous speech the children showed mastery of subject-verb agreement (94% of the 906 utterances recorded showed appropriate agreement). When asked to repeat sentences where subject and verb did not agree, there was a significant tendency for the children to correct them. However, nonverbal tests aimed to determine whether the children could extract number information just from the verbal inflection produced only chance performance. This suggests, according to Keeney & Wolfe, that the children had acquired a syntactic rule, but had no comprehension of the semantics of the agreement marker. This is another piece of evidence against the suggestion that agreement in English might be purely semantic (§1.2). For more on the acquisition of English agreement see Radford (1994), and for German see Clahsen & Penke (1992). A study of the acquistion of agreement in Brazilian Portuguese suggested that the system is acquired piecemeal (Rubino & Pine 1998). There is a tradition of work on Bantu languages. Early on, Suzman (1982) pointed out that four children learning Zulu (where the children have extensive evidence on agreement since there are so many agreement targets) adopted rather different strategies.[5] Work on Bantu is surveyed by Demuth (2003). There is recent work by Deen (2004) on the acquisition of Swahili agreement, confronting the old problem of object agreement / pronominalization (§3.8.2) and the role of specificity (§6.7.2).

There is a group of children whose language learning is of particular interest here. They have difficulty acquiring language, particularly morphology, but for whom there is no obvious related problem. That is, their mental age is as expected from their chronological age, and they have no hearing or behavioural problem. Such children are called 'specifically-language impaired' (SLI). There are competing suggestions as to the cause of the problem. In a set of papers Harald Clahsen has suggested that the problem is precisely in establishing agreement relations, hence this approach is called the 'grammatical agreement deficit'.

---

[5] Suzman's work is also relevant for the issue of radical alliterative agreement (§3.5.2). Given the alliterative nature of much of Zulu agreement, we might expect children to overgeneralize in this direction. However, such extensions of alliterative agreement were 'exceptional within the child's own data' (1982: 64). 'The scarcity and exceptional nature of these few utterances indicate that concord was not generally perceived as a phonological copying process' (1982: 64). Kupisch, Müller & Cantone (2002: 141–2) give instances in the acquisition of Italian of the form of the article being made to match that of the noun and, importantly, the form of the noun being made to match that of the article.

Clahsen & Hansen (1997) describe work with four German SLI children (aged 6;1 to 6;11). At the beginning of the study the children had evident problems with subject-verb agreement, since regular verbs appeared 76% of the time as the stem or the infinitive. Word order was in general not a problem, except for the verb-second rule. Around ninety therapy sessions were organized for each child, over a fourteen-month period, using material specifically designed to help with the aquisition of agreement. By the end the children used agreement forms in adult-like ways in 97% of the cases. And once subject-verb agreement was acquired, the figures for verb-second increased substantially, even though this had not been subject to therapy.

9.4 Psycholinguistic research

Psycholinguists have worked very seriously on agreement. 'In English, the linguistic dependency represented in subject-verb agreement exemplifies one of the classic explanatory problems in psycholinguistics . . .' (Bock & Eberhard 1993: 57–8). Agreement is an attractive topic since the agreement features offer discrete choices of values, while the displacement of information offers a window into structural properties. Given this interest and the volume of work it has produced, the psycholinguistic approach to agreement is given special prominence in this chapter. It is true that only a limited range of languages is tackled: the typologically rather odd system of English figures prominently, together with a few other familiar languages. This limits investigation to features with few possible values (see §4.3 and §5.2). On the other hand, the psycholinguistic literature includes insightful experimental designs and meticulous care in controlling for irrelevant factors. There is remarkable and encouraging convergence with linguistic research: results obtained in the carefully controlled conditions of the laboratory match well with results obtained by linguists by examining large amounts of text, as we shall see. To give an idea of the variety of psycholinguistic work, I will structure this section by looking at some of the different techniques used. I divide the studies into two broad groups: production studies (§§9.4.1–9.4.3) and comprehension studies (§§9.4.4–9.4.7).

9.4.1 Observation of spontaneously occurring errors

One way of coming to understand a system is to observe what happens when things go wrong. Since the pioneering work of Fromkin (1971) and Garrett (1975), psycholinguists have been interested in observing errors, for what they may reveal about the normal system. Of course, error is a tricky notion, in that what one researcher counts as an error may be considered an instance of variation or indication of diachronic shift by someone else. Yet we recognize the existence of 'slips of the tongue', when we know that what we said was not what was intended. Careful analysis of potential instances of errors, considering instances of self-correction and examining the environment in which they occur, can allow us to treat some examples as errors (see Bock & Miller 1991: 52–4, 85–6). Fortunately, there is a substantial study of errors in one of our key languages. Rusakova (2001) gathered 542 examples of errors in attributive position in Russian, mainly by personal observation. In many instances it was possible to establish the intended utterance. Consider this example:

Russian speech error (Rusakova 2001: 81):
(17)   Ja   èt-o   čita-l-a   v   **odn-om**   knig-e.
         1SG.NOM this-N.SG.ACC read-PST-F.SG   in one-M/N.SG.LOC   book(F)-SG.LOC
         'I read this in a book.' (woman speaking)

The error is *odnom* 'one', which could be masculine or neuter, and so fails to agree with the head noun *kniga* 'book'. In Rusakova's interpretation the intention was to use the noun *roman* 'novel', which is masculine, and the error results from a switch to *kniga* 'book', which is feminine. The errors as a whole reveal a clear pattern:

(18)   Speech errors in attributive position in Russian (Rusakova 2001: 61)

feature	number of errors
animacy	6
case	38
number	93
gender	395

Recall that in Russian attributive modifiers regularly precede the head. The pattern in (18) confirms the claim in §4.3.4 that these features differ in their nature. In Russian, animacy (§4.2.1) matches semantics almost perfectly. Hence the speaker is referring to an animate or an inanimate and there is little to invoke errors. The opposite situation obtains with gender. There are many nouns for which gender is not semantically justified (§4.3.1); hence it is easy for speakers to begin a noun phrase which makes good semantic sense in context while still not having a unique choice of head noun. This is also possible, but much less likely, with number, since number in Russian matches semantics more closely. And case, being a property of the noun phrase as a whole (§4.4.1), is less likely still to give errors in attributive position (though of course it is not a direct feature (§4.2.4), that is, it does not have the semantic justification which makes animacy so secure).[6]

---

[6] For naturally occurring agreement errors in German see Pfau (2001). A helpful review of psycholinguistic work on agreement errors involving gender can be found in Schriefers & Jeschhniak (1999). Errors of second-language learners may throw further light on agreement systems; Fisher (1985) reports on Swedish learners of English, Clahsen & Hong (1995) investigate Korean learners of German, White, Valenzuela, Kozlowska-MacGregor & Leung (2004) worked with English and French learners of Spanish, while Hawkins & Franceschina (2004) are concerned with English learners of French and Spanish. O'Grady & Yamashita (2002) examine the way Japanese learners of English tackle agreement in coordinate structures for which they would not have received instruction and find that they behave remarkably like native speakers.

9.4.2   Experimental error elicitation

A natural experimental approach is to present speakers with carefully chosen fragments, whether in spoken or written form, and to ask them to continue. For instance, Bock & Miller (1991) start from the attraction/proximity effects noted by Strang (1966), and others (see §2.4 and §7.4.2). The effect is seen in examples like this one:

TV witness cited by Francis (1986: 318)
(19)   The thrust of those allegations **are** baseless.

Here we have 'attraction' of the verbal agreement by the nearer noun phrase. Based on this type of error, Bock & Miller asked participants to repeat preambles such as *The key to the cabinets* . . . and to complete them. The idea was to see whether there would be errors in experimental conditions; in this particular case the plural *cabinets* might induce plural agreement. Participants were encouraged to repeat the preamble and to add their continuation rapidly. There were relatively few responses which were classified as errors (under 5%); if the figure were significantly higher, then of course we might ask whether 'error' was an appropriate term. They were typically in examples with the preamble like that in (19), that is, in instances where the head noun and its dependent are of different numbers, with the verb then agreeing with the nearer one, being plural in our case, rather than with the head. Thus the errors induced in the laboratory conform to those found in natural speech. Extending the dependent phrase (*to the ornate Victorian cabinet(s)*) did not affect the error rates. Several experiments have been carried out along these lines, and we can discuss only some of them.

Bock & Eberhard (1993) used a similar methodology to investigate the basic question of what determines agreement. They asked whether it might be the overt marking of the feature. Thus they investigated phrases of the type *The player on the course* to see whether the final /s/ might induce errors (which would be plausible if agreement were driven by phonological form). Such examples failed to induce errors; we may see this as supporting the notion of phonology-free syntax and running counter to the claims of radical alliterative agreement (§3.5.2). They also tested for regular versus irregular morphology (*The trap for the rats* versus *the trap for the mice*). Again there were no significant effects for regular versus irregular; this supports the notion of morphology-free syntax (§6.3.1). Their results fit with a feature-based view of agreement for English:

> The surprise, then, is the degree to which subcategorised number seems to control verb marking even at the edges of the agreement system. We have therefore argued that the implementation of agreement is directly affected by an abstract marking of number that is not equivalent to notional number or to overt number inflection.   (Bock & Eberhard 1993: 94)

This outcome is consonant with the inferential-realizational approach to morphology (§3.1).

There is a significant asymmetry in the errors found. Consider this example, noticed by Eberhard (1997: 149) in the abstract to an article on agreement (!):

(20)   Grammatical findings indicate that the grammatical number of English
         verbs **are** determined by agreement with the noun.

The dependent noun *verbs* is the likely cause of the agreement error. The asymmetry is that we find examples of this type (singular head, plural dependent, plural verb) but only rarely of the reverse type (plural head, singular dependent, singular verb). This argues against a simple proximity account, which would lead us to expect both types of error with similar frequency. Thus the values of the feature number are not of the same standing (§4.2.6). Work by Nicol & Wilson (2000) on Russian (using examples like *ščet ot buxgalterov* 'the bill from the accountants') gave comparable findings. This is one of the instances where the problem cries out for psycholinguistic work on languages with features with more than two values, where different types of effect can be teased apart. Thus the plural occurs less frequently than the singular and it is difficult to control for this; in a language with a dual, which will be less frequent than the plural, it is possible to take account of this effect. Work using the same basic technique includes Bock, Nicol & Cutting (1999), who investigated nouns like *audience* and *committee*; they found more plurals in agreeing pronouns than in verbs. This finding is as we would expect, given the work on the Agreement Hierarchy reported in §7.2.4. However, it is still reassuring that the psycholinguistic results mirror those of typology and of corpus work.

Vigliocco, Butterworth & Semenza (1995) used the basic methodology of Bock and her colleagues, and applied it to Italian, which allowed them to investigate agreement in gender and number. They found errors in number agreement comparable to those found for English, but extremely few errors in gender agreement. They found evidence that information about the referent of the controller (specifically distributivity) can have an effect (§5.4), as did Eberhard (1999). This latter effect was also found for Spanish (Vigliocco, Butterworth & Garrelt 1996) and for Dutch and French (Vigliocco, Hartsuiker, Jarema & Kolk (1996).

Vigliocco & Franck (1999) worked on French and Italian, and established the effect on agreement of gender when semantically based (where there is semantic assignment §4.3.1). Then, in an interesting departure (2001), they again contrasted French and Italian, but used more subtle data. They brought in nouns like Italian *vittima* 'victim'; this takes feminine agreements in positions to the left of the Agreement Hierarchy, irrespective of the sex of the victim, though anaphoric pronouns may take semantic agreement. They found that 'In both languages, errors were most common when the sex of the referent and the gender of the noun were incongruent' (2001: 378), and they found differences between the two languages. These results fit closely with the regularities I have established: agreement options often result from mismatches, they are subject to the Agreement Hierarchy, and similar mismatches do not give exactly the same results in different languages (as shown in §7.3).

It has generally been assumed that errors of the type in (19) are due to the proximity of the plural noun and the verb. Vigliocco & Nicol (1998) checked this by asking participants to complete fragments, as in the usual methodology, but then in a second experiment they asked them to produce questions. Given the prompt *safe*, and then *The helicopter for the flights*, participants were expected to produce *The helicopter for the flights is safe* (or, if an error was induced, *are safe*). In this first experiment the results confirmed earlier studies. In the second experiment, given similar items, participants were expected to produce: *Is the helicopter for the flights safe?* (or *Are the helicopter for . . .*). If the source for errors is proximity, then there should be fewer errors in the second experiment. In fact the results were comparable between the two. According to Vigliocco & Nicol (1998: 24) 'these results suggest an architecture in which assigning grammatical roles and building hierarchical structure are separate from assigning word order.'

A major study in this paradigm is that of Bock, Eberhard & Cutting (2004), which involves five completion task experiments, comparing verb agreement and the form of pronouns. They found that pronouns are subject to attraction, like verbs (giving more evidence for the claim that both are agreement targets, §2.2.2). They confirmed that with *committee* nouns plural agreement of the pronoun is considerably more likely than that of the verb (§7.2.4).

Sentence completion was also used by Berg (1998), but this time in writing. A comparison of German and English participants revealed a conflict of syntactic and semantic influences on agreement, but with a stronger impact of semantic factors in English. This is what we would expect, given the unusually strong impact of semantic factors on agreement in English (§1.2).

9.4.3   Errors by impaired speakers

Building on the understanding of the experimental technique gained with unimpaired speakers (§9.4.2), Vigliocco, Butterworth, Semenza & Fossella (1994) extended it to use with two aphasic speakers of Italian. This research is developed in Vigliocco & Zilli (1999), working with impaired speakers of Italian in contrast with unimpaired speakers.[7] Both types of speaker used semantic and formal cues for gender assignment (§4.3.1). The results are of undoubted interest in showing how the production of sentences, including the appropriate agreement, can be disrupted in speakers with aphasia.

Almor, MacDonald, Kempler, Andersen & Tyler (2001) investigated number agreement in patients with probable Alzheimer's disease. They found that these patients were less sensitive than the control participants to a lack of agreement between antecedent and anaphoric pronoun, while performing at a similar level to the control participants for subject-verb agreement violations. The researchers suggest that working memory deficits affect processing across sentences but not within sentences, while also pointing to a possible statistical interpretation (they

---

[7] For work with aphasics on gender agreement in Czech see Lehečková (2000).

consider that verb agreement is more frequent than antecedent-pronoun dependencies, and the patients in question become impaired in comprehending structures according to frequency). This indicates both how agreement is used as a means to understand other problems (here, the nature of the impairment caused by Alzheimer's disease) and the difficulty of interpreting some experimental results, however carefully the data are gathered.

9.4.4   Use of response times

We now switch to comprehension studies, those in which participants' understanding is the key; one way of measuring it is through response times. Garnham, Oakhill, Ehrlich & Carreiras (1995) investigated speakers of French and Spanish. They looked at the interpretation of pronouns, which matched or failed to match an antecedent. Participants were asked to respond to examples by pressing a 'yes' or 'no' key. It was not just the answers that were of interest; the reaction times were also measured for analysis. Given the nature of the gender systems of French and Spanish, the researchers were able to contrast examples (involving humans) where the gender is semantically motivated from others where it is not. Their main result is that information about syntactic gender is used in determining the antecedent of a pronoun (suggesting that pronouns are indeed agreement targets, §2.2.2 and §7.6.1) but that as real distance increases, so the effect of syntactic gender diminishes (§7.7.4). These experiments thus give a clear reflection of the gender assignment rules (§4.3.1).

9.4.5   Grammaticality judgements

Working on French, Kail & Bassano (1997) use the same type of material as Bock and others, but instead of inducing errors they asked participants to spot them. Participants heard examples like this:

French (ungrammatical test sentence, Kail & Bassano (1997: 33))
(21)   les=élève-s   de l'=original et   prestigieux professeur veut !   lire . . .
        DEF.PL=pupil-PL of DEF=first   and prestigious teacher   want.SG read.INF . . .
        'the pupils of the first and prestigious teacher wants ! to read . . .'

The participants heard the examples, and in those containing errors a timer was started at the offset of the word with the agreement error (marked '!' in (21)). Participants were asked to indicate, by pressing a button, whether each example was grammatical, which meant that the experimenters could establish the time between the violation and the participant's response. The participants made few incorrect judgements, and 96% of the violations were detected. Analyses were therefore based on the different lengths of time it took for participants to detect a violation. At first sight the results are as we might expect: of the various errors presented to them, participants took longest to detect errors in sentences with a complex noun phrase including a mismatch in number values. There was a less expected result, however. Generalizing over the stimuli with complex noun phrases (with matches and mismatches), we find that participants took longer to detect errors when the head noun was plural (994 milliseconds) than when it was singular (777 milliseconds). The authors suggest this may be because of the specifics of number marking in French. In the examples, as is normally the case in French, it is the articles which give the number of the noun phrases unambiguously. The verbs used were *vouloir* 'want' (as here) and *pouvoir* 'can, may' since with these the relevant agreement is audible (the plural involves an additional segment). However, this result also relates to the effect of number noted in the discussion of example (20). This study shows how an experiment can both give a predictable result (complex noun phrases gave longer decision times) and offer a problem (the errors depended in part on the number of the noun phrase).

9.4.6   Experiments involving event-related brain potentials (ERPs)

Event-related potentials are recorded from electrodes placed on the participant's scalp. They give a picture of electroencephalographic activity (the brain at work). Earlier experiments established that when participants are given sentences with semantic or with syntactic anomalies the two produce *different* observable patterns. Osterhout & Mobley (1995) asked what would happen with agreement violations. When confronted with agreement errors (**Most cats likes to play outside*) participants produced ERP patterns like those established for syntactic anomalies. Moreover, when faced with mismatching pronouns (*The actress . . . he . . .*) the effect also patterned with syntactic anomalies. It is highly significant that the two give similar results (compare §2.2.2 and §7.6.1). The general technique which gives an insight into semantic versus formal effects is one which offers great promise for a deeper understanding of agreement. Thus Brown, van Berkum & Hagoort (2000), working on Dutch, show how discourse-semantic information can lead participants to go against the clear evidence provided by agreement information (in other words, the information provided by the functioning of agreement (§9.2) can be outweighed during the comprehension of spoken language).

9.4.7   Experiments involving tracking of eye movement

Another way of investigating how long processing of agreement takes is by tracking eye movement, as participants read examples on a screen. Deutsch (1998) used this technique to work on agreement in Hebrew. The first experiment varied the distance between subject and predicate, in examples with appropriate agreement and others with agreement errors (in gender, in number or in both). Errors when subject and predicate were relatively close caused the participants to gaze longer at the predicate before moving on, while greater distance caused the effect largely to disappear (compare §7.7.4). The second experiment contrasted subject-predicate and predicate-subject examples. When there were errors, participants gazed longer at the predicate when it preceded the subject (compare §6.1.3) than when it followed. This approach is complemented by an ERP study in Deutsch & Bentin (2001). As Deutsch suggests, part of the explanation for the interesting result observed may be in the asymmetry of agreement (§4.1). The longer gaze resulted when the point at which the participant is first confronted with the error is the predicate, while the feature values make semantic sense only when interpreted with the subject noun phrase.

9.5   Conclusion

I have given a typology of agreement, a phenomenon which pervades some languages, like Russian and Tsakhur, is more limited but still challenging in others, like Kayardild and English, and is absent in others. We have seen the value of the canonical approach in typology, in allowing us to analyse these widely varying systems. This approach will become increasingly useful, I believe, for tackling the more difficult topics in typology. From that starting point we looked at controllers, targets, domains, features and conditions in turn, noting the range of their behaviour and the way they are realized in the morphology. We then looked at the remarkable variety of agreement choices, and showed how this variation is constrained by the Agreement Hierarchy. We tackled the interesting issue of conjoining and the resolution of feature specifications. Finally, we have considered other approaches to agreement, and the results obtained there, notably in psycholinguistics, show encouraging convergence with those from our typological study.

There are areas where significant progress has been made in recent years, both in the range of relevant data established and in the accounts of those data in different formal models. And yet the data I have been able to incorporate into our typology represent considerable challenges for syntactic theory. There is much more still to understand about agreement.

References

This bibliography contains just those items referred to in the text. For further references on agreement see Tiberius, Corbett & Barron (2002) available at:http://www.surrey.ac.uk/LIS/SMG/projects/agreement/agreement_bib.htm.

Abbott, Miriam. 1991. Macushi. In: Desmond C. Derbyshire & Geoffrey K. Pullum (eds.) *Handbook of Amazonian Languages III*, 23–160. Berlin: Mouton de Gruyter.

Abondolo, Daniel M. 1988. *Hungarian Inflectional Morphology*. Budapest: Akadémiai Kiadó.

Ackema, Peter & Neeleman, Ad. 2003. Context-sensitive spell-out. *Natural Language and Linguistic Theory* 21.681–735.

Aikhenvald, Alexandra. Y. 2003. *A Grammar of Tariana, from Northwest Amazonia*. Cambridge: Cambridge University Press.

Aissen, Judith. 1990. Towards a theory of agreement controllers. In: Paul M. Postal & Brian D. Joseph (eds.) *Studies in Relational Grammar 3*, 279–320. Chicago: University of Chicago Press.

Almor, Amit; MacDonald, Maryellen C.; Kempler, Daniel; Andersen, Elaine D. & Tyler, Lorraine K. 2001. Comprehension of long distance number agreement in probable Alzheimer's disease. *Language and Cognitive Processes* 1.35–63.

Alpher, Barry. 1982, Dalabon dual-subject prefixes, kinship categories, and generation skewing. In: Jeffrey Heath, Francesca Merlan & Alan Rumsey (eds.) *The Languages of Kinship in Aboriginal Australia* (Oceania Linguistic Monograph 24), 19–30. Sydney: The University of Sydney.

Ambrazas, Vytautas (ed.) 1997. *Lithuanian Grammar*. Vilnius: Baltos Lankos.

Anderson, Stephen C. 1980. The noun class system of Amo. In: Larry M. Hyman (ed.) *Noun Classes in the Grassfields Bantu Borderland* (Southern California Occasional Papers in Linguistics 8), 155–78. Los Angeles: Department of Linguistics, University of Southern California.

Anderson, Stephen R. 1982. Where's morphology? *Linguistic Inquiry* 13.571–612.

1984. On representations in morphology: case, agreement and inversion in Georgian. *Natural Language and Linguistic Theory* 2.157–218.

1992. *A-Morphous Morphology* (Cambridge Studies in Linguistics 62). Cambridge: Cambridge University Press.

2001. On some issues in morphological exponence. In: Geert Booij & Jaap van Marle (eds.) *Yearbook of Morphology 2000*, 1–17. Dordrecht: Kluwer.

Andersson, Erik. 2000. How many gender categories are there in Swedish? In: Barbara Unterbeck, Matti Rissanen, Terttu Nevalainen & Mirja Saari (eds.) *Gender in Grammar and Cognition: I: Approaches to Gender, II: Manifestations of Gender* (Trends in Linguistics: Studies and Monographs 124), 545–59. Berlin: Mouton de Gruyter.

Andrews, Avery D. 1971. Case agreement of predicate modifiers in Ancient Greek. *Linguistic Inquiry* 2.127–52.

  1982. Long distance agreement in Modern Icelandic. In: Pauline Jacobson & Geoffrey K. Pullum (eds.) *The Nature of Syntactic Representation*, 1–33. Dordrecht: Reidel.

Anward, Jan. 1988. Verb-verb agreement in Swedish. In: Denise Fekete & Zofia Laubitz (eds.) *McGill Working Papers in Linguistics: Special Issue on Comparative Germanic Syntax (May 1988)*, 1–34. Montreal: McGill University.

Aoun, Joseph & Benmamoun, Elabbas. 1999. Gapping, *PF* merger and patterns of partial agreement. In: Shalom Lappin & Elabbas Benmamoun (eds.) *Fragments: Studies in Ellipsis and Gapping*, 175–92. New York: Oxford University Press.

Ariel, Mira. 2000. The development of person agreement markers: from pronouns to higher accessibility markers. In: Michael Barlow & Suzanne Kemmer (eds.) *Usage-Based Models of Language*, 197–260. Stanford: Center for the Study of Language and Information.

Aronoff, Mark. 1998. Gender agreement as morphology. In: Geert Booij, Angela Ralli & Sergio Scalise (eds.) *Proceedings of the First Mediterranean Conference of Morphology* (Mytilene, Greece, 19–21 September 1997), 7–18. Patras: University of Patras.

Aronoff, Mark; Meir, Irit & Sandler, Wendy. 2005. The paradox of sign language morphology. *Language* 81.301–44.

Aronson, Howard I. 1982. *Georgian: A Reading Grammar*. Columbus, OH: Slavica.

Asher, R. E. 1996. Japanese and Tamil: some typological analogies. *Asian Cultural Studies* 22 (International Christian University Publications III-A), 109–20.

Askedal, John O. 1973. *Neutrum Plural mit persönlichem Bezug im Deutschen: Unter Berücksichtigung des germanischen Ursprungs*. (Germanistische Schriftenreihe der norwegischen Universitäten und Hochschulen 4.) Trondheim: Universitetsforlaget.

Austin, Peter & Bresnan, Joan. 1996. Non-configurationality in Australian Aboriginal languages. *Natural Language and Linguistic Theory* 14. 215–68.

Avgustinova, Tania & Uszkoreit, Hans. 2003. Towards a typology of agreement phenomena. In: William E. Griffin (ed.) *The Role of Agreement in Natural Language: Proceedings of the Fifth Annual Texas Linguistics Society Conference*, 167–80. Available at: http://uts.cc.utexas.edu/~tls/2001tls/2001proceeds.html.

Baerman, Matthew; Brown, Dunstan & Corbett, Greville G. 2005. *The Syntax-Morphology Interface: A Study of Syncretism*. Cambridge: Cambridge University Press.

Baker, Brett J. 2002. How referential is agreement? The interpretation of polysynthetic disagreement in Ngalakgan. In: Nicholas Evans & Hans-Jürgen Sasse (eds.) *Problems of Polysynthesis* (Studia typologica 4), 51–85. Berlin: Akademie Verlag.

Baker, Mark. 1996. *The Polysynthesis Parameter*. New York: Oxford University Press.

Bakker, Dik. 2005. Expression and agreement: some more arguments for the dynamic expression model. In: Kees Hengeveld & Casper de Groot (eds.) *Morphosyntactic Expression in Functional Grammar*, 1–40. Berlin: Mouton de Gruyter.

Bakker, Peter. 1997. *A Language of Our Own: The Genesis of Michif, the Mixed Cree-French Language of the Canadian Métis*. Oxford: Oxford University Press.

Bakker, Peter & Papen, Robert A. 1997. Michif: a mixed language based on Cree and French. In: Sarah G. Thomason (ed.) *Contact Languages: A Wider Perspective*, 295–363. Amsterdam: John Benjamins.

Bani, Ephraim. 1987. Garka a ipika: masculine and feminine grammatical gender in Kala Lagaw Ya. *Australian Journal of Linguistics* 7.189–201.

Barbu, Cătălina; Evans, Richard & Mitkov, Ruslan. 2002. A corpus based investigation of morphological disagreement in anaphoric relations. In: Manuel González Rodríguez & Carmen Paz Suárez Araujo (eds.) *LREC2002: Third International Conference on Language Resources and Evaluation: Proceedings: VI*, 1995–9. Paris: European Language Resources Association.

Barlow, Michael. 1991. The agreement hierarchy and grammatical theory. In: Laurel A. Sutton, Christopher Johnson & Ruth Shields (eds.) *Proceedings of the Seventeenth Annual Meeting of the Berkeley Linguistics Society, February 15–18, 1991: General Session and Parasession on the Grammar of Event Structure*, 30–40. Berkeley: Berkeley Linguistics Society, University of California.

   1992. *A Situated Theory of Agreement*. New York: Garland. [Published version of 1988 doctoral dissertation, Stanford.]

Barlow, Michael & Ferguson, Charles A. (eds.) 1988. *Agreement in Natural Language: Approaches, Theories, Descriptions*. Stanford: CSLI.

Bartos, Huba. 1997. On 'subjective' and 'objective' agreement in Hungarian. *Acta Linguistica Hungarica* 44.363–84.

Bauer, Winifred; with Parker, William & Evans, Te Kareongawai. 1993. *Maori* (Descriptive Grammars Series). London: Routledge.

Bayer, Sam & Johnson, Mark. 1995. Features and agreement. *Proceedings of the 33rd Annual Conference of the Association for Computational Linguistics (ACL-'95)*, 70–6. Cambridge, MA: ACL.

Bejar, Susana. 2003. Phi-syntax: a theory of agreement. Unpublished PhD thesis, University of Toronto.

Belletti, Adriana. 2001. Agreement projections. In: Mark Baltin & Chris Collins (eds.) *The Handbook of Contemporary Syntactic Theory*, 483–510. Oxford: Blackwell.

Belnap, R. Kirk. 1999. A new perspective on the history of Arabic: variation in marking agreement with plural heads. In: Greville G. Corbett (ed.) *Agreement* (Special issue of *Folia Linguistica* 33/2), 169–85.

Belnap, R. Kirk & Gee, John. 1994. Classical Arabic in contact: the transition to near categorical agreement patterns. In: Mushira Eid, Vincente Cantarino & Keith Walters (eds.) *Perspectives on Arabic Linguistics VI: Papers from the Sixth Annual Symposium on Arabic Linguistics* (Amsterdam Studies in the Theory and History of Linguistic Science 115), 121–49. Amsterdam: John Benjamins.

Bentley, Delia. 2004. Definiteness effects: evidence from Sardinian. *Transactions of the Philological Society* 102.57–101.

Berg, Helma van den. 1995. *A Grammar of Hunzib (with texts and lexicon)*. Munich: Lincom Europa.

   1999. Gender and person agreement in Akusha Dargi. In: Greville G. Corbett (ed.) *Agreement* (Special issue of *Folia Linguistica* 33/2), 153–68. Berlin: Mouton de Gruyter.

Berg, René van den. 1989. *A Grammar of the Muna Language* (Verhandelingen van het Koninklijk Instituut voor Taal-, Land- en Volkenkunde 139). Dordrecht: Foris.

Berg, Thomas. 1998. The resolution of agreement conflicts in English and German agreement patterns. *Linguistics* 36.41–70.

Bergel´son, Mira B.; Zaliznjak, Anna A. & Kibrik, Aleksandr E. 1982. Konstrukcii s sen-
tencial´nym aktanktom v tabasaranskom jazyke. In: *Tabasaranskie ètjudy: Materialy
Dagestanskoj èkspedicii 1979* (Publikacii otdelenija strukturnoj i prikladnoj lingvistiki 15, series editor V. A. Zvegincev), 44–65. Moscow: Izdatel´stvo Moskovskogo
Universiteta.

Bickel, Balthasar. 2000. On the syntax of agreement in Tibeto-Burman. *Studies in Language* 24.583–609.

2003. Referential density in discourse and syntactic typology. *Language* 79.708–36.

Bickel, Balthasar; Bisang, Walter & Yādava, Yogendra P. 1999. Face vs. empathy: the
social foundation of Maithili verb agreement. *Linguistics* 37.481–518.

Bickel, Balthasar & Nichols, Johanna. forthcoming. Inflectional morphology. In: Tim-
othy Shopen (ed.) *Language Typology and Syntactic Description*, revised edition.
Cambridge: Cambridge University Press.

Bickel, Balthasar & Yādava, Yogendra P. 2000. A fresh look at grammatical relations in
Indo-Aryan. *Lingua* 110.343–73.

Blake, Barry J. 1990. *Relational Grammar* (Croom Helm Linguistic Theory Guides).
London: Croom Helm.

1994. *Case*. Cambridge: Cambridge University Press.

Blevins, James P. 2000. Markedness and agreement. *Transactions of the Philological
Society* 98.233–62.

2003. Passives and impersonals. *Journal of Linguistics* 39.473–520.

forthcoming. Feature-based grammar. In: Robert D. Borsley & Kersti Börjars (eds.)
Non-Transformational Syntax. Oxford: Blackwell.

Bloomfield, Leonard. 1933. *Language*. New York: Holt, Rinehart and Winston.

Bobaljik, Jonathan D. 1998. Pseudo-ergativity in Chukotko-Kamchatkan agreement systems. In: Léa Nash (ed.) *Ergativité: Recherches linguistiques de Vincennes* 27, 21–44.
Saint Denis: PUV.

2003. Realizing Germanic inflection: why morphology does not drive syntax. *Journal
of Comparative Germanic Linguistics* 6.129–67.

Bobaljik, Jonathan D. & Wurmbrand, Susi. 2002. Notes on agreement in
Itelmen. *Linguistic Discovery* 1/1. Available at: http://linguistic-discovery.
dartmouth.edu/WebObjects/Linguistics.

2005. The domain of agreement. *Natural Language and Linguistic Theory* 23.809–65.

Bobaljik, Jonathan D. & Yatsushiro, Kazuko. Forthcoming. Problems with honorification-
as-agreement in Japanese: A reply to Boeckx & Niinuma. *Natural Language and
Linguistic Theory*.

Bock, Kathryn & Eberhard, Kathleen M. 1993. Meaning, sound and syntax in English
number agreement. *Language and Cognitive Processes* 8.57–99.

Bock, Kathryn; Eberhard, Kathleen M. & Cutting, J. Cooper. 2004. Producing number agreement: how pronouns equal verbs. *Journal of Memory and Language*
51.251–78.

Bock, Kathryn & Miller, Carol. 1991. Broken agreement. *Cognitive Psychology* 23.45–93.

Bock, Kathryn; Nicol, Janet & Cutting, J. Cooper. 1999. The ties that bind: creating
number agreement in speech. *Journal of Memory and Language* 40.330–46.

Boeckx, Cedric. 2000. Quirky agreement. *Studia Linguistica* 54.354–80.

Boeckx, Cedric & Niinuma, Fumikazu. 2004. Conditions on agreement in Japanese.
Natural Language and Linguistic Theory 22.453–80.

Boel, Else. 1976. Le genre des noms désignant les professions et les situations féminines en français moderne. *Revue romane* 11.16–73.

Bogdanov, V. N. 1968. Osobyj slučaj dialektnogo soglasovanija skazuemogo s podležaščim po smyslu i kategorija predstavitel'nosti. *Naučnye doklady vysšej školy: filologičeskie nauki* 4.68–75.

Bokamba, Eyamba G. 1985. Verbal agreement as a noncyclic rule in Bantu. In: Didier L. Goyvaerts (ed.) *African Linguistics: Essays in Memory of M. W. K. Semikenke* (Studies in the Sciences of Language 6), 9–54. Amsterdam: Benjamins.

Bolt, Janet E.; Hoddinott, William C. & Kofod, Frances M. 1970. An elementary grammar of the Nungali language. Unpublished manuscript, held at AIATSIS, Canberra.

Booij, Geert. 1994. Against split morphology. In: Geert Booij & Jaap van Marle (eds.) *Yearbook of Morphology 1993*, 27–49. Dordrecht: Kluwer.

   1996. Inherent versus contextual inflection and the split morphology hypothesis. In: Geert Booij & Jaap van Marle (eds.) *Yearbook of Morphology 1995*, 1–15. Dordrecht: Kluwer.

   2002. *The Morphology of Dutch.* Oxford: Oxford University Press.

Borer, Hagit. 1989. Anaphoric AGR. In: Osvaldo Jaeggli & Kenneth J. Safir (eds.) *The Null Subject Parameter* (Studies in Natural Language and Linguistic Theory 15), 69–109. Dordrecht: Kluwer.

Börjars, Kersti & Chapman, Carol. 1998. Agreement and pro-drop in some dialects of English. *Linguistics* 36.71–98.

Börjars, Kersti & Donohue, Mark. 2000. Much ado about nothing: features and zeroes in Germanic noun phrases. *Studia Linguistica* 54.309–53.

Borsley, Robert D. 2005. Against ConjP. *Lingua* 115.461–82.

Branigan, Phil & MacKenzie, Marguerite. 2002. Altruism, Ā-movement, and object agreement in Innu-aimûn. *Linguistic Inquiry* 22.385–407.

Brentari, Diane; Larson, Gary N. & MacLeod, Lynn A. (eds.) 1988. *CLS 24: Papers from the 24th Annual Regional Meeting of the Chicago Linguistic Society: Part II: Parasession on Agreement in Grammatical Theory.* Chicago: Chicago Linguistic Society.

Bresnan, Joan. 2001a. *Lexical-Functional Syntax.* Oxford: Blackwell.

   2001b. The emergence of the unmarked pronoun. In: Géraldine Legendre, Jane Grimshaw & Sten Vikner (eds.) *Optimality-Theoretic Syntax*, 113–42. Cambridge, MA: MIT Press.

Bresnan, Joan & Mchombo, Sam. 1987. Topic, pronoun, and agreement in Chicheŵa. *Language* 63.741–82.

Bresnan, Joan & Moshi, Lioba. 1990. Object asymmetries in comparative Bantu syntax. *Linguistic Inquiry* 21.147–85.

Brown, Dunstan; Corbett, Greville G. & Tiberius, Carole (eds.) 2003. *Agreement: A Typological Perspective* (Special issue of *Transactions of the Philological Society* 101/2). Oxford: Blackwell.

Brown, Colin; Berkum, Jos J. A. van & Hagoort, Peter. 2000. Discourse before gender: an event-related brain potential study on the interplay of semantic and syntactic information during spoken language understanding. *Journal of Psycholinguistic Research* 29.53–68.

Brown, Lea. 2003. Nias: an exception to universals of argument-marking. Paper presented at the Association for Linguistic Typology, V, Sardinia, 15–18 September 2003.

2005. Nias. In: Alexander Adelaar & Nikolaus P. Himmelmann (eds.) *The Austronesian Languages of Asia and Madagascar*, 562–89. London: Routledge.

Bruening, Benjamin. 2001. Syntax at the edge: cross-clausal phenomena and the syntax of Passamaquoddy. Unpublished PhD dissertation, MIT.

Butt, Miriam. 2001. Case, agreement, pronoun incorporation and pro-drop in South Asian languages. Paper read at the workshop on 'The Role of Agreement in Argument Structure', Utrecht 31 August to 1 September 2001.

    forthcoming. The role of pronominal suffixes in Punjabi. In: Jane Grimshaw, Joan Maling, Chris Manning, Jane Simpson and Annie Zaenen (eds.) *Architectures, Rules, and Preferences: A Festschrift for Joan Bresnan*. Cambridge, MA: MIT Press.

Bybee, Joan. 1985. *Morphology: A Study of the Relation between Meaning and Form* (Typological Studies in Language 9). Amsterdam: John Benjamins.

Bynon, Theodora. 1992. Pronominal attrition, clitic doubling and typological change. *Folia Linguistica Historica* 13.27–63 (=Werner Abraham (ed.) *Grammatikalisierung und Reanalyse: Konfrontation*).

Camacho, José. 2003. *The Structure of Coordination: Conjunction and Agreement Phenomena in Spanish and Other Languages* (Studies in Natural Language and Linguistic Theory 57). Dordrecht: Kluwer.

Cameron, Richard. 1993. Ambiguous agreement, functional compensation, and non-specific *tú* in the Spanish of San Juan, Puerto Rico, and Madrid, Spain. *Language Variation and Change* 5.305–34.

Carstens, Vicki. 2000. Concord in Minimalist Theory. *Linguistic Inquiry* 31.319–55.

Casillas Martínez, Luis D. 2003. Gender mismatches in Spanish and French N_1/A de N_2 affective constructions: index agreement vs. morphosyntactic concord. In: Jong-Bok Kim & Stephen Wechsler (eds.) *Proceedings of the 9th International Conference on Head-Driven Phrase Structure Grammar*, 1–17. Stanford: CSLI. Available at: http://cslipublications.stanford.edu/HPSG/3/hpsg02.htm.

Chapman, Shirley & Derbyshire, Desmond C. 1991. Paumarí. In: Desmond C. Derbyshire & Geoffrey K. Pullum (eds.) *Handbook of Amazonian Languages III*, 161–352. Berlin: Mouton de Gruyter.

Chekili, Ferid. 2004. The position of the postverbal subject and agreement asymmetries in Arabic. *PhiN: Philologie im Netz* 27.35–46.

Choi, Incheol. 2003. A constraint-based approach to Korean partial honorific agreement. In: W. E. Griffin (ed.) *The Role of Agreement in Natural Language: TLS 5 Proceedings*, 157–66. Available at: http://uts.cc.utexas.edu/~tls/2001tls/2001proceeds.html.

Chomsky, Noam. 1995. *The Minimalist Program*. Cambridge, MA: MIT Press.

    2000. Minimalist inquiries: the framework. In: Roger Martin, David Michaels & Juan Uriagereka (eds.) *Step by Step: Essays on Minimalist Syntax in Honor of Howard Lasnik*, 89–155. Cambridge, MA: MIT Press.

    2001. Derivation by phase. In: Michael Kenstowicz (ed.) *Ken Hale: A Life in Language*, 1–52. Cambridge, MA: MIT Press.

Chung, Sandra. 1998. *The Design of Agreement: Evidence from Chamorro*. Chicago: University of Chicago Press.

Clahsen, Harald & Hansen, Detlef. 1997. The grammatical agreement deficit in specific language impairment: evidence from therapy experiments. In: Myrna Gopnik (ed.)

The Inheritance and Innateness of Grammars, 141–60. New York: Oxford University Press.

Clahsen, Harald & Hong, Upyong. 1995. Agreement and null subjects in German L2 development: new evidence from reaction-time experiments. *Second Language Research* 11.57–87.

Clahsen, Harald & Penke, Martina. 1992. The acquisition of agreement morphology and its syntactic consequences: new evidence on German child language from the Simone-corpus. In: Jürgen M. Meisel (ed.) *The Acquisition of Verb Placement: Functional Categories and V2 Phenomena in Language Acquisition* (Studies in Theoretical Psycholinguistics 16), 181–223. Dordrecht: Kluwer.

Comrie, Bernard. 1975. Polite plurals and predicate agreement. *Language* 51.406–18.

1980. Morphology and word order reconstruction: problems and prospects. In: Jacek Fisiak (ed.) *Historical Morphology* (Trends in Linguistics, Studies and Monographs 17), 83–96. The Hague: Mouton. [Reprinted in *Mouton Classics*, 359–72. Berlin: Mouton de Gruyter.]

1989a. Some general properties of reference-tracking systems. In: Doug Arnold, Martin Atkinson, Jacques Durand, Claire Grover & Louisa Sadler (eds.) *Essays on Grammatical Theory and Universal Grammar*, 37–51. Oxford: Clarendon Press.

1989b. *Language Universals and Linguistic Theory: Syntax and Morphology*, 2nd edition. Oxford: Blackwell. [1st edition 1981.]

1995. The typology of predicate case marking. In: Joan Bybee, John Haiman & Sandra A. Thompson (eds.) *Essays on Language Function and Language Type: Dedicated to T. Givón*, 39–50. Amsterdam: Benjamins.

2003. When agreement gets trigger-happy. In: Dunstan Brown, Greville Corbett & Carole Tiberius (eds.) *Agreement: A Typological Perspective*. (Special issue of *Transactions of the Philological Society* 101/2), 313–37. Oxford: Blackwell.

Comrie, Bernard & Polinsky, Maria. 1998. The great Daghestanian case hoax. In: Anna Siewierska & Jae Jung Song (eds.) *Case, Typology and Grammar: In Honor of Barry J. Blake*, 95–114. Amsterdam: Benjamins.

Comrie, Bernard; Stone, Gerald & Polinsky, Maria. 1996. *The Russian Language in the Twentieth Century*. Oxford: Clarendon Press.

Connell, Bruce. 1987. Noun classification in Lower Cross. *Journal of West African Languages* 17.110–25.

Copestake, Ann. 1995. The representation of group denoting nouns in a lexical knowledge database. In: Patrick Saint-Dizier & Evelyne Viegas (eds.) *Computational Lexical Semantics*, 207–30. Cambridge: Cambridge University Press.

2002. *Implementing Typed Feature Structure Grammars* (CSLI lecture notes 110). Stanford: CSLI.

Corbett, Greville G. 1978. Universals in the syntax of cardinal numerals. *Lingua* 46.355–68.

1979. The agreement hierarchy. *Journal of Linguistics* 15.203–224. [Reprinted in: Francis X. Katamba (ed.) 2003. *Morphology: Critical Concepts in Linguistics: IV: Morphology and Syntax*, 48–70. London: Routledge.]

1981. A note on grammatical agreement in *Šinel'. Slavonic and East European Review* 59.59–61.

1983. *Hierarchies, Targets and Controllers: Agreement Patterns in Slavic*. London: Croom Helm.

1986. Agreement: a partial specification, based on Slavonic data. *Linguistics* 24.995–1023.

1987. The morphology/syntax interface: evidence from possessive adjectives in Slavonic. *Language* 63.299–345.

1991. *Gender.* Cambridge: Cambridge University Press.

1993. The head of Russian numeral expressions. In: Greville G. Corbett, Norman M. Fraser & Scott McGlashan (eds.) *Heads in Grammatical Theory*, 11–35. Cambridge: Cambridge University Press.

1995a. Slavonic's closest approach to Suffix Copying: the possessive adjective. In: Frans Plank (ed.) *Double Case: Agreement by Suffixaufnahme*, 265–82. New York: Oxford University Press.

1995b. Agreement (research into syntactic change). In: Joachim Jacobs, Arnim von Stechow, Wolfgang Sternefeld & Theo Vennemann (eds.) *Syntax: An International Handbook of Contemporary Research: II*, 1235–44. Berlin: de Gruyter.

(ed.) 1999a. *Agreement* (Special issue of *Folia Linguistica* 33/2). Berlin: Mouton de Gruyter.

(ed.) 1999b. Resolution rules for gender agreement in Tsakhur. In: Ekaterina V. Rakhilina & Yakov G. Testelets (eds.) *Tipologija i teorija jazyka: Ot opisanija k ob´jasneniju: K 60-letiju Aleksandra Evgen´eviča Kibrika*, 400–11. Moscow: Jazyki russkoj kul´tury.

2000. *Number.* Cambridge: Cambridge University Press.

2003a. Types of typology, illustrated from gender systems. In: Frans Plank (ed.) *Noun Phrase Structure in the Languages of Europe* (Empirical Approaches to Language Typology EUROTYP 20–7), 289–334. Berlin: Mouton de Gruyter.

2003b. Agreement: the range of the phenomenon and the principles of the Surrey Database of Agreement. In: Dunstan Brown, Greville G. Corbett & Carole Tiberius (eds.) *Agreement: A Typological Perspective* (Special issue of *Transactions of the Philological Society* 101/2), 155–202.

2005. The number of genders, Sex-based and non-sex-based gender systems, and gender assignment systems (three maps). In: Martin Haspelmath, Matthew Dryer, David Gil & Bernard Comrie (eds.) *World Atlas of Language Structures*, 126–37. Oxford: Oxford University Press.

Corbett, Greville G. & Fraser, Norman. 1993. Network morphology: A DATR account of Russian nominal inflection. *Journal of Linguistics* 29.113–142. [Reprinted in: Francis X. Katamba (ed.) 2003. *Morphology: Critical Concepts in Linguistics: VI: Morphology: Its Place in the Wider Context*, 364–96. London: Routledge.]

Corbett, Greville G. & Hayward, Richard J. 1987. Gender and number in Bayso. *Lingua* 73.1–28.

Corbett, Greville G. & Mtenje, Alfred D. 1987. Gender agreement in Chichewa. *Studies in African Linguistics* 18.1–38.

Cormier, Kearsey; Wechsler, Stephen & Meier, Richard P. 1999. Locus agreement in American Sign Language. In: Gert Webelhuth, Jean-Pierre Koenig & Andreas Kathol (eds.) *Lexical and Constructional Aspects of Linguistic Explanation*, 215–29. Stanford: CSLI.

Cornish, Francis. 1986. *Anaphoric Relations in English and French: A Discourse Perspective*. London: Croom Helm.

Crawford, William J. 2005. Verb agreement and disagreement: a corpus investigation of concord variation in existential *there + be* constructions. *Journal of English Linguistics* 33.35–61.

Crockett, Dina B. 1976. *Agreement in Contemporary Standard Russian.* Cambridge, MA: Slavica.

Croft, William. 2001. *Radical Construction Grammar: Syntactic Theory in Typological Perspective.* Oxford: Oxford University Press.

Culy, Christopher. 1996. Agreement and Fula pronouns. *Studies in African Linguistics* 25.1–26.

Curzan, Anne. 2003. *Gender Shifts in the History of English.* Cambridge: Cambridge University Press.

Cysouw, Michael. 2003. *The Paradigmatic Structure of Person Marking.* Oxford: Oxford University Press.

Dahl, Östen. 2000. Animacy and the notion of default gender. In: Barbara Unterbeck, Matti Rissanen, Terttu Nevalainen & Mirja Saari (eds.) *Gender in Grammar and Cognition: I: Approaches to Gender, II: Manifestations of Gender* (Trends in Linguistics: Studies and Monographs 124), 99–115. Berlin: Mouton de Gruyter.

Dalrymple, Mary & Kaplan, Ronald M. 2000. Feature indeterminacy and feature resolution. *Language* 76.759–98.

Dalrymple, Mary & Nikolaeva, Irina. 2004. Syntax of natural and accidental coordination: evidence from agreement. Paper read at the Linguistics Association of Great Britain, Oxford, August 2004.

Davison, Alice. 1988. Constituent structure and the realization of agreement features. In: Diane Brentari, Gary N. Larson & Lynn A. MacLeod (eds.). *CLS 24: Papers from the 24th Annual Regional Meeting of the Chicago Linguistic Society: Part II: Parasession on Agreement in Grammatical Theory*, 41–53. Chicago: Chicago Linguistic Society.

Deen, Kamil Ud. 2004. Subject agreement, object agreement and specificity in Nairobi Swahili. In: Jacqueline van Kampen & Sergio Baauw (eds.) *Proceedings of GALA 2003*, 139–50. Utrecht: LOT.

DeLancey, Scott. 1989. Verb agreement in Proto-Tibeto-Burman. *Bulletin of the School of Oriental and African Studies* 52.315–33.

1992. The historical status of the conjunct/disjunct pattern in Tibeto-Burman. *Acta Linguistica Hafniensia* 25.39–62.

Delsing, Lars-Olof. 1993. *The Internal Structure of Noun Phrases in the Scandinavian Languages: A Comparative Study.* Lund: Department of Scandinavian Languages, University of Lund.

Demuth, Katherine. 2003. The acquisition of Bantu languages. In: Derek Nurse & Gérard Philippson (eds.) *The Bantu Languages*, 209–22. London: Routledge.

Demuth, Katherine & Johnson, Mark. 1989. Interaction between discourse functions and agreement in Setawana. *Journal of African Languages and Linguistics* 11.21–35.

Dench, Alan C. 1995. *Martuthunira: A Language of the Pilbara Region of Western Australia* (Pacific Linguistics C-125). Canberra: Department of Linguistics, Research School of Pacific and Asian Studies, Australian National University.

Dench, Alan C. & Evans, Nicholas. 1988. Multiple case-marking in Australian languages. *Australian Journal of Linguistics* 8.1–47.

Depraetere, Isle. 2003. On verbal concord with collective nouns in British English. *English Language and Linguistics* 7.85–127.

Derganc, Aleksandra. 2003. The dual in Slovenian. *Sprachtypologie und Universalienforschung* 56.165–82.

Deutsch, Avital. 1998. Subject-predicate agreement in Hebrew: interrelations with semantic processes. *Language and Cognitive Processes* 13.575–97.

Deutsch, Avital & Bentin, Shlomo 2001. Syntactic and semantic factors in processing gender agreement in Hebrew: evidence from ERPs and eye movements. *Journal of Memory and Language* 45.200–24.

Dikken, Marcel den. 1999. On the structural representation of possession and agreement: the case of (anti-)agreement in Hungarian possessed nominal phrases. In: István Kenesei (ed.) *Crossing Boundaries: Advances in the Theory of Central and Eastern European Languages* (Amsterdam Studies in the Theory and History of Linguistic Science, Series IV, Current Issues in Linguistic Theory 182), 137–78. Amsterdam: John Benjamins.

   2001. 'Pluringulars', pronouns and quirky agreement. *Linguistic Review* 18.19–41.

Dixon, R. M. W. 1977. Semantic neutralization for phonological reasons. *Linguistic Inquiry* 8.598–602.

   1994. *Ergativity*. Cambridge: Cambridge University Press.

   2000. Categories of the noun phrase in Jarawara. *Journal of Linguistics* 36.487–510.

Dobrin, Lise M. 1995. Theoretical consequences of literal alliterative concord. In: Audra Dainora, Rachel Hemphill, Barbara Luka, Barbara Need & Sheri Pargman (eds.) *CLS 31: Papers from the 31st Regional Meeting of the Chicago Linguistic Society: I: The Main Session*, 127–42. Chicago: Chicago Linguistic Society.

   1998. The morphosyntactic reality of phonological form. In: Geert Booij & Jaap van Marle (eds.) *Yearbook of Morphology 1997*, 59–81. Dordrecht: Kluwer.

   1999. Phonological form, morphological class, and syntactic gender: the noun class systems of Papua New Guinea Arapeshan. Unpublished PhD dissertation, University of Chicago.

Dončeva, Liljana. 1975. Nabljudenija vărxu kvantitativnija aspekt na nominativnite lični mestoimenija v ruski i v bălgarski ezik. *Bălgarski ezik* 25/1.9–20.

Dončeva-Mareva, Liljana. 1978. Săglasuvaneto na učtivoto *Vie* săs skazuemoto v bălgarskija i ruskija ezik ot dvantitativno gledište. *Săpostavitelno ezikoznanie* 3.70–5.

Donohue, Mark. 1999. A most agreeable language. Paper presented at the meeting of the Australian Linguistics Society, Perth, 30 September 1999.

   2000. Pronouns and gender: exploring nominal classification systems in Northern New Guinea. *Oceanic Linguistics* 39.339–49.

   2003a. Agreement in the Skou language: a historical account. *Oceanic Linguistics* 43.479–98.

   2003b. Review of: Sandra Chung 'The Design of Agreement: Evidence from Chamorro'. *Linguistic Typology* 7.285–92.

Donohue, Mark & Maclachlan, Anna. 2000. What agreement in Chamorro? In: Carolyn Smallwood & Catherine Kitto (eds.) *Proceedings of AFLA VI: The Sixth Meeting of the Austronesian Formal Linguistics Association*, 121–32. Toronto: Toronto Working Papers in Linguistics.

Dowty, David & Jacobson, Pauline. 1989. Agreement as a semantic phenomenon. In: Joyce Powers & K. de Jong (eds.) *Proceedings of the Fifth Eastern States*

Conference on Linguistics (ESCOL '88), 95–108. Columbus, OH: Ohio State University.

Drabbe, P. 1955. *Spraakkunst von het Marind: Zuidkust Nederlands Nieuw-Guinea* (Studia Instituti Anthropos 11). Wien-Mödling: Drukkerij van het Missiehuis St. Gabriel.

Driem, George van. 1991. Tangut verbal agreement and the patient category in Tibeto-Burman. *Bulletin of the School of Oriental and African Studies* 54.520–34.

———. 1993. The Proto-Tibeto-Burman verbal agreement system. *Bulletin of the School of Oriental and African Studies* 56.292–334.

———. 1995. Black Mountain conjugational morphology, Proto-Tibeto-Burman morphosyntax, and the linguistic position of Chinese. In: Yoshio Nishi, James A. Matisoff & Yasuhiko Nagano (eds.) *New Horizons in Tibeto-Burman Morphosyntax* (Senri Ethnological Studies 41), 229–59. Osaka: National Museum of Ethnology.

Dryer, Matthew. 2002. Case distinctions, rich verb agreement, and word order type (Comments on Hawkins' paper). *Theoretical Linguistics* 28.151–7.

Durie, Mark. 1986. The grammaticization of number as a verbal category. In: Vassiliki Nikiforidou, Mary VanClay, Mary Niepokuj & Deborah Feder (eds.) *Proceedings of the Twelfth Annual Meeting of the Berkeley Linguistics Society: February 15–17, 1986*, 355–70. Berkeley, CA: Berkeley Linguistics Society, University of California.

Dyła, Stefan. 1988. Quasi-comitative coordination in Polish. *Linguistics* 26.383–414.

Dziwirek, Katarzyna. 1990. Default agreement in Polish. In: Katarzyna Dziwirek, Patrick Farrell & Errapel Majías-Bikandi (eds.) *Grammatical Relations: A Cross-theoretical Perspective*, 147–61. Stanford: Stanford Linguistics Association/CSLI.

Eberhard, Kathleen M. 1997. The marked effect of number on subject-verb agreement. *Journal of Memory and Language* 36.147–64.

———. 1999. The accessibility of conceptual number to the processes of subject-verb agreement in English. *Journal of Memory and Language* 41.560–78.

Enger, Hans-Olav. 2004. Scandinavian pancake sentences as semantic agreement. *Nordic Journal of Linguistics* 27.5–34.

Enrique-Arias, Andrés. 2002. Accounting for the position of verbal agreement morphology with psycholinguistic and diachronic explanatory factors. *Studies in Language* 26.1–31.

Evans, Nicholas. 1994. The problem of body parts and noun class membership in Australian languages. *University of Melbourne Working Papers in Linguistics* 14.1–8.

———. 1995. *A Grammar of Kayardild, with Historical-Comparative Notes on Tangkic.* Berlin: Mouton de Gruyter.

———. 1997. Head classes and agreement classes in the Mayali dialect chain. In: Mark Harvey & Nicholas Reid (eds.) *Nominal Classification in Aboriginal Australia* (Studies in Language Companion Series 37), 105–46. Amsterdam: John Benjamins.

———. 1999. Why argument affixes in polysynthetic languages are not pronouns: evidence from Bininj Gun-wok. *Sprachtypologie und Universalienforschung* 52.255–81 [Slightly revised version appeared 2002, as The true status of grammatical object affixes: evidence from Bininj Gun-wok. In: Nicholas Evans & Hans-Jürgen Sasse (eds.), *Problems of Polysynthesis* (Studia typologica 4), 15–50. Berlin: Akademie Verlag.]

———. 2000. Iwaidjan, a very un-Australian language family. *Linguistic Typology* 4.91–142.

———. 2003. Typologies of agreement: some problems from Kayardild. In: Dunstan Brown, Greville G. Corbett & Carole Tiberius (eds.) *Agreement: A Typological Perspective*

(Special issue of *Transactions of the Philological Society* 101/2), 203–34. Oxford: Blackwell.

Evans, Nicholas; Brown, Dunstan & Corbett, Greville G. 2002. The semantics of gender in Mayali: partially parallel systems and formal implementation. *Language* 77.111–55.

Evans, Nicholas & Sasse, Hans-Jürgen. 2002. Introduction: problems of polysynthesis. In: Nicholas Evans & Hans-Jürgen Sasse (eds.) *Problems of Polysynthesis* (Studia typologica 4), 1–13. Berlin: Akademie Verlag.

Everett, Daniel L. & Kern, Barbara. 1997. *Wariʾ: The Pacaas Novos Language of Western Brazil* (Descriptive Grammars Series). London: Routledge.

Faarlund, Jan Terje. 1977. Embedded clause reduction and Scandinavian gender agreement. *Journal of Linguistics* 13.239–57.

Fabra, Pompeu. 1956. *Gramàtica catalana*. Barcelona: Teide.

Fabri, Ray. 1993. *Kongruenz und die Grammatik des Maltesischen*. (Linguistische Arbeiten 292). Tübingen: Niemeyer.

2001. Definiteness marking and the structure of the NP in Maltese. *Verbum* 23.153–72.

Farkaş, Donka F. & Zec, Draga. 1995. Agreement and pronominal reference. In: Guglielmo Cinque & Giuliana Giusti (eds.) *Advances in Roumanian Linguistics* (Linguistik Aktuell 10), 83–101. Amsterdam: John Benjamins.

Faßke, Helmut. 1981. *Grammatik der obersorbischen Schriftsprache der Gegenwart: Morphologie*. Bautzen: Domowina Verlag.

1996. *Sorbischer Sprachatlas 15: Syntax*. Bautzen: Domowina Verlag.

Ferguson, Charles A. 1989. Grammatical agreement in Classical Arabic and the modern dialects: a response to Versteegh's pidginization hypothesis. *Al-ᶜArabiyya* 22.5–17.

1996. Variation and drift: loss of agreement in Germanic. In: Charles A. Ferguson *Sociolinguistic Perspectives: Papers on Language and Society 1959–1994*. Edited by Thom Huebner, 241–60. New York: Oxford University Press.

Findreng, Ådne. 1976. *Zur Kongruenz in Person und Numerus zwischen Subjekt und finitem Verb im modernen Deutsch*. Oslo: Universitetsforlaget.

Fisher, Ulla T. 1985. *The Sweet Sound of Concord: A Study of Swedish Learners' Concord Problems in English* (Lund Studies in English 73). Malmö: CWK Gleerup.

Francis, W. N. 1986. Proximity concord in English. *Journal of English Linguistics* 19.309–18.

Franks, Steven. 1995. *Parameters of Slavic Morphosyntax* (Oxford Studies in Comparative Syntax). New York: Oxford University Press.

Fraser, Norman M. & Corbett, Greville G. 1995. Gender, animacy and declensional class assignment: a unified account for Russian. In: Geert Booij & Jaap van Marle (eds.) *Yearbook of Morphology 1994*, 123–50. Dordrecht: Kluwer.

1997. Defaults in Arapesh. *Lingua* 103.25–57.

Friðjónsson, Jón. 1989. *Samsettar myndir sagna*. Reykjavík: Málvísindastofnun Háskóla Íslands.

Friedman, Victor A. 1993. Macedonian. In: Bernard Comrie & Greville G. Corbett (eds.) *The Slavonic Languages*, 249–305. London: Routledge.

Fromkin, Victoria A. 1971. The non-anomalous nature of anomalous utterances. *Language* 47.27–52.

Fuß, Eric. 2005. *The Rise of Agreement: A Formal Approach to the Syntax and Grammaticalization of Verbal Inflection.* Amsterdam: Benjamins.

Garnham, Alan; Oakhill, Jane; Ehrlich, Marie-France & Carreiras, Manuel. 1995. Representations and processes in the interpretation of pronouns: new evidence from Spanish and French. *Journal of Memory and Language* 34.41–62.

Garrett, Andrew. 1990. The origin of NP split ergativity. *Language* 66.261–96.

Garrett, Merrill F. 1975. The analysis of sentence production. In: Gordon H. Bower (ed.) *The Psychology of Learning and Motivation: Advances in Research and Theory 9,* 133–77. New York: Academic Press.

Gazdar, Gerald; Klein, Ewan; Pullum Geoffrey K. & Sag, Ivan A. 1985. *Generalized Phrase Structure Grammar.* Blackwell: Oxford.

Gelderen, Elly van. 1997. *Verbal Agreement and the Grammar behind its Breakdown: Minimalist Feature Checking* (Linguistische Arbeiten 364). Tübingen: Max Niemeyer Verlag.

Genetti, Carol. 1994. *A Descriptive and Historical Account of the Dolakha Newari Dialect* (Monumenta Serindica 24). Tokyo: Institute for the Study of Languages and Cultures of Asia and Africa.

Georgopoulos, Carol P. 1991. *Syntactic Variables.* Dordrecht: Kluwer.

Getty, Michael. 1997. *Machds, daß-ds wegkummds!* The mystery of inflected complementizers. In: Irmengard Rauch & Gerald F. Carr (eds.) *Insights in Germanic Linguistics II: Classic and Contemporary* (Trends in Linguistics, Studies and Monographs 94), 47–62. Berlin: Mouton de Gruyter.

Gil, David. 2001. Noun-phrase types and the number marking of anaphors. *Sprachtypologie und Universalienforschung* 54.3–25.

Givón, Talmy. 1970. The resolution of gender conflicts in Bantu conjunction: when syntax and semantics clash. In: *Papers from the Sixth Regional Meeting, Chicago Linguistic Society,* 250–61. Chicago: Chicago Linguistic Society.

1971. Some historical changes in the noun-class system of Bantu, their possible causes and wider implications. In: Chin-Wu Kim & Herbert Stahlke (eds.) *Papers in African Linguistics* (Current Inquiry into Language and Linguistics 1), 33–54. Edmonton: Linguistic Research.

1976. Topic, pronoun and grammatical agreement. In: Charles N. Li (ed.) *Subject and topic,* 149–88. New York: Academic Press.

1984. *Syntax: A Functional-Typological Introduction: I.* Amsterdam: John Benjamins.

2001. *Syntax: An Introduction: I.* Amsterdam: John Benjamins.

Godfrey, Elizabeth & Tagliamonte, Sali. 1999. Another piece for the verbal -*s* story: evidence from Devon in southwest England. *Language Variation and Change* 11.87–121.

Gotteri, Nigel. 1984. The evasive neuter in Polish. In: Frank E. Knowles & J. Ian Press (eds.) *Papers in Slavonic Linguistics II,* 1–8. Birmingham: Department of Modern Languages, University of Aston in Birmingham.

Graudina, L. K.; Ickovič, V. A. & Katlinskaja, L. P. 1976. *Grammatičeskaja pravil'nost' russkoj reči.* Moscow: Nauka

Green, Lisa J. 2002. *African American English: A Linguistic Introduction.* Cambridge: Cambridge University Press.

Greenberg, Joseph H. 1963. Some universals of grammar with particular reference to the order of meaningful elements. In: Joseph H. Greenberg (ed.) *Universals of*

Language, 73–113. Cambridge, MA: MIT Press. [Paperback edition published 1966; page references to this edition.]

1978. How does a language acquire gender markers? In: Joseph H. Greenberg, Charles A. Ferguson & Edith A. Moravcsik (eds.) *Universals of Human Language: III: Word Structure*, 47–82. Stanford: Stanford University Press.

Greenberg, Robert D. 2004. *Language and Identity in the Balkans: Serbo-Croatian and its Disintegration.* Oxford: Oxford University Press.

Grevisse, Maurice. 1964. *Le bon usage*, 8th edition. Gembloux: J. Duculot.

Grinevald, Colette. 2000. A fieldwork squib. In: Jorge Hankamer WebFest. Available at: http://ling.ucsc.edu/Jorge/grinevald.html.

Grönberg, Anna Gunnarsdotter. 2002. Masculine generics in current Icelandic. In: Marlis Hellinger & Hadumod Bußmann (eds.) *Gender across Languages: The Linguistic Representation of Men and Women: Volume 2*, 163–85. Amsterdam. John Benjamins.

Haegeman, Liliane. 1992. *Theory and Description in Generative Syntax: A Case Study in West Flemish.* Cambridge: Cambridge University Press.

Haiman, John. 1974. *Targets and Syntactic Change.* The Hague: Mouton.

Halle, Morris & Marantz, Alec. 1993. Distributed morphology and the pieces of inflection. In: Kenneth Hale & Samuel Jay Keyser (eds.) *The View from Building 20: Essays in Linguistics in Honor of Sylvain Bromberger*, 111–76. Cambridge, MA: MIT Press.

Hallman, Peter. 2000. The structure of agreement failure in Lebanese Arabic. In: Roger Billerey & Brook Danielle Lillehaugen (eds.) *WCCFL 19: Proceedings of the 19th West Coast Conference on Formal Linguistics*, 178–90. Somerville, MA: Cascadilla Press.

Halpern, Aaron L. 1998. Clitics. In: Andrew Spencer & Arnold Zwicky (eds.) *The Handbook of Morphology*, 101–22. Oxford: Blackwell.

Hargreaves, David. ms. Intentional action in Kathmandu Newar[i]. Unpublished paper, Western Oregon University.

Harmer, L. C. & Norton, F. J. 1957. *A Manual of Modern Spanish*, 2nd edition. London: University Tutorial Press [1st edition 1935].

Harris, Alice C. 1981. *Georgian Syntax: A Study in Relational Grammar.* Cambridge: Cambridge University Press.

1984. Case marking, verb agreement, and inversion in Udi. In: David Perlmutter & Carol Rosen (eds.) *Studies in Relational Grammar* 2, 243–58. Chicago: University of Chicago Press.

1994. Ergative-to-nominative shift in agreement: Tabassaran. In: Howard I. Aronson (ed.) *NSL.7: Linguistic Studies in the Non-Slavic Languages of the Commonwealth of Independent States and the Baltic Republics*, 113–31. Chicago: Chicago Linguistic Society.

2002. *Endoclitics and the Origins of Udi Morphosyntax.* Cambridge: Cambridge University Press.

Harris, James W. 1987. Disagreement rules, referral rules and the Spanish feminine article *el. Journal of Linguistics* 23.177–83.

Haspelmath, Martin. 1999. Long distance agreement in Godoberi (Daghestanian) complement clauses. In: Greville G. Corbett (ed.) *Agreement* (Special issue of *Folia Linguistica* 33/2), 131–51.

Haude, Katherine. 2003. Clasificadores en Movima. Paper presented at the International Congress of Americanists, Chile, 15 July 2003.

Hawkins, John A. 2002. Symmetries and asymmetries: their grammar, typology and parsing. *Theoretical Linguistics* 28.95–149.

Hawkins, Roger & Franceschina, Florencia. 2004. Explaining the acquisition and non-acquisition of determiner-noun gender concord in French and Spanish. In: Philippe Prévost & Johanne Paradis (eds.) *The Acquisition of French in Different Contexts: Focus on Functional Categories* (Language Acquisition and Language Disorders 32), 175–205. Amsterdam: John Benjamins.

Hayward, Richard J. 1979. Bayso revisited: some preliminary linguistic observations – II. *Bulletin of the School of Oriental and African Studies* 42.101–32.

1998. The origins of the North Ometo verb agreement systems. *Journal of African Languages and Linguistics* 19.93–111.

Hayward, Richard J. & Corbett, Greville G. 1988. Resolution rules in Qafar. *Linguistics* 26.259–79.

Hayward, Richard J. & Orwin, Martin. 1991. The prefix conjugation in Qafar-Saho: the survival and revival of a paradigm – Part I. *African Languages and Cultures* 4.157–76.

Hazen, Kirk. 2000. Subject-verb concord in a postinsular dialect. *Journal of English Linguistics* 28.127–44.

Heap, David. 2000. *La variation grammaticale en géolinguistique: les pronoms suject en roman central* (Lincom Studies in Romance Linguistics 11). Munich: Lincom Europa.

Helmbrecht, Johannes. 1996. The syntax of person agreement in East Caucasian languages. *Sprachtypologie und Universalienforschung* 49.127–48.

Henry, Alison. 1995. *Belfast English and Standard Englist: Dialect Variation and Parameter Setting*. Oxford: Oxford University Press.

Herbert, Robert K. & Nykiel-Herbert, Barbara. 1986. Explorations in linguistic sexism: a contrastive sketch. *Papers and Studies in Contrastive Linguistics* 21.47–85.

Hewitt, B. G. 1979. *Abkhaz* (Lingua Descriptive Studies 2). Amsterdam: North Holland.

Hoeksema, Jack 1986. Some theoretical consequences of Dutch complementizer agreement. In: Vassiliki Nikiforidou, Mary VanClay, Mary Niepokuj & Deborah Feder (eds.) *Proceedings of the Twelfth Annual Meeting of the Berkeley Linguistics Society: February 15–17, 1986*, 147–58. Berkeley, CA: Berkeley Linguistics Society, University of California.

Holes, Clive. 1990. *Gulf Arabic*. London: Routledge.

Hook, Peter E. & Chauhan, Mohabbat S. M. S. 1988. The perfective adverb in Bhitrauti. *Word* 39.177–86.

Hook, Peter E. & Joshi, Dayashankar M. 1991. Concordant adverbs and postpositions in Gujarati. *Indian Linguistics* 52.1–14.

Hosokawa, Komei. 1996. 'My face *am* burning!' quasi-passive, body parts, and related issues in Yawuru grammar and cultural concepts. In: Hilary Chappell & William McGregor (eds.) *The Grammar of Inalienability: A Typological Perspective on Body Parts and the Part-Whole Relation* (Empirical Approaches to Language Typology 14), 155–92. Berlin: Mouton de Gruyter.

Høybye, Poul. 1944. *L'Accord en français contemporain: essai de grammaire descriptive*. Copenhagen: Høst & Søns Forlag.

Hoyt, Frederick M. L. 2000. Agreement, specificity effects, and phrase structure in rural Palestinian Arabic existential constructions. MA thesis, Cornell University.

2002. Impersonal agreement as a specificity effect in rural Palestinian Arabic. In: Dilworth B. Parkinson & Elabbas Benmamoun (eds.) *Perspectives on Arabic Linguistics XIII–XIV: Papers from the Thirteenth and Fourteenth Annual Symposia on Arabic Linguistics* (Current Issues in Linguistic Theory 230), 111–41. Amsterdam: John Benjamins.

Hualde, José Ignacio. 1992. Metaphony and count/mass morphology in Asturian and Cantabrian dialects. In: Christiane Laeufer & Terrell A. Morgan (eds.) *Theoretical Analyses in Romance Linguistics: Selected Papers from the Nineteenth Linguistic Symposium on Romance Languages (LSRL XIX): The Ohio State University, 21–23 April 1989* (Current Issues in Linguistic Theory 74), 99–114. Amsterdam: John Benjamins.

Huang, Yan. 2000. *Anaphora: A Cross-linguistic Approach.* Oxford: Oxford University Press.

Hudson, Richard. 1999. Subject-verb agreement in English. *Journal of English Language and Linguistics* 3.173–207.

Hulk, Aafke & Tellier, Christine. 1999. Conflictual agreement in Romance nominals. In: J.-Marc Authier, Barbara E. Bullock & Lisa Reed (eds.) *Formal Perspectives on Romance Linguistics: Selected Papers from the 28th Linguistic Symposium on Romance Languages (LSRL XXVIII), University Park, 16–19 April 1998* (Current Issues in Linguistic Theory 185), 179–95. Amsterdam: John Benjamins.

Hundt, Marianne. 1998. *New Zealand English Grammar – Fact or Fiction? A Corpus-Based Study in Morphosyntactic Variation* (Varieties of English round the World 23). Amsterdam: John Benjamins.

Huntley, David. 1989. Grammatical and lexical features in number and gender agreement in Old Bulgarian. *Paleobulgarica* 13.21–32.

Hyman, Larry M. 2003. Basaá (A.43). In: Derek Nurse & Gérard Philippson (eds.) *The Bantu Languages*, 257–82. London: Routledge.

Igartua, Iván. 2004. Sobiratel´nye suščestvitel´nye i ierarxija soglasovanija v drevnerusskom jazyke. *Die Welt der Slaven* 49.229–46.

Ingham, Richard. 1998. Tense without agreement in early clause structure. *Language Acquisition* 7.51–81.

Jaeggli, Osvaldo & Safir, Kenneth J. 1989. The null subject parameter and parametric theory. In: Osvaldo Jaeggli & Kenneth J. Safir (eds.) *The Null Subject Parameter* (Studies in Natural Language and Linguistic Theory 15), 1–44. Dordrecht: Kluwer.

Janaš, Pětr. 1984. *Niedersorbische Grammatik*, 2nd edition. Bautzen: Domowina-Verlag [1st edition 1976].

Janda, Richard D. & Varela-García, Fabiola. 1991. On lateral hermaphroditism and other variation in Spanish 'feminine' *el*. In: Lise M. Dobrin, Lynn Nichols & Rosa M. Rodríguez (eds.) *CLS 27: Papers from the 27th Regional Meeting of the Chicago Linguistic Society 1991: Part I The General Session*, 276–90. Chicago: Chicago Linguistic Society.

Janko-Trinickaja, N. A. 1966. Naimenovanie lic ženskogo pola suščestvitel´nymi ženskogo i mužskogo roda. In: A. E. Zemskaja & D. N. Šmelev (eds.) *Razvitie slovoobrazovanija sovremennogo russkogo jazyk*a, 167–210. Moscow: Nauka.

Jelinek, Eloise. 1984. Empty categories, case, and configurationality. *Natural Language and Linguistic Theory* 2.39–76.

Johannessen, Janne Bondi. 1996. Partial agreement and coordination. *Linguistic Inquiry* 27.661–76.

Johnson, David E. 1977. On relational constraints on grammars. In: Peter Cole & Jerrold M. Sadock (eds.) *Syntax and Semantics 8: Grammatical relations*, 151–78. New York: Academic Press.

Johnson, David & Lappin, Shalom. 1997. A critique of the minimalist program. *Linguistics and Philosophy* 20.273–333.

Kail, Michèle & Bassano, Dominique. 1997. Verb-agreement processing in French: a study of on-line grammaticality judgements. *Language and Speech* 40.25–46.

Källström, Roger. 1993. *Kongruens i svenskan* (Nordistica Gothoburgensia 16). Gothenburg: Acta Universitatis Gothoburgensis.

1994. Language universals, linguistic typology and Nordic agreement. In: Jens Allwood, Bo Ralph, Paula Andersson, Dora Kós-Dienes & Åsa Wengelin (eds.) *Proceedings of the XIVth Scandinavian Conference of Linguistics and the VIIIth Conference of Nordic and General Linguistics* (Gothenburg Papers in Theoretical Linguistics 69), I, 187–201. Gothenburg: Department of Linguistics, Gothenburg University.

Kathman, David. 1995. Verb agreement and grammatical relations. In: Clifford S. Burgess, Katarzyna Dziwirek & Donna Gerdts (eds.) *Grammatical Relations: Theoretical Approaches to Empirical Questions*, 153–70. Stanford: CSLI.

Kathol, Andreas. 1999. Agreement and the syntax-morphology interface in HPSG. In: Robert D. Levine & Georgia M. Green (eds.) *Studies in Contemporary Phrase Structure Grammar*, 223–74. Cambridge: Cambridge University Press.

Kathol, Andreas. 2001. Positional effects in a monostratal grammar of German. *Journal of Linguistics* 37.35–66.

Kazenin, Konstantin I. 1999. Ličnoe soglasovanie v lakskom jazyke: markirovannost´i nejtralizacija In: Ekaterina V. Raxilina & Jakov G. Testelec (eds.) *Tipologija i teorija jazyka: Ot opisanija k ob˝jasneniju: K 60-letiju Aleksandra Evgen´eviča Kibrika*, 383–99. Moscow: Jazyki russkoj kul´tury.

2002. Focus in Daghestanian and word order typology. *Linguistic Typology* 6.289–316.

Keenan, Edward. 1974. The functional principle: generalizing the notion 'subject of'. In: Michael W. La Galy, Robert A. Fox & Anthony Bruck (eds.) *Papers from the Tenth Regional Meeting, Chicago Linguistic Society, April 19–21, 1974*, 298–309. Chicago: Chicago Linguistic Society.

1976. Towards a universal definition of 'subject'. In: Charles N. Li (ed.) *Subject and Topic*, 303–33. New York: Academic Press.

1978. On surface form and logical form. In: Braj B. Kachru (ed.) *Linguistics in the Seventies: Directions and Prospects* (Studies in the Linguistic Sciences 8/2), 163–203. Urbana, IL: Department of Linguistics, University of Illinois.

Keenan, Edward L. & Comrie, Bernard. 1977. Noun phrase accessibility and universal grammar. *Linguistic Inquiry* 8.63–99.

Keenan, Edward L. & Polinsky, Maria. 1998. Malagasy (Austronesian). In: Andrew Spencer & Arnold Zwicky (eds.) *The Handbook of Morphology*, 563–623. Oxford: Blackwell.

Keeney, Terrence J. & Wolfe, Jean. 1972. The acquisition of agreement in English. *Journal of Verbal Learning and Verbal Behavior* 11.698–705.

Kibrik, Aleksandr. E. 1972. O formal´nom vydelenii soglasovatel´nyx klassov v arčinskom jazyke. *Voprosy jazykoznanija* 1.124–31.

1977a. *Opyt strukturnogo opisanija arčinskogo jazyka II: Taksonomičeskaja grammatika* (Publikacii otdelenija strukturnoj i prikladnoj lingvistiki 12). Moscow: Izdatel'stvo Moskovskogo universiteta.

1977b. *Opyt strukturnogo opisanija arčinskogo jazyka III: Dinamičeskaja grammatika* (Publikacii otdelenija strukturnoj i prikladnoj lingvistiki 13). Moscow: Izdatel´stvo Moskovskogo universiteta.

1979. Canonical ergativity and Daghestan languages. In Frans Plank (ed.) *Ergativity: Towards a Theory of Grammatical Relations*, 61–77. London: Academic Press.

1985. Toward a typology of ergativity. In: Johanna Nichols & Anthony C. Woodbury (eds.) *Grammar inside and outside the Clause*, 268–323. Cambridge: Cambridge University Press.

1994. Archi. In: Rieks Smeets (ed.) *Indigenous Languages of the Caucasus IV: North East Caucasian Languages II: Presenting the Three Nakh Languages and Six Minor Lezgian Languages*, 297–365. Delmar, NY: Caravan Books.

1995. Direct-oblique agreement of attributes in Daghestanian. In: Frans Plank (ed.) *Double Case: Agreement by Suffixaufnahme*, 216–39. New York: Oxford University Press.

2003. *Konstanty i peremennye jazyka*. Saint Petersburg: Aletheia.

Kibrik, A. E.; Kazenin, K. I.; Ljutikova, E. A. & S. G. Tatevosov (eds.) 2001. *Bagvalinskij jazyk: Grammatika: Teksty: Slovari*. Moscow: Nasledie.

Kibrik, A. E.; Kodzasov, S. V.; Olovjannikova, I. P. & Samedov, D. S. 1977a. *Opyt strukturnogo opisanija arčinskogo jazyka: I: Leksika, fonetika* (Publikacii otdelenija strukturnoj i prikladnoj lingvistiki 11). Moscow: Izdatel´stvo Moskovskogo universiteta.

1977b. *Arčinskij jazyk: Teksty i slovari* (Publikacii otdelenija strukturnoj i prikladnoj lingvistiki 14). Moscow: Izdatel´stvo Moskovskogo universiteta.

Kibrik, A. E. & Seleznev, M. G. 1982. Sintaksis i morfologija glagol´nogo soglasovanija v tabasaranskom jazyke. In: *Tabasaranskie ètjudy: Materialy Dagestanskoj èkspedicii 1979* (Publikacii otdelenija strukturnoj i prikladnoj lingvistiki 15), 17–33. Moscow: Izdatel´stvo Moskovskogo universiteta.

Kibrik, Aleksandr E.; Tatevosov, Sergej G. & Eulenberg, Alexander (eds.) 1996. *Godoberi* (Lincom Studies in Caucasian Linguistics 2). Munich: Lincom Europa.

Kibrik, Aleksandr E. & Testelec, Jakov G. (eds.) 1999. *Èlementy grammatiki caxurskogo jazyka v tipologičeskom osveščenii*. Moscow: Nasledie Press.

King, Tracey Holloway & Dalrymple, Mary. 2004. Determiner agreement and noun conjunction. *Journal of Linguistics* 40.69–104.

Kirby, Simon. 1999. *Function, Selection and Innateness: The Emergence of Language Universals*. Oxford: Oxford University Press.

Kiss, Katelin É. 2002. *The Syntax of Hungarian*. Cambridge: Cambridge University Press.

Kitajgorodskaja, M. V. 1976. Variativnost´ v vyraženii roda suščestvitel´nogo pri oboznačenii ženščin po professii. In: L. P. Krysin & D. N. Šmelev (eds.) *Social´no-lingvističeskie issledovanija*, 144–55. Moscow: Nauka.

Koopman, Hilda. 2003. The locality of agreement and the structure of the DP in Maasa. In: William E. Griffin (ed.) *The Role of Agreement in Natural Language: Proceedings of the Fifth Annual Texas Linguistics Society Conference*, 207–27. Available at: http://uts.cc.utexas.edu/~tls/2001tls/2001proceeds.html.

Koppen, Marjo van. 2005. *One Probe – Two Goals: Aspects of Agreement in Dutch Dialects*. (PhD thesis, University of Leiden) Utrecht: LOT.

Kühner, Raphael & Stegmann, Carl. 1955. *Ausführliche Grammatik der lateinischen Sprache: Satzlehre: Erster Teil*, 3rd edn. Leverkusen: Gottschalksche Verlagsbuchhandlung.

Kupisch, Tanja; Müller, Natascha & Cantone, Katja F. 2002. Gender in monolingual and bilingual first language acquisition: comparing Italian and French. *Lingue e Linguaggio* 1.107–49.

Laidig, Wyn D. & Laidig, Carol J. 1990. Larike pronouns: duals and trials in a Central Moluccan language. *Oceanic Linguistics* 29.87–109.

Lambrecht, Knud. 1981. *Topic, Anti-topic and Verb Agreement in Non-standard French* (Pragmatics and Beyond 2/6). Amsterdam: John Benjamins.

    1994. *Information Structure and Sentence Form: Topic, Focus, and the Mental Representations of Discourse Referents*. Cambridge: Cambridge University Press.

Lambrecht, Knud & Michaelis, Laura A. 1998. Sentence accent in information questions: default and projection. *Linguistics and Philosophy* 21.477–544.

Lambrecht, Knud & Polinsky, Maria. 1997. Typological variation in sentence-focus constructions. In: Kora Singer, Randall Eggert & Gregory Anderson (eds.) *CLS 33: Papers from the Panels: On Linguistic Ideologies in Conflict; Universal Grammar, Parameters and Typology; the Perception of Speech and Other Acoustic Signals*, 189–206. Chicago: Chicago Linguistic Society.

Lapointe, Steven G. 1988. Toward a unified theory of agreement. In: Michael Barlow & Charles A. Ferguson (eds.) *Agreement in Natural Language: Approaches, Theories, Descriptions*, 67–87. Stanford: CSLI.

    1996. Review article on 'Agreement and anti-agreement: A syntax of Luiseño.' By Susan Steele. *Language* 72.372–9.

LaPolla, Randy, J. 1992. On the dating and nature of verb agreement in Tibeto-Burman. *Bulletin of the School of Oriental and African Studies* 55.298–315.

Lasnik, Howard. 2002. Feature movement or agreement at a distance? In: Artemis Alexiadou, Elena Anagnostopoulou, Sjef Barbiers and Hans-Martin Gaertner (eds.) *Dimensions of Movement: From Features to Remnants*, 189–208. Amsterdam: John Benjamins.

Lehečková, Helena. 2000. Use and misuse of gender in Czech. In: Barbara Unterbeck, Matti Rissanen, Terttu Nevalainen & Mirja Saari (eds.) *Gender in Grammar and Cognition I: Approaches to Gender, II: Manifestations of Gender* (Trends in Linguistics: Studies and Monographs 124), 749–70. Berlin: Mouton de Gruyter.

Lehmann, Christian. 1982. Universal and typological aspects of agreement. In: Hansjakob Seiler & Franz J. Stachowiak (eds.) *Apprehension: Das sprachliche Erfassen von Gegenständen II: Die Techniken und ihr Zusammenhang in Einzelsprachen*, 201–67. Tübingen: Narr.

Leigh, John & Woodhouse, David. 2004. *Football Lexicon*. London: Faber and Faber.

Leko, Nedžad. 1986. Syntax of noun headed structures in Serbo-Croatian and corresponding phrasal structures in English. PhD dissertation, Indiana University. Distributed by UMI, Ann Arbor, reference 86–28003.

    2000. Syntactic vs. semantic agreement in the Oslo corpus. In: Tracy Holloway King & Irina A. Sekerina (eds.) *Annual workshop on Formal Approaches to Slavic Linguistics 8: The Philadelphia Meeting 1999* (Michigan Slavic Materials 45), 259–78. Ann Arbor, MI: Michigan Slavic Publications.

Lenček, Rado L. 1972. O zaznamovanosti in nevtralizaciji slovnične kategorije spola v slovenskem knjižnem jeziku. *Slavistična revija* 20.55–63.

Leslau, Wolf. 1995. *Reference Grammar of Amharic*. Wiesbaden: Olto Harrassowitz.

LeTourneau, Mark S. 2003. Interpretability, feature strength, and impoverished agreement in Arabic. In: Dilworth B. Parkinson & Samira Farwaneh (eds.) *Perspectives on Arabic Linguistics XV: Papers from the Fifteenth Annual Symposia on Arabic Linguistics, Salt Lake City 2001* (Current Issues in Linguistic Theory 247), 85–131. Amsterdam: John Benjamins.

Levi, Jaakov. 1987. *Die Inkongruenz im biblischen Hebräisch.* Wiesbaden: Otto Harrassowitz.

Levin, Magnus. 2001. *Agreement with Collective Nouns in English* (Lund Studies in English 103). Stockholm: Almqvist & Wiksell.

Levinson, Stephen C. 1983. *Pragmatics.* Cambridge: Cambridge University Press.

Lichtenberk, Frantisek. 2000. Inclusory pronominals. *Oceanic Linguistics* 39.1–32.

Lieber, Rochelle. 1992. *Deconstructing Morphology: Word Formation in Syntactic Theory.* Chicago: University of Chicago Press.

Loporcaro, Michele. 1998. *Sintassi comparata dell'accordo participiale romanzo.* Turin: Rosenberg & Sellier.

Lötzsch, Ronald. 1965. Das sog. Possessivadjektiv im Slawischen, speziell im Sorbischen, und seine Stellung im System der Redeteile. *Forschungen und Fortschritte* 39/12.377–9.

Lyons, John. 1968. *Introduction to Theoretical Linguistics.* Cambridge: Cambridge University Press.

McCoy, Svetlana. 1998. Individual level predicates and pronoun doubling in colloquial Russian. In: Željko Bošković, Steven Franks and William Snyder (eds.) *Annual Workshop on Formal Approaches to Slavic Linguistics: The Connecticut Meeting 1997* (Michigan Slavic Materials 43), 231–51. Ann Arbor, MI: Michigan Slavic Publications.

McKay, Graham. 2000. Ndjébbana. In: R. M. W. Dixon & Barry J. Black (eds.) *The Handbook of Australian Languages* V, 154–354. Melbourne: Oxford University Press.

McLaughlin, Fiona. 1996. Inflection and phonological form in Wolof. In: Frances Ingemann (ed.) *1994 Mid-America Linguistics Conference Papers* II, 436–46. Lawrence, KS: The University of Kansas Department of Linguistics.

1997. Noun classification in Wolof: when affixes are not renewed. *Studies in African Linguistics* 26.1–28.

Mahajan, Anoop K. 1989. Agreement and agreement phrases. In: Itziar Laka & Anoop K. Mahajan (eds.) *MIT Working Papers in Linguistics* X, 217–52. Cambridge, MA: MIT.

Mallinson, Graham & Blake, Barry J. 1981. *Language Typology: Cross-Linguistic Studies in Syntax* (North-Holland linguistic series 46). Amsterdam: North-Holland.

Marchese, Lynell. 1988. Noun classes and agreement systems in Kru: a historical approach. In: Michael Barlow & Charles A. Ferguson (eds.) *Agreement in Natural Language: Approaches, Theories, Descriptions*, 323–41. Stanford: CSLI.

Marković, Svetozar V. 1954. O kolebljivosti slaganja u rodu kod imenica čiji se prirodni i gramatički rod ne slažu (i o rodu ovih imenica). *Pitanja književnosti i jezika* (Sarajevo) 1.87–110.

Marten, Lutz. 2005. The dynamics of agreement and conjunction. *Lingua* 115.527–47.

Matthews, Peter H. 1972. *Inflectional Morphology: A Theoretical Study Based on Aspects of Latin Verb Conjugation.* Cambridge: Cambridge University Press.

1997. *Oxford Concise Dictionary of Linguistics.* Oxford: Oxford University Press.

Maurice, Florence. 2001. Deconstructing gender – The case of Romanian. In: Marlis Hellinger & Hadumod Bußmann (eds.) *Gender across Languages: The Linguistic Representation of Men and Women*: I, 229–52. Amsterdam. John Benjamins.

Megaard, John. 1976. Predikatets kongruens i serbokroatisk i setninger med koordinerte subjektsnominalfraser. Unpublished dissertation, University of Oslo.

Meir, Irit. 2002. A cross-modality perspective on verb agreement. *Natural Language and Linguistic Theory* 20.413–50.

Mel čuk, Igor. 1993. Agreement, government, congruence. *Lingvisticae Investigationes* 17.307–72.

Mereu, Lunella. 1999. Agreement, pronominalization and word order in pragmatically-oriented languages. In: Lunella Mereu (ed.) *Boundaries of Morphology and Syntax* (Current Issues in Linguistic Theory 180), 231–50. Amsterdam: John Benjamins.

Meyerhoff, Miriam. 2000. *Constraints on Null Subjects in Bislama (Vanuatu): Social and Linguistic Factors* (Pacific Linguistics 506). Canberra: Pacific Linguistics, Research School of Pacific and Asian Studies, The Australian National University.

Michalopoulou, Ioanna. 1994. *Die Kategorie des Genus im Neugriechischen: Grundstudiumsarbeit*. Cologne: Institut für Sprachwissenschaft.

Miller, Philip H. & Sag, Ivan A. 1997. French clitic movement without clitics or movement. *Natural Language and Linguistic Theory* 15.573–639.

Minkoff, Seth. 2000. Animacy hierarchies and sentence processing. In: Andrew Carnie & Eithnre Guilfoyle (eds.) *The Syntax of Verb Initial Languages*, 201–12. Oxford: Oxford University Press.

Miranda, Rocky V. 1975. Indo-European gender: a study in semantic and syntactic change. *Journal of Indo-European Studies* 3.199–215.

Mithun, Marianne. 1986. When zero isn't there. In: Vassiliki Nikiforidou, Mary VanClay, Mary Niepokuj & Deborah Feder (eds.) *Proceedings of the Twelfth Annual Meeting of the Berkeley Linguistics Society: February 15–17, 1986*, 195–211. Berkeley: Berkeley Linguistics Society, University of California.

1988. The grammaticization of coordination. In: John Haiman & Sandra A. Thompson (eds.) *Clause Combining in Grammar and Discourse* (Typological Studies in Language 18), 331–59. Amsterdam: John Benjamins.

1991. The development of bound pronouns. In: W. P. Lehmann & H.-J. J. Hewitt (eds.) *Language Typology 1988: Typological Models in Reconstruction* (Current Issues in Linguistic Theory 81), 85–104. Amsterdam: John Benjamins.

1999. *The Languages of Native North America*. Cambridge: Cambridge University Press.

2003. Pronouns and agreement: the information status of pronominal affixes. In: Dunstan Brown, Greville G. Corbett and Carole Tiberius (eds.) *Agreement: A Typological Perspective* (Special issue of *Transactions of the Philological Society* 101/2), 235–78. Oxford: Blackwell.

Mladenova, Olga M. 2001. Neuter designations of humans and norms of social interactions in the Balkans. *Anthropological Linguistics* 43.18–53.

Mohammad, M. A. 1988. Nominative case, I-subjects, and subject-verb agreement. Diane Brentari, Gary N. Larson & Lynn A. MacLeod (eds.) *CLS 24: Papers from the 24th Annual Regional Meeting of the Chicago Linguistic Society: Part II: Parasession on Agreement in Grammatical Theory*, 223–35. Chicago: Chicago Linguistic Society.

2000. *Word Order, Agreement and Pronominalization in Standard and Palestinian Arabic* (Current Issues in Linguistic Theory 181). Amsterdam: John Benjamins.

Mohanan, Tara. 1994. *Argument Structure in Hindi* (Dissertations in Linguistics). Stanford: CSLI.

Moore, John & Perlmutter, David. 2000. What does it take to be a dative subject? *Natural Language and Linguistic Theory* 18.373–416.

Moosally, Michelle. 1998. Noun phrase coordination: Ndebele agreement patterns and cross-linguistic variation. PhD Dissertation, University of Texas at Austin. Distributed by UMI, Ann Arbor, reference 9937102.

Moravcsik, Edith A. 1978. Agreement. In: Joseph H. Greenberg, Charles A. Ferguson & Edith A. Moravcsik (eds.) *Universals of Human Language: IV: Syntax*, 331–74. Stanford: Stanford University Press.

1988. Agreement and markedness. In: Michael Barlow & Charles A. Ferguson (eds.) *Agreement in Natural Language: Approaches, Theories, Descriptions*, 89–106. Stanford: CSLI.

2003. Non-compositional definiteness marking in Hungarian. In: Frans Plank (ed.) *Noun Phrase Structure in the Languages of Europe* (Empirical Approaches to Language Typology EUROTYP 20–7), 397–466. Berlin: Mouton de Gruyter.

Morgan, Jerry L. 1972. Verb agreement as a rule of English. In: Paul M. Peranteau, Judith N. Levi & Gloria C. Phares (eds.) *Papers from the Eighth Regional Meeting of the Chicago Linguistic Society*, 278–86. Chicago: Chicago Linguistic Society.

1984. Some problems of agreement in English and Albanian. In: Claudia Brugman, Monica Maccauley, Amy Dahlstrom, Michele Emanatian, Birch Moonwoman & Catherine O'Connor (eds.) *Proceedings of the Tenth Annual Meeting of the Berkeley Linguistics Society*, 233–47. Berkeley: Berkeley Linguistics Society, University of California.

Morgan, Jerry L. & Green, Georgia M. 2005. Why verb agreement is not the poster child for formal theory. In: Salikoko S. Mufwene, Elaine J. Francis & Rebecca S. Wheeler (eds.) *Polymorphous Linguistics: Jim McCawley's Legacy*, 454–78. Cambridge, MA: MIT Press.

Mosel, Ulrike & Hovdhaugen, Even. 1992. *Samoan Reference Grammar.* Oslo: Scandinavian University Press.

Napoli, Donna Jo. 1975. A global agreement phenomenon. *Linguistic Inquiry* 6.413–35.

Naro, Anthony J. 1981. The social and structural dimensions of a syntactic change. *Language* 57.63–98.

Nathan, Geoffrey S. 1981. What's these facts about. *Linguistic Inquiry* 12.151–3.

Nichols, Johanna. 1985. The directionality of agreement. In: Mary Niepokuj, Mary VanClay, Vassiliki Nikiforidou & Deborah Feder (eds.) *Proceedings of the Eleventh Annual Meeting of the Berkeley Linguistics Society, February 16–18, 1985*, 273–86. Berkeley: Berkeley Linguistics Society, University of California.

1986. Head marking and dependent marking grammar. *Language* 62.56–119.

1989. The Nakh evidence for the history of gender in Nakh-Daghestanian. In: Howard I. Aronson (ed.) *The Non-Slavic Languages of the USSR: Linguistic Studies*, 158–73. Chicago: Chicago Linguistic Society.

1992. *Linguistic Diversity in Space and Time.* Chicago: University of Chicago Press.

Nichols, Johanna; Rappaport, Gilbert & Timberlake, Alan. 1980. Subject, topic and control in Russian. In: Bruce R. Caron et al. (eds.) *Proceedings of the Sixth Annual Meeting of the Berkeley Linguistics Society*, 372–86. Berkeley: Berkeley Linguistics Society, University of California.

Nicol, Janet & Wilson, Rachel. 2000. Agreement and case-marking in Russian: a psycholinguistic investigation of agreement errors in production. In: Tracy Holloway King & Irina A. Sekerina (eds.) *Annual Workshop on Formal Approaches to Slavic Linguistics 8: The Philadelphia Meeting 1999* (Michigan Slavic Materials 45), 314–27. Ann Arbor: Michigan Slavic Publications.

Nikolaeva, Irina. 1999. Object agreement, grammatical relations and information structure. *Studies in Language* 23.331–76.

2001. Secondary topic as a relation in information structure. *Linguistics* 39.1–49.

2005. Modifier-head person concord. In: *Morphology and Linguistic Typology: Online Proceedings of the Fourth Mediterranean Morphology Meeting (MMH4) Catania, 21–23 September 2003*. Available at: http://morbo.lingue.unibo.it/mmm/mmm4-proceedings.php.

forthcoming. Agreement and situation construal. In: Jocelyne Fernandez-Vest (ed.) *Uralic Languages Today*. Paris.

Nishi, Yoshio. 1995. A brief survey of the controversy in verb pronominalization in Tibeto-Burman. In: Yoshio Nishi, James A. Matisoff & Yasuhiko Nagano (eds.) *New Horizons in Tibeto-Burman Morphosyntax* (Senri Ethnological Studies 41), 1–16. Osaka: National Museum of Ethnology.

Nocentini, Alberto. 1999. Topical constraints in the verbal agreement of spoken Italian (Tuscan variety). *Rivista di Linguistica* 11.315–39.

Norman, Boris. 2001. Substantivnoe podležaščee pri glagolax v 1-m lice množestvennogo čisla v bolgarskom jazyke (*dvama studenti tărsim rabota*). In: Alexander Kiklevič (ed.) *Količestvennost´ i gradual´nost´ v estestvennom jazyke* (Die Welt der Slaven 11), 77–86. Munich: Otto Sagner.

Nuessel, Frank. 1984. (Dis)agreement in Spanish. *Papers in Linguistics* 17.267–81.

Nunberg, Geoffrey D. 1996. Transfers of meaning. In: James Pustejovsky & Branimir Boguraev (eds.) *Lexical Semantics: The Problem of Polysemy*, 109–32. Oxford: Clarendon.

O'Grady, William & Yamashita, Yoshi. 2002, Partial agreement in second-language acquisition. *Linguistics* 40.1011–19.

O'Herin, Brian. 2002. *Case and Agreement in Abaza* (SIL International and The University of Texas at Arlington Publications in Linguistics 138). Dallas: SIL International.

Ortmann, Albert & Popescu, Alexandra. 2000. Romanian definite articles are not clitics. In: Birgit Gerlach & Janet Grijzenhout (eds.) *Clitics in Phonology, Morphology and Syntax* (Linguistik Aktuell 36), 295–324. Amsterdam: John Benjamins.

Osenova, Petya N. 2003. On subject-verb agreement in Bulgarian (An HPSG-based account). In: Peter Kosta, Joanna Błaszcyak, Jens Frasek, Ljudmila Geist & Marzena Żygis (eds.) *Investigations into Formal Slavic Linguistics: Contributions of the Fourth European Conference on Formal Description of Slavic Languages – FDSL IV, 2001, II*, 661–72. Frankfurt: Peter Lang.

Osterhout, Lee & Mobley, Linda A. 1995. Event-related brain potentials elicited by failure to agree. *Journal of Memory and Language* 34.739–73.

Paducheva, Elena V. & Uspenskij, Vladimir A. 1997. Binominativnoe predloženie: problema soglasovanija svjazki. In: Leonid Krysin (ed.) *Oblik slova: Sbornik statej pamjati D. N. Šmeleva*, 170–82. Moscow: Institut russkogo jazyka im. V. V. Vinogradova, Rossijskaja Akademija Nauk.

Palmer, F. R. 1994. *Grammatical roles and relations*. Cambridge: Cambridge University Press.

Pandharipande, Rajeshwari P. 1997. *Marathi*. London: Routledge.

Panevová, Jarmila. 1991. Některé otázky shody selektivní a shody paradigmatické. In: Maciej Grochowski & Daniel Weiss (eds.) *'Words Are Physicians for an Ailing Mind'* (Sagners Slavistische Sammlung 17), 323–8. Munich: Otto Sagner.

Panevová, Jarmila & Petkevič, Vladimír. 1997. Agreement in Czech and its formal account. In: Uwe Junghanns & Gerhild Zybatow (eds.) *Formale Slavistik*, 321–33. Frankfurt: Vervuert Verlag.

Parker, Enid M. & Hayward, Richard J. 1985. *An Afar–English–French Dictionary (with Grammatical Notes in English)*. London: School of Oriental and African Studies, University of London.

Payne, John R. 1995. Inflecting postpositions in Indic and Kashmiri. In: Frans Plank (ed.) *Double Case: Agreement by Suffixaufnahme*, 283–98. New York: Oxford University Press.

Pensalfini, Robert. 2003. *A Grammar of Jingulu: An Aboriginal Language of the Northern Territory* (Pacific Linguistics 536). Canberra: Pacific Linguistics.

Perlmutter, David M. 1972. A note on syntactic and semantic number in English. *Linguistic Inquiry* 3.243–6.

(ed.) 1983a. *Studies in Relational Grammar 1*. Chicago: University of Chicago Press.

1983b. Personal vs. impersonal constructions. *Natural Language and Linguistic Theory* 1.141–200.

Perlmutter, David & Moore, John. 2002. Language-internal explanation: the distribution of Russian impersonals. *Language* 78.619–50.

Perlmutter, David & Rosen, Carol (eds.) 1984. *Studies in Relational Grammar 2*. Chicago: University of Chicago Press.

Peterson, Peter G. 1986. Establishing verb agreement with disjunctively conjoined subjects: strategies vs principles. *Australian Journal of Linguistics* 6.231–49.

Pfau, Roland. 2001. Defective feature copy and anti-agreement in language production. In: William E. Griffin (ed.) *The Role of Agreement in Natural Language: Proceedings of the Fifth Annual Texas Linguistics Society Conference*, 95–107. Available at: http://uts.cc.utexas.edu/~tls/2001tls/2001proceeds.html.

Pietsch, Lukas. 2005. *Variable Grammars: Verbal Agreement in Northern Dialects of English* (Linguistische Arbeiten 496). Tübingen: Niemeyer.

Plank, Frans. 1984. Romance disagreements: phonology interfering with syntax. *Journal of Linguistics* 20.329–439.

(ed.) 1995. *Double Case: Agreement by Suffixaufnahme*. New York: Oxford University Press.

Polinsky, Maria. 1995. Non-terms in complex predicates: from incorporation to reanalysis. In: Clifford S. Burgess, Katarzyna Dziwirek & Donna Gerdts (eds.) *Grammatical Relations: Theoretical Approaches to Empirical Questions*, 359–90. Stanford: Center for the Study of Language and Information.

2002. Efficiency preferences: Refinements, rankings, and unresolved questions. *Theoretical Linguistics* 28.177–202.

2003. Non-canonical agreement is canonical. In: Dunstan Brown, Greville Corbett & Carole Tiberius (eds.) *Agreement: A Typological Perspective* (Special issue of *Transactions of the Philological Society* 101/2), 279–312. Oxford: Blackwell.

Polinsky, Maria & Comrie, Bernard. 1999. Agreement in Tsez. In: Greville G. Corbett (ed.) *Agreement* (Special issue of *Folia Linguistica* 33/2), 109–30. Berlin: Mouton de Gruyter.

Polinsky, Maria & Potsdam, Eric. 1999. Cross-linguistic view of a long-distance agreement. Paper presented at the Third International Conference of the Association for Linguistic Typology, University of Amsterdam, August 1999.

2001. Long-distance agreement and topic in Tsez. *Natural Language and Linguistic Theory* 19.583–646.

2002. Backward control. *Linguistic Inquiry* 33.245–82.

Pollard, Carl & Sag, Ivan A. 1994. *Head-Driven Phrase Structure Grammar.* Chicago: University of Chicago Press.

Poplack, Shana & Tagliamonte, Sali. 1989. There's no tense like the present: verbal *-s* inflection in Early Black English. *Language Variation and Change* 1.47–84.

1994. *-S* or nothing: marking the plural in the African American diaspora. *American Speech* 69.227–59.

Popović, Ljubomir. 1991. Honorifička i semantička kongruencija pri učtivom obraćanju. *Književnost i jezik* 38.38–53.

Posner, Rebecca. 1985. Non-agreement on Romance disagreements. *Journal of Linguistics* 21.437–51.

Postal, Paul M. & Joseph, Brian D. (eds.) 1990. *Studies in Relational Grammar 3.* Chicago: University of Chicago Press.

Priestly, T. M. S. 1983. On 'drift' in Indo-European gender systems. *Journal of Indo-European Studies* 11.339–63.

1984. O popolni izgubi srednega spola v selščini: enodobni opis. *Slavistična revija* 32.37–47.

1993. Slovene. In: Bernard Comrie & Greville G. Corbett (eds.) *The Slavonic Languages*, 388–451. London: Routledge.

Przepiórkowski, Adam. 2001. Predicative case agreement with quantifier phrases in Polish. In: Adam Przepiórkowski & Piotr Banski (eds.) *Generative Linguistics in Poland: Syntax and Morphosyntax*, 159–69. Warsaw: Polish Academy of Sciences.

Pullum, Geoffrey K. 1984. How complex could an agreement system be? In: Gloria Alvarez, Belinda Brodie & Terry McCoy (eds.) *ESCOL '84: Proceedings of the First Eastern States Conference on Linguistics*, 79–103. Columbus, OH: Ohio State University.

Pullum, Geoffrey K. & Zwicky, Arnold. 1988. The syntax-phonology interface. In: Frederick J. Newmeyer (ed.) *Linguistics: The Cambridge Survey: I: Linguistic Theory: Foundations*, 255–80. Cambridge: Cambridge University Press.

Radford, Andrew. 1994. Tense and agreement variability in child grammars of English. In: Barbara Lust, Margarita Suñer & John Whitman (eds.) *Syntactic Theory and First Language Acquisition: Cross-Linguistic Perspectives I: Heads, Projections, and Learnability*, 135–57. Hillsdale, NJ: Lawrence Erlbaum.

2004. *Minimalist Syntax: Exploring the Structure of English.* Cambridge: Cambridge University Press.

Rangan, K. & Suseela, M. 2003. A comparison of agreement system in Old Tamil and Modern Tamil. In: B. Ramakrishna Reddy (ed.) *Agreement in Dravidian Languages,* 28–50. Chennai: International Institute of Tamil Studies.

Reid, Nicholas. 1997. Class and classifier in Ngan'gityemmeri. In: Mark Harvey & Nicholas Reid (eds.) *Nominal Classification in Aboriginal Australia* (Studies in Language Companion Series 37), 165–228. Amsterdam: John Benjamins.

Rizzi, Luigi. 1990. *Relativized Minimality.* Cambridge, MA: MIT Press.

Robblee, Karen E. 1993a. Predicate lexicosemantics and case marking under negation in Russian. *Russian Linguistics* 17.209–36.

1993b. Individuation and Russian agreement. *Slavic and East European Journal* 37.423–41.

1997. The interaction of word order, agreement and case marking. In: Anne-Marie Simon-Vandenbergen, Kristin Davidse & Dirk Noël (eds.) *Reconnecting Language: Morphology and Syntax in Functional Perspectives,* 227–48. Amsterdam: John Benjamins.

Roberts, Ian G. 1985. Agreement parameters and the development of English modal auxiliaries. *Natural Language and Linguistic Theory* 3.21–58.

Roberts, Ian & Roussou, Anna. 2003. *Syntactic Change: A Minimalist Approach to Grammaticalization.* Cambridge: Cambridge University Press.

Rohrbacher, Bernard. 1999. *Morphology-Driven Syntax: A Theory of V to I Raising and Pro-Drop* (Linguistik Aktuell 15). Amsterdam: John Benjamins.

Rothstein, Robert A. 1980. Gender and reference in Polish and Russian. In: Catherine V. Chvany & Richard D. Brecht (eds.) *Morphosyntax in Slavic,* 79–97. Columbus, OH: Slavica.

1993. Polish. In: Bernard Comrie & Greville G. Corbett (eds.) *The Slavonic Languages,* 686–758. London: Routledge.

Rubino, Rejane B. & Pine, Julian M. 1998. Subject-verb agreement in Brazilian Portuguese: what low error rates hide. *Journal of Child Language* 25.35–59.

Rusakova, Marina V. 2001. Imennaja slovoforma flektivnogo jazyka (soglasovanie v russkom atributivnom slovosočetanii). Unpublished PhD dissertation, St Petersburg: Gosudarstvennyj pedagogičeskij universitet im. A. I. Gercena.

Sadler, Louisa. 2003. Coordination and asymmetric agreement in Welsh. In: Miriam Butt & Tracey Holloway King (eds.) *Nominals: Inside and Out,* 85–117. Stanford: CSLI Publications.

Saeed, John I. 1993a. Adpositional clitics and word order in Somali. *Transactions of the Philological Society* 91.63–93.

1993b. *Somali Reference Grammar (Second Revised Edition).* Kensington, MD: Dunwoody.

1999. *Somali* (London Oriental and African Language Library 10). Amsterdam: John Benjamins.

Sand, Diane E. Z. 1971. Agreement of the Predicate with Quantitative Subjects in Serbo-Croatian. PhD dissertation, University of Pennsylvania. Distributed by UMI, Ann Arbor, reference 72–17420.

Sauvageot, Serge. 1967. Sur la classification nominale en baïnouk. In: *La classification nominale dans les langues négro-africaines*, 225–35. Paris: Centre national de la recherche scientifique.

Scatton, Ernest A. 1993. Bulgarian. In: Bernard Comrie & Greville G. Corbett (eds.) *The Slavonic Languages*, 188–248. London: Routledge.

Schiffman, Harold F. 1999. *A Reference Grammar of Spoken Tamil*. Cambridge: Cambridge University Press.

Schmidt, Peter. forthcoming. The limits of grammatical agreement: a critical assessment of semantic solutions to the domain problem. In: Peter Lauwers & Pierre Swiggers (eds.) *Linguistic Currents and Concepts: Proceedings of the 34th SLE Meeting: Language Study in Europe at the Turn of the Millennium, Leuven, 28–31 August 2001*. Leuven: Peeters.

Schmidt, Peter & Lehfeldt, Werner. 1995. *Kongruenz, Rektion, Adjunktion: Systematische und historische Untersuchungen zur allgemeinen Morphosyntax und zu den Wortfügungen (slovosočetanija) im Russischen* (Specimina philologiae slavicae supplement 37). Munich: Otto Sagner.

Schriefers, Herbert & Jescheniak, Jörg D. 1999. Representation and processing of grammatical gender in language production: a review. *Journal of Psycholinguistic Research* 28.575–600.

Schroeder, Christoph. 1999. *The Turkish Nominal Phrase in Spoken Discourse* (Turcologica 40). Wiesbaden: Olto Harrassowitz.

Schuh, Russell G. 1989. Number and gender in Miya. In: Zygmunt Frajzyngier (ed.) *Current Progress in Chadic Linguistics: Proceedings of the International Symposium on Chadic Linguistics: Boulder, Colorado, 1–2 May, 1987* (Current Issues in Linguistic Theory 62), 171–81. Amsterdam: John Benjamins.

1998. *A Grammar of Miya* (University of California Publications in Linguistics 130). Berkeley: University of California Press.

Schultze, Wolfgang M. 2004. Review article of Alice C. Harris 'Endoclitics and the Origins of Udi Morphosyntax'. *Studies in Language* 28.419–41.

Schultze-Berndt, Eva & Himmelmann, Nikolaus P. 2004. Depictive secondary predicates in cross-linguistic perspective. *Linguistic Typology* 8.59–131.

Schütze, Carson T. 1999. English expletive constructions are not inflected. *Linguistic Inquiry* 30.467–84.

Seidl, Amanda & Dimitriadis, Alexis. 1997. The discourse function of object marking in Swahili. In: Kora Singer, Randall Eggert & Gregory Anderson (eds.) *CLS 33: Papers from the Main Session, April 17–19, 1997*, 373–87. Chicago: Chicago Linguistic Society.

Seifart, Frank. 2004. Nominal classification in Miraña, a Witotoan language of Colombia. *Sprachtypologie und Universalienforschung (STUF)* 57.228–46.

Seo, Seunghyun. 2001. The frequency of null subject in Russian, Polish, Czech, Bulgarian and Serbo-Croatian: an analysis according to morphosyntactic environments. PhD dissertation, Indiana University. Distributed by UMI, Ann Arbor, reference 3038515.

Šewc-Schuster, Hinc. 1976. *Gramatika hornjoserbskeje rěče, 2. zwjazk: syntaksa*. Bautzen: Ludowe nakładnistwo Domowina.

Sgall, Petr; Hajičová, Eva & Panevová, Jarmila. 1986. *The Meaning of the Sentence in its Semantic and Pragmatic Aspects*. Edited by Jacob L. Mey. Dordrecht: Reidel.

Shevelov, George Y. 1963. *The Syntax of Modern Literary Ukrainian: The Simple Sentence*. The Hague: Mouton.

Shieber, Stuart M. 1986. *An Introduction to Unification-Based Approaches to Grammar* (CSLI lecture notes 4). Stanford: CSLI.

Siewierska, Anna. 1996. Word order type and alignment type. *Sprachtypologie und Universalienforschung (STUF)* 49.149–76.

1998. Variation in major constituent order: a global and a European perspective. In: Anna Siewierska (ed.) *Constituent Order in the Languages of Europe* (Empirical Approaches to Language Typology: EUROTYP 20–1), 475–551. Berlin: Mouton de Gruyter.

1999. From anaphoric pronoun to grammatical agreement marker: why objects don't make it. In: Greville G. Corbett (ed.) *Agreement* (Special issue of *Folia Linguistica* 33/2), 225–51. Berlin: Mouton de Gruyter.

2004a. On the discourse basis of person agreement marking. In: Tuija Virtanen (ed.) *Approaches to Cognition through Text and Discourse*, 33–48. Berlin: Mouton de Gruyter.

2004b. *Person*. Cambridge: Cambridge University Press.

Sigler, Michele. 1992. Number agreement and specificity in Armenian. In: Costas P. Canakis, Grace P. Chan & Jeanette Marshall Denton (eds.) *Papers from the 28th Regional Meeting of the Chicago Linguistic Society 1992 I: The Main Session*, 499–514. Chicago: Chicago Linguistic Society.

Sigurðsson, Halldór Ármann. 1996. Icelandic finite verb agreement. *Working Papers in Scandinavian Syntax* 57.1–46.

2002. To be an oblique subject: Russian vs. Icelandic. *Natural Language and Linguistic Theory* 20.691–724.

Silverstein, Michael. 1976. Hierarchy of features and ergativity. In: R. M. W. Dixon (ed.) *Grammatical Categories in Australian Languages*, 112–71. Canberra: Australian Institute of Aboriginal Studies.

Simon, Horst J. 2003. From pragmatics to grammar: tracing the development of respect in the history of the German pronouns of address. In: Irma Taavitsainen & Andreas H. Jucker (eds.) *Diachronic Perspectives on Address Term Systems*, 85–123. Amsterdam: John Benjamins.

2004. Respekt – die Grammatik der Höflichkeit im Bairischen. In: Stephan Gaisbauer & Hermann Scheuringer (eds.) *Linzerschnitten: Beiträge sur 8. Bayerisch-österreichischen Dialektologentagung, zugleich 3. Arbeitstagung zu Sprache und Dialekt in Oberösterreich, in Linz, September 2001*, 355–70. Linz: Adalbert-Stifter-Institut.

Simpson, Jane & Bresnan, Joan. 1983. Control and obviation in Warlpiri. *Natural Language and Linguistic Theory* 1.49–64.

Skorik, Petr Ja. 1961. *Grammatika čukotskogo jazyka I: Fonetika i morfologija imennyx častej reči*. Moscow: Izd. Akademii Nauk SSSR.

Smith, John C. 1995. Perceptual factors and the disappearance of agreement between past participle and direct object in Romance. In: John C. Smith & Martin Maiden (eds.) *Linguistic Theory and the Romance Languages* (Current Issues in Linguistic Theory 122), 161–80. Amsterdam: John Benjamins.

Sobin, Nicholas. 1997. Agreement, default rules, and grammatical viruses. *Linguistic Inquiry* 28.318–43.

Sparks, Randall B. 1984. Here's a few more facts. *Linguistic Inquiry* 15.179–83.

Spencer, Andrew. 1991. *Morphological Theory: An Introduction to Word Structure in Generative Grammar*. Oxford: Blackwells.

——— 1992. Nominal inflection and the nature of functional categories. *Journal of Linguistics* 28.313–41.

——— 2000. Agreement morphology in Chukotkan. In: Wolfgang U. Dressler, Oskar E. Pfeiffer, Markus A. Pöchtrager & John R. Rennison (eds.) *Morphological Analysis in Comparison* (Current Issues in Linguistic Theory 201), 191–222. Amsterdam: John Benjamins.

Sridhar, S. N. 1990. *Kannada* (Descriptive grammars series). London: Routledge.

Stassen, Leon. 2003. Noun phrase conjunction: the coordinative and the comitative strategy. In: Frans Plank (ed.) *Noun Phrase Structure in the Languages of Europe* (Empirical Approaches to Language Typology: EUROTYP 20–7), 761–817. Berlin: Mouton de Gruyter.

Steele, Susan. 1978. Word order variation: a typological study. In: Joseph H. Greenberg, Charles A. Ferguson & Edith A. Moravcsik (eds.) *Universals of Human Language IV: Syntax*, 585–623. Stanford: Stanford University Press.

——— 1990. *Agreement and Anti-Agreement: A Syntax of Luiseño* (Studies in Natural Language and Linguistic Theory 17). Dordrecht: Kluwer.

——— 1995. Towards a theory of morphological information. *Language* 71.260–309.

Steinberg, Elisa & Caskey, Alexander F. 1988. The syntax and semantics of gender (dis)agreement: an autolexical approach. In: Diane Brentari, Gary N. Larson & Lynn A. MacLeod (eds). *CLS 24: Papers from the 24th Annual Regional Meeting of the Chicago Linguistic Society: Part II: Parasession on Agreement in Grammatical Theory*, 291–303. Chicago: Chicago Linguistic Society.

Stone, Gerald 1993. Sorbian (Upper and Lower). In: Bernard Comrie & Greville G. Corbett (eds.) *The Slavonic Languages*, 593–685. London: Routledge.

Strang, Barbara M. H. 1966. Some features of S-V concord in present-day English. In: Ilva Cellini & Giorgio Melchiori (eds.) *English Studies Today: Fourth Series*, 73–87. Rome: Edizioni di Storia e Letteratura.

Stump, Gregory T. 2001. *Inflectional Morphology: A Theory of Paradigm Structure*. Cambridge: Cambridge University Press.

Stump Gregory T. & Yadav, Ramawater. 1988. Maithili verb agreement and the control agreement principle. In: Diane Brentari, Gary N. Larson & Lynn A. MacLeod (eds.) *CLS 24: Papers from the 24th Annual Regional Meeting of the Chicago Linguistic Society: Part II: Parasession on Agreement in Grammatical Theory*, 304–21. Chicago: Chicago Linguistic Society.

Subbarao, K. V. 2003. Language types and agreement in South Asian languages. In: B. Ramakrishna Reddy (ed.) *Agreement in Dravidian Languages*, 1–27. Chennai: International Institute of Tamil Studies.

Sumbatova, Nina R. 2003. Glagol´naja sistema jazyka landuma. In: V. A. Vinogradov & I. N. Toporova (eds.) *Osnovy afrikanskogo jazykoznanija: Glagol*, 325–56. Moscow: Vostočnaja literatura.

Sumbatova, Nina R. & Mutalov, Rasul O. 2003. *A Grammar of Icari Dargwa* (Languages of the World/Materials 92). Munich: Lincom Europa.

Sun, Hongkai. 1995. A further discussion on verb agreement in Tibeto-Burman languages. In: Yoshio Nishi, James A. Matisoff, & Yasuhiko Nagano (eds.) *New Horizons in Tibeto-Burman Morphosyntax* (Senri Ethnological Studies 41), 17–29. Osaka: National Museum of Ethnology.

Suprun, A. E. 1957. K upotrebleniju roditel´nogo i imenitel´nogo padežej množestvennogo čisla prilagatel´nyx v sočetanijax s čislitel´nymi *dva, tri, četyre* v sovremennom russkom jazyke. *Učenye zapiski Kirgizskogo gosudarstvennogo pedagogičeskogo instituta* 3.72–84.

—— 1969. *Slavjanskie čislitel´nye (stanovlenie čislitel´nyx kak osoboj časti reči).* Minsk: Belorussian State University.

Suzman, Susan M. 1982. Strategies for acquiring Zulu concord. *South African Journal of African Linguistics* 2.53–67.

Švedova, N. Ju. (ed.) 1980. *Russkaja grammatika II.* Moscow: Nauka.

Taraldsen, Knut Tarald. 1980. On the nominative island condition, vacuous application, and the *That* -trace filter. Distributed by Indiana University Linguistics Club, Bloomington, Indiana.

Tasmowski, Liliane & Verluyten, S. Paul. 1985. Control mechanisms of anaphora. *Journal of Semantics* 4.341–70.

Terrill, Angela. 2003. *A Grammar of Lavukaleve* (Mouton Grammar Library 30). Berlin: Mouton de Gruyter.

Testelec, Jakov G. 2001. *Vvedenie v obščij sintaksis.* Moscow: Rossijskij gosudarstvennyj gumanitarnyj universitet.

Tiberius, Carole; Brown, Dunstan & Corbett, Greville G. 2002a. *The Surrey Database of Agreement.* http://www.smg.surrey.ac.uk/

—— 2002b. A typological database of agreement. In: Manuel González Rodríguez & Carmen Paz Suarez Araujo (eds.) *Proceedings of LREC2002, the Third International Conference on Language Resources and Evaluation* VI, 1843–6. Las Palmas, Spain. Available at: http://www.surrey.ac.uk/LIS/SMG/projects/agreement/outputs.html.

Tiberius, Carole; Corbett, Greville G. & Barron, Julia. 2002. *Agreement: A Bibliography.* Available at: http://www.surrey.ac.uk/LIS/SMG/projects/agreement/agreement_bib.htm.

Timberlake, Alan. 1988. Case agreement in Lithuanian. In: Michael Barlow & Charles A. Ferguson (eds.) *Agreement in Natural Language: Approaches, Theories, Descriptions*, 181–99. Stanford: CSLI.

—— 1993. Russian. In: Bernard Comrie & Greville G. Corbett (eds.) *The Slavonic Languages*, 827–86. London: Routledge.

—— 2004. *A Reference Grammar of Russian.* Cambridge: Cambridge University Press.

Timmermans, Mark; Schriefers, Herbert; Dijkstra, Tom & Haverkort, Marco. 2004. Disagreement on agreement: person agreement between coordinated subjects and verbs in Dutch and German. *Linguistics* 42.905–29.

Toivonen, Ida. 2000. The morphosyntax of Finnish possessives. *Natural Language and Linguistic Theory* 18.579–609.

—— 2003. Grammatical functions and Inari Sami verbal agreement. Paper read at the 19th Scandinavian Conference of Linguistics, revised ms under review.

Trask, R. L. 1997. *A Student's Dictionary of Language and Linguistics.* London: Arnold.

Troike, Rudolf C. 1981. Subject-object concord in Coahuilteco. *Language* 57.658–73.

Tsunoda, Tasaku. 1981. Interaction of phonological, grammatical, and semantic factors: an Australian example. *Oceanic Linguistics* 20.45–92.

Tuite, Kevin. 1998. *Kartvelian Morphosyntax: Number Agreement and Morphosyntactic Orientation in the South Caucasian Languages.* Munich: Lincom Europa.

Valentine, J. Randolph. 2001. *Nishnaabemwin Reference Grammar.* Toronto: University of Toronto Press.

Valenzuela, Pilar. 1999. Adverbials, transitivity and switch-reference in Shipibo-Konibo. In: Sabrina J. Billings, John P. Boyle & Aaron M. Griffith (eds.) *CLS 35: Part 2: Papers from the Panels*, 355–71. Chicago: Chicago Linguistic Society.

Valiouli, Maria. 1997. Grammatical gender clash: slip of the tongue or shift of perspective? *Linguistics* 35.89–110.

Van Valin, Robert D. & LaPolla, Randy J. 1997. *Syntax: Structure, Meaning and Function.* Cambridge: Cambridge University Press.

Vanek, Anthony L. 1970. *Aspects of subject-verb agreement.* Edmonton: Department of Slavic Languages, University of Alberta. [Republished 1977 in the series Current Inquiry into Language and Linguistics 23. Edmonton: Linguistic Research.]

Velázquez-Castillo, Maura. 1991. The semantics of Guarani agreement markers. In: Laurel A. Sutton, Christopher Johnson with Ruth Shields (eds.) *Proceedings of the Seventeenth Annual Meeting of the Berkeley Linguistics Society, February 15–18, 1991: General Session and Parasession on the Grammar of Event Structure*, 324–35. Berkeley: Berkeley Linguistics Society, University of California.

Veselovská, Ludmila. 2001. Agreement patterns of Czech group nouns and quantifiers. In: Norbert Corver & Henk van Riemsdijk (eds.) *Semi-Lexical Categories: The Function of Content Words and the Content of Function Words* (Studies in Generative Grammar 59), 274–320. Berlin: Mouton de Gruyter.

Vigliocco, Gabriella; Butterworth, Brian & Garrett, Merrill F. 1996. Subject-verb agreement in Spanish and English: Differences in the role of conceptual constraints. *Cognition* 61.261–98.

Vigliocco, Gabriella; Butterworth, Brian & Semenza, Carlos. 1995. Constructing subject-verb agreement in speech: the role of semantic and morphological factors. *Journal of Memory and Language* 34.186–215.

Vigliocco, Gabriella; Butterworth, Brian; Semenza, Carlos & Fossella, Sabrina. 1994. How two aphasic speakers construct subject-verb agreement. *Journal of Neurolinguistics* 8.19–25.

Vigliocco, Gabriella & Franck, Julie. 1999. When sex and syntax go hand in hand: gender agreement in language production. *Journal of Memory and Language* 40.455–78.

2001. When sex affects syntax: contextual influences in sentence production. *Journal of Memory and Language* 45.368–90.

Vigliocco, Gabriella; Hartsuiker, Robert J.; Jarema, Gonia & Kolk, Herman H. J. 1996. One or more labels on the bottles? Notional concord in Dutch and French. *Language and Cognitive Processes* 11.407–42.

Vigliocco, Gabriella & Nicol, Janet. 1998. Separating hierarchical relations and word order in language production: is proximity concord syntactic or linear? *Cognition* 68.13–29.

Vigliocco, Gabriella & Zilli, Tiziana. 1999. Syntactic accuracy in sentence production: gender disagreement in Italian language-impaired and unimpaired speakers. *Journal of Psycholinguistic Research* 28.623–48.

Vinogradov, V. V. & Istrina, E. S. (eds.) 1954. *Grammatika russkogo jazyka II: Sintaksis, čast'pervaja.* Moscow: AN SSSR.

Wald, Benji. 1975. Animate concord in Northeast Coastal Bantu: its linguistic and social implications as a case of grammatical convergence. *Studies in African Linguistics* 6.267–314.

Ward, Gregory. 2004. Equatives and deferred reference. *Language* 80.262–89.

Wechsler, Stephen. forthcoming. Elsewhere in gender resolution. In: Kristin Hanson & Sharon Inkelas (eds.) *The Nature of the Word: Essays in Honor of Paul Kiparsky.* Cambridge, MA: MIT Press.

Wechsler, Stephen & Zlatić, Larisa. 2000. A theory of agreement and its application to Serbo-Croatian. *Language* 76.799–832.

2003. *The Many Faces of Agreement.* Stanford: CSLI.

Weiss, Daniel. 1993. How many sexes are there? (reflections on natural and grammatical gender in contemporary Polish and Russian). In: Gerd Hentschel & Roman Laskowski (eds.) *Studies in Polish Morphology and Syntax*, 71–105. Munich: Otto Sagner.

Weiß, Helmut. 2005. Inflected complementizers in Continental West Germanic dialects. *Zeitschrift für Dialektologie und Linguistik* 72.148–66.

Welmers, William E. 1973. *African Language Structures.* Berkeley: University of California Press.

Wheeler, Max. 1995. 'Underspecification' and 'misagreement' in Catalan lexical specifiers. In: John C. Smith & Martin Maiden (eds.) *Linguistic Theory and the Romance Languages* (Current Issues in Linguistic Theory 122), 201–29. Amsterdam: John Benjamins.

White, Lydia; Valenzuela, Elena; Kozlowska-MacGregor, Martyna & Leung, Yan-Kit Ingrid. 2004. Gender and number agreement in nonnative Spanish. *Applied Psycholinguistics* 25.105–33.

Wilson, W. A. A. 1962. Temne, Landuma and the Baga languages. *Sierra Leone Language Review* 1.27–38.

Wintner, Shuly. 2000. Definiteness in the Hebrew noun phrase. *Journal of Linguistics* 36.319–63.

Woolford, Ellen. 2000. Ergative agreement systems. *University of Maryland Working Papers in Linguistics* 10.157–91.

2003. Clitics and agreement in competition: ergative cross-referencing patterns. In: Angela Carpenter, Andries Coetzee & Paul de Lacy (eds.) *Papers in Optimality Theory II* (University of Massachusetts Occasional Papers in Linguistics (UMOP) 26), 421–49. Amherst, MA: GLSA.

Xajdakov, S. M. 1980. *Principy imennoj klassifikacii v dagestanskix jazykax.* Moscow: Nauka.

Yadav, Ramawatar. 1996. *A Reference Grammar of Maithili* (Trends in Linguistics: Documentation 11). Berlin: Mouton de Gruyter.

Zarę ba, Alfred. 1984–85. Osobliwa zmiana rodzaju naturalnego w dialektach polskich. *Zbornik Matice srpske za filologiju i lingvistiku* 17–18.243–7.

Zemskaja, E. A. & Kapanadze, L. A. (eds.) 1978. *Russkaja razgovornaja reč: teksty.* Moscow: Nauka.

Zubin, David A. & Köpcke, Klaus-Michael. 2005. Gender – where is the system? Paper read at the DGfS Annual Meeting, Cologne, 23 February 2005.

Zwart, Jan-Wouter. 1993. Clues from dialect syntax: complementizer agreement. In: Werner Abraham & Josef Bayer (eds.) *Dialektsyntax (Linguistische Berichte* special issue 5), 246–70. Opladen: Westdeutscher Verlag.

Zwicky, Arnold M. 1977. Hierarchies of person. In: Woodford A. Beach, Samuel E. Fox & Shulamith Philosoph (eds.) *Papers from the Thirteenth Regional Meeting: Chicago Linguistic Society: April 14–16, 1977*, 714–33. Chicago: Chicago Linguistic Society.

1986a. Agreement features: layers or tags? *Ohio State University Working Papers in Linguistics* 32.146–8.

1986b. German adjective agreement in GPSG. *Linguistics* 24.957–90.

1987. Phonologically conditioned agreement and purely morphological features. Report SRC-87–06 of the Syntax Research Center, Cowell College, University of California, Santa Cruz.

1992. Jottings on adpositions, case inflections, government, and agreement. In: Diane Brentari, Gary N. Larson & Lynn A. MacLeod (eds.) *The Joy of Grammar: A Festschrift in Honor of James D. McCawley*, 369–83. Amsterdam: John Benjamins.

1996. Syntax and phonology. In: Keith Brown & Jim Miller (eds.) *Concise Encyclopedia of Syntactic Theories*, 300–5. Oxford: Elsevier Science.

Zwicky, Arnold M. & Pullum, Geoffrey K. 1983. Phonology in syntax: the Somali optional agreement rule. *Natural Language and Linguistic Theory* 1.385–402.

Author index

Language index

When available, the Ethnologue (15th edition) three-letter code is given for identification. Where there is no code, information is given when the language is first mentioned, either directly in the text or through a reference.

Subject index